Generic Composition in
Greek and Roman
Poetry

to Colin Macleod

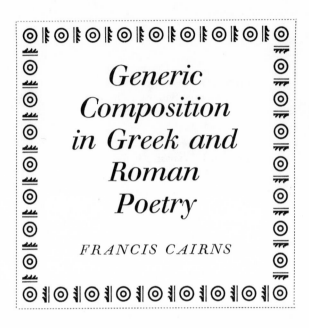

Generic Composition in Greek and Roman Poetry

FRANCIS CAIRNS

EDINBURGH

University Press

© F. J. Cairns 1972
EDINBURGH UNIVERSITY PRESS
22 George Square, Edinburgh
ISBN 0 85224 224 7
North America
Aldine · Atherton, Inc.
529 South Wabash Avenue, Chicago
Library of Congress
Catalog Card Number 72-77763
Printed in Great Britain by
T. and A. Constable Ltd, Edinburgh

Preface

The aim of this work is to suggest an approach whereby the subject-matter of ancient literature may be better understood. I have confined myself to poetic examples for reasons of space, although generic considerations are equally applicable to ancient prose. Within the sphere of poetry, epic and drama have contributed less material than have minor forms. This is partly a matter of personal taste and partly to avoid unnecessary difficulties of exposition.

The method adopted throughout has been to suggest principles of analysis rather than attempt to produce complete lists of genres, or generic examples, or topoi – an impossible task until much more work has been done in the field. Throughout I have tried to move from familiar to unfamiliar and from easy to difficult. This has meant concentrating on genres already familiar to students of ancient literature, or on genres made familiar in the course of the book. Needless to say, the genres most frequently used are not necessarily more complex or more interesting than the others.

Greek generic names have been employed mainly, but not exclusively, in the form ending in *on* (i.e. *propemptikon* for *propemptikos logos*, *propemptike lalia* and *propemptikos hymnos*), even though this is not normal ancient practice. Latin generic names are unchanged. Where no ancient name has survived for a genre, a modern name is accepted or invented.

Where an ancient text has been discussed at length or in detail it has been quoted in all cases where this has been practical. The basis of most of these quotations is the relevant Oxford Classical Text published by the Clarendon Press. I am indebted to the Delegates of the Clarendon Press for permission to make use of their copyright material in this way. It should be noted, however, that I have departed from the readings of the Oxford Classical Texts where I felt it necessary to do so. All the ancient texts quoted are translated, the translations of fragmentary Greek texts or of extracts from Menander the Rhetor appearing in the body of the work while the remainder form an appendix. In this way it is hoped that the book will be useful to readers unacquainted with ancient languages.

Material known to be derived from the work of a particular scholar is acknowledged. I apologize to any scholar whose ideas I may have unwittingly used or whose views I may have misrepresented.

Several individual debts incurred in connection with this book must be acknowledged. Mr J. G. Howie revised those translations from Greek which appear in the body of the work and frequently bettered them. Professor I. M. Campbell, Professor R. G. M. Nisbet, and Professor D. A. West scrutinized one or other of my several drafts. I hope that they will welcome the absence of errors they detected and the tempering of excesses they censured. They will certainly recognize their own insights and suggested improvements which I have gratefully incorporated. My own obstinacy is to be blamed for what mistakes and follies remain.

I owe also a general debt to my colleagues, past and present, in the Classical Departments of Edinburgh University. Over the past eight years they have placed their learning and judgment at my disposal with unfailing generosity. I have also benefited greatly from the advice and encouragement of Mr A. Turnbull, Secretary to Edinburgh University Press. Finally, I should like to thank those members of his staff responsible for editing the text and designing the book and dustjacket, and also Mr Peter McIntyre for compiling the analytical index, and Mrs Cathy Dennis and Miss Jeanette Walsh, who typed the manuscript.

FRANCIS CAIRNS
Edinburgh 1971

Contents

Abbreviations

References to these works will be to page numbers. In the case of Menander both page and line numbers will be given. Other abbreviations used are self-explanatory.

Burgess   T. C. Burgess *Epideictic Literature*, Studies in Classical Philology, vol. III, pp. 89 ff. Chicago 1902.

Copley   F. O. Copley *Exclusus Amator, A Study in Latin Love Poetry*, Philological Monographs published by the American Philological Association no. XVII, 1956.

Jäger   F. Jäger *Das antike Propemptikon und das 17. Gedicht des Paulinus von Nola*, Rosenheim 1913.

Menander   Menander Rhetor Περὶ Ἐπιδεικτικῶν in *Rhetores Graeci* ed. L. Spengel, vol. III, pp. 331 ff. Leipzig 1856.

N–H I   R. G. M. Nisbet and M. Hubbard *A Commentary on Horace Odes Book I*, Oxford 1970.

Williams   G. Williams *Tradition and Originality in Roman Poetry*, Oxford 1968.

PART ONE

Genres and Topoi

1

In Medias Res

Non ego nunc Hadriae uereor mare noscere tecum,
    Tulle, neque Aegaeo ducere uela salo,
cum quo Rhipaeos possim conscendere montis
    ulteriusque domos uadere Memnonias;
5 sed me complexae remorantur uerba puellae,
    mutatoque graues saepe colore preces.
illa mihi totis argutat noctibus ignis,
    et queritur nullos esse relicta deos;
illa meam mihi iam se denegat, illa minatur,
10   quae solet irato tristis amica uiro.
his ego non horam possum durare querelis:
    a pereat, si quis lentus amare potest!
an mihi sit tanti doctas cognoscere Athenas
    atque Asiae ueteres cernere diuitias,
15 ut mihi deducta faciat conuicia puppi
    Cynthia et insanis ora notet manibus,
osculaque opposito dicat sibi debita uento,
    et nihil infido durius esse uiro?
tu patrui meritas conare anteire securis,
20   et uetera oblitis iura refer sociis.
nam tua non aetas umquam cessauit amori,
    semper at armatae cura fuit patriae;
et tibi non umquam nostros puer iste labores
    afferat et lacrimis omnia nota meis!
25 me sine, quem semper uoluit fortuna iacere,
    hanc animam extremae reddere nequitiae.
multi longinquo periere in amore libenter,
    in quorum numero me quoque terra tegat.
non ego sum laudi, non natus idoneus armis:
30   hanc me militiam fata subire uolunt.
at tu seu mollis qua tendit Ionia, seu qua
    Lydia Pactoli tingit arata liquor;
seu pedibus terras seu pontum carpere remis

ibis, et accepti pars eris imperii:
35 tum tibi si qua mei ueniet non immemor hora,
    uiuere me duro sidere certus eris.
        Propertius 1 6

In this, the sixth elegy of his first published book, Propertius addresses
the man who is both his patron and the book's dedicatee, the young
nobleman L. Volcacius Tullus.[1] The occasion of the address is Tullus'
imminent departure from Rome to take up an official post in the province
of Asia. It cannot be doubted that Propertius meant his farewell to Tullus
to be friendly and complimentary. But a critical reader may well feel
that some of what Propertius says is not easily reconcilable with this
view.

At the beginning of the elegy Propertius employs the classical commonplace that willingness to go anywhere with a person is a sign of one's
friendship for that person.[2] He does so in order to make a strong declaration of his friendship for Tullus (1-4). Propertius then immediately
refuses to go with Tullus to Asia. He produces as the main reason for his
refusal to do so the fact that his mistress Cynthia is putting pressure on
him. This takes the form of changes of complexion, nagging, and threats
directed at Propertius because he plans to accompany Tullus (5-18).

It is clear from this abrupt juxtaposition that Propertius intended his
readers to be struck by the contrast between these protestations of
friendship for Tullus and his reason for refusing to go with Tullus.
Propertius has intensified the contrast in two ways: he has ruled out
fear on his own part as a motive for refusal (1-2), and he has used the
commonplace about friendship in a novel and extended form (3-4). Normally the commonplace goes something like '*x* would accompany *y to
the ends of the earth therefore x is a friend to y*'. Propertius says 'I
would accompany you to and *beyond* the ends of the earth'.[3]

On one side, therefore, Propertius places his great friendship for
Tullus, a friendship which is more than personal and includes his poet-
patron relationship with Tullus; on the other side Propertius places
Cynthia's threats, and he submits to the latter. In ancient literature it
is impossible that a poem addressed to a patron-cum-dedicatee should be
uncomplimentary. Despite appearances, therefore, this contrast cannot
be uncomplimentary to Tullus. How then can we explain it? We might
suggest that in elegiac poetry there is a convention by which the ena-
moured elegiac poet prefers his mistress's love to everything, including

the needs of friend and patron; but this is not in fact true. Tibullus in 1 3 describes how he was in the same position as Propertius is in 1 6. Unlike Propertius, Tibullus left his mistress Delia to go abroad with his friend, patron and dedicatee, Messalla, despite Delia's attempts to restrain him.[4] Nevertheless, the amorous character of the elegiac poet may to some extent soften Propertius' decision. A second suggestion would be more helpful: Propertius' seeming insult to Tullus may be indirectly encomiastic to Tullus because it is part of the character contrast which Propertius constructs throughout the poem between Tullus the man of war, proof against love and devoted to the service of his country (cp. 19ff.), and Propertius the worthless lover, suffering from moral blemishes that have been specifically chosen to high-light the opposite virtues in Tullus.

These two suggestions would probably constitute an adequate if not complete explanation and justification of the contrast between 1-4 and 5-18, if the poem did not contain another similar and apparently unencomiastic contrast to which this sort of explanation is inapplicable. From 19 on Propertius compliments Tullus as a soldier and contrasts Tullus in this role with himself, the weak poet-lover; but at 31 a startling reversal of these compliments seems to occur. The language of this and the following lines is carefully chosen to suggest the luxury and wealth of Asia with its irrigated cornland watered by the gold-bearing Pactolus (31-2), and to imply the ease with which Tullus will travel (33) and the security of Tullus' position (34), all of which[5] contrast with Propertius' own hard life (36, where *duro* contrasts with *mollis*, 31). This contrast is also without doubt intentional and again seems at first sight highly unflattering to Tullus. The man who at 19ff. was a tough soldier is now said, or so it appears, to have an easy life in store for him. Such an interpretation must again be wrong, but this time no elegiac conventions or easy theories of indirect encomium are available to explain how this section of the poem can be reconciled with Tullus' role as a man of war. The fact that this problem does not yield to conventional approaches strengthens any residual doubts about the satisfactoriness of the conventional explanations of the contrast between 1-4 and 5-18.

These two difficulties presented by Propertius 1 6 are characteristic of a whole class of difficulties in classical literature. Often the logic of a classical poem or speech appears to be intentionally incomplete or inconsistent. The overall solution to such difficulties which this book sets out to explore is one that involves an acceptance of the validity and meaningfulness of these difficulties. This solution is that the poems and speeches of classical antiquity are not internally complete, individual works but are members of classes of literature known in antiquity as γένη or εἴδη, which will be described in this book as *genres*. Genres in this sense are not classifications of literature in terms of form as are epic, lyric, elegy, or epistle, but classifications in terms of content; for example *propemptikon* (the farewell to the departing traveller), and *komos*, often incorrectly termed *paraclausithyron*[6] (the song and actions of a lover who is usually excluded[7]). It may be felt that it is confusing to call classifications in terms of content genres (although this is commonly done) since classifications in terms of form are also commonly called genres. On the other hand it can be argued that an already established term, for all its potential ambiguity, is preferable to a new coinage since the ambiguity can be removed by definition.

For the purposes of analysis every genre can be thought of as having a set of primary or logically necessary elements which in combination distinguish that genre from every other genre. For example, the primary elements of the propemptikon are in these terms someone departing, another person bidding him farewell, and a relationship of affection between the two, plus an appropriate setting. The primary elements of the komos are a lover, a beloved, and the lover's attempts to come to the beloved, plus an appropriate setting. These primary elements will be present in every example of the genre, either explicitly or implicitly, with those exceptions discussed in Chapter 5. This is because it is only by recognizing these primary elements that an ancient audience could know to which genre a poem or speech belonged.

As well as containing the primary elements of its genre every generic example contains some secondary elements (*topoi*). These topoi are the smallest divisions of the material of any genre useful for analytic purposes. Their usefulness lies in the fact that they are the commonplaces which recur in different forms in different examples of the same genre. They help, in combination with the primary elements, to identify a generic example. But the primary elements are the only final arbiters of generic identity since any particular individual topos (secondary element) can be found in several different genres.

The logical incompleteness and apparent internal inconsistencies of many ancient writings are a consequence of their non-individual character, that is, their membership of genres in the sense defined. These writings assume in the reader a knowledge of the circumstances and content of the particular genre to which they belong, and they exploit this knowledge to allow logical connexions and distinctions to remain implicit or be omitted altogether. In ages and civilizations where, as is the case today, writer and audience do not share a common body of knowledge and expectation, such features of literary works may well be faults of composition. But in situations where, as in classical antiquity, writer and audience do have this common background, they can be part of a greater sophistication in the conveying of information.

Propertius 1 6 belongs to the genre propemptikon.[8] It is not a propemptikon of the best known variety, that is, it does not contain *schetliasmos*. A *schetliastic propemptikon* is one in which the speaker attempts by complaints and protests to persuade the traveller who is intending to depart not to do so but rather to stay behind. Most of the propemptika which have been recognized and discussed by scholars are schetliastic, and it is this type of propemptikon which is fully exemplified in one of the two important works on epideictic genres attributed to Menander the Rhetor, a writer of the third century A D. But although Propertius 1 6 is not a schetliastic propemptikon it is nevertheless a propemptikon, as Felix Jacoby first noted[9] without further comment; and as Propertian scholars have not realized, it exemplifies another variety of propemptikon mentioned but not elaborated upon by Menander.

The section of his treatise in which Menander discusses the varieties of the single genre propemptikon is worth quoting at this point for three reasons. First, it is relevant to Propertius 1 6; second, it will provide the basis for important distinctions made in Chapter 9; and third, it will exemplify the kind of thinking which is valid in generic studies in general.

πολλοὶ δὲ τῆς προπεμπτικῆς τρόποι. εἰς μὲν ὁ δυνάμενος συμβουλεύειν κατὰ μέρος δέξασθαι τῶν λοιπῶν μερῶν δεχομένων καὶ ἐγκώμια καὶ λόγους ἐρωτικούς, εἰ βούλεται προστιθέναι καὶ ταῦτα ὁ λέγων· δύναται δὲ συμβουλὴν ἐπιδέξασθαι, ὅταν ὁ πολλῷ κρείττων προπέμπῃ τὸν ἥττονα, ὡς ὅταν ὁ παιδευτὴς προπέμπῃ τὸν ἀκροατήν· δίδωσι γὰρ αὐτῷ συμβουλευτικὸν ἦθος τὸ οἰκεῖον ἀξίωμα. ἕτερος δὲ τρόπος ἂν γένοιτο, ἐν ᾧ δυνήσεταί τις ἐνδείξασθαι ἦθος ἐρωτικὸν καὶ διάπυρον περὶ τὸν προπεμπόμενον συμβουλὴν μὴ καταμιγνὺς τῆς ἀξίας ὑπαρχούσης ἐφαμίλλου καὶ τῆς δόξης ἴσης τῷ προπέμποντι καὶ

7

τῷ προπεμπομένῳ, ὅταν ἑταῖρος ἑταῖρον προπέμπῃ· καὶ γὰρ
εἰ βελτίων εἴη ὁ προπέμπων ἐνταῦθα τοῦ ἀπαίροντος, ἀλλ᾽ οὖν
ἡ κοινωνία τοῦ ὀνόματος καὶ τὸ ἀμφοτέρους εἶναι φίλους
ἀφαιρεῖται τὸ ἀξίωμα τῆς συμβουλῆς τὸν λέγοντα. γένοιτο δ᾽
ἂν καὶ ἄλλος τρόπος πλείονα διατριβὴν ἔχων περὶ τὰ ἐγκώμια
μᾶλλον, σχεδὸν δὲ εἰπεῖν μικροῦ σύμπασαν, ὅταν ἐθέλῃ προ-
ΐστασθαι τῷ μὲν δοκεῖν προπεμπτικὸν λόγον, τῇ δ᾽ ἀληθείᾳ
ἐγκώμιον. ὥσπερ ἂν εἰ μέλλοιμεν προπέμπειν ἄρχοντα ἢ τῆς
ἀρχῆς πεπαυμένον ἢ ἀφ᾽ ἑτέρας εἰς ἑτέραν πόλιν μέλλοντα
ἀπιέναι. λέγω δὲ ταῦτα οὐκ ἀποστερῶν οὐδένα τῶν προει-
ρημένων τρόπων τῆς προπεμπτικῆς τῶν ἐρωτικῶν παθῶν·
χαίρει γὰρ ἡ προπεμπτικὴ πανταχοῦ τούτοις, ἀλλ᾽ ἐνδεικ-
νύμενος ὅτι ὅπου μὲν μᾶλλόν ἐστιν αὐτῷ καταχρῆσθαι, ὅπου
δὲ ἐπ᾽ ἔλαττον. παραλήψῃ δὲ ἐπὶ τοῦ ἄρχοντος καὶ πόθον
πόλεων ὁλοκλήρων περὶ αὐτὸν καὶ ἔρωτας.

Menander 395 4-32

'There are many sorts of propemptikon.

One sort can be made up partly of advice and partly of encomium
and affectionate addresses, should the speaker wish to add these latter
too. Advice can be included when someone of a much higher status is
bidding farewell to someone of inferior status, for example, a teacher
saying goodbye to a pupil, since in such a case the teacher's status
allows him to display the character of a counsellor.

The second sort is when the speaker can display a burning feeling
of affection for the person to whom he is bidding farewell, without
including advice. In this case the pair will be of equal standing and
reputation, two friends for example; and their friendship and their
common right to the name "friend" deprives the speaker of any right
to give advice, even if the friend saying goodbye should be superior
in status to the friend going away.

A third sort is much more, or rather, almost totally concerned with
praise, when the speaker's intent is to produce an encomium in the
guise of a propemptic speech; for example, if we were going to bid
farewell to a governor laying down office or leaving one city for
another.

In saying all this I do not mean to exclude from any of the sorts of
propemptikon mentioned the expression of feelings of affection. For
the propemptikon universally revels in them. I am only pointing out
that in some cases they are to be used more than in others. When a

governor is the addressee you will bring in the unanimous love of the cities for him and how much they will miss him.'

Menander distinguishes between three sorts of propemptikon. Since his rambling style does not make for clarity, it may be worth while to summarize the three categories:

1. The propemptikon of superior to inferior which has advice as its distinguishing characteristic, e.g. teacher's propemptikon to pupil.

2. The propemptikon of equal to equal which has affection as its distinguishing characteristic, e.g. friend's propemptikon to friend.

3. The propemptikon of inferior to superior which has encomium as its distinguishing characteristic, e.g. orator's propemptikon to governor.

When Menander goes on to give detailed instructions for the composition of a propemptikon, these instructions are for an example of the second sort, that of equal to equal. This example is schetliastic and in this respect resembles the majority of known propemptika. This does not mean, of course, that all propemptika of equal to equal are necessarily schetliastic,[10] or even that all schetliastic propemptika are those of equal to equal.[11] That Menander should thus have chosen to exemplify the second•sort of propemptikon and not the third is somewhat surprising. In the case of other genres with variant types, it is always those addressed to officials and cities to which he devotes most of his space, his purpose being to give tuition in public oratory. Hence we might have expected that the third type of propemptikon, that addressed to a governor, would be the one exemplified in full. The primary reason why Menander chose to exemplify the second sort is probably that he was very concerned to impress on his readers the intimate connexion between all sorts of propemptika and expressions of affection. He may have felt that the best way to drive home this lesson was to exemplify the sort of propemptikon characterized principally by such expressions. Some of the details of Menander's example of the propemptikon of equal to equal hint at a secondary reason. These details make it clear that the imagined circumstances of delivery are that one pupil of a rhetorical school is going home after completing his rhetorical studies and that he is being addressed by a fellow-pupil who is staying behind at the school.[12] This suggests that Menander, and doubtless other teachers of rhetoric, exploited the departures of pupils who had completed their courses as occasions to exercise their remaining pupils in the delivery of this kind of speech, and therefore that the prescription by Menander of the equal to equal variant was meant to help his pupils to compose propemptika in these circumstances. This suggestion is confirmed by another detail of Menander's account. He gives as an example of the superior to inferior type the propemptikon delivered by a teacher saying goodbye to his pupil.[13] Doubtless, when a pupil departed, the teacher of rhetoric led off or crowned the propemptic efforts of his remaining pupils towards their departing comrade.

The choice by Menander of the propemptikon of equal to equal for full exemplification does not mean that the contents of the other two sorts must remain unknown to us. They can be derived partly from literary examples[14] and partly from the prescription for the second sort. For although variants of the same genre differ in content to some extent, they very often have much in common, and this is the case with the propemptikon.

Propertius 1 6 is a propemptikon of Menander's third sort. Tullus, the addressee, is a governor in the broad sense of the word.[15] There are two small differences between the situation in Propertius and that envisaged by Menander. Menander imagines his third sort of propemptikon as being directed by a public orator speaking on behalf of a city or cities towards a governor either demitting office and going home or leaving one city in his province for another. However, in 1 6, Propertius speaks as a private individual not as a public representative, and he addresses Tullus when Tullus is leaving Rome to take up his appointment and not when he is leaving his province or moving about within it. But differences of these two kinds, although they are of some interest and will be treated later in this book,[16] do not affect the generic assignment of Propertius 1 6.

Menander's third type of propemptikon is characterized by encomium. Thus the generic assignment of Propertius 1 6 confirms the common-sense view of the elegy in terms of Propertius' attitude to Tullus. However odd Propertius' remarks at the two places discussed above may seem, they must be intended to be encomiastic. Lines 1-4 can easily be understood in terms of the emotions which characterize the genre in general and Menander's third type of the genre in particular. Propertius' affection for Tullus is expressed in his strong declaration of friendship in these lines. Some compliment to Tullus is implied in 1-2: Propertius makes it clear that the Adriatic and Aegean, traditionally dangerous seas, might terrify some sailors, but not himself or Tullus, and only Tullus will be sailing them! What then of the excuses of 5-18? One might assume that other surviving examples of type 3 propemptika would help with this problem since some of them also contain reasons or excuses for the speaker's inability to accompany a departing official. In fact the frequency of such reasons or excuses suggests that they sometimes play the same role in type 3 propemptika as schetliasmos sometimes plays in type 2, namely that, whereas the equal speaker may reproach the addressee, the inferior speaker may excuse himself to the addressee. However, just as all type 2 propemptika are not schetliastic, so all type 3 propemptika are not necessarily excusatory.

Excusatory sections of three other surviving type 3 excusatory propemptika and one type 2 excusatory propemptikon are:

> me tenet ignotis aegrum Phaeacia terris:
> abstineas auidas Mors modo nigra manus.
> Tibullus 1 3 3-4

> utrumne iussi persequemur otium,
> non dulce, ni tecum simul.
> Horace *Epode* 1 7-8

> cur nobis ignauus amor? sed pectore fido
> numquam abero longisque sequar tua carbasa uotis.
> Statius *Siluae* 3 2 99-100

> sed licet teneamur aegri
> corporis nexu, tamen euolamus
> mentibus post te, Dominoque tecum
> dicimus hymnos.
> Paulinus *Carmina* 17 93-6

The excuses are of different sorts; illness in Tibullus 1 3; the orders of Maecenas in Horace *Epode* 1;[17] faint-heartedness in love in *Siluae* 3 2. In *Siluae* 3 2 Statius employs the preceding imaginary pictures of all the things he might have done abroad with Maecius Celer (90-5) to reinforce his lame excuse for refusing to accompany Celer in real life. Statius then goes on to declare that he will be with Celer in mind. This elaboration gives Statius' handling of the idea that he might go abroad with his addressee a more conventional air than that of Tibullus and Horace. In Paulinus *Carmina* 17 the excuse is rather a statement of fact, namely that Paulinus is mortal and so can only be in one place at a time.

This implies that he himself has a diocese to look after just as Nicetas has. Paulinus goes on to employ the same notion as Statius uses, when he says that he will be with Nicetas in spirit. In spite of their differences, none of these excuses could be misread as insults to the addressee. The encomiastic sense is manifest. An examination of these other examples of the same topos in the same variant of the same genre is therefore unhelpful for Propertius 1 6.

The excuse offered at Propertius 1 6 5-18 can be considered generically in the following way. Propertius' excuse for not accompanying Tullus in a type 3 excusatory propemptikon is that Cynthia, when told by Propertius that he intends to accompany Tullus, has been expressing her disapproval in various ways. The report of this in 5-18 is an example of a type 2 schetliastic propemptikon in which Cynthia is the speaker and Propertius the addressee. The principle which allows this narration of Cynthia's behaviour to be considered a propemptikon is one which is valid for all genres and will recur in this book.[18] It is that, although surviving rhetorical prescriptions for genres are naturally prescriptions for direct first-person speeches, nevertheless literary examples of genres can just as well consist of narrated speeches, either accompanied or unaccompanied by descriptions of related relevant actions; or they can even consist simply of narrations of relevant actions. Cynthia's narrated and imagined speeches, and her related actions of 5-18, are the schetliasmos of a schetliastic propemptikon. The pleas and threats and reproaches of these lines are characteristic of propemptic schetliasmoi and, as though to confirm this, Propertius uses the verb *queror* (8) and the noun *querelae* (11), which appear to be the Latin renderings of the Greek σχετλιάζω, σχετλιασμός.[19] Other propemptic topoi which may be noted in these lines are:

(i) The accusation of breach of faith. There is a hint of this topos in 8 where the gods concerned must, because of the proximity of *ignis* in 7, be those by whom their mutual oaths of love have been sworn. The topos occurs openly in 18.[20]

(ii) Reproaches of hardness of heart, etc. (10, 18).[21]

(iii) Reflections on Propertius' motives for departure, summed up in touristic language as a desire to visit those resorts of learning and wealth, Athens and the famous cities of Asia (13-14).[22]

(iv) The prayers of Cynthia that Propertius' ship will be held up (17).[23]

The propemptikon of Cynthia to Propertius consists of schetliasmos and nothing more. It can nevertheless be considered a member of the genre propemptikon in spite of the absence of the normal second section. Such omissions of material from generic examples without destruction of their generic identity will be discussed in Chapter 5.[24]

Propertius then in 1 6 has yielded to Cynthia's schetliastic propemptikon to him. A parallel for this is Cynthia's yielding to Propertius' schetliastic propemptikon to her in Propertius 1 8. In 1 6 Propertius uses Cynthia's type 2 schetliastic propemptikon to himself in his type 3 excusatory propemptikon to Tullus as his own main excuse for not going to Asia with Tullus. The literary procedure involved here, namely the inclusion within one example of a genre of an example of another variant of the same genre, will be discussed at greater length in Chapter 7 and will be exemplified there and elsewhere. Inclusion was familiar to Propertius' audience, so that to the non-generic explanations of the significance of the contrast between 1-4 and 5-18 can now be added the generic explanation that the contrast was devised by Propertius so that he could demonstrate his skill and originality by using this striking and sophisticated device. In other words the audience, knowing that 1 6 was a propemptikon, would not have expected internal logical completeness in this striking generic innovation, would have accepted 1-18 without asking overprecise questions about internal consistency, and would have understood them in the encomiastic spirit in which they were written. Characteristically what would in a non-generic poem have been a hiatus of thought is not so within this generic elegy. This is because the generic formula and the principle of inclusion are, in a sense, as much parts of the elegy as the elegy itself in as much as the reader would approach the elegy with a prior knowledge of them. This poem is therefore, like all generic works, not a thing in itself. It exists against the background of the reader's generic expectation which it uses as its starting-point.

In the second part of the included propemptikon (13-18), Propertius adds to the description of Cynthia's actual schetliasmos to him in the past (5-12) an anticipation of her future schetliastic activity should he fail to yield to her pleas. This section also paves the way for the contrast between Propertius as poet-lover and Tullus as man of war that will follow in 19-30. The anticipation occurs in 13-14, in which Propertius imagines his own residence abroad not in terms of 1-4 where, in conjunction with Tullus, he was bravely facing the sea-storms, but rather in terms of solitary touring of those standard places of resort in antiquity, Athens with its university and Asia with its wealthy cities. With this prospect he contrasts the further potential propemptic activity on

Cynthia's part – Cynthia on the sea-shore shouting at his departing ship, tearing her face, hoping the winds will be contrary to him and attacking his harshness and lack of fidelity. Thus 13-18 are also a thematic repetition-cum-variation of 1-12.[25]

At line 19 the second half of the propemptikon to Tullus and with it pure encomium of Tullus begins. The first section of this encomium, in which the *persona* of Tullus as a man of war is contrasted with the *persona* of Propertius (19-30), can be interestingly paralleled from Menander's prescription for the type 2 schetliastic propemptikon. Menander recommends that the speaker, while praising the good looks of the traveller, should guard against any impression that the traveller's morals may consequently be faulty by stressing his integrity.[26]

ἐπειδὴ δὲ εἰς εὐδαιμονίαν συντελεῖ καὶ σώματος κάλλος, γράψον καὶ τὸν νεανίαν, οἶος μὲν ἰδεῖν, οἶος δ'ὀφθῆναι. ἐν ᾧ διαγράψεις αὐτοῦ καὶ ἴουλον καὶ ὀφθαλμοὺς καὶ κόμην καὶ τὰ λοιπά. ἵνα δὲ τὸν λόγον σεμνὸν ποιῇς τὸν περὶ τῆς γραφῆς καὶ τὴν διαβολὴν ἐκφύγῃς τὴν ἐκ τοῦ κάλλους, ἀπέργασαι τὸ ἦθος σεμνότερον, λέγων ὅτι κοσμεῖ δὲ τὸ εἶδος τῇ τῶν ἠθῶν ἐγκρατείᾳ, καὶ τῷ μὴ πολλοῖς ῥᾳδίως ἑαυτὸν ἐκδιδόναι, ἀλλὰ μόνον συνεῖναι τῶν ἀνδρῶν τοῖς ἀρίστοις καὶ λόγοις καὶ βιβλίοις.

Menander 398 14-23

'Since physical beauty makes up part of general well-being, describe the young man, how he looks at people and what he is like to look at. Describe in this section his first growth of beard, his eyes, his hair, etc. But in order to make your description serious and to shield him from the kind of insinuations which beauty attracts, you must give some seriousness to his character. Say that his physical attributes are disciplined by his strict morals, by his aversion to associating with the common herd and by his habit of communing only with the best men, speeches and books.'

Propertius does not go into detailed rhapsodies over Tullus' beauty, but he does specify that Tullus is a young man,[27] and immediately goes on to picture him as an anti-love soldier.[28] All this simply intensifies the problem of 31-6. Propertius has been openly laudatory in the previous lines. How then do 31-6 continue this encomium in spite of seeming to be unflattering? This problem, unlike the first, can be solved by direct reference to the generic formula. It is caused simply by the occurrence of a topos at the place specified for it by the generic formula. Since the

14

topos so occurs the author is excused from producing explicit links with its context because these links already exist in the generic formula known to both author and audience.

The topos is described by Menander in the post-encomiastic part of his instructions for the propemptikon as follows:

κἂν μὲν πεζεύειν μέλλῃ, διάγραφε τὴν ὁδὸν καὶ τὴν γῆν δι᾽ἧς πορεύεται, οἷος μὲν ἔσται, ἐὰν οὕτω τύχῃ διὰ τῆς Θρᾴκης διιών, ἐπαινούμενος καὶ προπεμπόμενος ἐπὶ τοῖς λόγοις, θαυμαζόμενος δὲ διὰ Λυδίας καὶ Φρυγίας.

Menander 398 29-399 1

'And if he is going to journey by land, describe the route and the land he will journey through and what sort of traveller he will be, praising and escorting him in your speech (?) if, for example, he is going by land through Thrace, congratulating him if he is going through Lydia and Phrygia.'

What this amounts to is that if the traveller's road is through rough terrain, he is to be praised for his endurance; if it is through a pleasant country, he is to be congratulated on his good fortune. Tullus does in fact pass through Lydia, one of Menander's two examples of pleasant terrain (32). Ionia, the other place he is said to be visiting, is adjacent to and shares the characteristics of Lydia and Phrygia. Hence Propertius lays emphasis on the luxuriousness of Lydia and Ionia, and on the ease of Tullus' passage through and residence in them as a form of laudatory congratulation of Tullus. In doing so, and in placing the topos at this point, Propertius is conforming with the precepts of the rhetorical schools. The general position of the topos in Propertius 1 6 as well as the content of the topos conforms with the generic formula. In Propertius 1 6 as in Menander's prescription (397 21ff.) it is part of the encomium section of the propemptikon. Moreover, in Propertius 1 6 it is followed by the propemptic 'remember me' topos (35-6), a topos which in Menander's prescription immediately precedes in the same sentence the instructions to describe the traveller in accordance with the nature of the terrain he is to traverse (398 26-9).[29]

Two more aspects of the second half of Propertius 1 6 are worth mentioning. Lines 19-36, as well as contrasting Propertius and Tullus to the latter's advantage, also add, by implication for the most part but sometimes openly (e.g. 29-30), to the excusatory tendencies of the first half. Their message is that Propertius is an unwarlike person suited by fate and by his bad character only to the warfare of love. In representing himself in this way, Propertius is producing, as well as the unusual excuse of 5-18, another type of excuse familiar in the context of excusatory propemptika. When Statius in *Siluae* 3 2, in similar circumstances, pleads faint-heartedness as his excuse, he has previously explained that he is militarily useless (94-8). Horace, when in *Epode* 1 he considers the possibility of excusing himself and then decides to go with Maecenas after all, is careful to point out that the decision to go is made in spite of the fact that he is a military nonentity (15-16).

The second aspect of 19-36 is characteristic of the generic practice of ancient poets, who love to disappoint their audiences' expectations on one level and at the same time fulfil them on another level. There is no explicit schetliasmos addressed to Tullus in Propertius 1 6; but in 19-36 Propertius manages to portray himself as a lonely, wretched character strongly reminiscent of the speaker of a schetliastic propemptikon – tearful, woeful, dying. Naturally Propertius nowhere says or implies that his miserable condition has anything to do with Tullus' absence, for to suggest this would be an insult to Tullus' performance of his duty to the state. Propertius blames it all on the fact that he himself is a lover. We might easily believe that the resemblance between this self-portrait and that of the schetliastic speaker was accidental, if the same sort of thing did not happen in other non-schetliastic propemptika.[30] These examples indicate that when ancient poets wrote a non-schetliastic propemptikon they often compensated for the lack of an explicit schetliasmos by some such device.

The choice of Propertius 1 6 as a first example of the usefulness of generic studies was, paradoxically, dictated by the relatively unproblematic nature of the elegy. The two problems of the poem which have been discussed above have never troubled scholars. Moreover, the generic solution to the first of them must be supplemented by conventional approaches. The point of choosing an example of this kind was to avoid suggesting that generic studies are a panacea, that they are in conflict with other branches of classical studies, or that they are worthy of attention only because they solve problems. Their value is that they yield understanding of the compositional methods and intents of ancient writers. This is not to say that they cannot sometimes solve very difficult problems which have long baffled conventional scholarship.

The second example of the utility of generic studies concerns a poem which has puzzled its two most distinguished commentators in the last hundred years.

Ἦλυθες, ὦ φίλε κοῦρε· τρίτῃ σὺν νυκτὶ καὶ ἠοῖ
ἤλυθες· οἱ δὲ ποθεῦντες ἐν ἤματι γηράσκουσιν.
ὅσσον ἔαρ χειμῶνος, ὅσον μῆλον βραβίλοιο
ἥδιον, ὅσσον ὄις σφετέρης λασιωτέρη ἀρνός,
5 ὅσσον παρθενικὴ προφέρει τριγάμοιο γυναικός,
ὅσσον ἐλαφροτέρη μόσχου νεβρός, ὅσσον ἀηδών
συμπάντων λιγύφωνος ἀοιδοτάτη πετεηνῶν,
τόσσον ἔμ᾽ εὔφρηνας σὺ φανείς, σκιερὴν δ᾽ ὑπὸ φηγόν
ἠελίου φρύγοντος ὁδοιπόρος ἔδραμον ὥς τις.
10 εἴθ᾽ ὁμαλοὶ πνεύσειαν ἐπ᾽ ἀμφοτέροισιν Ἔρωτες
νῶιν, ἐπεσσομένοις δὲ γενοίμεθα πᾶσιν ἀοιδή·
'δίω δή τινε τώδε μετὰ προτέροισι γενέσθην
φῶθ᾽, ὃ μὲν εἴσπνηλος, φαίη χ᾽ Ὠμυκλαϊάζων,
τὸν δ᾽ ἕτερον πάλιν, ὥς κεν ὁ Θεσσαλὸς εἴποι, ἀίτην.
15 ἀλλήλους δ᾽ ἐφίλησαν ἴσῳ ζυγῷ. ἦ ῥα τότ᾽ ἦσαν
χρύσειοι πάλιν ἄνδρες, ὅτ᾽ ἀντεφίλησ᾽ ὁ φιληθείς.'
εἰ γὰρ τοῦτο, πάτερ Κρονίδη, πέλοι, εἰ γάρ, ἀγήρῳ
ἀθάνατοι, γενεῆς δὲ διηκοσίῃσιν ἔπειτα
ἀγγείλειεν ἐμοί τις ἀνέξοδον εἰς Ἀχέροντα·
20 'ἡ σὴ νῦν φιλότης καὶ τοῦ χαρίεντος ἀίτεω
πᾶσι διὰ στόματος, μετὰ δ᾽ ἠιθέοισι μάλιστα.'
ἀλλ᾽ ἤτοι τούτων μὲν ὑπέρτεροι Οὐρανίωνες·
ἔσσεται ὡς ἐθέλουσιν. ἐγὼ δέ σε τὸν καλὸν αἰνέων
ψεύδεα ῥινὸς ὕπερθεν ἀραιῆς οὐκ ἀναφύσω.
25 ἢν γὰρ καί τι δάκῃς, τὸ μὲν ἀβλαβὲς εὐθὺς ἔθηκας,
διπλάσιον δ᾽ ὤνησας, ἔχων δ᾽ ἐπίμετρον ἀπῆλθον.
Νισαῖοι Μεγαρῆες, ἀριστεύοντες ἐρετμοῖς,
ὄλβιοι οἰκείοιτε, τὸν Ἀττικὸν ὡς περίαλλα
ξεῖνον ἐτιμήσασθε, Διοκλέα τὸν φιλόπαιδα.
30 αἰεί οἱ περὶ τύμβον ἀολλέες εἴαρι πρώτῳ
κοῦροι ἐριδμαίνουσι φιλήματος ἄκρα φέρεσθαι·
ὃς δέ κε προσμάξῃ γλυκερώτερα χείλεσι χείλη,
βριθόμενος στεφάνοισιν ἑὴν ἐς μητέρ᾽ ἀπῆλθεν.
ὄλβιος ὅστις παισὶ φιλήματα κεῖνα διαιτᾷ·
35 ἦ που τὸν χαροπὸν Γανυμήδεα πόλλ᾽ ἐπιβῶται
Λυδίῃ ἶσον ἔχειν πέτρῃ στόμα, χρυσὸν ὁποίη

πεύθονται, μὴ φαῦλος, ἐτήτυμον ἀργυραμοιβοί.
Theocritus *Idyll* 12

Wilamowitz made four main points about this idyll.[31] He could not believe that 3-9, with their chain of ornate images, could be taken seriously; he jibbed at the introduction of the glossographical matter of 13-14 into a love poem; he held that 23-4, coming as they do after the high-sounding prayers of 10-21, constitute bathos; and finally he felt that the kissing contest of the Dioclea was something that would have appeared naïve to Theocritus' sophisticated readers. Wilamowitz explained all these points not very convincingly by suggesting that Theocritus was not serious in the idyll but was being deliberately humorous.

In his commentary on Theocritus Gow took a different view.[32] He accepted the validity of Wilamowitz's four points but rejected his explanation of them. Gow's verdict on the idyll was that if, as he himself believed, the poem is serious, then it shows 'lack of emotional restraint', 'untimely display of learning' and 'incongruous juxtaposition of the two'. Gow concluded: 'If it is wholly serious, it displays more conspicuous deficiencies of tact and taste than are to be found elsewhere in Theocritus'.

Idyll 12 belongs to a genre which in this book will be called *prosphonetikon*. This genre is the welcome to a traveller who has arrived at the place where the speaker is. In antiquity it appears that such a speech could be described as either a *prosphonetikos*[33] or, with a cognate term, a *prosphonematikos*[34] *logos*, or as an *epibaterios*[35] *logos*. The name *prosphonetikon* will be used here because the term *epibaterios logos* is also applied in antiquity to something quite different – the speech of the traveller who has arrived somewhere. The reason for the dual nomenclature may be conjectured. Ancient rhetoricians, with their usual disregard of logic and concern for convenience, could impose names on pre-existent and well-known generic patterns with a view to emphasizing either the distinctions between the primary elements of different genres or the similarity between the secondary elements of different genres. The primary elements of the *prosphonetikon* (speech of welcomer) and *epibaterion* (in the sense of speech of arriver) are as different as those of the *propemptikon* (speech *to* the departing traveller) and *syntaktikon* (speech *of* the departing traveller). But as many of the secondary elements (topoi) of the *prosphonetikon* and the *epibaterion* (speech of arriver) are similar, some rhetoricians therefore applied the term *epibaterion* to both categories.

Menander calls the speech of the welcomer both prosphonetikon and epibaterion. In his second treatise on epideictic genres he gives the name prosphonetikon to one genre (414ff.). This is clearly a speech of welcome. But in the same treatise, in his discussion of the genre epibaterion, Menander says:

Ἐπιβατήριον ὁ βουλόμενος λέγειν δῆλός ἐστι βουλόμενος προσφωνῆσαι ἢ τὴν ἑαυτοῦ πατρίδα ἐξ ἀποδημίας ἥκων, ἢ πόλιν ἑτέραν, εἰς ἣν ἂν ἀφίκηται, ἢ καὶ ἄρχοντα ἐπιστάντα τῇ πόλει.

Menander 377 32-378 3

'A person pronouncing an epibaterion is clearly wishing either to address his own country on return from abroad or to address another city at which he has arrived or to address the governor appointed to rule over the city.'

Menander continues with a long prescription for the last circumstance, which makes it clear that the last kind of address is made to a governor arriving at one's city. Thus the speech is a speech of welcome pronounced in exactly the same situation as is found in the prosphonetikon as defined by Menander.

Menander himself is not unaware of or entirely comfortable about this overlapping of nomenclature. At the end of his discussion of the epibaterion (speech of welcome) he attempts to define the difference between the prosphonetikon and this supposed epibaterion.

δοκεῖ δὲ περιττὸν ἔχειν ὁ ἐπιβατήριος λόγος κατὰ τοῦ προσφωνητικοῦ τὸ ἐκ περιχαρείας κεφάλαιον μετὰ τὰ προοίμια, καὶ ταῦτα ἐκ περιχαρείας λαμβανόμενα· ὅμως δὲ οὐδὲν κωλύει μετὰ τὰ προοίμια τελείαν ἐργασίαν τῶν κεφαλαίων δίδοσθαι· χρήσῃ δὲ ἐν ταῖς τοιαύταις ὑποθέσεσι ταῖς τῶν προσφωνητικῶν καὶ τῶν ἐπιβατηρίων ἢ ἑνὶ προοιμίῳ ἢ καὶ δευτέρῳ πολλάκις, ἔστι δὲ ὅτε καὶ τρισὶ χρήσῃ, ὅταν ἀπαιτῇ καὶ τοῦτο ἡ ὑπόθεσις.

Menander 382 1-9

'It appears that the epibaterion has when compared to the prosphonetikon an additional section after the prologues dealing with the great pleasure ⟨ felt by the speaker ⟩, the prologues also dealing with his great pleasure. There is, however, nothing to prevent a full working

out of the subsequent sections of the epibaterion after the prologues. When dealing with such subjects, that is, the subjects of
prosphonetika and epibateria, you will employ either one prologue
or often two, and sometimes three, when this is demanded by the
subject-matter.'

It is not absolutely clear what Menander means in this extract. If his
meaning is as the translation above suggests, he is simply distinguishing
between prosphonetikon and epibaterion in terms of the amount of
treatment each gives to the expressions of pleasure by the welcomer.
Such a distinction, namely the amount of treatment of subject-matter
rather than the presence or absence of subject-matter, concerns secondary elements rather than primary elements and so is topical rather than
generic. It is not the kind of distinction between genres made elsewhere
in Menander or by other authors.

The term prosphonetikon can therefore be used with some confidence
to refer to the speech of the welcomer, and the term epibaterion ignored.
From the point of view of literary welcomes Libanius' use of the term
prosphonetikon is of most interest. In his prosphonetikos to the Emperor
Julian (5) he quotes Alcaeus *Fr.* 350 (LP), a typical poetic welcome,
thus showing that he believes it to belong to the same genre as his speech.
But although we may reject the name epibaterion for a welcome,
Menander's prescription for the epibaterion (speech of welcome) remains valid as material for the study of the genre prosphonetikon.

Menander's detailed instructions for the propemptikon were for a
variant of that genre in which speaker and addressee were equal (type 2)
and both were private citizens. But the propemptikon we have been
discussing, Propertius 1 6, was one in which the addressee was a superior
(type 3) and a man in public life. Our discussion of Propertius 1 6 relied
both on the Menandrian type 2 prescription and on literary examples of
type 3. Theocritus *Idyll* 12 will be analysed with the help of a slightly
different combination of material.

Menander's instructions for the genre prosphonetikon, both those for
the prosphonetikon proper (414ff.) and for the epibaterion (speech of
welcome) (378ff.), are for examples addressed to important and superior
public personalities like governors. Theocritus *Idyll* 12 is an example
addressed to an equal private person. The Menandrian prosphonetic
prescriptions bear some relationship to literary prosphonetika addressed
both to equals and to superiors. But because these parts of Menander's

treatise are more of a practical guide to rhetoric than the section on the propemptikon, they are not as close to literary prosphonetika or as helpful in treating them as is his propemptic prescription with regard to literary propemptika. Consequently although there are striking differences between private and public literary prosphonetika, they can for present purposes be combined to provide a topical list in the light of which examples of the genre can be discussed. The relevance and occasional utility of the Menandrian prescriptions should not of course be forgotten (see below). Theocritus *Idyll* 12 will therefore be discussed as a prosphonetikon with reference to such a topical list. The following poetic examples form a representative sample of easily recognisable prosphonetika:

Homer *Odyssey* 16 11-67, 187-234; 17 28-60; 23 205-350; 24 345-412; Alcaeus *Fr.* 350 (LP); Theognis 1 511-22; Aeschylus *Agamemnon* 855-974; Euripides *Heracles* 531-3; Aristophanes *Aves* 676-84; Catullus 9; Horace *Odes* 1 36; Ovid *Amores* 2 11 37-56; Statius *Siluae* 3 2 127-43; Juvenal 12.

The order of the topoi in the list is not necessarily the order in which they are found in any particular example. Bracketed references are to implicit allusions to the topoi rather than to explicit occurrences of them. The formal principles of equivalence of direct speech and narrated speech and of action and description of action, formulated above with reference to Propertius 1 6 5-18, apply in these examples of the prosphonetikon and in the topical list derived from them, as indeed in all examples of all genres.

A. *Primary Elements, i.e. the Persons, Situation, Function, Communication logically necessary for the genre*

1. The person arriving (Ar)
2. The Welcomer (We)
3. A relationship between them of friendship or love
4. The welcome of Ar by We

These primary elements are found in all members of the genre, except those affected by the processes discussed in Chapters 5-9.

B. *Secondary Elements, i.e. some of the topoi commonly but not necessarily included*

1. An announcement of the arrival of Ar by means of a verb of arriving, etc., with, on occasion, a repetition of this verb (see below): Hom. *Od.* 16 23; 17 41; 24 399; Alc. *Fr.* 350 1 (LP); Theogn. 1 511; Eur. *Her.* 531; Arist. *Av.* 680; Cat. 9 3, 5; Juv. 12 15.

2. The place where Ar has been: Hom. *Od.* 17 42; Alc. *Fr.* 350 1 (LP); Cat. 9 6; Hor. *O.* 1 36 4.

3. Expressions of affection of We for Ar or of mutual affection: Hom. *Od.* 16 23; 17 41; 24 401; Theogn. 1 513-22; Aesch. *Ag.* 855-7, 905; Eur. *Her.* 531; Arist. *Av.* 678-80; Cat. 9 1-2, 5, 10-11; Hor. *O.* 1 36 10; St. *Sil.* 3 2 131; Juv. 12 1, 16, 93-5.

4. Demonstrations of such affection, e.g. kisses, embraces, tears on the part of We and sometimes also Ar: Hom. *Od.* 16 14-22, 190-1, 213-20; 17 35, 38-9; 23 206-8; 24 344-5, 396-7; (Aesch. *Ag.* 887-91); Cat. 9 8-9; Hor. *O.* 1-36 6; Ov. *Am.* 2 11 45-6; St. *Sil.* 3 2 132-4.

5. Emphasis on return *home* of Ar if this is the case: Hom. *Od.* 23 258-9; Cat. 9 3.

6. Divine assistance to Ar: Hom. *Od.* 16 237-8; 24 31-2, 401; Hor. *O.* 1 36 2-3; Juv. 12 62-6.

7. Emphasis on safety of Ar: Hom. *Od.* 16 21; Eur. *Her.* 531; Cat. 9 6; Hor. *O.* 1 36 4; Juv. 12 16.

8. Dangers and sufferings undergone by Ar: Hom. *Od.* 16 21, 189; 17 (41-2), 47; (23 234-8); Aesch. *Ag.* 865-76, 882-3; Juv. 12 15-82.

9. Achievements of Ar: Hom. *Od.* 23 310-41; Alc. *Fr.* 350 3-7 (LP); Aesch. *Ag.* 907; Juv. 12 37-51.

10. Sufferings of We because of absence of Ar: Hom. *Od.* 23 210-12, 230-1; Aesch. *Ag.* 858-76, 887-95, 904-5.

11. The joys and benefits conferred on We by Ar's arrival with/without *exempla* to emphasize: Hom. *Od.* 23 233-40; Aesch. *Ag.* 895-905, 966-75; Arist. *Av.* 681; Cat. 9 5, 10-11.

12. Priority or preferred status of We: Hor. *O.* 1 36 7-8; Ov. *Am.* 2 11 43; St. *Sil.* 3 2 133.[36]

13. Narrations of Ar (*with a humorous hit at them): (Hom. *Od.* 17 44-6); Hom. *Od.* 16 226-32; 23 306-41; Cat. 9 6-7; Ov. *Am.* 2 11 49-52; St. *Sil.* 3 2 135-41; Juv. 12 17-82(?); *Cat. 9 8; *Ov. *Am.* 2 11 53.

14. Narrations of We: Hom. *Od.* 23 302-5; St. *Sil.* 3 2 135, 142-3.

15. Vows previously made by We for Ar: Aesch. *Ag.* 963-5; Hor. *O.* 1 36 2; Ov. *Am.* 2 11 46; St. *Sil.* 3 2 131; Juv. 12 2-16.

16. Sacrifices by We in fulfilment of vows: Aesch. *Ag.* 958-62 (cp. 1035); Hor. *O.* 1 36 1-3; Ov. *Am.* 2 11 46; St. *Sil.* 3 2 131-2; Juv. 12 2-16, 83-92.

17. The other(s) welcoming Ar and seconding or taking We's place in his various activities: Hom. *Od.* 17 31-5; 24 386-412; (Aesch. *Ag.*

855-7); Eur. *Her.* 531-2; Cat. 9 3-4; Hor. *O.* 1 36 5.
18. Celebratory banquet with accoutrements: Hom. *Od.* 16 46-55(?); 24 363-412(?);[37] Hor. *O.* 1 36 11-20; Ov. *Am.* 2 11 47-9.
19. Amatory activities of Ar or others: Hom. *Od.* 254-5, 300; Hor. *O.* 1 36 17-20; Ov. *Am.* 2 11 54.
20. Previous shared activities of Ar and We: Arist. *Av.* 678-9; Hor. *O.* 1 36 7-9.

In some examples these topoi occur inextricably bound up with others. In the above list I have recorded only those occurrences which can be readily distinguished. More examples of these topoi and others can be found in additional prosphonetika treated elsewhere in this book.

Theocritus *Idyll* 12 belongs to the genre prosphonetikon because it has all the logically necessary elements of the genre (a person arriving, a person welcoming him, and a suitable relationship between them), and because it also has a number of common though not strictly necessary topoi of the genre in an easily recognisable form:

(i) The formal announcement of return (B 1) employing here the verb ἔρχομαι (*uenio*) (1-2) (cp. Homer *Odyssey* 16 23; 17 41, Alcaeus *Fr.* 350 1 (LP), Euripides *Heracles* 532, Theognis 511, Menander 378 10) in this case in the emphatic repeated form as in

ἦλθες ἦλθες ὤφθης
Aristophanes *Aves* 680

and with a slight variation in

Verani, omnibus e meis amicis
antistans mihi milibus trecentis,
uenistine domum ad tuos penates
fratresque unanimos anumque matrem?
uenisti. o mihi nuntii beati!
        Catullus 9 1-5

cf. also

ἦλθ' ἦλθε χελιδών
Poetae Melici Graeci 848 1

(ii) The formal assertion of affection by We for Ar (1) and other statements and demonstrations of affection throughout (B3 and 4). These sometimes refer in examples of the genre, as here, to sexual affection, e.g. Homer *Odyssey* 23 205ff.; Ovid *Amores* 2 11 37ff.

(iii) The happiness Ar confers on We by his return (B 11), emphasized

23

by *exempla* stressing this and further emphasizing the affection of We for Ar (3-9). We may compare:

ὡς δ' ὅτ' ἂν ἀσπάσιος γῇ νηχομένοισι φανήῃ,
ὧν τε Ποσειδάων εὐεργέα νῆ' ἐνὶ πόντῳ
235 ῥαίσῃ ἐπειγομένην ἀνέμῳ καὶ κύματι πηγῷ
παῦροι δ' ἐξέφυγον πολιῆς ἁλὸς ἤπειρόνδε
νηχόμενοι, πολλὴ δὲ περὶ χροῒ τέτροφεν ἅλμη,
ἀσπάσιοι δ' ἐπέβαν γαίης, κακότητα φυγόντες·
ὡς ἄρα τῇ ἀσπαστὸς ἔην πόσις εἰσοροώσῃ,
240 δειρῆς δ' οὔ πω πάμπαν ἀφίετο πήχεε λευκώ.

Homer *Odyssey* 23 233-40

895 νῦν ταῦτα πάντα τλᾶσ', ἀπενθήτῳ φρενὶ
λέγοιμ' ἂν ἄνδρα τόνδε τῶν σταθμῶν κύνα,
σωτῆρα ναὸς πρότονον, ὑψηλῆς στέγης
στῦλον ποδήρη, μονογενὲς τέκνον πατρί,
καὶ γῆν φανεῖσαν ναυτίλοις παρ' ἐλπίδα,
900 κάλλιστον ἦμαρ εἰσιδεῖν ἐκ χείματος,
ὁδοιπόρῳ διψῶντι πηγαῖον ῥέος.
τερπνὸν δὲ τἀναγκαῖον ἐκφυγεῖν ἅπαν.
τοιοῖσδέ τοί νιν ἀξιῶ προσφθέγμασιν.
....
ῥίζης γὰρ οὔσης φυλλὰς ἵκετ' ἐς δόμους,
σκιὰν ὑπερτείνασα σειρίου κυνός.
καὶ σοῦ μολόντος δωματῖτιν ἑστίαν,
θάλπος μὲν ἐν χειμῶνι σημαίνεις μολόν·
970 ὅταν δὲ τεύχῃ Ζεὺς ἀπ' ὄμφακος πικρᾶς
οἶνον, τότ' ἤδη ψῦχος ἐν δόμοις πέλει,
ἀνδρὸς τελείου δῶμ' ἐπιστρωφωμένου.

Aeschylus *Agamemnon* 895-903, 966-72

(iv) The statement regarding time and affection (2), which although not paralleled often enough to be called a topos of the genre is worth comparing with

ὡς δὲ πατὴρ ὃν παῖδα φίλα φρονέων ἀγαπάζῃ
ἐλθόντ' ἐξ ἀπίης γαίης δεκάτῳ ἐνιαυτῷ,
μοῦνον τηλύγετον, τῷ ἔπ' ἄλγεα πολλὰ μογήσῃ
Homer *Odyssey* 16 17-19

where Telemachus is being welcomed by Eumaeus, and Telemachus' short absence is compared (by the poet not by Eumaeus) to a long one – a

24

comparison which in its details (father and son) also hints covertly at the presence of the disguised Odysseus. The idea is also found in a brief epigram which probably belongs to the same genre:[38]

Τὸν καλόν, ὡς ἔλαβες, κομίσαις πάλι πρός με θεωρὸν
Εὐφραγόρην, ἀνέμων πρηΰτατε Ζέφυρε,
εἰς ὀλίγων τείνας μηνῶν μέτρον. ὡς καὶ ὁ μικρὸς
μυριετὴς κέκριται τῷ φιλέοντι χρόνος.

    A.P. 12 171 (Dioscorides)

The occurrence of these topoi in the first few lines of Theocritus *Idyll* 12, together with the elements of persons and situation revealed in these lines, were for Theocritus' original audience an unmistakable announcement of the generic identity of the idyll. Such indirect initial announcements of the genre of a piece are common in ancient literature,[39] and they play an important part in generic communication between author and audience. Their function is sometimes to alert the audience to the further occurrence of standard topoi in less obvious and more sophisticated forms.

The difficulties Wilamowitz found in *Idyll* 12 can be resolved and the merit of the idyll revealed by the assignment of it to the genre prosphonetikon, by the application to it of the principle that a clear generic announcement precedes sophisticated use of generic topoi, and by appreciation of the emotional complexities which these generic subtleties depict.

It has already been noted that the content of *Idyll* 12 3-9 is paralleled by similar chains of images in Aeschylus' *Agamemnon*, and it will have been observed that the correspondences between the two authors extend at two points to details. Theocritus 8-9 present an image in terms of coolness and shade almost identical to part of *Agamemnon* 966-72, and an image to do with a wayfarer occurs both in Theocritus 8-9 and *Agamemnon* 901. These correspondences are probably not due to imitation of Aeschylus by Theocritus but to the influence of the genre within which both are working. Similarly, *Agamemnon* 898 employs the same image, that of the father and his only son, in almost the same words as Homer *Odyssey* 16 17-19, *Agamemnon* 899 the same notion (land and shipwrecked sailors) as *Odyssey* 23 233-40, and *Agamemnon* 900 probably reflects that standard phrase γλυκερὸν φάος, which is used twice in prosphonetic circumstances in the *Odyssey*,[40] and which finds its parallel built into Menander's instructions for the genre:

ἀλλ' ἥκεις μὲν ἐπ' αἰσίοις συμβόλοις ἄνωθεν λαμπρός, ὥσπερ
ἡλίου φαιδρά τις ἀκτὶς ἄνωθεν ἡμῖν ὀφθεῖσα.
Menander 378 10-12; cp. 21-3, 381 15-18.
'You have come accompanied by good omens, a man of high and illus-
trious ancestry, like some glittering beam of the sun seen by us on
high.'

Three conclusions can be drawn from all this: first, that at least a single
comparison or metaphor of some kind or other enhancing the effects of
the arrival was commonplace in the genre; second, that a chain of such
images was probably not unusual in the genre; third, that some of the
material of the imagery was commonplace in the genre. None of these
considerations would be in the least affected if those scholars were right
who wish to expel some lines from the first *Agamemnon* passage quoted
as spurious later additions.[41] For if some of these lines were added later
than Aeschylus, they were added in accordance with the generic formula
and practice which they thus illustrate further.

Idyll 12 3-9 must therefore be approached on the assumption that
Theocritus' readers expected, once they knew the genre of *Idyll* 12,
that at least one if not more enhancing comparisons of just the sort found
in 3-9 would occur in the idyll. Their surprise at the appearance of the
sequence of comparisons of 3-9 must for this reason have been much less
than that of Wilamowitz and Gow. This is not to say that generic considerations explain the intensity and emphasis of the many comparisons.
However, the similar chain of comparisons at *Agamemnon* 896-903, part
of another member of the genre, offers some assistance here. Dindorf
bracketed 895-902 and remarked: 'This sounds like Theodorus Pro-
dromus and poets like him'. Dindorf's brackets were, of course, unnecessary; but they had the good effect of leading Fraenkel[42] to explain
the significance of Aeschylus' piling up of images in this speech of
Clytemnestra to Agamemnon: 'The lack of discretion in this string of
eulogies is exactly appropriate to the manner of speech of the lady who
doth protest too much'.

In Theocritus *Idyll* 12 3-9, a different but similar emotional reason
lies behind the apparent oddness of the chain of comparisons. This emotional reason will be discussed below in relation both to this and the
other seeming oddities of the poem. For the moment it may be concluded
that the occurrence in two widely separate examples of the genre,
between which direct influence is most unlikely, of the same kind of

'indiscreet' or exaggerated comparisons, is enough to show that comparisons of this kind – not merely comparisons or chains of comparison in themselves – are at home in the genre; Theocritus' readers are unlikely to have been surprised even by this feature of 5-9. But it is at the same time legitimate to see 5-9 as setting the emotional tone for the rest of the poem and establishing an atmosphere of tension in which exaggerations and oddities of kinds perhaps not elsewhere attested in the genre may be found.

Lines 10-21 contain expressions of the wish that the two men were equally in love and that their love would become one of the great loves of tradition. One of the standard prosphonetic themes already mentioned is the affection the welcomer feels for the person who has arrived (B5). Often this affection is implied or stated to be reciprocated by the addressee of the prosphonetikon. Indeed, it may even be that the addressee is specifically stated to have preferential feelings for the welcomer (B12), for example:

> . . . cum me magna ceruice ligatum
> attolles umeris atque in mea pectora primum
> incumbes e puppe nouus . . .
>   Statius *Siluae* 5 2 152-4

In Theocritus *Idyll* 12 10-21, instead of an elaborate statement of outstanding mutual love and affection, we have an elaborate wish for this. Such alterations in mood are among those formal alterations which occur often both in whole generic examples and in single topoi, and which will be discussed in Chapter 5.[43] An alteration of mood in the opposite direction, from wish to statement, occurs in a well-known Theocritean propemptikon:

> Ἔσσεται Ἀγεάνακτι καλὸς πλόος ἐς Μιτυλήναν,
> χὤταν ἐφ' ἑσπερίοις Ἐρίφοις νότος ὑγρὰ διώκῃ
> κύματα, χὠρίων ὅτ' ἐπ' ὠκεανῷ πόδας ἴσχει,
> 55 αἴ κα τὸν Λυκίδαν ὀπτεύμενον ἐξ Ἀφροδίτας
> ῥύσηται· θερμὸς γὰρ ἔρως αὐτῷ με καταίθει.
>   Theocritus *Idyll* 7 52-6

The normal propemptic speaker utters good wishes for the departing traveller.[44] But Lycidas, instead of wishing Ageanax a good voyage and so forth, states that he will have a good voyage. The striking alteration of mood paves the way for the second major sophistication of these lines. Whereas the normal propemptic speaker utters unconditional good wishes, Lycidas makes statements about Ageanax's future, statements which he then proceeds to make conditional on Ageanax favouring himself.

As in Theocritus *Idyll* 7 52-6, so in Theocritus *Idyll* 12 10-21 the alteration of mood calls the reader's attention to the alteration of concept involved. The speaker of *Idyll* 12 feels, like the standard prosphonetic speaker, strong affection for his addressee. But unlike the standard speaker he cannot feel any confidence whatsoever that his feelings are reciprocated. He can only wish for this.

Within the speaker's wish occurs the glossographical passage (13-14), the second difficulty Wilamowitz found in the idyll. Contemporary views of Alexandrian learning are not as extreme as those of some earlier scholars. Especially since the appearance of R. Pfeiffer's monumental edition of Callimachus, we have learnt to recognize that learning is by no means incompatible with the sincere portrayal of deep emotions.

Furthermore, a better understanding of the significance of the two places mentioned may help to soften any impression that the lines are irrelevant pedantry. Most ancient place names have several associations.[45] However, there is one link between the Laconian town of Amyclae and Thessaly which may well be relevant to what Theocritus is saying. Pindar's tenth Pythian Ode begins:

'Ολβία Λακεδαίμων
μάκαιρα Θεσσαλία
1-2

It is not known whether some such dictum was proverbial before or indeed after Pindar made it the beginning of this ode, although Sparta is later proverbial as a 'good thing'.[46] But the sentiment it expresses agrees well with the sense of Theocritus *Idyll* 12 10-21; for there the speaker wishes that the mutual love of himself and his addressee may make the pair spoken of as 'godlike' (12) and 'men of the golden age' (16), which also means god-like since Hesiod speaks as follows of the men of the golden age:

ὥς τε θεοὶ δ' ἔζωον ἀκηδέα θυμὸν ἔχοντες
νόσφιν ἄτερ τε πόνων καὶ ὀιζύος...
    Opera et Dies 112-13

The adjectives ὄλβιος and μάκαρ, with their frequent associations with the gods, accord well with the sentiments of 10-21. It is of further interest that the adjective ὄλβιος occurs later in *Idyll* 12 at 28 in a passage of similar import, that is of indirect wishes for reciprocation of love. If this is the significance of the allusions to Amyclae and Thessaly, they strengthen the picture of the god-like bliss which the speaker wishes for himself.

Wilamowitz's next difficulty, the 'bathos' of 23-4, can be divided into a question about the idea expressed in the two lines and a question about its mode of expression. The idea expressed in the two lines appears to be a rare but natural prosphonetic topos. It seems that where the prosphonetic addressee is in a position to confer favours on the welcomer, or might be thought to be in this position, the speaker may stress that no flattery or self-seeking is involved in the praise and affection that he is pouring upon his addressee:

> neu suspecta tibi sint haec, Coruine, Catullus,
> pro cuius reditu tot pono altaria, paruos
> tres habet heredes.
> Juvenal 12 93-5

In *Idyll* 12, 23-4 fulfil this function. They are a denial of sycophancy. The mode of expression of this idea is certainly, at first sight, odd. The explanation of this oddity is partly cultural, partly one of characterization. Modern tastes are not ancient tastes. In any case, no one has criticized Theocritus for drawing an omen from a twitch of the eye at *Idyll* 3 37, although this is just as trivial as pimples. Moreover, we do not know the social status of the speaker of *Idyll* 12. If he is a rustic, as 3-9 would suggest, then the image, like that of *Idyll* 3 37, is appropriate and a part of Theocritus' character-drawing. It may also help to portray the mental state of the speaker of *Idyll* 12 (see below). It is followed immediately by an easily recognizable topos of the prosphonetikon, the recompense which the addressee brings for the misery his absence has meant (B11, 25-6).

The final passage of *Idyll* 12, 27-37, which Wilamowitz again found odd, is not difficult once the sense and generic element (B4) involved have been understood. The normal welcomer expects to embrace and kiss the returned traveller:

> . . . applicansque collum
> iucundum os oculosque suauiabor.
> Catullus 9 8-9

excipiamque umeris et multa sine ordine carpam
oscula . . .
Ovid *Amores* 2 11 45-6

The underprivileged lover of *Idyll* 12 cannot with confidence anticipate such embraces and kisses. All he can do is request the kisses in an indirect way by congratulating Diocles, the Nisean Megarians and the judge at the kissing contest, and by giving a description of the contest and its origin.

These explanations of the difficulties of *Idyll* 12 pave the way for a fairer assessment of it, based on an understanding of how the author has used sophisticated variants of standard topoi of the prosphonetikon to portray the emotional state of his speaker. The welcomer is represented as being in a well-known human condition. He is completely in love but his beloved, the returning traveller, is apparently not so enthusiastic. If any compliance on the beloved's part is implied, it is small. There is therefore a tension in the mind of the lover between his desire to produce greater response from his beloved and his fear of losing what response he already has. This kind of alternation between fear and hope in the mind of a lover is typically Theocritean. It can be seen also in *Idyll* 11 in the soliloquy of the Cyclops (19-81) and in *Idyll* 3.

Here in *Idyll* 12 this ambivalence is worked out in a subtle succession of passages alternatively asserting on one hand the pleasure the lover receives from his beloved's present limited response and on the other his wish that the beloved would be more compliant. Since the lover is the traditional humble lover of antiquity, more or less enslaved to the beloved and terrified of upsetting him, the idyll with its sudden transitions between the two emotions should be seen not as a clumsy union of discreet and sometimes pedantically obscure remarks but as the reflection of a state of mind where the lover, because of the conflict within him, can suddenly move from excessive enthusiasm (3-9) to controlled sophistication (10-21), to eager and pathetic naïvety (23-6), and back to controlled subtlety (27-37). The indirectness of the passages where the lover is in command of himself, and complains and begs through comparisons and wishes, is as much a sign of his terror and eagerness as are the more obvious manifestations of these emotions in the passages where he expresses himself in a more open manner. *Idyll* 12 is therefore a typical piece of Alexandrian poetry, combining emotional sophistication, generic sophistication, and glossological and aetiological learning.

As has been illustrated, generic analysis can illuminate the logic and thought processes of classical writers, by showing what connexions of thought were built into the formulae behind particular writings, and can also solve major traditional problems. But important as these two functions are, they are not the most important role of generic studies. The theory which underlies this book is that the whole of classical poetry is written in accordance with the sets of rules of the various genres, rules which can be discovered by a study of the surviving literature itself and of the ancient rhetorical handbooks dealing with this subject. If this theory is correct, then generic studies are essential to any rational literary criticism of the conceptual side of ancient poetry. Until the genre of a particular piece is known, many assessments of the motives, methods or merits of its author are bound to be subjective. Once a correct assignment to a genre has been made, the generic formula, that is, the raw material available to the author before he began to compose, can be invoked and the author's own individual contribution to the piece can be isolated. Only then can questions of originality and quality of thought be discussed on an objective basis, and only then can detailed factual information about the thought processes and intellectual activity of the ancient writer be obtained. Such an approach makes unnecessary the psychoanalytic examinations, the inopportune hypotheses of irony, the anachronistic applications of the out-of-date critical techniques of scholars in other fields, and the verbose and emotional 'appreciations' which are sometimes thought to assist in the understanding of Greek and Roman poetry.

It may well be asked why, if generic studies are so useful, they are not a fully explored and established part of classical curricula everywhere rather than, as is the case, a field treated partially and seldom. Several answers can be given to this question. Generic studies are difficult; the field is full of pitfalls, confusion is easy and errors are inevitable. Moreover, the ancient authors who treat generic matters are not famous or easy to read, nor are their works enjoyable or inspiring. These little-known and late rhetoricians lack the glamour of their rivals, those writers who are usually thought of as the only literary critics of antiquity – Aristotle and Horace in their Arts of Poetry and Longinus in his work on the Sublime. Again, the kind of information which generic studies give about ancient literature, although completely consonant with everything else we know about antiquity, may well be unwelcome on a personal level to some classical scholars; for this information may appear to detract from the personalities and sometimes the good characters of ancient poets – although it does not in fact do so – and those classical scholars who study and identify with a single classical writer may resent this.

Another reason why generic studies are neglected is that they are not as friendly as they might be to two cardinal concepts of classical studies – development and imitation. Classical scholars like to talk about development because it gives them an intellectual tool with which to shape and link masses of amorphous information. Some development did indeed take place in the ancient world over the eleven hundred or so years between the appearance of the Homeric poems and the disappearance of Latin as a spoken language of ordinary people. But in a very real sense antiquity was in comparison with the nineteenth and twentieth centuries a time-free zone. Generic studies reflect this fact and show as much development in the genres and no more than is found for instance in ancient technology.

Imitation is another favourite concept of classical scholars. There is certainly a very great deal of direct imitation in ancient literature and classical scholars rightly lay emphasis on it. But generic studies often produce paradoxical results in this field. Authors displaying the closest similarity in their use of topoi or of generic sophistications are frequently authors in whose cases imitation is most unlikely to have been involved. The existence in antiquity of very many formulae of subject-matter that were passed down from one generation to another means that great care must precede judgments upon imitation and that a fair amount of verbal as well as conceptual similarity is necessary before imitation can with any degree of security be postulated.

The last and most important reason for the failure of generic studies to receive due attention, and an explanation also of the instant hostility which sometimes greets generic theory, is basically historical. Incredible as it may seem to scholars working in other literatures, there is a continued, wide acceptance among persons interested in ancient literature of 'Romantic' ideas about poetry; to such persons generic studies are a desecration of their ideas about poetry. Poetry, according to them, should be the beautiful, simple product of individual writers of deep feeling. Generic studies with their emphasis on what is commonplace, sophisticated and intellectual therefore seem to be almost sacrilegious. Such persons suffer partly from misconceptions about poets and poetry and partly from an inability to understand the end-product of generic studies. The sum of the accounts of their own activity given by practising poets of all ages can hardly be said to confirm the notions of the 'Romantic' reader of poetry, who is often in any case someone with a limited range of appreciation and more a devotee of sentimentality than of literature. Moreover, generic studies do not attempt to detract from the poet's individuality. They seek in fact, by separating what is commonplace from what is not, to isolate the individual poet's individuality.

It would have been possible in this book to have treated genre after genre singly, analysing the contents and examples of each genre and so, perhaps, to have ended up by convincing a doubting reader that classical literature ought to be treated generically. Such a procedure would, however, have left no room for more important matters and would have been boring and insulting to readers whose own experience of ancient literature has already led them to think of it in generic terms. I have therefore arranged my material so that within the book sufficient evidence is, I believe, set down to convince any fair-minded person initially unwilling to approach classical literature in this way that the generic approach is indeed valid. But this evidence has been set down, not simply to validate generic studies, but to carry them forward into an investigation of the antiquity and development of the genres, of their categories, of the modes of originality in the use of topoi and of the major mode of originality in the use of genres themselves.

2

The Antiquity and Development of the Genres

The genres are as old as organized societies; they are also universal. Within all human lives there are a number of important recurrent situations which, as societies develop, come to call for regular responses, both in words and in actions. Because literature, which in early society means poetry, concerns itself with these situations, it is natural that renderings and descriptions of these responses should become the staple subject-matter of literature. Of very great importance in early societies, both on a personal and a public level, is religion, which performs many functions allotted to secular disciplines in more developed societies. Hence, among the standard responses to standard situations incapsulated in literature, a large and important group will be of a religious nature. Our classical genres are therefore in essence older than recorded Greek literature and already established in the cultural heritage of the Greeks long before the Homeric poems or their ancestors were composed.

The purpose of this book is not, however, to look at ancient literature from a sociological point of view but to see it through the eyes of its contemporary audience. Although the origin of the genres in real life must not be forgotten by us and was in one sense known and appreciated in antiquity, in another sense people in antiquity did not think that the genres, or most of them, arose from real life. And up to a point this opinion must, in view of the purpose of this book, be accepted as valid and made the basis for our investigation.

Menander the Rhetor at two points expresses and implies his opinion about the antiquity of the genres he is discussing.

Ὅμηρος ὁ θεῖος ποιητὴς τά τε ἄλλα ἡμᾶς ἐπαίδευσε καὶ τὸ τῆς μονῳδίας εἶδος οὐ παραλέλοιπε.
Menander 434 11-12
'That divine poet Homer taught us the genres including the genre *monodia*.'

προὔλαβε μὲν ὁ θεῖος Ὅμηρος καὶ τοῦτο τὸ εἶδος.
Menander 430 12-13

34

'Divine Homer was the first to compose an example of this genre ⟨ syntaktikon ⟩.'

Since Menander is writing about epideictic genres, his belief that Homer invented these genres can be considered part of one view of the relationship between Homer and the whole of rhetoric which was widely held in ancient times.[1] The many texts assembled and cited by Radermacher[2] to illustrate this view show that, from the fifth century BC onwards, the Homeric heroes were frequently regarded as the first exemplars of rhetorical abilities and Homer himself as the inventor of all branches and aspects of the art of rhetoric.

In one sense it is totally incorrect to regard Homer as the inventor of rhetoric. From the historical standpoint the real origins of systematic rhetorical theory and practice, as opposed to skilful oratory, lie in a period later than the Homeric corpus. Radermacher is therefore right from this point of view to give to the source material concerning these later and genuine origins (A 4) the title *Initia Vera*. But from another point of view Homer can justly be considered the inventor of ancient rhetoric. It is not simply that those classical rhetoricians and orators who held the historically false view of Homer's relations with rhetoric imitated Homer in those parts of his work which were considered to be rhetorical, and thereby brought about subsequent verification of the false historical view; it is also that Homer's work, which assembled in its first definitive form all the important components of early Greek social life, including notably its eloquence, became for all later generations of Greeks an encyclopaedic guide to all areas of human activity. It must therefore have influenced those first rhetoricians who were conscious of being original systematizers just as much as it influenced those later Greeks and Romans who, accepting the unhistorical view, regarded Homer, and not its true inventors, as the father of rhetoric.

But in agreeing with Menander in tracing the genres, as far as they can be traced, back to Homer, we are not merely assenting to a part of the general theory that Homer invented rhetoric in the sense in which this theory can be said to be true. Many other sections of rhetorical theory formed no part of the conscious procedure of the Homeric poets, who simply employed natural wit and everyday eloquence. But there is plentiful evidence that the Homeric poets were conscious of generic matters, that with full self-awareness they frequently wrote set-pieces,[3] and that sometimes these set-pieces could be sophisticated generic examples.[4] Moreover, the early Greek lyric poets showed their recognition of the Homeric generic examples by consciously using and varying the Homeric models of the different genres.

So even if rhetoric is left out of the question completely, the generic patterns can be traced quite independently through poetic examples in unbroken line to Homer. It is of course neither desirable nor necessary to leave rhetoric out of consideration, since in antiquity there was no fixed boundary between poetry and rhetoric at any period.[5] In addition, although the rhetoricians doubtless distorted generic patterns, they nevertheless do appear, until the very latest antiquity, to have remained remarkably faithful to the generic material they received from the poets, when the very different purposes of rhetoricians and poets are taken into account.

In conclusion, therefore, Homeric examples can be cited as prototypes of particular rhetorical genres. For example, Menander introduces Odysseus' farewells to Alcinous and the Phaeacians, and to Arete,[6] as examples of syntaktika (430 12ff.) and describes the laments of Andromache, Priam and Hecuba for Hector as monodiae (434 11ff.);[7] Jäger cites Homeric propemptika;[8] and we have treated Homeric prosphonetika in Chapter 1. But this is not all we mean when we agree with Menander in calling Homer the inventor of the genres. We also mean that by the time the rhetoricians came to set down prescriptions for the rhetorical genres, there was already in existence in literature a body of generic examples stemming from Homer which to a large extent dictated the contents of the rhetoricians' prescriptions. It is for this reason that, from our position as observers trying to reconstruct the generic patterns from a fragmentary knowledge of ancient literature and its background and attempting to understand what in ancient eyes was important in ancient literature, even the late and heavily schematized prescriptions found in Pseudo-Dionysius and Menander are useful for the interpretation of the earliest poetry. It is for this reason too that the ability to trace a thought-pattern or situation back to Homer is one of the soundest guarantees that it genuinely constitutes the basis for an ancient genre. All that has been said about Homer so far in this chapter applies also to the early Greek lyric poets, who were thought of to a lesser extent as inventors or early exemplars of rhetorical genres.[9]

So much for genres, which, later than their origin, came to be categorized under one or other branch of oratory. Non-rhetorical genres and their origin will be treated in Chapter 3. It is inevitable with regard to genres found originally in Homer that some question should arise about their development in the subsequent period. Such a development is envisaged by Menander when he discusses how he is going to produce a prescription for the genre monodia:

χρὴ τοίνυν λαβόντας παρὰ τοῦ ποιητοῦ τὰς ἀφορμὰς ἐπεξερ-
γάζεσθαι ταύτας γνόντας τὸ θεώρημα, ὁποῖον ὁ ποιητὴς
παρέδωκεν.

Menander 434 16-18

'We must therefore take our raw material from Homer and work it keeping to the framework laid down by him.'

But Menander, although admitting the concept of development, is nevertheless in this passage adumbrating the substance of two cardinal principles of generic development in antiquity:

1. That the development is limited by the necessity of keeping to the generic material and framework.

2. That the developing 'generic formulae' used by successive generations of ancient writers were regarded by them as expansions of Homeric, or similar prototypes rather than as syntheses of contemporary sophisticated generic examples.

It is for these reasons that generic development in antiquity presents a different appearance from developments in some other literatures. Naturally the 'generic formulae' to which all writers looked were not simply analyses into topoi of the Homeric models. Had they been so, Menander's claims of Homeric ancestry for his own prescriptions would be patently absurd, because they often differ very much from the Homeric models. The generic formulae were formulae similar to the Menandrian prescriptions but broader and more adaptable than them. They can be thought of, although ancient writers probably did not consider them in this mechanical fashion, as full lists of the primary elements and topoi of each genre. They could be used in all kinds of prose and poetry. The generic formulae were not confined to the narrow purposes of rhetorical instruction but were part of the cultural and social heritage of all educated men in antiquity. But it is worth emphasizing that throughout antiquity men regarded the developing generic formulae both for genres taught and not taught in the rhetorical schools as having that relationship with Homeric material which Menander claims for his monodia prescription.

The best beginning of a discussion of the development of the genres

37

from Homer onwards which will not anticipate too many of the principles of generic criticism as yet unintroduced would seem to be an examination of a single genre suitable as a model. I have chosen the syntaktikon – the farewell of a departing traveller.

I shall treat this genre by setting down one of the Homeric prototypes cited by Menander (Homer *Odyssey* 13 38-46), followed by an analysis of the Menandrian prescription for the genre and then by considering a representative sample of members of the genre from the intermediate period – Solon *Fr.* 7 (19) D; Sophocles *Philoctetes* 1452-71; Catullus 46; Tibullus 1 10; Juvenal 3; Rutilius Namatianus 1 1-164.[10]

> Ἀλκίνοε κρεῖον, πάντων ἀριδείκετε λαῶν,
> πέμπετέ με σπείσαντες ἀπήμονα, χαίρετε δ' αὐτοί·
> 40 ἤδη γὰρ τετέλεσται ἅ μοι φίλος ἤθελε θυμός,
> πομπὴ καὶ φίλα δῶρα, τά μοι θεοὶ Οὐρανίωνες
> ὄλβια ποιήσειαν· ἀμύμονα δ' οἴκοι ἄκοιτιν
> νοστήσας εὕροιμι σὺν ἀρτεμέεσσι φίλοισιν.
> ὑμεῖς δ' αὖθι μένοντες ἐϋφραίνοιτε γυναῖκας
> 45 κουριδίας καὶ τέκνα· θεοὶ δ' ἀρετὴν ὀπάσειαν
> παντοίην, καὶ μή τι κακὸν μεταδήμιον εἴη.

Homer *Odyssey* 13 38-46

Odysseus is leaving the foreign city of the Phaeacians to come home to Ithaca. Menander takes this situation into account when he considers the possible sets of circumstances in which a syntaktikon could be delivered – first when the speaker is leaving another city to come home (Odysseus' situation) and second when he is leaving home to go to another city. In fact, Menander even mentions briefly a third situation where the speaker is leaving one foreign city to go to another. The distinction between home and another city creates variant types not only in this genre but in all the travel genres. The mention of the third variant is a sign of the practical intent of Menander's treatise. He knew that some of his pupils' lives would be those of peripatetic rhetors.

Menander's prescription (430-4) is one for a tripartite speech. Parts 1 and 3 are identical for the three variants of the syntaktikon mentioned by Menander:

(*a*) on leaving another city for home
(*b*) on leaving home for another city
(*c*) on leaving one foreign city for another.

Part 2 differs. Menander's variants will be respected in the analysis of

38

his prescription detailed below. But in the subsequent discussion of literary syntaktika, the somewhat over-mechanical rhetorical divisions will be given only as much respect as they deserve and no surprise will be felt if topoi occur rather more freely in examples of the three variants than Menander would have us believe.

Menander's prescription amounts in essence to:

Part 1 (a), (b), (c): The speaker's expressions of sorrow at his departure, grateful praise of the city he is leaving on the basis of attributes relevant to it (e.g. fame, buildings, institutions) (see below), praise of the people of the city, both the public functionaries and the character of the people in general, that is, their kindness, hospitality, etc., sadness at the prospect of his departure from the excellences of the city being emphasized throughout this whole section.

Part 2 (a): Stress on the speaker's natural longing for home, praise of his home, emphasis on the necessity of his going home in spite of his affection for other city, mention of his family at home.

(b) and (c): 'How shall the foreigners treat me?', followed by praise of the city he is going to, with emphasis on his reason for going.

(b): Promise of his return and praise of home once more.

Part 3 (a), (b), (c): Prayer and good wishes for the people being left behind, together with undertakings not to forget them and to spread their fame everywhere, and finally prayers for his own good voyage and safe journey.

As with his monodia prescription, Menander regarded his syntaktikon prescription as an elaboration which nevertheless remained faithful to the Homeric models. He prefaces his syntaktikon prescription with this remark:

ἐπειδὴ δὲ δεῖ τὸν ῥήτορα καὶ περιεργότερον χρῆσθαι τῷ εἴδει καὶ ἐξεργασίᾳ πλείονι, φέρε μὴ ἀφιστάμενοι τοῦ Ὁμηρικοῦ ἔθους διέλωμεν.

Menander 430 28-30

'Since the rhetor must employ the genre in a more elaborate and highly-wrought way ⟨than Homer did⟩, let us divide it into parts without departing from the customary Homeric manner.'

It is therefore fairly clear how Menander would have viewed the elements of his Homeric models, especially those of the one quoted above, the syntaktikon of Odysseus to Alcinous and the Phaeacians (*Odyssey* 13 38-46), as compared with the elements of his prescription. He would have seen 38 as praise of Alcinous, 40-1 as an expression of gratitude to Alcinous and to the Phaeacians, 42-3 as expressing Odysseus' reasons for departure in a reference to his wife and kinsfolk at home (this being encomium of his native land), 39 and 44-6 as prayers and good wishes for the Phaeacians, 41-2 as a good wish for himself, and finally ἀπήμονα in 39 as a wish for his own safe departure. Nor would Menander, in spite of his emphasis on his own pupils sticking to the correct order of topics (433 19-20), have been much concerned about what is possibly the slightly disordered nature of the Homeric example as compared with his own formula. In another section of his work, he discusses what he calls *lalia* (388ff.). This is not a separate genre but an informal un-ordered way of treating the same subject-matter of any genre as is treated formally by the appropriate *logos*. Menander mentions among the genres which can be treated by means of a lalia the syntaktikon, and he gives a brief account of a *syntaktike lalia* (393 31-394 12). This account is apparently abbreviated and does not, as far as it goes, have a different order of topoi from the *syntaktikos logos*. But the general principle which Menander puts forward to distinguish lalia and logos (391 19ff.) makes it likely that, if he thought Homer did not in any respect correspond in order of treatment of material to his own prescription, he would have explained this by saying that Odysseus was uttering the less formal lalia but was still producing a prototype for his own logos prescription.

Homer and Menander may, for our practical purposes, be considered as the first and last stages of whatever development the genre syntaktikon saw in antiquity, although there are in fact surviving post-Menandrian syntaktika which show further development.[11] The sample of syntaktika written in the interval begins with a short example addressed by Solon to his host Philokypros, King of Soloi in Cyprus:

> νῦν δὲ σὺ μὲν Σολίοισι πολὺν χρόνον ἐνθάδ' ἀνάσσων
> τήνδε πόλιν ναίοις καὶ γένος ὑμέτερον·
> αὐτὰρ ἐμὲ ξὺν νηὶ θοῇ κλεινῆς ἀπὸ νήσου
> ἀσκηθῆ πέμποι Κύπρις ἰοστέφανος·
> 5 οἰκισμῷ δ' ἐπὶ τῷδε χάριν καὶ κῦδος ὀπάζοι
> ἐσθλὸν καὶ νόστον πατρίδ' ἐς ἡμετέρην.
> Solon *Fr.* 7 (19) D

The basic Menandrian elements are present in fairly explicit form, in contrast to *Odyssey* 13 38ff., where some of them are indirectly expressed, a fact which demonstrates that even this Homeric model is not a simple but a sophisticated example of the genre.[12] After the good wishes to Philokypros (1-2), a variant of the topos found in *Odyssey* 13 39 occurs. Instead of saying 'Send me off safely' (ἀπήμονα), as does Odysseus to Alcinous and the Phaeacians, Solon says 'May Kypris (Aphrodite, goddess of Cyprus and of the sea) send me off safely' (ἀσκηθῆ) and adds 'from this celebrated island'. In this way Solon is combining the request for safe despatch with the prayers to the gods and also with praise of Cyprus and therefore of Soloi.[13] In similar fashion in 5-6, continuing his prayer and also summing up 1-4, he asks that the goddess give χάρις and glory to Soloi; by mentioning glory and making a pun on χάρις he combines good wishes for Soloi with an expression of his own gratitude for the hospitality he has received. Solon then employs the verb (may she give) in 5 to express a prayer in 6 for his own return home. Solon's syntaktikon is short like that of Odysseus to Alcinous and the Phaeacians; but it cannot be described as more or less sophisticated than the Homeric example. It is less simple in some ways than Homer but more simple in others: the elements are varied and combined more subtly than in Homer, but in themselves they occur in a more obvious and less indirect form than in Homer.

Solon's syntaktikon, like that of Odysseus, was delivered on leaving a foreign city for home – Menander's variant (*a*). The next example is, like the first two, delivered on the occasion of departure from another country. But another aspect of it is different: the people delivering it are not going home, but to yet another foreign place – Menander's variant (*c*):

ΦΙΛΟΚΤΗΤΗΣ
φέρε νυν στείχων χώραν καλέσω.
χαῖρ᾽, ὦ μέλαθρον ξύμφρουρον ἐμοί,
Νύμφαι τ᾽ ἔνυδροι λειμωνιάδες,
1455 καὶ κτύπος ἄρσην πόντου προβολῆς,
οὗ πολλάκι δὴ τοὐμὸν ἐτέγχθη
κρᾶτ᾽ ἐνδόμυχον πληγῇσι νότου,
πολλὰ δὲ φωνῆς τῆς ἡμετέρας
Ἑρμαῖον ὄρος παρέπεμψεν ἐμοὶ
1460 στόνον ἀντίτυπον χειμαζομένῳ.
νῦν δ᾽, ὦ κρῆναι Λύκιόν τε ποτόν,
λείπομεν ὑμᾶς, λείπομεν ἤδη,

δόξης οὔ ποτε τῆσδ᾽ ἐπιβάντες.
χαῖρ᾽, ὦ Λήμνου πέδον ἀμφίαλον,
1465 καί μ, εὐπλοίᾳ πέμψον ἀμέμπτως,
ἔνθ᾽ ἡ μεγάλη Μοῖρα κομίζει,
γνώμη τε φίλων χὠ πανδαμάτωρ
δαίμων, ὃς ταῦτ᾽ ἐπέκρανεν.

ΧΟΡΟΣ
χωρῶμεν δὴ πάντες ἀολλεῖς,
1470 Νύμφαις ἁλίαισιν ἐπευξάμενοι
νόστου σωτῆρας ἱκέσθαι.

Sophocles *Philoctetes* 1452-71

Because Menander says so little specifically on the subject of the syntaktikon delivered when its speaker is going from one foreign place to another, and because literary syntaktika of this kind are hard to find,[14] it
is not easy to say with certainty what topoi of this part of Sophocles'
Philoctetes are being used in a normal or abnormal way. Caution is
necessary. To begin with, a generic rather than a topical sophistication
may be noted in Philoctetes' speech. It is addressed throughout not to
a man or a *polis* (which is a collection of men)[15] but to the land, *chora*
(cp. p. 221) – a device to increase the pathos of Philoctetes' departure
by emphasizing the deserted nature of his place of exile. Philoctetes is a
positive counter-example to Menander's precept that the syntaktic
speaker must either be sorry to be leaving or affect sorrow. But when the
matter is considered, it will be remembered that Odysseus and Solon
did not in fact regret leaving Phaeacia and Cyprus, nor did they affect
such regret. The explanation is probably that Menander was thinking
in terms of the professional rhetor. When Menander's prescription
characterizes the genre syntaktikon in terms of positive sorrow or pretence of sorrow at separation, he is generalizing from the characteristic
emotion felt by people leaving home – variant (*b*) – and is being motivated to do so by the need of the professional rhetor to be complimentary
in all circumstances, whether he was leaving home or leaving another
city. But since Philoctetes is leaving a foreign place and is not a rhetor,
sorrow cannot be expected of him.

In topical terms a heavy emphasis is laid in Philoctetes' syntaktikon
on Lemnos, the place being left. Although Philoctetes is not unhappy
to leave Lemnos, he is not hostile to it. It has, after all, sheltered his
exile. He says goodbye to it (1453) and elaborates this into a farewell

to various geographical features of the island – rivers, headlands, mountain springs. Although these features are not mentioned in an explicitly encomiastic way and indeed in some cases are introduced in connexion with Philoctetes' unpleasant experiences in Lemnos, the passage has, albeit indirectly, the function of that part of the Menandrian prescription which runs:

ἐπαινέσεις δὲ αὐτήν, ὁπόθεν ἂν ὁ καιρὸς αὐτῇ διδῷ τὰ ἐγκώμια, οἷον ἀπὸ τῶν ἀρχαίων εἴ τι σεμνὸν ἔχοις, ἀπὸ τῶν ἀέρων, ἀπὸ τοῦ εἴδους τοῦ κάλλους, οἷον ἀπὸ στοῶν καὶ λιμένων καὶ ἀκροπόλεως καὶ ἱερῶν πολυτελῶν καὶ ἀγαλμάτων.

Menander 430 31-431 5

'. . . and you will praise the city ⟨which you are leaving⟩ on grounds relevant to that particular city, for example, some ancient distinction, if there is one, the climate, the city's particular beauties, its porticos and harbours, the acropolis, its rich sacred places and statues.'

After this elaborate address by Philoctetes to the place he is leaving, the place to which he is going is mentioned only briefly and obscurely (1466). Sophocles is being deliberately brief about Troy in contrast with the elaboration of his treatment of Lemnos. Here topoi are being given dramatic functions connecting them with the play as a whole. The elaboration of the address to Lemnos in contrast with the silence about Troy recalls Philoctetes' previous deep desire to return home to Greece and his equally deep reluctance to go to Troy. Earlier in the play he wanted to stay in Lemnos rather than go to Troy. The generally unsatisfactory circumstances of Philoctetes' recall are also underlined by this device, which in addition probably represents Philoctetes' misgivings about his reception at Troy, the next foreign place to which he will come, misgivings Menander's rhetor is recommended to express (431 18-19).

Lines 1465 and 1470-1 contain the prayers of Philoctetes and the chorus, respectively, for a good voyage and safety for themselves, a clear and straightforward use of this particular topos.[16] Lines 1466-8, however, contain topoi of the genre in sophisticated forms, again with dramatic function. Philoctetes refers to fate, the counsel of friends and the omnipotent deity, all of which have brought about his departure. The syntaktic speaker sometimes speaks of his loved ones,[17] and pleads necessity or compulsion as an excuse or reason for departure.[18] The topos on fate and necessity is given an added dimension when it is remembered that Philoctetes is leaving in accordance with a recent direct command of the gods relayed by Heracles. The reference to friends is both pathetic in view of the genuine affection between Neoptolemus and Philoctetes (the development of which is one of the play's chief themes), and also ominous in view of Philoctetes' hatred for the Atreidae, the leaders of the army at Troy to which he is going. As well as alluding subtly to two topoi of the genre, these lines give an air of resignation to the end of the play and suggest that, although Philoctetes may have reservations about his reception at Troy, he feels that, even if still far from home, he will not be without friends there.

Sophocles' use of the topoi, like that of Solon, remains on one level fairly straightforward. They appear, all of them, in an easily recognizable form. On another level, however, he is sophisticated in his operations with the topoi. It is not only that they are sometimes subtly combined: Sophocles' elaborate and allusive uses of some topoi, his dissociation of others from their normal functions, and his overall dramatic use of topoi show considerable self-consciousness and skill in generic composition.

The next example, Catullus 46, is another syntaktikon of a man leaving one foreign place for another, although he is going home eventually:

Iam uer egelidos refert tepores,
iam caeli furor aequinoctialis
iucundis Zephyri silescit auris.
linquantur Phrygii, Catulle, campi
5 Nicaeaeque ager uber aestuosae:
ad claras Asiae uolemus urbes.
iam mens praetrepidans auet uagari,
iam laeti studio pedes uigescunt.
o dulces comitum ualete coetus,
10 longe quos simul a domo profectos
diuersae uarie uiae reportant.
    Catullus 46

Lines 1-3 announce that it is spring, which means in this poem that it is good sailing weather. A reference to or description of the coming of spring is a favourite way of beginning a poem among lyric poets.[19]

The reference to spring in Catullus 46 stands in Catullus' syntaktikon in place of the normal prayer for a good voyage. The substitution is of a type already discussed on pp. 27-8, one of statement for wish. Catullus then goes on to announce his departure from the province of Bithynia, which he praises as fertile and productive in 4-5, and to state as his destination the cities of Asia, also praised in the adjective *claras* (6). So far Catullus conforms more or less to the generic pattern. But two features of his syntaktikon stand out as unusual. First, when making his farewells, he does not address the people of the province. Instead he employs self-apostrophe, announcing his departure by means of jussive subjunctives addressed to himself (*linquantur* 4, *uolemus* 6), followed by an address to his friends who are setting out for home by different routes at the same time as he himself is leaving. The second unusual feature is that Catullus goes beyond the normal practice of poetic syntaktic speakers who fail to show regret at going home (see above). Catullus shows positive pleasure at leaving, and moreover expresses eagerness to go not as an excuse but as the sole motive for going.

The first of these features, Catullus' failure to address the people of the province, is probably justified by his position. As a Roman in the entourage of a governor, Catullus had no definable relationship with any provincials. He was therefore able to transfer the encomiastic farewells from them mainly to those friends who had also been part of the entourage. The second feature, Catullus' positive joy at leaving, is possibly not as unusual as it might seem. The normal emotion in antiquity on going home is joy, on leaving it sorrow, and Menander's description of the syntaktikon, in characterizing it as marked by expressions of sorrow at departure, is (as was noted above) very much biased towards the needs of practising rhetoricians. But it is probably true that open joy at departure is not the normal characteristic of the syntaktikon, and that Catullus was able to express his joy as fully as he does because he had excluded the provincials as addressees and substituted for them fellow Romans who, since they were going home too, would share his own pleasure.

This technical ingenuity does have a poetic purpose. It allows Catullus without attacking Bithynia to exclude any circumstances conducive to sorrow, and so to reap the paradoxical literary benefits of using a genre normally not associated with expressions of pleasure as a vehicle for expressions of the highest pleasure. Catullus then, for all the brevity of his use of the topoi, has exploited the genre to fit his particular situation. At the same time the main topoi remain clearly recognizable.

The next syntaktikon to be treated, Tibullus 1 10, is a case where the speaker is leaving home to go abroad – variant (*b*). In this long elegy Tibullus has taken advantage of the traditional Roman opposition between home and war (*domi militiaeque*) to depict himself as leaving home not to go to another specific place but to go to war. This sophistication makes generic identification of the elegy more difficult than it would otherwise be and the difficulty is increased by two other factors. The first consists of Tibullus' divergences from the Menandrian prescription. Menander directs that home shall be treated first and abroad second. Tibullus treats war (abroad) first and home second. Moreover, Menander prescribes praise for abroad whereas Tibullus attacks war (abroad). The second factor increasing the difficulty of generic identification is the large presence in this epilogue to Tibullus' first book of the kind of autobiographical material so often used for programmatic purposes in prologues and epilogues. In all these sophistications Tibullus is showing a greater complexity and allusiveness in his use of topoi than has been found in the previous examples, and in this and in the repetition of some themes of 1-29 in 30ff. he is approaching the elaboration of treatment prescribed for rhetoricians by Menander.

Tibullus' hostile treatment of war is not unduly surprising, although the ancient reader was doubtless meant to experience a slight shock at vituperation, where encomium was expected. But because Tibullus is not a rhetor but an elegiac love-poet and is leaving home to go, not to another place but to war, the antithesis of love, his attack is acceptable within the limits of normal topical variation.[20] In 1-10 Tibullus delivers a strong and elaborate attack on war, and on gold as the cause of wars. Lines 11-12 explain why this denigration has prefaced the elegy. If there were no wars, Tibullus would not be leaving home. At 13 he alludes in the words 'now I am dragged off to the wars' to a topos of the genre – the compulsion put upon the traveller to depart.[21] He gives no explanation of this compulsion because to do so would have meant casting an aspersion on his patron Messalla, who was responsible for the poet's plight. Such an aspersion would have been unthinkable in view of the relations between Tibullus and Messalla. At 15ff. Tibullus turns to prayer for his own safety, another topos; he prays to the *Lares* here and at 22ff. This is partly because his devotion to the *Lares* is part of his ostentatiously Roman religious image. It is also because the *Lares*, with their countryside associations, form a good frame for a set of allusions (19-24) to the old-fashioned countryside, which in his poetic *persona* Tibullus regards as his home. Finally, the *Lares* are protectors of travellers on journeys.[22]

At 30 the sequence of themes already treated in the elegy begins to repeat itself.[23] Tibullus once more rejects war and martial glory (29-32), stressing again, this time at greater length, the companion of war, death (33-8). In contrast with war and death he paints an ideal picture of home. In his case home is the countryside flourishing in peace: this is the kind of life he wishes for himself (39-52). In 53-66 he describes the playful erotic wars of peace which are the only kind of wars congenial to him. There is no doubt that Tibullus 1 10 does show development in terms of complexity and originality in the use of topoi from those syntaktika previously discussed.

The last two syntaktika to be treated, Juvenal 3 and Rutilius Namatianus 1 1-164, are both long and elaborate, although it is only in length and greater formal approximation to the Menandrian rhetorical formula for the genre and not in subtlety and complexity that they show a development upon Tibullus 1 10. They differ from one another in one notable respect. The second (Rutilius Namatianus 1 1-164), although composed later than Menander's treatise, may be included as the last of this selection of syntaktika showing development from Homer to Menander because it is a pagan syntaktikon that does not contain material of the kind which entered the genre in the Christian period. It is strictly speaking a farewell to a foreign place by a man going home. But Rome had been for Rutilius a place of long residence, where he had attained high office, so that it is hardly surprising that his syntaktikon displays strong sorrow at departure and encomium of the place being left. However, the first (Juvenal 3), although a farewell to his home by one leaving for foreign parts, attacks the home he is leaving. It is, therefore, what will be described later in this chapter and in Chapter 5 as an 'inverse' example of the genre. Like other members of other genres treated there and elsewhere in this book and described as 'inverse', it preserves the generic characters and situation but substitutes the opposite function for that normally associated with the particular genre. Here, in the speech of Umbricius, the departing traveller feels no regrets whatsoever about leaving his home town Rome and indeed subjects Rome to a lengthy attack on a great many counts. This attack should not be confused with the mere lack of enthusiasm for the foreign places being left in some of the syntaktika discussed above, nor with the praise of the places to which travellers are going in these and other syntaktika. Inversion in the syntaktikon consists not in failing to express regret at departure, or even in failing to laud the place one is leaving, but in open hostility to the place being left behind, which is equivalent to denigration of the addressee.[24] In cases where the traveller is leaving a foreign place, his perfectly normal joy at the prospect of returning home may, although this is not inevitable, quite naturally diminish the encomium of the foreign place being left. Therefore, a writer wishing to compose an inverse syntaktikon upon leaving a foreign place would have to make it clear by vicious attacks on that place what he was doing. In the case of someone leaving home, the very failure to regret this fact and praise home enthusiastically would itself be odd, although again this alone would not constitute attack on home and make it clear that inversion was taking place. Juvenal, characteristically, and to make his intentions wholly unambiguous, causes Umbricius to attack his home viciously in no uncertain terms. Hence the effectiveness of Umbricius' expressed desire to leave his native land (29), which follows the general explanation of his intentions and reasons for departure.

The inverse syntaktikon of Umbricius is of course a mere pretext to allow Juvenal to indulge in almost 300 lines of satirical attack on Rome in all its aspects. At 170 the attack on the capital and its populace begins to be enlivened through the exploitation of another set of syntactic commonplaces. Umbricius is made to attack Rome by comparing her with country places of the sort in which he intends to settle – a comparison which is of course to Rome's detriment. These topical praises of places typical of the one to which Umbricius is going continue off and on up to 231, when Umbricius resorts once more to uninterrupted attacks on Rome. At 315 Umbricius departs with injunctions to Juvenal not to forget him – a neat variation, since the friendly syntactic speaker claims that he will never forget the place he is leaving.[25] Umbricius also asks for an invitation to Juvenal's home town of Aquinum should Juvenal be there. By this last request Umbricius says indirectly that he will never return to Rome – the inversion of the normal final topos of the syntaktikon of someone leaving home.[26]

Rutilius devotes to praise of Rome most of the syntactic first 164 lines of the *hodoiporikon* in which he describes his journey back from Rome to Gaul. The first section (1-18), among other encomia of Rome and regrets for his own departure, congratulates those for whom Rome is their native city (5ff.). At 19 Rutilius topically explains that his fortune takes him away from his beloved Rome since Gaul, his home, is summoning him back. In this section, in which he should in accordance with the generic prescription praise his native land, the ravaged state of that country prompts him rather to express his pity and love for Gaul.

These feelings afford more sophisticated motives for the affection he states for Gaul, along with impatience to be there, at the end of the section of which Gaul is the subject:

ipsi quin etiam fontes si mittere uocem
  ipsaque si possent arbuta nostra loqui,
cessantem iustis poterant urgere querelis
  et desideriis addere uela meis.
iam iam laxatis carae complexibus urbis
  uincimur et serum uix toleramus iter.

Rutilius Namatianus 1 31-6

Lines 37-42 describe his choice of the sea as his route, a choice dictated by considerations of safety. Like Catullus he states here the conditions conducive to safety instead of praying for safety, although he later includes a prayer also. The final section of the syntaktikon (43-164) is a long prayer – to the goddess Rome. This prayer, which Rutilius regards as an atonement for the sin of leaving Rome, fulfils all the encomiastic requirements of the genre several times over. Rome's Empire, her ancient glories, her temples, aqueducts, beauties, climate – the Menandrian topoi and many others besides – find their place in this elaborate prayer. At the end of it (155-64) Rutilius prays to Rome for a calm voyage, asks, like Solon, that Venus be his guide and smooth his way, and finally begs Rome not to forget him. This last variation on the generic topos is here encomiastic, unlike the similar but not identical variation noted above in Juvenal 3.

The genre syntaktikon and these particular examples of it have been chosen to illustrate development in the use of topoi throughout the classical period because they are as typical in this respect as any one genre and examples of it could be. From these syntaktika it would appear that the poets' treatment of topoi develops: as time goes on, there is a general increase in the complexity, subtlety, allusiveness and variation of their use of topoi. Moreover, generic examples, and hence individual topoi, become longer and more elaborate. But at the same time a counter-current of conformity is gathering force. The later a poem, the more likely it is to conform to the rhetorical prescription for its genre in terms of presenting a large proportion of the appropriate topoi in standard order. There are of course many exceptions to both these principles. The development described appears to have taken place slowly and there are no milestones in it or hard and fast rules. This is not to say that an exhaustive study of development in the use of topoi, based on as yet unavailable detailed analyses of a large number of genres, may not at some time in the future yield a much more precise description of the process. Such a description would of course take account of the general increase in elaboration, rigidity of topical order and length of generic examples, of the influence of the rhetorical schools from the time of their emergence, and of the increasing dominance of rhetoric, especially in the first and subsequent centuries A D. But it would probably continue to lay stress on the slow pace of development, on the importance of the purposes and abilities of individual writers, and on the great sophistication of which authors of early date were capable.

One part of the question of topical development is virtually untreatable: this is the matter of the dates at which particular topoi entered genres. Had classical literature survived in entirety and were all generic examples assigned to their genres, those would be well known. As it is, the fact that a topos first appears in a known member of a genre at a particular date is not significant. It may well have appeared in a lost member long before this, or may well appear in a surviving but unassigned member. The development of generic sophistications cannot be discussed in any detail in this chapter since such a discussion would anticipate material from Chapters 5-9. In general, however, the results of the enquiries in these chapters in terms of development are similar to those obtained by a study of topical development.

At this point it may be worth exemplifying topical sophistication in early Greek poetry. This is because there is a natural and wrong inclination to believe that in ancient poetry 'early' means 'simple' and that real sophistication in ancient literature is something which first occurs after the emergence of rhetoric. No purpose would be served by attempting the difficult task of proving the existence in Homer of topically, and indeed generically sophisticated examples of genres as well as simple examples.[27] It is easier and just as satisfactory to exemplify topical sophistication in early Greek lyric poetry. Since religious examples might be considered as special cases and conclusions drawn from them not to be capable of wider application, four non-religious poems will be treated. The first of these is a propemptikon:

τεθνάκην δ' ἀδόλως θέλω·
ἄ με ψισδομένα κατελίμπανεν

πόλλα καὶ τόδ' ἔειπ.[
ὤιμ' ὠς δεῖνα πεπ[όνθ]αμεν·
5 Ψάπφ', ἦ μάν σ' ἀέκοισ' ἀπυλιμπάνω.
τὰν δ' ἔγω τάδ' ἀμειβόμαν·
χαίροισ' ἔρχεο κἄμεθεν
μέμναισ'· οἶσθα γὰρ ὤς σε πεδήπομεν.
αἰ δὲ μή, ἀλλά σ' ἔγω θέλω
10 ὄμναισαι[... (.)][.. (.)]..αι
..[   ] καὶ κάλ' ἐπάσχομεν·
πό[λλοις γὰρ στεφάν]οις ἴων
καὶ βρ[όδων   ]κίων τ' ὔμοι
κα..[   ] πὰρ ἔμοι περεθήκαο,
15 καὶ πόλλαις ὐπαθύμιδας
πλέκταις ἀμφ' ἀπάλᾳ δέρᾳ
ἀνθέων .[   ] πεποημμέναις,
καὶ π.....[   ]. μύρῳ
βρενθείῳ .[   ]ρυ[..]ν
20 ἐξαλείψαο καὶ βασιληίῳ,
καὶ στρώμν[αν ἐ]πὶ μολθάκαν
ἀπάλαν πα.[   ]...ων
ἐξίης πόθο[ν   ].νιδων,
κωὔτε τις [   ]..τι
25 ἶρον οὐδυ[   ]
ἔπλετ' ὄππ[οθεν ἄμ]μες ἀπέσκομεν,
οὐκ ἄλσος .[   ].ρος
                    ]ψοφος
                    ]...οιδιαι
        Sappho *Fr*. 94 (LP)

'I really want to die'
She parted from me weeping
copiously and said this.
'Alas, what misery we have suffered,
5 Sappho. I swear to you I leave you against my will.'
But I answered her thus.
'Go with my blessing and remember me,
for you know how much we cherished you.
If you do not, then I want
10 to remind you ...
    ... and the good times we had.

For many crowns of violets
and roses and . . . together
. . . you put around you by my side
15 and many plaited garlands . . .
you put round your soft neck
of blossoms . . .
and . . . with perfume
of flowers . . .
20 and with myrrh of royal quality you anointed yourself
and on soft beds
tender . . .
you satisfied your desire . . .
and neither was there any . . . nor any
25 temple nor even . . .
from which we were absent . . .
There was no grove . . .

Topoi used in standard fashion are:
(i) The formal 'go' or 'you will go' with good wishes (7).[28]
(ii) The request 'remember me' (7-8).[29]
(iii) The statement of affection (8).[30]
The statement of affection leads to a set of propemptic topoi used in a novel and sophisticated way. At the end of the second non-schetliastic section of Menander's prescription for the propemptikon, occurs the following precept:

εἶτα ἐπὶ τούτοις ἅπασιν ἀξιώσεις αὐτὸν μεμνῆσθαι τῆς πάλαι
συνηθείας, τῆς εὐνοίας, τῆς φιλίας, καὶ παραμυθεῖσθαι τὴν
ἀπόστασιν μνήμαις καὶ λόγοις.

Menander 398 26-9

'Then after all this you will ask him to bear in mind your long association and kind friendship with him and to assuage his separation from you by remembering these and speaking about them.'

This is what Sappho is doing in 10-29. Having asked the traveller not to forget her, and assured the traveller of her affection, Sappho reinforces this request and protestation through a fictional assumption[31] that the traveller does not know how much Sappho loved and cared for her. This assumption allows Sappho to recall to the traveller their shared love-making and other shared experiences. Besides its basic propemptic function of displaying affection, the passage has a second function: that of consoling the departing traveller. But on closer examination Sappho's material also resembles another section of the Menandrian prescription – this time part of the schetliasmos:

προϊὼν δὲ τῷ λόγῳ ὑπομνησθήσῃ, ἂν οὕτω τύχῃ, καὶ ἀσκήσεως κοινῆς καὶ παλαίστρας καὶ γυμνασίων τῶν αὐτῶν.... εἰσάξεις πρὸς ἐποχὴν δῆθεν καὶ τὰ τῆς πόλεως ἐγκώμια. οὐδ' οὕτως ὁ τῶν Ἀθηναίων αἱρεῖ σε πόθος, οὐδὲ μυστηρίων καὶ τελετῶν, οὐδὲ μουσεῖα καὶ θέατρα λόγων... ;

Menander 396 21-3, 25-8

'Continuing in your speech, you will remind ⟨the traveller⟩, if it is relevant, of how you practised together in the same wrestling school and the same gymnasia . . . then you will introduce after this praises of the city with the supposed purpose of holding the traveller back. You will say, for example, ''are you not in love with ⟨ and so held back by⟩ Athens, by the mysteries and their hierophants, by the schools of literature and the exhibitions of oratory . . .?'' '

Some of this section of Menander appears to be reflected in another propemptikon, Ovid *Amores* 2 11

ecce fugit notumque torum sociosque Penates
fallacisque uias ire Corinna parat.

7-8

where, as part of his schetliasmos to the departing Corinna, Ovid recalls their common activities in the erotic field (7) and follows this by the punning allusion in *fallaces* to Corinna's faithlessness to him. In the same way the Menandrian passage quoted above is followed by one of the frequent accusations of faithlessness made by Menander's propemptic speaker.

Sappho's material overlaps with that of Menander. She reminds the traveller, as does Ovid, of their common love-making at some length (10-23). Sappho then, or so it would appear from what remains of the lines, goes on to talk of temples or sacred rites or offerings and of a sacred grove (24-9) at which she and the departing traveller were constantly together. Here Sappho can be credited with a minor topical sophistication. In the Menandrian prescription, and hence probably in ancient literature in general, common activities and praise of the religious life of the city are separate sections. Sappho has combined the two notions so that her mention of sacred matters is part of her reminiscences about things done by herself and the traveller. The two of them, she says, together took part in the sacred rites at the sacred places being mentioned. But the major topical sophistication is that Sappho has used as the substance of her consolatory reminiscences material normally associated with schetliasmos. This sophistication resembles a similar device in Propertius 1 6 and it is paralleled in other non-schetliastic propemptika.[32] Sappho's consolation is rendered all the more effective by the paradox that the material contained in it is normally associated with schetliasmos and that its purpose is usually to deter the traveller from leaving, not as here to comfort the departing traveller's grief at separation from the speaker.

This topical sophistication occurs in Sappho along with three generic sophistications. The first two are of a kind already mentioned on p. 12 and discussed at greater length in Chapter 5: they affect the 'form' of the poem. Sappho's first 'formal' sophistication is that her propemptikon is narrated as having been uttered in the past as a direct speech, rather than, as is normal, simply occurring in the present. The second 'formal' sophistication is that the poem is in dialogue form. Both these sophistications help to explain the absence of a schetliasmos in this propemptikon of equal to equal. By placing her propemptikon in the past Sappho shows that a schetliasmos, if she had included one, would certainly have been ineffectual. For although most schetliasmoi fail, some succeed,[33] and success is always a possibility.

However, since Sappho's propemptikon, although narrated as having been spoken in the past, is reported in the tense of its delivery (the present tense), a schetliasmos could from a logical point of view have been included in it. But the second formal sophistication, the dialogue form, is used to explain further the absence of a schetliasmos as well as to introduce the third generic sophistication, which resembles one already mentioned on p. 13 in connexion with Propertius 1 6. There we discussed the ' inclusion ' within a member of a genre of an example of another variant of the same genre. This and the related sophistication found here, the inclusion within a generic example of an example of a related genre, will be discussed again in Chapter 7. In Sappho *Fr.* 94 (LP) the dialogue form is exploited to allow the syntaktikon of the traveller (1-5) to be included at the beginning of a poem whose overall genre is propemptikon. Thus an example of one travel genre is included within an example of another. The included syntaktikon contains only two of the most important syntactic topoi, the departing traveller's unhappiness at departure (1-2, 4) and her unwillingness to go (5).

Both of these imply further generic material: the topos that she is going of necessity and, also topical, the affectionate praise of Sappho whom she is leaving. This included syntaktikon explains completely the omission of a schetliasmos. The purpose of a schetliasmos is to dissuade from departing someone who wishes to depart. In this case the departing traveller is going against her will.

The temporal sophistication of Sappho *Fr.* 94 (LP), whereby the propemptikon is narrated as having been delivered in the past, has a superficial resemblance to what occurs in another lyric propemptikon – Horace *Odes* 1 3. There the propemptikon is spoken directly in the present tense, but the traveller has already departed, and there also no schetliasmos is found. But the resemblance is no more than superficial. Besides the difference between the temporal sophistications of the two lyrics, they differ also in belonging to different variants of the propemptikon. While Sappho *Fr.* 94 (LP) is of the equal to equal variant, Horace *Odes* 1 3 is a propemptikon of inferior to superior. In Horace, therefore, a schetliasmos would have been doubly inappropriate: logically ridiculous because the traveller was already gone, and generically odd, though not impossible, because schetliasmos is not normally associated with this variant of the genre.

Sappho then, in *Fr.* 94 (LP), has combined several topical and generic sophistications. The apparent simplicity of the result is a tribute to her art. The second early Greek poem which exemplifies topical sophistication is also a propemptikon. It is attributed either to Archilochus – *Fr.* 79aD – or to Hipponax – *Fr.* 115 (Masson):

π.[   ]ν[...]....[
    κύμ[ασι] πλα[ζόμ]ενος.
κἀν Σαλμυδ[ησσ]ῷ γυμνὸν εὐφρονέσ[τατα]
    Θρήικες ἀκρό[κ]ομοι
5 λάβοιεν – ἔνθα πόλλ' ἀναπλήσει κακὰ
    δούλιον ἄρτον ἔδων –
ῥίγει πεπηγότ' αὐτόν. ἐκ δὲ τοῦ χνό‹ο›υ
    φυκία πόλλ' ἐπέχοι,
κροτέοι δ' ὀδόντας ὡς [κύ]ων ἐπὶ στόμα
10   κείμενος ἀκρασίῃ
ἄκρον παρὰ ῥηγμῖνα κυμαντῷ [.].[.].ι
    ταῦτ' ἐθέλοιμ' ἂν ἰδεῖν,

ὅς μ' ἠδίκησε, λ[ὰ]ξ δ' ἐπ' ὀρκίοισ' ἔβη
τὸ πρὶν ἑταῖρος [ἐ]ών.

. . . . .

... carried here and there on the waves
and I hope that naked on Salmydessus
the top-knotted Thracians receive him
5 most kindly – there he shall endure many troubles
eating the bread of slavery –
yes, stiff with cold and when he comes out of the sea scum
I hope many a strand of seaweed covers him
and his teeth chatter as he lies
10 helpless on his face like a dog
on the beach by the breakers.
I would like to see these things happen
to the man who did me an injustice, who trampled on his oaths,
though once he was my friend.

This propemptikon, like Horace *Epode* 10 which is recognized as being
an imitation of it, employs the principle of 'inversion' which has already
been referred to in this chapter in connexion with Juvenal 3. In inverse
propemptika the speaker displays hatred instead of affection for the
departing traveller: he wishes him a rough voyage and an evil end to his
journey in shipwreck (see pp. 130-5). All the topoi which in normal
propemptika express the speaker's encomiastic affection are inverted.
In this fragment the evil wishes for the traveller are long, involved and
spiteful. Only at the very end is the reason for the speaker's hatred
given, namely that the traveller was once the speaker's comrade but
treated him unjustly, breaking his oath to him.

The links of comradeship were an important factor in Greek culture,
especially early Greek culture, and the institution had political aspects.
Moreover, in a society where the duty of a good man was thought to
consist of benefiting his friends and harming his enemies, harm done to
friends was regarded as all the more dreadful because it was more un-
expected and less necessary, since one's enemies provided a socially
acceptable field for evil-doing. The structure of the poem is therefore
fairly comprehensible in non-generic terms. The author has created
tension in his audience by pronouncing a series of vicious curses, the
reason for which or at the least the main reason for which (since nothing
can be assumed with certainty about the lost beginning of this fragment)

he postpones until the end of the poem. When the reason comes, it is that the person upon whom the ill-wishes are being heaped has committed a crime among the worst in contemporary estimation.[34]

In generic terms the author may well have had another motive in his choice of reason and postponement of it, namely a wish to employ a standard topos of the genre in unusual circumstances. This topos is one which Menander makes much of in his prescription for the schetliasmos of the propemptikon of friend to friend. It is that the two friends have entered into a compact of friendship which the departing traveller, by his departure, is breaking (396-7). At one point he makes his propemptic speaker quote Homer (almost correctly):

πῇ δὴ συνθεσίαι καὶ ὅρκια βήσεται ἡμῖν;
Iliad 2 339

The emphasis placed by Menander on this notion seems to be reflected in some literary propemptika:

et queritur nullos esse relicta deos.
et nihil infido durius esse uiro.
   Propertius 1 6 8, 18

sed quocumque modo de me, periura, mereris,
   Propertius 1 8 17

dissimulare etiam sperasti, perfide, tantum
posse nefas tacitusque mea decedere terra?
nec te noster amor nec te data dextera quondam
nec moritura tenet crudeli funere Dido?
   Virgil *Aeneid* 4 305-8

ecce fugit notumque torum sociosque Penates
fallacisque uias ire Corinna parat.
   Ovid *Amores* 2 11 7-8

An accusation of perfidy appears to be one of the principal schetliastic topoi and can therefore be accepted as forming a part of the generic formula throughout antiquity. In the Archilochus-Hipponax fragment the breach of friendship is not of course the departure of the traveller, but something else. But the occurrence of this standard schetliastic topos of the friendly propemptikon at the end of an inverse propemptikon as a justification for the contents of the latter is a splendidly original device. Its effect, when reinforced by contemporary morality, upon the original audience, must have been devastating.

Two Alcaic examples where the poet makes sophisticated use of topoi follow. The first is a fragmentary prosphonetikon restored mainly from Strabo 13 617 and also referred to by Libanius (*Orationes* 13 5). Its generic identification is guaranteed externally by this Libanian allusion which occurs in the prologue of the prosphonetikos to the Emperor Julian.

Ἦλθες ἐκ περάτων γᾶς ἐλεφαντίναν
λάβαν τὼ ξίφεος χρυσοδέταν ἔχων...
τὸν ἀδελφὸν Ἀντιμενίδαν...φησὶν Ἀλκαῖος Βαβυλωνίοις
συμμαχοῦντα τελέσαι
ἄεθλον μέγαν, εὐρύσαο δ' ἐκ πόνων,
κτένναις ἄνδρα μαχαίταν βασιληίων
παλάσταν ἀπυλείποντα μόναν ἴαν
παχέων ἀπὺ πέμπων...

Alcaeus *Fr.* 350 (LP)

You have come from the ends of the earth,
with an ivory and gold bound sword-hilt . . .
Alcaeus says that his brother Antimenidas, fighting beside the Babylonians, performed
a great feat and you saved them from their troubles
by killing a warrior, whose height
was only one palm's breadth short
of five royal cubits.

Internal confirmation comes from the contents of the fragment. It begins with the standard announcement of arrival (B 1), followed immediately by the place from which the returning traveller, in this case Alcaeus' brother Antimenidas, has returned, namely the ends of the earth (B 2). The remainder of the fragment describes Antimenidas' sword-hilt of ivory bound with gold, which he has brought back with him, and recounts an exploit performed by him abroad – his killing of a giant enemy while he was fighting as a mercenary of the Babylonians. This account contains an alteration of a standard topos which demonstrates very well Alcaeus' sophistication in the handling of topoi. In some prosphonetika mention is made of the troubles which the returning traveller has endured (B8) and of his safe deliverance from them (B7). Alcaeus stands this topos on its head: the troubles are there but they are not those of Antimenidas. We hear of safe deliverance, but Antimenidas' safety is not in question. Alcaeus makes this topos do duty as part of the narrative of the achievements of the returning traveller – another standard prosphonetic theme (B9) – and speaks of Antimenidas saving the Babylonians from their troubles. The alteration of the topos, coming as it does contrary to expectation and alluding as it does to the normal and expected sentiment, constitutes a significant enhancement of the encomium upon Antimenidas.

A similar treatment of a major topos of a genre can be found in Alcaeus *Fr.* 130 (LP):[35]

ἀγνοισ.. ϲβιότοισ ισ.. ὸ τάλαις ἔγω
ζώω μοῖραν ἔχων ἀγροϊωτίκαν
ἰμέρρων ἀγόρας ἄκουσαι
καρυ[ζο]μένας ὦγεσιλαΐδα
20 καὶ β[ό]λλας· τὰ πάτηρ καὶ πάτερος πάτηρ
κα..[.].ηρας ἔχοντες πεδὰ τωνδέων
τὼν [ἀ]λλαλοκάκων πολίταν
ἔ.[..ἀ]πὺ τούτων ἀπελήλαμαι
φεύγων ἐσχατίαισ', ὡς δ' 'Ονυμακλέης
25 ἔνθα[δ'] οἶος ἐοίκησα λυκαιμίαις
.[   ]ον [π]όλεμον· στάσιν γὰρ
πρὸς κρ.[....]. οὐκ ἄμεινον ὀννέλην·
.].[...].[..]. μακάρων ἐς τέμ[ε]νος θέων
ἐοι[.....]μϵ[λ]αίνας ἐπίβαις χθόνος
30 χλι.[.].[.].[.]ν συνόδοισί μ' αὔταις
οἴκημ⟨μ⟩ι κ[ά]κων ἔκτος ἔχων πόδας,
ὄππα Λ[εσβί]αδες κριννόμεναι φύαν
πώλεντ' ἐλκεσίπεπλοι, περὶ δὲ βρέμει·
ἄχω θεσπεσία γυναίκων
35 ἴρα[ς ὸ]λολύγας ἐνιαυσίας
         ].[.].[.]. ἀπὺ πόλλων πότα δὴ θέοι
      ].[   ]οκ...ν 'Ολύμπιοι;
         ]......
.γα[   ]...μεν.

Alcaeus *Fr.* 130 16-39 (LP)

... miserable

I live the life of a rustic,

longing to hear the summons

to the assembly, Agesilaidas,

20 and to the council. The rights that my father and my father's father

... had among those
citizens who harm each other,
I am deprived of those.
I am an exile on the outskirts and, like Onymacles,
25 I live there alone in a country infested by wolves (?)
... war. It is
... not to end civil strife (?)
... to the sacred enclosure of the blessed gods
... standing on the black earth
30 ... in the heart of the gatherings
I live with my feet clear of trouble
where the women of Lesbos, being judged for their beauty,
go by with trailing gowns and about me
the marvellous cry of women sounds,
35 the annual sound of the ritual *ololyge*
... When, from many, gods
... of Olympus ... ?

The genre involved is the epibaterion, the speech which a traveller
makes on arrival either at his home or at some other place.[36] Alcaeus *Fr.*
130 16-39 (LP) is an inverse epibaterion in the sense in which the
Archilochus-Hipponax fragment and Horace *Epode* 10 are inverse
propemptika and in which the speech of Umbricius in Juvenal 3 is an
inverse syntaktikon. The sentiments of the speakers towards their
addressees in each genre are the opposite of what they normally are in
that genre.[37] The normal epibateric speaker shows goodwill towards
the place to which he has come. He says how he has longed for it, mentions its special beauties in enthusiastic terms, expresses his joy at being
there, tells how painful it was for him not to be there, and describes
the place and its people at great length in friendly and complimentary
terms.

Rhetoricians did not produce prescriptions for the inverse epibaterion
any more than for inversions of any other epideictic genres. Hence
ancient poets composed inversions of the epibaterion (as of many other
genres) within a purely literary tradition. It is necessary therefore, as a
preliminary to generic analysis of Alcaeus *Fr.* 130 16-39 (LP), to examine other literary members of the genre in order to discover the
raw material with which Alcaeus was working. The fact that this poem
of Alcaeus must be discussed against a literary background is not un-

welcome since it affords an opportunity to examine at this point some members of yet another travel genre.

The following passage may be the Homeric exemplar of the inverse epibaterion:

"Ὦ μοι ἐγὼ δειλός, τί νύ μοι μήκιστα γένηται;
300 δείδω μὴ δὴ πάντα θεὰ νημερτέα εἶπεν,
ἥ μ' ἔφατ' ἐν πόντῳ, πρὶν πατρίδα γαῖαν ἱκέσθαι,
ἄλγε' ἀναπλήσειν· τὰ δὲ δὴ νῦν πάντα τελεῖται,
οἵοισιν νεφέεσσι περιστέφει οὐρανὸν εὐρὺν
Ζεύς, ἐτάραξε δὲ πόντον, ἐπισπέρχουσι δ' ἄελλαι
305 παντοίων ἀνέμων· νῦν μοι σῶς αἰπὺς ὄλεθρος.
τρισμάκαρες Δαναοὶ καὶ τετράκις οἳ τότ' ὄλοντο
Τροίῃ ἐν εὐρείῃ, χάριν Ἀτρεΐδῃσι φέροντες.
ὡς δὴ ἐγώ γ' ὄφελον θανέειν καὶ πότμον ἐπισπεῖν
ἤματι τῷ ὅτε μοι πλεῖστοι χαλκήρεα δοῦρα
310 Τρῶες ἐπέρριψαν περὶ Πηλείωνι θανόντι.
τῷ κ' ἔλαχον κτερέων, καί μευ κλέος ἦγον Ἀχαιοί·
νῦν δέ με λευγαλέῳ θανάτῳ εἵμαρτο ἁλῶναι.
Homer *Odyssey* 5 299-312

The situation in which Odysseus finds himself here is not arrival at some land uncongenial to him – for to a man in his position all land was welcome – but shipwreck by a storm at sea. However, Odysseus' position would not have seemed as different in antiquity from the generic situation as it might seem today. This is because, in antiquity, the same vocabulary could be used of being severely damaged by a storm at sea, but not sunk, and of being cast up shipwrecked on land. Therefore, the situation of Propertius in 1 17 (another inverse epibaterion, see below), where Propertius is shipwrecked, could have been described in the same language then as the situation of Odysseus in *Odyssey* 5 299-312. The position of some other speakers of inverse epibateria is not very different.

In these lines Odysseus bewails his fate (299), recollects the advice and warnings of the goddess Calypso (300ff.), describes his stormbound condition and how divine action is being taken against him (303ff.), declares that death awaits him (305), congratulates those of the Greeks who died at Troy (306-7), and wishes he had died there and received proper burial and mourning from his fellows (308-12).

The other four members of the genre to be discussed here are Latin:

Catullus 63 50-73, Tibullus 1 3, Propertius 1 17, and Horace *Odes* 3
27 37-66. They show varying degrees of similarity to the Homeric
exemplar.

50 patria o mei creatrix, patria o mea genetrix,
  ego quam miser relinquens, dominos ut erifugae
  famuli solent, ad Idae tetuli nemora pedem,
  ut aput niuem et ferarum gelida stabula forem
  et earum omnia adirem furibunda latibula,
55 ubinam aut quibus locis te positam, patria, reor?
  cupit ipsa pupula ad te sibi derigere aciem,
  rabie fera carens dum breue tempus animus est.
  egone a mea remota haec ferar in nemora domo?
  patria, bonis, amicis, genitoribus abero?
60 abero foro, palaestra, stadio et guminasiis?
  miser a miser, querendumst etiam atque etiam, anime.
  quod enim genus figuraest, ego non quod obierim?
  ego mulier, ego adolescens, ego ephebus, ego puer,
  ego gymnasi fui flos, ego eram decus olei:
65 mihi ianuae frequentes, mihi limina tepida,
  mihi floridis corollis redimita domus erat,
  linquendum ubi esset orto mihi sole cubiculum.
  ego nunc deum ministra et Cybeles famula ferar?
  ego Maenas, ego mei pars, ego uir sterilis ero?
70 ego uiridis algida Idae niue amicta loca colam?
  ego uitam agam sub altis Phrygiae columinibus,
  ubi cerua siluicultrix, ubi aper nemoriuagus?
  iam iam dolet quod egi, iam iamque paenitet.
    Catullus 63 50-73

Of all these examples Catullus is the most rhetorical. Attis addresses his
native land in terms of high praise and expresses his longing to be back
in it. By these means and by direct statement he makes clear his abhor-
rence of the place in which he finds himself, Ida, represented as a cold
snowy wilderness, the haunt of wild beasts (cp. Horace below). In all
this Catullus is employing two ideas not found in Homer, but topical in
the genre. He makes his character praise his homeland as a means of
attacking the place in which he finds himself (a topos that also occurs in
Propertius, Tibullus and Horace), and he makes him describe the place
he is in as a desert, as opposed to a city, as does Propertius and Horace's

speaker. It should be noticed, however, that Homer's failure to employ these two topoi may be due to particular circumstances in which his hero finds himself. As regards the first, it might be argued that Troy was Odysseus' point of departure and that he had spent ten years there so that he naturally thinks of Troy rather than Ithaca in contrast to the sea. Or it may be that when Homer makes Odysseus wish he had died at Troy this is a sophisticated variant on the 'longing-for-home' theme: Odysseus is so desperate that he longs not for home and life but for the land of the enemy and death there. As regards the second topos absent from Homer, it would have been ludicrous for Odysseus to emphasize that the sea is not a city.

The encomium by Attis of his home includes many of the standard rhetorical commonplaces for the praise of a city – its buildings and places of resort (60), its people (59), and the speaker's own activities there (62-7). Attis implies, as Odysseus states, the part played by a deity, in his case Cybele, in bringing him to the situation he is in. Throughout, we see the opposite of the joy at arrival and encomium of the place of arrival which Menander defines as the main characteristics of the epibaterion. Attis displays the utmost misery at his position and repents bitterly of the actions which have brought him to it.

Tibullus 1 3 and Propertius 1 17 show such great similarities to each other in material that they may be treated together. Since Tibullus 1 3 is fairly long (94 lines) I have quoted only the sections containing the most relevant material.

> me tenet ignotis aegrum Phaeacia terris:
>> abstineas auidas Mors modo nigra manus.
> 5 abstineas, Mors atra, precor: non hic mihi mater
>> quae legat in maestos ossa perusta sinus,
> non soror, Assyrios cineri quae dedat odores
>> et fleat effusis ante sepulcra comis,
> Delia non usquam quae, me cum mitteret urbe,
> 10 dicitur ante omnes consuluisse deos.
> illa sacras pueri sortes ter sustulit: illi
>> rettulit e trinis omnia certa puer.
> cuncta dabant reditus: tamen est deterrita numquam
>> quin fleret nostras respiceretque uias.
> 15 ipse ego solator, cum iam mandata dedissem,
>> quaerebam tardas anxius usque moras.

aut ego sum causatus aues aut omina dira
Saturniue sacram me tenuisse diem.
o quotiens ingressus iter mihi tristia dixi
20   offensum in porta signa dedisse pedem!
audeat inuito ne quis discedere Amore,
aut sciat egressum se prohibente deo.
quid tua nunc Isis mihi, Delia, quid mihi prosunt
illa tua totiens aera repulsa manu,
25   quidue, pie dum sacra colis, pureque lauari
te, memini, et puro secubuisse toro?
nunc, dea, nunc succurre mihi (nam posse mederi
picta docet templis multa tabella tuis)
ut mea uotiuas persoluens Delia uoces
30   ante sacras lino tecta fores sedeat
bisque die resoluta comas tibi dicere laudes
insignis turba debeat in Pharia.
at mihi contingat patrios celebrare Penates
reddereque antiquo menstrua tura Lari.

. . . . .

at tu casta precor maneas, sanctique pudoris
adsideat custos sedula semper anus.
85   haec tibi fabellas referat positaque lucerna
deducat plena stamina longa colu;
at circa grauibus pensis adfixa puella
paulatim somno fessa remittat opus.
tunc ueniam subito, nec quisquam nuntiet ante,
90   sed uidear caelo missus adesse tibi.
tunc mihi, qualis eris longos turbata capillos,
obuia nudato, Delia, curre pede.
hoc precor, hunc illum nobis Aurora nitentem
Luciferum roseis candida portet equis.
    Tibullus 1 3 3-34, 83-94

Et merito, quoniam potui fugisse puellam!
nunc ego desertas alloquor alcyonas.
nec mihi Cassiope saluo uisura carinam,
omniaque ingrato litore uota cadunt.
5   quin etiam absenti prosunt tibi, Cynthia, uenti:
aspice, quam saeuas increpat aura minas.

nullane placatae ueniet fortuna procellae?
haecine parua meum funus harena teget?
tu tamen in melius saeuas conuerte querelas:
10   sat tibi sit poenae nox et iniqua uada.
an poteris siccis mea fata reponere ocellis,
ossaque nulla tuo nostra tenere sinu?
a pereat, quicumque ratis et uela parauit
primus et inuito gurgite fecit iter!
15 nonne fuit leuius dominae peruincere mores
(quamuis dura, tamen rara puella fuit),
quam sic ignotis circumdata litora siluis
cernere et optatos quaerere Tyndaridas?
illic si qua meum sepelissent fata dolorem,
20   ultimus et posito staret amore lapis,
illa meo caros donasset funere crinis,
molliter et tenera poneret ossa rosa;
illa meum extremo clamasset puluere nomen,
ut mihi non ullo pondere terra foret.
25 at uos, aequoreae formosa Doride natae,
candida felici soluite uela choro:
si quando uestras labens Amor attigit undas,
mansuetis socio parcite litoribus.
Propertius 1 17

Both poets express their desire for their home throughout; both emphasize that the place at which they find themselves is not their home (Tibullus 3, Propertius 2), Propertius adding the information that he is in a strange and solitary place (2) and mentioning this feature of it again later (17-18), with emphasis on various aspects of the storm which has wrecked him there (5-10, cp. Homer *Odyssey* 5 303ff.). Both poets think, like Odysseus above and Europa below, on the possibility of death (Tibullus 4ff., 50ff.; Propertius 11-12, 19ff.). Both also think of the kind of funeral they would have had at Rome had they died there with, in Tibullus' case, his mother, sister and mistress Delia in attendance, and in Propertius' case, his mistress Cynthia. Although neither of them wish they had died at Rome, both are employing the same topos as Homer puts into Odysseus' mouth when he makes him wish to have died at Troy and to have received funeral rites from his comrades. Both Tibullus and Propertius recollect the pleas of their mistresses that they

E   *65* should not go (Tibullus 9ff., Propertius 5ff., cp. Calypso at *Odyssey* 5 300ff.), Tibullus adding that he did not want to go (Tibullus 15-16). Both state that love was against their departure (Tibullus 21-2, Propertius 1), Propertius saying he has deserved what has befallen him for acting unlike a lover. In both cases the gods have been of no avail (Tibullus 23ff., Delia's gods, Propertius 4, his own?). But the gods have not actively brought about the poet's situation, as have the gods in the cases of Odysseus, Attis and Europa, unless one is meant to assume that the god Love, since he disapproved of their departures, brought about their predicaments. However, despite the uselessness of the gods, or perhaps because the gods have not actively and explicitly brought them to this pass, both Tibullus and Propertius, unlike the other three, pray to the gods to assist their return (Tibullus 27ff., 93ff.; Propertius 25ff.), Tibullus being optimistic enough to envisage his return in some detail (83-92).

Only a section of Horace *Odes* 3 27 is an inverse epibaterion.[38]

'pater, o relictum
35 filiae nomen, pietasque' dixit
'uicta furore!
unde quo ueni? leuis una mors est
uirginum culpae. uigilansne ploro
turpe commissum, an uitiis carentem
40   ludit imago
uana, quae porta fugiens eburna
somnium ducit? meliusne fluctus
ire per longos fuit, an recentis
carpere flores?
45 si quis infamem mihi nunc iuuencum
dedat iratae, lacerare ferro et
frangere enitar modo multum amati
cornua monstri.
impudens liqui patrios Penatis,
50 impudens Orcum moror. o deorum
si quis haec audis, utinam inter errem
nuda leones!
antequam turpis macies decentis
occupet malas teneraeque sucus
55 defluat praedae, speciosa quaero
pascere tigris.

"uilis Europe," pater urget absens:
"quid mori cessas? potes hac ab orno
pendulum zona bene te secuta
60   laedere collum.
siue te rupes et acuta leto
saxa delectant, age te procellae
crede ueloci, nisi erile mauis
    carpere pensum
regius sanguis, dominaeque tradi
barbarae paelex.'''
    34-66

In this passage the generic pattern may not at first sight be very obvious. However, both the general situation – arrival at a foreign place – and the miserably unappreciative attitude of the traveller to the place characterize this speech of Europa as a member of the genre. Secondary elements confirm this assignment. Although Europa does not address her home (*patria*) or describe it, except when recollecting her flower-picking there (43-4), she does address her father (*pater*) and lay stress on *pietas* – her duty to father, native land and gods (34ff.). She imagines the words of her father (56ff.) and throughout regards her own abandonment of her native land, parent and gods (49) as a crime. Like Odysseus, Propertius, and Tibullus she envisages her own death and does so at length and in many forms, but she does not, as they do, envisage death as a consequence of illness or shipwreck but as a self-inflicted punishment for the crime of abandoning her home. There is indirect description of Crete in the references to trees and rocks (58ff.), wild beasts (51ff.), and barbarian inhabitants (67). This probably means that Europa thinks she is in a desert or solitary place as were Attis and Propertius, in spite of the fact that the reader of the ode has already been told that Crete is not like this:

quae simul centum tetigit potentem
oppidis Creten
    Horace *Odes* 3 27 33-4

The inverse epibateric section has therefore many similarities to the other inverse epibateria being treated here. But it is worth asking why Horace makes Europa so reticent about her native land, leaves out any notion of her being buried at home, fails to make her blame gods knowingly or pray to gods, and why he makes her think of Crete as a desert after 33-4, where the reader has been informed differently. We might also ask why her words about Crete sound like the fantasies of an over-imaginative girl.

What is happening is probably this: Horace knows his story will have a happy ending, that Europa will settle in Crete, make it her home and bear sons who will be kings of Crete. So, just as the story as a whole is leading up to a reconciliation between Jupiter and Europa and a justification of the ways of the god to her, the lament of Europa is carefully modulated to take account of this coming resolution by being already annulled or easily annullable. This is why there is no great emphasis on Europa's former home, only a mention of picking flowers; no cogent attack on Crete or direct description of it as a wilderness, and no thoughts of Europa's burial at home. No hostile gods are present in the lament because the bull she is blaming is Jupiter and so the attack, which replaces one on a god, will become meaningless when the bull's identity is revealed. Europa does not pray to gods for help because it is already on its way unasked. In this fashion, once the truth of her situation is revealed to her, her lament is swept away instantly. Her censure of the bull and her impiety to her father are annulled because she is the wife of Jupiter; her thoughts of suicide are therefore meaningless; and her sons will be kings of those hundred cities of Crete. The themes which Horace has omitted or distorted are those which at the end of the poem turn out to have been irrelevant.

Alcaeus *Fr.* 130 16-39 (LP) can now be seen to be an inversion of the same genre, the epibaterion. Alcaeus is in exile from his native city. He begins by emphasizing his misery and the rustic uncivilized life he leads (17). This emphasis is later reiterated at 24ff., where he again stresses that he lives in the countryside and compares himself with Onymacles, who must then have been a proverbial anti-social or rustic personality. Thus, like Attis, Propertius and Europa, he characterizes the place he is in as a wilderness. Also, like most inverse epibateric speakers, he longs for home (18ff.), which he associates particularly with the public assembly and council. These are not only aspects of his native city which he longs for; they are also chosen for their political associations. Mention of his father's and grandfather's rights in Mytilene (20-1) leads to a specific statement that Alcaeus is deprived of these rights and is in exile from his own land. Immediately the reason for his exile follows and, unlike that produced by some other epibateric speakers, his excuse brings no discredit to him, for it is civil strife (28). At 36-7 he appears

68

(like Tibullus and Propertius) to be praying to the gods to bring his exile to an end.

The topical sophistication of the poem occurs at 28ff. There, only two lines after the reiterated description of his life in the wilderness (24ff.), we suddenly find Alcaeus taking part in a festival at a shrine. He is free of troubles, attending the women's beauty competition and listening to the ritual cry of the women. The change of scene from the woe and wilderness of the first three stanzas to the temple of the fourth and fifth is astonishing and deliberate. What makes it ingenious is this. An exile would normally imagine a scene of this kind as taking place in his own city and would long unavailingly to be a participant at it.[39] Alcaeus has placed the scene in his exile at a place other than his own native city. He has done so, as far as can be judged, to emphasize something about his exile which probably was stated in 26ff., namely that his exile is a choice, that he has deliberately set himself up against the government now in power in his own city and has chosen exile, in spite of his longings for home, because of his political principles. These principles mean more to him than home, although he loves his home dearly; and he shows this by placing himself free of cares abroad in a setting which his readers would have expected to find in his own city. By this device he turns what began as an exile's lament into a political manifesto.

It is clear then from these examples that topical sophistications of a highly developed kind occur in the work of the early Greek lyric and iambic poets. Some of the equally developed generic sophistications to be found in their work have been illustrated in this chapter and more will be demonstrated later in this book in Chapters 5-9.

3

The Categories of Genres

All the genres originate in important, recurrent, real-life situations. The categorization of the genres attempted in this chapter, which is not a categorization in terms of subject-matter, might therefore seem *a priori* vain and artificial. But the discussion of the origin of the genres in Chapter 2 was able to take useful account of the unhistorical ancient belief that Homer invented the genres, or at least some of them. So in this chapter it will be found useful to categorize the genres in terms of another ancient belief equally untrue from a historical point of view but equally useful in practice. This belief is that rhetoric and poetry are two branches of the same activity, that the rules, procedures and excellences of the two are closely connected and that some, if not all, genres found in poetry are rhetorical genres.[1]

The historical falsehood of this second ancient belief is even more apparent than that of the first. It was not held and could not have been held until rhetoric had come to a developed form, so that it was quite unknown to pre-fourth-century Greeks. Nevertheless its practical truth and utility for us are considerable. Ancient poets wrote within genres which in some cases, as far as we know, had no names at any point in antiquity and in other cases received their names late in antiquity at the hands of rhetoricians. In spite of this lack of generic names, ancient writers and audiences, because they had an education based on intimate knowledge of Homer, of rhetoric once it had developed, and of contemporary social habits and traditions, were able almost instinctively to distinguish between different genres. Modern students of classical literature have none of these advantages. For us genres are a jungle of indistinct patterns requiring patient elucidation and distinction. If we are to avoid even avoidable errors in these processes, we must have recourse to the surviving generic names and descriptions, which in many cases derive from the classificatory activities of rhetoricians of late antiquity. Access to these names and descriptions involves a willingness to accept the useful untruth that some, if not all, genres can be categorized in accordance with rhetorical distinctions.

The first major category of genres comprises those which can be described in the full sense as rhetorical, that is, those genres which were taught and exercised in the rhetorical schools and practised where relevant in ancient public life. This category falls into four subdivisions consisting of the three kinds of practical oratory and the elementary exercises which were a preparation for them.

Dicanic. There are two dicanic genres—the accusation (κατηγορία, *accusatio*) and the defence (ἀπολογία, *defensio*). Several ancient accounts of their composition are extant. These are concerned with the composition of real speeches of accusation and defence for use in the law-courts.[2] There are also numerous examples of such court speeches.

In poetry, examples of the dicanic genres may be modelled closely on real court speeches. This means that they can be placed in the imaginary context of a trial and can adhere to all the conventions of a real-life court situation. An 'official' accusation of this kind is Herodas' second mime, which pretends to be a real speech made in court by a brothel-keeper bringing an action against a young man who has broken into his brothel and assaulted both him and the girls. In this accusation much of the humour derives from the contrast between the low character of the speaker and his complaint on the one hand, and his affected efforts to conform with the requirements of the genre on the other, efforts which produce linguistic and conceptual absurdities.

Examples of dicanic genres can also be much less 'official'. While preserving the form and topoi of a dicanic genre they can have as background not a formal court-case but a setting from lay life. Propertius 1 18, a defensio, is of this kind.[3] The distinction made here between 'official' and 'unofficial' examples of genres is useful since it can be applied to the other two branches of practical oratory also.

Symbouleutic. As with dicanic there are several ancient treatises on symbouleutic. Again as with dicanic, symbouleutic falls essentially into genres, *protreptic* and *apotreptic*.[4] An instance of an 'official' example of a symbouleutic genre in poetry is Horace *Epode* 16, where the poet imagines himself as addressing a political body in a situation of public decision-making and as uttering a protreptic speech. Advice of a political sort could also be given in unofficial circumstances (e.g. Alcaeus *Fr.* 6 (LP)) and of course advice could be of a purely personal kind given privately (e.g. Horace *Odes* 2 10).

Moreover, all ancient didactic literature was probably thought to fall under the heading of symbouleutic. The function of the teacher in antiquity was regarded not as the conveyance of facts but the giving of precepts and therefore as a kind of advising. Conversely the giver of advice was a teacher. When Oceanus comes to advise Prometheus about his future conduct (Aeschylus *Prometheus Vinctus* 307-29) he begins:

ὁρῶ, Προμηθεῦ, καὶ παραινέσαι γέ σοι
θέλω τὰ λῷστα . . .
307-8

and in the course of his advice says:

οὔκουν ἔμοιγε χρώμενος διδασκάλῳ
πρὸς κέντρα κῶλον ἐκτενεῖς . . .
322-3

The fact that in antiquity didactic literature was probably regarded as symbouleutic does not mean, for example, that *Georgica* and *Cynegetica* should be thought of simply as protreptics. Here, as elsewhere within the generic framework,[5] it is more convenient to regard specialized forms of genres as genres in themselves, although at the same time their generic relationships should not be forgotten. A well-known specialized didactic genre is one which A. L. Wheeler, who collected and analysed many examples of it, called *erotodidaxis*.[6] This genre, which is of great importance for Roman elegy, consists of erotic precepts. One fragmentary example of the genre, of which Wheeler could not take account since it was first published after his articles on erotodidaxis, is especially interesting as it clearly belongs to the genre and at the same time proclaims itself to be advice. This is Callimachus, *Iambi* 5. Callimachus proclaims the symbouleutic nature of *Iambi* 5 in its first two lines:

Ὦ ξεῖνε, συμβουλὴ γὰρ ἕν τι τῶν ἱρῶν,
ἄκουε τἀπὸ καρδ [ίης,   ]
1-2

That it belongs to the genre erotodidaxis is clear from the *diegesis*:

Γραμματο[δ]ιδάσκαλ[ο]ν, ὄνομα ’Απολλώνι-
ον, οἱ δὲ Κλέωνά τινα, ἰαμβίζει ὡς
τοὺς ἰδίους μαθητὰς καταισχύνον-
τα, ἐν ἤθει εὐνοίας ἀπαγ[ο]ρεύων τούτῳ δρᾶν, μὴ ἁλῷ.

Moreover it is confirmed by a topos contained in two of the few lines which survive entire:

ἐγὼ Βάκις τοι καὶ Σίβυλλα [καὶ] δάφνη
καὶ φηγός.

31-2

This claim to be as reliable as an oracle is also found in a Propertian claim to be a teacher of love:

non me Chaoniae vincant in amore columbae
dicere, quos iuuenes quaeque puella domet.

Propertius 1 9 5-6

and in other didactic situations.[7] It goes without saying that *Iambi* 5 is highly ironic. Callimachus' professions of goodwill and good advice are a device to make a scathing attack upon an enemy and the choice of the erotodidactic framework is probably a further indirect piece of humour at the expense of the addressee's profession of school teacher. From our point of view, the amenability of the genre to this sort of use implies a pre-Callimachean tradition of serious erotodidaxis[8] and a full recognition by Callimachus of the symbouleutic relationships of didactic poetry.

Epideictic. Two ancient treatises on epideictic survive, that of Pseudo-Dionysius of Halicarnassus (second century A D) and that which consists of two works attributed to Menander the Rhetor, who lived in the third century A D. Since epideictic genres are exemplified very widely in ancient poetry, many examples of them are treated in this book. The prescriptions which Pseudo-Dionysius and Menander offer for epideictic speeches are naturally influenced by the purpose and date of their authors. But although in them the traditional generic formulae are altered and added to by these influences, Pseudo-Dionysius and Menander are nevertheless good witnesses to the literary practice of the whole of antiquity. In this they are at one with the authors of the treatises on dicanic and symbouleutic speeches and on *progymnasmata*, which are likewise remarkably conservative in their content.

Just as didactic genres were described above as specialized forms of symbouleutic, so there appear to be specialized forms of epideictic genres which merit a separate generic identity because of their numbers and importance. The genre *soteria* is one example. This is the speech of rejoicing, congratulations and thanksgiving for the safety of someone who has been rescued from danger or has recovered from illness. Some members of the genre are Catullus 44; [Tibullus] 3 10 = 4 4; Propertius 2 28; Horace *Odes* 2 17,[9] 3 8; Statius *Siluae* 1 4; Himerius *Orationes* 45 (Colonna). The soteria has clear relations with various forms of the genre *eucharistikon*, in which formal thanksgiving is made. It stands somewhere between the *eucharistikos logos* and the *eucharistikos hymnos*, although strictly speaking the hymnic element is subordinate. The soteria's thanksgiving is addressed to a god, but at the same time the soteria is honorific in intent and this honour is directed towards the man whose recovery or safety is being celebrated; so it is he who, strictly speaking, is the addressee (object) of the speech.[10] However, the form of the generic title soteria, which refers properly to the sacrifices made in thanksgiving for recovery,[11] is probably a sign of the importance of the subordinate religious element in the generic situation. The soteria, then, is a specialized form of eucharistic utterance. The genre eucharistikon is not prescribed as an epideictic speech by Pseudo-Dionysius or Menander; but it was considered in antiquity to be an epideictic genre and was taught as such in the rhetorical schools. Thanksgiving is classified under epideictic by Quintilian (*Institutio Oratoria* 3 4 3) and given equal importance to panegyrics and protreptics by him at *Institutio Oratoria* 11 3 153. 'Official' eucharistika (*gratiarum actiones*) were regular features of Roman public life.[12]

The form of generic specialization which leads the soteria to be established in literature and rhetoric, and perhaps even taught in rhetorical schools as a separate genre, is paralleled in Menander's work by his treatment of the *stephanotikos logos*. This speech, which Menander prescribes to accompany the award of a crown to the Emperor, has as its distinguishing feature a strong eucharistic content (422 28ff.); and yet it is prescribed by Menander as an independent epideictic genre.

Another less exalted genre with a similar relation to the eucharistikon is the everyday thanksgiving utterance with which individuals thank each other formally for meals, gifts, and other services.[13] The essence of the specialization which entitles it to be regarded as a separate genre is not restriction in its field of applicability, since apparently it could be adapted to give thanks for almost any gift or service, but is its restricted social status as an 'unofficial' utterance. The epideictic *kletikon* (speech of official invitation) has a parallel specialized 'unofficial' form, the informal invitation (*uocatio*), often to a meal and so known as *uocatio ad cenam*.[14]

It is clear that the distinctions one makes or accepts from antiquity between different genres fulfilling the same kind of function are to a great extent arbitrary and dictated purely by convenience. At the same time the relationships claimed between the different kinds of thanksgiving and invitation illustrate one of the great difficulties about classifying genres. Beginning with the certainly epideictic eucharistikon we have moved to the soteria, a genre which may well have been taught and practised in the rhetorical schools, although I know no evidence of this except Himerius *Orationes* 45 (Colonna). We have then moved on to the thanksgiving for a meal, which almost certainly was not taught in the schools and might well be regarded as thoroughly unrhetorical. Similarly the certainly rhetorical kletikon appears to be related to the certainly unrhetorical uocatio ad cenam. It is not surprising that the validity of the distinction between rhetorical and non-rhetorical genres will be defended below only in a restricted sense and with the proviso that in antiquity some or all non-rhetorical genres must at times have been thought to be rhetorical.

Progymnasmata. Many ancient treatises on progymnasmata have survived. The reason why progymnasmata are classed as a distinct category of genres is historical, not logical. Some of the progymnasmata could, if one wished, be classified with a little thought under one or other of the major branches of rhetoric. The historical reason for not doing so but for regarding progymnasmata as a separate category of genres is that these school-exercises, which were used as preparatory work for schoolboys aspiring to be instructed in and to practise major branches of rhetoric, were assembled together for this purpose at a fairly early date,[15] remained together for this purpose, and entered the consciousness of all later antiquity as a group. A subsidiary reason is that, because they were childhood exercises, they can be considered as the minimum formal rhetorical equipment of any literate person from the Hellenistic period on. Poetic examples of progymnasmata are not uncommon. Perhaps the best known is Propertius 2 12 (a *kataskeue*), where not only the rhetorical framework but also the particular subject-matter is known to correspond with that of a real-life Roman school-exercise (see Quintilian *Institutio Oratoria* 2 4 26). Another well-known poetic progymnasma is Juvenal 6, an inflated example of the *thesis* 'Ought a man to marry'.

The genres mentioned so far in this chapter, although in many cases they certainly arose and in other cases they may have arisen before the birth of rhetoric, are all subsumable into the rhetorical system. However, certain important recurrent human situations produced genres which were never embraced by rhetoric and were never taught and practised in the rhetorical schools. These constitute another major division of genres and may fairly, with the proviso mentioned above and below, be called non-rhetorical genres. An excellent example of a non-rhetorical genre is the komos. In komoi we find the words and actions of lovers who, within the ancient tradition of post-symposiastic visits to the beloved, are attempting, usually in vain,[16] to reach the object of their love. Some komoi will be treated elsewhere in this book.

Less well known but equally interesting is a genre whose examples were first collected and analysed by F. Jacoby.[17] This genre, for which no name has come down from antiquity, is of symposiastic origin and its essentials are that the addressee, a lover, displays symptoms of love which arouse speculation or interrogation about the love by the speaker. The speaker asks or surmises the cause of the symptoms and/or identity of the beloved and may comment upon the beloved. This genre will for convenience be called 'symptoms of love'. It is easy to see why this genre and the komos were never, at any rate formally, incorporated into the rhetorical framework.

A third non-rhetorical ancient genre may be called for lack of an attested ancient name 'public advertisement'. We know that public announcements were regularly made in antiquity and that notices were posted in public places informing the public of auction sales, runaway slaves and the rewards for their recapture, lost goods, and so forth.[18] Literary versions of these public advertisements are sometimes found. One amusing example is Moschus I (*"Ερως Δραπέτης*) which advertises a reward for the runaway Eros as though he was a fugitive slave. Another, which is more complicated, is Propertius 3 23:

> Ergo tam doctae nobis periere tabellae,
> > scripta quibus pariter tot periere bona!
> has quondam nostris manibus detriuerat usus,
> > qui non signatas iussit habere fidem.
> 5 illae iam sine me norant placare puellas,
> > et quaedam sine me uerba diserta loqui.
> non illas fixum caras effecerat aurum:
> > uulgari buxo sordida cera fuit.
> qualescumque mihi semper mansere fideles,
> 10 > semper et effectus promeruere bonos.
> forsitan haec illis fuerint mandata tabellis:
> > 'Irascor quoniam es, lente, moratus heri.
> an tibi nescio quae uisa est formosior? an tu

non bona de nobis crimina ficta iacis?'
15 aut dixit: 'Venies hodie, cessabimus una:
   hospitium tota nocte parauit Amor,'
   et quaecumque dolens reperit non stulta puella
   garrula cum blandis ducitur hora dolis.
   me miserum, his aliquis rationem scribit auarus
20 et ponit diras inter ephemeridas!
   quas si quis mihi rettulerit, donabitur auro:
   quis pro diuitiis ligna retenta uelit?
   i puer, et citus haec aliqua propone columna,
   et dominum Esquiliis scribe habitare tuum.

It is not absolutely clear whether the actual advertisement to be posted consists of 1-22 plus Propertius' address or whether the elegy is a meditation-cum-expansion upon the subject-matter of a much briefer actual advertisement. Poetic fantasy knows no bounds, so that the elaboration of the elegy is no argument against the first possibility, although 19-20 are somewhat out of keeping with it. On the whole the second possibility is more likely. But the question is not important since the difference is only one of form (see pp. 127-8). It is therefore irrelevant to the generic identification of Propertius 3 23 whether the elegy is the actual advertisement, in direct speech, or is a description of the contents of the advertisement plus a commentary upon relevant circumstances. In either case generic assignment and recognition of the topoi of the genre in the elegy are equally valid.

   The elegy consists of:
(i)   announcement of loss (1-2)
(ii) description of the article lost (3-18)
(iii) indirect reiteration of the fact of the loss (19-20)
(iv) offer of reward (21-2)
(v)   Propertius' address (24).
The topoi of the genre will be clear from the real and realistic examples collected at Bruns, *Fontes Iuris Romani* (7 ed. pp. 361-2 q.v.). They are: statement of loss of an article, offer of reward to any person returning it, description of the lost article, address for contact. Of these examples the following are worth quoting as illustrations:

urna aenia pereit de taberna. sei quis rettulerit, dabuntur HS LXV;
sei furem dabit und [. . .
   Corpus Inscriptionum Latinarum 4 6 n.64 (cp. p. 191)

Παῖς ἀνακεχώρηκεν ἐν Ἀλεξανδρείᾳ, ᾧ ὄνομα "Ερμων, ὡς ἐτῶν ιη΄, ἔχων περὶ τὸ σῶμα χλαμύδα καὶ περίζωμα. τοῦτον ὃς ἂν ἀναγάγῃ, λήψεται χαλκοῦ τ(ά)λ(αντα) β/γ, ἐφ᾽ ἱεροῦ δείξας τλ. α/β, παρ᾽ ἀνδρὶ ἀξιόχρεῳ, καὶ δωσιδίκῳ, τλ. γ/ε. μηνύειν δὲ τὸν βουλόμενον τοῖς παρὰ τοῦ στρατηγοῦ.
ἔστιν δὲ καὶ ὁ συναποδεδρακὼς αὐτῷ Βίων, δοῦλος, τοῦτον ὃς ἂν ἀναγ(άγ)ῃ, λήψεται ὅσα καὶ ὑπὲρ τοῦ προγεγραμμένου. μηνύειν δὲ καὶ ὑπὲρ τούτου τοῖς παρὰ τοῦ στρατηγοῦ.
Papyrus *Aegyptiaca* 146 BC (See Bruns loc. cit. for sources)

praeco cum seruo publico . . . haec proclamauit: 'Puer in balneo paulo ante aberrauit, annorum circa XVI, crispus, mollis, formosus, nomine Giton. Si quis eum reddere aut commonstrare uoluerit, accipiet nummos mille.'
Petronius *Satyricon* 97 (cp. Apuleius *Metamorphoses* 6 8)

The description of the writing-tablets in Propertius 3 23 is fairly long and involved. This is because it is contrived so as to be a description of writing-tablets which reflect the personality of their owner, the Alexandrian love-poet Propertius. The description therefore functions also as one of those oblique Alexandrian literary manifestos of which Propertius never tired.[19] The writing-tablets are learned (1 cp. *diserta* 6); they are small – if the diminutive of *tabulae* used in 1 implies this as well as showing Propertius' affection for them; they are heavily used (3); they have an individuality which makes them recognizable without the author's seal (4); they have power to win over women with their eloquence (5-6, 10); they are not expensively plated with gold but made of common box-wood and humble (not dirty) wax (7-8). These features of the writing-tablets are meant to reflect upon the writings of Propertius with which they are associated (2).[20] *Doctrina*, smallness, *labor* and individuality as Alexandrian motifs require no comment.[21] Power over women relates to the effectiveness of the Alexandrian erotic poet in this sphere, particularly in his role as teacher of love.

The lack of gold-plating and the cheapness of the tablets (*vulgari* and *sordida* (8) contrasting with *caras* (7) in one of its senses) may be another Alexandrian symbol. Luxurious materials (ivory, cloth of gold, incense) are anti-Alexandrian symbols in Propertius 2 13,[22] and Propertius speaks of his own poetry as *cera* (4 6 3) in an Alexandrian context.[23] The inexpensiveness of the tablets also allude to the traditional poverty of the poet, although in the case of elegiac poets this is highly relative. Box-wood is a durable wood proof against decay,[24] and the mention of it may reflect the common Alexandrian claim of immortality for the poet's work.[25] Box-wood also was so often used for making pipes (*tibiae*) that the word *buxum* is a common Latin poetic synonym for *tibia*. *Buxo* may therefore also, or as an alternative, be an allusion to the *tibia*, a common symbol of elegy. Lines 7-8 are more than a description of lost goods in a sense relevant to the advertisement. They tell a potential or actual finder that the goods are intrinsically valueless, a topos, perhaps, in situations where the return of goods is sought,[26] and anticipate 21-2.[27] In 19-20 the account-books and their money-loving owner may be another allusion to the contrast between wealth and Alexandrianism; similarly, the hardness of the account-books may allude to its antithesis, the characteristic softness of the elegiac love-poet. Propertius has thus taken the 'sentimental value only' topos and put it to ingenious use as part of a richly allusive Alexandrian programme.

Lines 12-18 are not Propertian reminiscences of past messages which the tablets have carried but speculations about the message which the lost tablets may at present have in them. Thus they are part of the description of the *tabellae*, for, with a humorous touch, Propertius pretends to be imagining what may possibly be written in the tablets so as to help a finder to identify them as his. Naturally these lines also contribute to the picture of the successful elegiac love-poet already sketched out in 5-6 and 10, for it will be observed that nowhere in the imagined message does Propertius mention the possibility of a refusal of his suit. In 15-16 he is told by the girl to come and be welcome. In 12-14 the girl goes even further. She is abjectly in love with Propertius and afraid of losing him to a rival or because of an imaginary grievance.

The identification of the lost writing tablets with his own love-poetry has a programmatic significance extending beyond 3 23. This is shown by the position of the elegy within the first three books of his *Elegies*. It stands immediately before the one (or two) *renuntiationes amoris* (3 24 and 25) which conclude, in a double sense, the erotic works of Propertius. *Elegy* 3 23 is an additional preliminary epilogue to the collection. Propertius has lost his tablets. His tablets are his love-poetry; so he will not be able to write any more love-poetry.

A fourth non-rhetorical genre will provide a model for the establishment and analysis into topoi of such a genre. This is the *renuntiatio amoris*. In the Graeco-Roman world friendship (φιλία, ἑταιρία, *amicitia*) was an important political and social institution as well as being personally significant.[28] In the Roman period there is evidence that, among prominent men at any rate, it was conducted in a formal way, and that its dissolution could be marked by an act of repudiation of friendship such as the sending of a communication to this effect. Since love and friendship are kindred sentiments, it is by no means unlikely that renuntiationes amoris, which are formal repudiations of love or the beloved, were influenced by these analogous repudiations of friendship. On the other hand there is no reason to think that the renuntiatio amoris is derived from the *renuntiatio amicitiae*. The situation of giving up love or a beloved is as old as the human race.

A representative sample of members of the genre is: Anacreon ap. Himerium *Orationes* 48 4 (Colonna);[29] Theocritus *Idyll* 30; *A.P.* 5 175, 179, 184 (Meleager); Catullus 8, 11, 58; *A.P.* 5 112 (Philodemus); Tibullus 1 9; Horace *Epode* 15; *Odes* 1 5, 3 26; Propertius 2 5, 3 24 and 25; Ovid *Amores* 3 11 and 11b; *A.P.* 12 201 (Strato); *A.P.* 5 245 (Macedonius).

The primary elements of the genre renuntiatio amoris are:
A. 1. The speaker (a lover).
   2. The addressee (the beloved).
   3. An act of renunciation of the addressee by the speaker.
The following appear to be the principal secondary elements (topoi) of the genre. Bracketed instances are ones in which the topos, although not directly stated, is strongly implied. Where no line numbers are given, the topos occurs widely or throughout the poem.
B. 1. The lover's previous sentiments for the beloved: Theocr. *Id.* 30 1-11; Cat. 8 3-8; 58 1-3; (Hor. *Epod.* 15 1-10; *O.* 1 5 9-13); Tib. 1 9 1-28, 41-50 esp. 47-50; Prop. 3 24 1-8; Ov. *Am.* 3 11 17-20; *A.P.* 5 112 1-2; otherwise implied generally.
   2. The lover's formal renunciation of his beloved/love: (?) Anacr.; *A.P.* 5 175 6; 179 9; 184 6; 112 3; Tib. 1 9 51-2; Prop. 3 25 9-10; Ov. *Am.* 3 11 2; *A.P.* 12 201 2.
   3. The lover's reasons for rejecting love/the beloved.
      (i) The lover's coming to the age of discretion/retirement from love: Theocr. *Id.* 30 12-23; Hor. *O.* 3 26; *A.P.* 5 112 3-6.
      (ii) The beloved's infidelity (*and perjury): **A.P.* 5 175; *184 1-5; (Cat. 11 17-24); *Tib. 1 9; Hor. *Epod.* 15 11ff. (*1-10); *Prop. 2 5 1-4; 3 25 1-2; Ov. *Am.* 3 11 9-15, *21-26.
      (iii) Unwillingness of beloved: Anacr.; Cat. 8 9-13; (?) Hor. *O.* 3 26 12; *A.P.* 12 201 1.

4. The lover's rivals/successors – treated by the poet with varying degrees of disparagement sometimes amounting to open hostility: *A.P.* 5 184 4; Cat. 11 17-20; 58 4-5; Tib. 1 9 53-75; Hor. *Epod.* 15 17-22; *O.* 1 5 1-5; Ov. *Am.* 3 11 11-15, 21-6.

5. The future miseries of the lover's rivals/successors, mainly ill-treatment and infidelity by the beloved: (Cat. 11 17-20); Tib. 1 9 53-74 (infidelity of rival's wife); Hor. *Epod.* 15 23-4; *O.* 1 5 5-13; Ov. *Am.* 3 11 28.

6. The future miseries of the beloved, mainly loss of this/ all lover(s): Cat. 8 14-18; Hor. *Epod.* 15 11; Tib. 1 9 79-80; Prop. 2 5 8, 15; 3 25 11-18.

7. The lover's present state of mind always implicitly, sometimes explicitly described as one of
 Conflict: Cat. 8; Ov. *Am.* 3 11 7-8, 35-44 (cf. also Observation II below).
 Contentment: Cat. 11 21-4; Tib. 1 9 81-4; Prop. 3 24 17-20; expressed occasionally through an image either of the shipwrecked sailor saved (Hor. *O.* 1 5 13-16; Prop. 3 24 11-18; Ov. *Am.* 3 11 29-30), or/and a dedication (Hor. *O.* 1 5 13-16; 3 26 1-8; Tib. 1 9 83-4; Prop. 3 24 19-20), or through another image (Cat. 11 21-4).

8. The beloved's attempts to win back the lover: (Cat. 11?); Prop. 3 25 5-6; Ov. *Am.* 3 11 31-2; *A.P.* 5 245 1-2.

9. The lover's resolve to find a better beloved: Hor. *Epod.* 15 14; Tib. 1 9 79-80; Prop. 2 5 5-8; *A.P.* 5 245 7-8.

Each member of the genre could be analysed in the light of this list of topoi and with the assistance of the later discussions of originality in the use of topoi (Chapter 4) and of the genres (Chapters 5-9).

For the moment a few observations arising simply from this list of topoi may be recorded, some of particular interest and some of general interest for the theme of this book.

I. It has been suggested that Horace *Odes* 1 5 1-5 contains references in chronological order to a particular act of love-making.[30] That the references are general and not confined to a specific act of love-making in chronological order and that *religas* (4) means 'bind up', the normal action of a courtesan preliminary to going to see a client (cp. Horace *Odes* 3 14 21), is confirmed by a similar set of interrogative references in Catullus 8 16-18. Some of them (17) are descriptive of general conditions and others (16, 18) refer to actions. But as a whole they do

F

not refer to a particular single act of love-making and do not have chronological significance.

> quis nunc te adibit? cui uideberis bella?
> quem nunc amabis? cuius esse diceris?
> quem basiabis? cui labella mordebis?
> Catullus 8 16-18

II. Conflict of mind on the part of the lover appears not only in descriptions but also in reversals by the lover of his renunciation of love/the beloved in Theocritus *Idyll* 30; *A.P.* 5 184; Horace *Odes* 3 26; Propertius 2 5; Ovid *Amores* 3 11; *A.P.* 12 201 (cf. Chapter 6).

III. Venus is the subject of two ex-lovers' dedications (see topos B 7) in Horace *Odes* 3 26 1-8 and Tibullus 1 9 83-4, and *Mens Bona* is the subject of a third in Prop. 3 24 19-20. These give further support to Zielinski's emendation *deae* for *deo* at Horace *Odes* 1 5 16 (recently defended N-H I ad loc), especially *Tibullus* 1 9 83-4, since the contexts of the renunciations of Tibullus 1 9 and Horace *Odes* 1 5 are very similar. That *Mens Bona* is dedicatee in Propertius 3 24 19-20 is no counter argument. She is the antithesis of love here and also, for example, at Ovid *Amores* 1 2 31-2. Thus it would appear that the normal dedicatees in such situations are either the love goddess or an anti-love deity but not a neutral figure.

IV. A clear distinction may be made in this genre between, on the one hand, places where thematic coincidence between different writers appears due to the influence of the generic pattern and, on the other hand, places where genuine reminiscences of one writer by another are probable. These latter are: Propertius 3 24 2-4 = Tibullus 1 9 47-8; Ovid *Amores* 3 11 7 = Catullus 8 11; Ovid *Amores* 3 11 23-4 = Propertius 3 25 1-2; Ovid *Amores* 3 11 29-30 = Propertius 3 24 15-16; Ovid *Amores* 3 11 45-8 = Propertius 2 5 17-18.

V. As is natural in a genre where reversal of attitude is often found (see Observation II above) the boundaries between decision, hypothetical decision and intent are narrow. Thus Anacreon ap. Himeriun *Orationes* 48 4 and *A.P.* 12 201 are conditional threats to renounce. Horace *Epode* 15, although near to a declaration of intent, remains conditional – *si certus intravit dolor* (16). Such temporal and modal differences within a genre are paralleled elsewhere and may constitute formal sophistications (see pp. 127-8).

It is obvious that errors can more easily occur in the identification and discussion of non-rhetorical genres than in the treatment of rhetorical genres. Names and descriptions are provided by antiquity for at least some rhetorical genres. For non-rhetorical genres names must often be invented – with all the dangers of false implication which imposed names bring – and the topoi must be derived from literary examples with the assistance of real-life examples where they survive. The most dangerous pitfall is the tendency to imagine genres which did not exist. Before a non-rhetorical genre can be established with any confidence some conditions must be fulfilled.

1. The social custom underlying the hypothesized genre must be clearly demonstrable, if possible by evidence independent of the examples of the genre.

2. The primary elements of the genre should be distinct from those of any other genre.

3. The correspondences of the secondary elements (topoi) throughout the examples of the genre should be such as to exclude random coincidence and the topoi, as a body, should be recognizably distinct from the topoi of any other genre.

4. A sufficient number of clear examples of the genre must be available. This number will vary depending on the ease of fulfilling the other conditions.

5. It is helpful, though not essential, if some early example of the genre survives, or is known of in Homer or in a lyric poet, which could have been treated as a model for the genre by later writers.

The distinction made above between rhetorical and non-rhetorical genres is a useful one and in so far as it is based on the facts of whether or not a genre was named, taught and exemplified in the rhetorical schools, a valid one. But it should not be assumed that ancient writers or critics would have considered the distinction valid or useful. Direct evidence cannot be cited on this point. But the discussion by Cicero and Quintilian of the divisions of rhetoric indicate the very wide sweep of material which could be considered to fall within the scope of oratory:

> sed tria an plura sint ambigitur. nec dubie prope omnes utique summae apud antiquos auctoritatis scriptores Aristotelen secuti, qui nomine tantum alio contionalem pro deliberatiua appellat, hac partitione contenti fuerunt. uerum et tum leuiter est temptatum, cum apud Graecos quosdam tum apud Ciceronem in libris de Oratore, et nunc maximo temporum nostrorum auctore prope inpulsum, ut non

modo plura haec genera sed paene innumerabilia uideantur. nam si laudandi ac uituperandi officium in parte tertia ponimus, in quo genere uersari uidebimur cum querimur, consolamur, mitigamus, concitamus, terremus, confirmamus, praecipimus, obscure dicta interpretamur, narramus, deprecamur, gratias agimus, gratulamur, obiurgamus, maledicimus, describimus, mandamus, renuntiamus, optamus, opinamur, plurima alia? ut mihi in illa vetere persuasione permanenti velut petenda sit venia, quaerendumque quo moti priores rem tam late fusam tam breviter adstrinxerint.

Quintilian *Institutio Oratoria* 3 4 1-4 (cp. Cicero *De Oratore* 2 11ff.)

Moreover, as we have seen, minor non-rhetorical genres may have come to be regarded as the poor relations of the rhetorical genres with similar functions. The process may have extended further, and other non-rhetorical genres with functions more disparate from those of rhetorical genres may have been falsely linked with them. This would be in keeping with the general rhetoricizing tendencies of antiquity in accordance with which Homer and the early Greek lyric poets were regarded as rhetorical exemplars and little difference was seen between rhetoric and poetry.[31] Hence it can easily be imagined that, for example, the renuntiatio amoris may have been thought to be related to the syntaktikon or the 'symptoms of love' to be a symbouleutic genre. A hint of this 'rhetoricization' process in action can perhaps be found in the comment of the scholiast (Σ) on Theocritus *Idyll* 18 upon a genre which we may call, adapting the scholiast's term, *diegertikon*.[32] It appears that in ancient Greece it was the custom for friends of a newly married couple to wake them up on the morning after the bridal night with singing, dancing, and so on. This inconsiderate custom is referred to in

55 ...ἐγρέσθαι δὲ πρὸς ἀῶ μὴ 'πιλάθησθε.
νεύμεθα κάμμες ἐς ὄρθρον, ἐπεί κα πρᾶτος ἀοιδός
ἐξ εὐνᾶς κελαδήσῃ ἀνασχὼν εὔτριχα δειράν.
Theocritus *Idyll* 18 55-7

as well as in Aeschylus *Fr.* 124 (Mette) and perhaps in Apollonius Rhodius *Argonautica* 4 1192-9 and Menander 406 3. What seems to be an actual diegertikon in fragmentary form survives (Sappho *Fr.* 30 (LP)). Moreover, the popular song in which a woman awakens her lover to speed him on his way before her husband's return (*Poetae Melici*

Graeci 853, cp. Plautus *Asinaria* 921ff.) should probably be regarded as a member of another variant of the genre; so too should the speech of Hypermnestra, at Horace *Odes* 3 11 37ff., to her husband on the morning after their nuptial night, and also *A.P.* 5 118 (Marcus Argentarius). This genre with its clear non-rhetorical origin and history is treated as though it was a variant of a rhetorical genre in scholium (*Σ*) to Theocritus *Idyll* 18. Commenting on 55-7 the scholiast says:

τῶν δὲ ἐπιθαλαμίων τινὰ μὲν ᾄδεται ἑσπέρας, ἃ λέγεται κατακοιμητικά, ἅτινα ἕως μέσης νυκτὸς ᾄδουσι· τινὰ δὲ ὄρθρια, ἃ καὶ προσαγορεύεται διεγερτικά.

It appears that he is attempting to assimilate the diegertikon to the *epithalamium*, and so to classify a non-rhetorical genre as a variant or specialized type of a rhetorical epideictic genre.

The distinction so far made between rhetorical and non-rhetorical genres, and the attempted subclassification of rhetorical genres, more or less exhaust the useful classification of genres other than by subject-matter. But three problems connected with this topic remain. *Did ancient writers think that topoi could gain the status of independent genres or that independent genres could become topoi of other genres?* No certain answer can be given to this question; but it is worth asking because a probable answer is available, and because the investigation affords an opportunity to examine some interesting generic phenomena. A genre, for which no specific ancient name survives, will form the basis for the first part of our investigation. It is one form of the general genre 'prophecy',[33] and it is exemplified often enough to be treated as an independent genre. Its basis is as follows. The speaker is in a situation not to his liking and the blame or responsibility for this lies, in his opinion, with the addressee. The speaker warns/prophesies/wishes that the addressee may in future find himself in a new position in which he will no longer incommode the speaker. The purpose of this threat is to induce the addressee to take faster action to relieve the speaker's present discomfort.

The genre is commonly used when the speaker is in love with the addressee and when the speaker is uncomfortable because the addressee will not yield to his passion. In such circumstances the speaker may warn the addressee that old age will come and render him unattractive (Theognis 1 1299-310; Theocritus *Idyll* 29; *A.P.* 12 33 (Meleager);

Horace *Odes* 4 10; *A.P.* 12 30 (Alcaeus of Messene); *A.P.* 12 31 (Phanias); *A.P.* 12 39 (Anon)); or/ and place the addressee in a plight similar to that of the speaker (Theognis 1 1299-310; Theocritus *Idyll* 29; Horace *Odes* 4 10; *A.P.* 12 30 (Alcaeus of Messene)). Or the speaker may, in sophisticated examples, simply say that the addressee's alternative love-relationship will come to no good, which resembles the previous threat (e.g. Horace *Odes* 1 13, see Ovid *Ars Amatoria* 3 69ff. for a comparable notion). Or – although this may be a different variant – the speaker can say that the addressee will grow to an age to feel the same sentiments as the speaker but with happy outcome. An example of this is Horace *Odes* 2 5, where the prophecy of reversal is not the norm 'you will grow older to old age, be in love with others, and be unsatisfied like me', but 'you will grow older to maturity, be in love with me and we shall both be satisfied'.

This kind of 'threat-prophecy' is found as the sole genre of the poems cited above. Moreover, it generates another genre also found as the sole genre of some poems, that is, the 'gloating over fulfilment' of such an erotic 'threat-prophecy'. 'Gloating over fulfilment' can thus be found in *A.P.* 5 107 (Philodemus); *A.P.* 5 21 (Rufinus); *A.P.* 12 32 (Thymocles). It is also possible that other poems describing how a once admired beauty is now aged and unattractive should be assigned to this latter genre, the prophecy having been omitted. (Such omissions of a primary element of a genre have already been mentioned in Chapter 1, will recur again in this chapter, and will be treated at greater length in Chapter 5.) The sophistication relies upon the ancient readers' sensitivity to the themes normally involved: he was expected to supply the missing 'I told you so'. Among these poems are *A.P.* 5 204 (Meleager); Horace *Odes* 3 15; *A.P.* 5 27 (Rufinus); *A.P.* 5 271 (Macedonius); *A.P.* 5 273 (Agathias); (cp. Epikrates ap. Athenaeum 570 B-D). Horace *Odes* 2 8 would be an inversion of this genre (see Chapter 5), the perjury spoken of amounting in this ode to erotic deprivation or infidelity.

A variation of the norm for the 'gloating over fulfilment' is found at *A.P.* 5 111 (Antiphilus). Here the speaker had prophesied that a young girl would come into her prime and fire all; now he himself is a victim of love for her.[34] Some interplay between the 'threat-prophecy' and 'gloating over fulfilment' occurs in *A.P.* 12 33 and 39, where the 'threat-prophecy' is backed up by a boastful 'gloating over fulfilment' in the case of another or others (cp. Tibullus 1 8 71-8).

But as well as the examples above, in which the 'threat-prophecy' and the 'gloating over fulfilment' are found as independent genres, both are found as topoi of other genres. The 'threat-prophecy' occurs in the komos, for example, *A.P.* 5 23 (Callimachus); *A.P.* 5 167 (Asclepiades); *A.P.* 5 191 (Meleager); Horace *Odes* 3 10 9-12, 19-20 (cp. Ovid *Ars Amatoria* 3 69ff.); (?) *A.P.* 5 103 (Rufinus).[35] It also occurs in the renuntiatio amoris, for example, Catullus 8; Horace *Epode* 15; Propertius 3 25, and in erotodidaxis, for example, Tibullus 1 8 71ff.; Ovid *Ars Amatoria* 3 69ff. The 'gloating over fulfilment' occurs in erotodidaxis (Propertius 1 9), a witty example of this genre which is used for Alexandrian literary manifesto purposes, that is, to advise: 'you, an epic poet, are in love, so write love-poetry, not epic, and you will be successful in love'.[36]

The behaviour of the two genres 'threat-prophecy' and 'gloating over fulfilment' is characteristic in this respect: many genres are also found as topoi of other genres (see Chapter 5). It is also typical that the erotic kind of 'threat-prophecy' is found as a topos of a small number of other genres, and most often of one, the komos; and in antiquity, such phenomena could possibly have given rise to the notion that some genres originated as topoi of other genres.

But there is an objection to the idea that the ancients thought in terms of topoi becoming independent genres, namely that there is no parallel concept in rhetorical theory. As will be seen below, the reverse notion, that independent genres could become topoi of other genres, is paralleled in ancient rhetorical theory; so it is more likely to have provided a model for ancient thought. On the other hand it is worth formulating the first notion since evidence to support it may at some time become available. In addition, the intimate connexion between the erotic 'threat-prophecy' and komos, revealed in the course of testing the idea, helps with the interpretation of a difficult Horatian ode:[37]

Parcius iunctas quatiunt fenestras
iactibus crebris iuuenes proterui,
nec tibi somnos adimunt, amatque
    ianua limen,

5 quae prius multum facilis mouebat
cardines; audis minus et minus iam
'me tuo longas pereunte noctes,
    Lydia, dormis?'

inuicem moechos anus arrogantis
10 flebis in solo leuis angiportu,

Thracio bacchante magis sub inter-
   lunia uento,
cum tibi flagrans amor et libido,
quae solet matres furiare equorum,
15 saeuiet circa iecur ulcerosum,
   non sine questu
laeta quod pubes hedera uirente
gaudeat pulla magis atque myrto,
aridas frondis hiemis sodali
20 dedicet Hebro
   Horace *Odes* 1 25

This ode appears at first sight to belong to the genre 'threat-prophecy'. If it does it is of the special type to which *A.P.* 5 103 3-4 (Rufinus), *A.P.* 12 30 (Alcaeus of Messene) and *A.P.* 12 31 (Phanias) also belong. In this type the warning is reinforced not, for example, as in *A.P.* 12 33, *A.P.* 12 39 and Tibullus 1 8 71-8, by the *exemplum* of someone else (see above) but even more pointedly by the *exemplum* of the addressee. The threat is therefore couched in the form 'it is happening to you already and will get worse'. In *Odes* 1 25 Horace says to Lydia 'you are getting fewer and fewer lovers coming to beg your favours as it is. The future has in store for you a worse fate. Far from anyone coming to you, you yourself will roam about frustrated, aged and unloved.' What is especially interesting about this 'threat-prophecy' is the way in which the komos is introduced into it. The fewer and fewer lovers who come to Lydia are komasts. They awaken her from sleep, throw stones at her windows, want to come through the door and plead outside it (1-8). Moreover, Lydia is threatened with the fate of herself becoming an aged komast, standing in a lane[38] in the cold wind, weeping at the haughtiness of her lovers who will not let her in (9) and lamenting because men no longer have any interest in her (16-20). In Roman sociological terms Lydia will be demoted within the ultra-snobbish and class-ridden demimonde,[39] and will be transformed from a high-class courtesan with her own house into a street walker plying her trade in the alley.

The import of this is as follows. In many short komoi, including the epigrams mentioned above (p. 87) where threat-prophecies occur as part of the komos, the komastic situation and therefore the genre of the poems are indicated only by hints, and some of the primary elements are left out.[40] Ancient sensitivity to generic contexts, always greater than ours, was especially fine with regard to the komos. This is what we would expect in view of the commonness of the genre, which made its contents very familiar to an ancient audience and inspired poets writing komoi to many innovations, including omission. The frequent omissions of some of the primary elements in komoi suggest that this is what is happening in Horace *Odes* 1 25. Horace intended his readers to gather from the emphasis on komastic situations that he is standing outside Lydia's house and saying 'You don't have many customers coming to you as it is and you will have to go out and look for them when you grow even older,' with the implication 'therefore admit me now'. It is no argument against this suggestion that Ovid *Ars Amatoria* 3 69ff., which speaks in similar terms of admitting a komast, is not part of a komos but occurs in erotodidaxis; for there Ovid has put on the mantle of the teacher of love, the mouthpiece of Venus, and is giving instructions to girls (57ff.). Horace has no such status in *Odes* 1 25. Since no other hypothesis gives Horace a reason for saying what he says to Lydia, it may be presumed that he is speaking on his own behalf and that the komastic emphasis within the threat-prophecy is meant to convey to the reader that the whole ode is a komos.

The most probable solution to the problem of whether ancient writers thought in terms of topoi becoming genres or vice versa is to be found through the analogy of rhetorical progymnasmata. These were genres in themselves; but they were taught and practised in the rhetorical schools so that they could later form sections of speeches belonging to the major rhetorical genres. As sections of major genres the progymnasmata lost their status as independent genres and were reduced to topoi or groups of topoi forming part of the examples of the major genres.

Consequently, when material which could have constituted an independent example of a genre forms an integral part of another generic example, an ancient critic would probably have thought that the subordinated material was behaving like a progymnasma. We have seen another case of such subordination in the use of the *anathematikon* (dedication), a genre capable of independent existence, as part of the renuntiatio amoris. The notion of a dedication to mark the end of love occurs in four examples of the genre (see above, topos B 7). In three cases the actual dedication is reproduced in the form of an anathematikon, incorporated into the renuntiatio amoris.

The absorption of a rhetorical progymnasma into another genre is not the same phenomenon as the 'inclusion' of one generic example within another example of the same or a related genre – an occurrence which has already been mentioned in Chapters 1 and 2 and will be treated at length in Chapter 7. When this latter phenomenon is found, the 'included' generic example, whose genre is just as important for the meaning of the poem as that of the overall generic example, retains its own separate generic identity, which is related to that of the including genre. This contrasts with the absorption of rhetorical progymnasmata whose genres are not so important for the meaning of the poem as a whole and whose generic functions are subordinated to those of the genres which absorb them.

But it would be idle to pretend that there is a watertight distinction between the absorption of progymnasmata and inclusion of the kind discussed in Chapter 7. It would be even more difficult to draw a line between inclusion and the absorption of the minor non-rhetorical genres which seem to behave in a way analogous to progymnasmata. This is because such minor genres are particularly difficult to identify and because the same minor genre may not always behave in the same way. The best way to think about the matter is in terms of a graduated scale with total absorption at one end and inclusion at the other. In the middle of the scale will be examples which incline to one or the other but which will not be definable in strict terms.

This can best be appreciated by consideration of the genre *mandata*, whose Greek title is probably *epistaltikon*.[41] In the 'public advertisement', Propertius 3 23, treated earlier in this chapter, 12-18 are described in 11 as mandata. This passage of mandata can easily be regarded as being absorbed like a progymnasma since its generic function is not important to the poem as a whole and is unrelated to that of the 'public advertisement'. In Horace *Odes* 2 11 a uocatio ad cenam ends with a set of mandata to slaves (18-24).[42] These mandata are also probably to be regarded in the same way. But the function of the uocatio, to invite or summon, is not too distant for that of mandata, to give instructions, and it is simply the subordination of mandata to uocatio in terms of the total meaning of the ode which allows us to think of the mandata as being treated like a progymnasma.

Even more difficult to classify are examples of yet another sort of mandata. Two Latin poetic *epikedia*[43] (Propertius 3 7 and Statius *Siluae* 5 1) contain passages which consist of the mandata of the dying person (Propertius 57-64, Statius 177-93). The *Elegiae in Maecenatem*, which in their MSS are a single poem and were divided by Scaliger into the two poems, as which they are generally printed nowadays, are probably another example of the same phenomenon. The 'first' elegy is an epikedion on Maecenas, the 'second' the mandata of the dying Maecenas. It may well be that the *Elegiae* should be treated as a single poem, an epikedion with a passage of mandata at the end. The passages of mandata in these epikedia belong to a genre which is a specialized form of the general genre and which may be called *mandata morituri*. It is useful to regard such mandata as a specialized genre in view of the social habit of uttering and recording such last injunctions.

Mandata morituri are exemplified as the genre of whole poems in Horace *Odes* 2 20 and in Propertius 1 21, a sometimes misunderstood elegy which is explicable as an example of the standard utterance of a dying man. Another example of the genre mandata morituri is Propertius 2 13, an elegy whose unity has, I believe, been firmly established by L. P. Wilkinson.[44] The unity question does not in fact affect a generic assignment of Propertius 2 13. If it is two elegies then 2 13B, which consists of a set of mandata uttered by Propertius in anticipation of his own death, is a member of the genre. If 2 13 is one elegy, then this one elegy is a member of the genre. It should be noted that the arguments for the unity of Propertius 2 13 are strengthened by the assignment to the genre mandata morituri of Horace *Odes* 2 10. This is also a programmatic poem, which functions as an epilogue; it also combines the themes of literary glory and death; and it is undoubtedly a single poem.

The mandata morituri found in epikedia are impossible to classify with any rigour as absorbed or included. In the case of Propertius 3 7 it is tempting to think of the mandata of the dying Paetus as behaving like a progymnasma. They do not affect the meaning of the poem to any great extent, and their function is different from that of the epikedion as a whole. But in *Siluae* 5 1 the mandata, although *qua* mandata they have a different function from the epikedion, in terms of content do have the same consolatory and encomiastic functions as the epikedion as a whole. Even more strongly is this the case with the second elegy on Maecenas, if it is in fact part of the first. Not only do the mandata share these functions of the epikedion but they are very important in terms of the meaning of the poem as a whole.

So the distinction is a useful one in clear-cut cases, in that the two different levels of originality are involved; but it cannot be applied in many instances.

Is hymn a genre in either sense of the word genre? Hymns were doubtless established as standard recurrent formulaic utterances long before many secular genres reached a fixed form. Moreover, Menander accords a separate treatise to them. But there is no genre 'hymn' in the sense in which the word is being used in this book. Hymns belong to various epideictic and other genres, the difference between them and other examples of those genres being simply in addressee:[45]

τῶν δὴ ἐπιδεικτικῶν τὸ μὲν ψόγος, τὸ δὲ ἔπαινος...ἔπαινος δέ τις γίνεται, ὀτὲ μὲν εἰς τὰ θεῖα, ὀτὲ δὲ εἰς τὰ θνητά, καὶ ὅτε μὲν εἰς θεούς, ὕμνους καλοῦμεν.

Menander 331 15-20
'Epideictic speeches divide into encomia and vituperations. . . . Encomia can be of gods and of men. When they are of gods, we call them hymns.'

Naturally this difference in addressee is reflected in differences of language in the address, but to say that a poem is a hymn is uninformative generically. We need to know whether, for example, it is a kletic, propemptic, or euktic hymn. Conversely, to say that a poem is, for example, a kletic hymn does not mean that it belongs to any genre other than the kletikon. The religious form of a genre, although perhaps older than the secular forms of it, need not be thought to have generated the secular forms. 'Hymn' therefore is not a genre in the sense in which propemptikon or komos is a genre. Nor is it a genre in the other common sense of the word, in which it is used to refer to kinds of literature like epic, elegy, or lyric; for these kinds of literature are each characterized by metre and length, and more important they are mutually exclusive. 'Hymn' is not characterized by metre or by length, and hymns can be found in epic, elegy, lyric, etc. One qualification must be made to what precedes: some specialized classes of hymns, such as *paean* and *dithyramb*, are genres in the sense in which propemptikon and komos are genres. This is so because at least some of the hymns classified in antiquity as dithyrambs or paeans are characterized by fixed subject-matter proper only to them.[46]

How far were native Roman genres Hellenized by Roman writers?
Roman society had institutions without parallels in Greek society. There is some evidence that when sophisticated Roman writers dealt with these institutions they sometimes sought to graft their Roman material on to pre-existent Greek genres so as to procure a respectable literary pedigree for their efforts. It is well known, for example, that Roman door-magic

and concern about doors was grafted on to the Greek genre komos, so that Roman examples of the komos have much more to do with doors than do Greek examples.[47] I have suggested elsewhere[48] that in *Odes* 1 30 Horace may be trying to graft on to the Greek kletic hymn the Roman institution of *euocatio* – a besieging general's appeal to his enemy's gods to defect. In these two cases the Roman material is not over-obtrusive. However, there were perhaps other cases of Hellenization of Roman institutions where the Roman material was more obtrusive and less tractable, and where the cultural fusion resulted in poems to which their authors would have given a Greek generic name but which probably do not deserve this name.

The first example of this process concerns the Roman institution of *flagitatio*, the subject of a seminal article by Herman Usener.[49] Flagitatio was a form of extra-legal or pro-legal self-help by which a man whose property had been stolen,[50] or more usually a creditor whose debtor was refusing to repay him,[51] could attempt to regain his property by subjecting the offender to a barrage of insults and demands for the return of his property.[52] Literary flagitationes mentioned or treated by Usener are: Plautus *Mostellaria* 568ff.; *Pseudolus* 357ff.; Catullus 25, 42, 55 9-10. Usener also collects other references to the practice.

Since Greece had no parallel institution, any Hellenization of flagitatio must have been to some extent strained. But the existence of a Greek genre which operated in a roughly parallel context makes it likely that Roman writers would have described their flagitationes as belonging to it. This Greek genre is *arai* (curses). Cursing of malefactors is a common human activity, both public and private. No actual Greek examples of arai named as such have survived but we know of several (see below) and we have Latin *dirae* (curses) which are probably of the Greek type – the poem entitled *Dirae* and Ovid's *Ibis*, the latter probably deriving from a homonymous poem by Callimachus (*Frr.* 381-2 (Pfeiffer)). Naturally not all arai were directed against persons who were retaining someone else's property but, as well as the *Dirae*, two of the Greek arai of which we know were concerned with just this situation. Information about the first, a work of the Alexandrian poetess Moero (*Fr. 4 Collectanea Alexandrina* ed. Powell) survives in Parthenius' 'Ερωτικὰ Παθήματα (*Love Stories*). The heading of the twenty-seventh legend is: 'Moero tells this story in her *Arai*', and the story concerns a lady called Alcinoe who came to a sorry end because of the anger of Athena, the patroness of spinners. She incurred Athena's wrath because she had hired a spinning woman named Nicandre and after a year had turned her out without her full wages. Nicandre's reaction to this treatment is narrated in the following words, in which we note the 'ambiguity' of ἀρᾶσθαι, which means both pray and curse:

> . . . τὴν δὲ ἀράσασθαι πολλὰ ᾿Αθηνᾷ τίσασθαι αὐτὴν ἀντ᾿ ἀδίκου στερήσεως.

Probably the tale of Alcinoe and Nicandre was not the main theme of Moero's *Arai*. The *Arai* was either just a collection of stories involving curses or a set of mythological illustrations designed to reinforce the ill-wishes which Moero herself was uttering (cp. Ovid's *Ibis* for this pattern). But the account of the story preserved in Parthenius is useful as evidence of one ground for arai, that is, unjust deprival of something owed. More evidence along these lines is provided by Euphorion *Fr.* 8 (*Collectanea Alexandrina*) ῞Οστις μεν κελέβην ᾿Αλυβήιδα μοῦνος ἀπηύρα. This fragment is assigned by Stephanus Byzantius to a work of Euphorion called ᾿Αραὶ ἢ Ποτηριοκλέπτης (*Curses, or the Beaker-Thief*), and by the scholiast on Theocritus *Idyll* 2 2 to a Ποτηριοκλέπτης of Euphorion.[53] Here we are instantly transported to the world of two of the Catullan flagitationes, Catullus 25 where the cause of the flagitatio is the theft of a cloak, napkin and writing tablets, and Catullus 12 where the theft of a napkin is in question. In this latter flagitatio, not identified as such by Usener, Catullus with characteristic humour employs a formal sophistication in the use of tenses (see p. 54). The effect is that the poem poses as a threat of flagitatio while actually being a flagitatio.

The clothes-thief and the man who stole from the dinner-table are familiar figures in classical literature and the coincidence that arai and flagitatio were both responses to these standard offences almost guarantees that they were regarded as one and the same genre by Roman writers. One factor which possibly made the identification easier is the 'ambiguity' of the verb *maledico* which, from the time of Plautus, meant both 'curse' and 'abuse'. Such 'ambiguities' in a language are not really cases of confusion or double-meaning. They are simply indications that a distinction of the sort other languages make was not found useful in that language. Just as the 'ambiguity' of words to do with shipwreck may have affected the inverse epibaterion (see p. 61) so the 'ambiguity' of *maledico* may have been influential here, since the word *maledicta* occurs as a description of the utterances characteristic of flagitatio.[54]

94

In all this, one distinction must be observed between arai and flagitationes. The purpose of flagitatio is to obtain the return of one's own property. In the surviving or known arai and dirae where the person cursing has been unjustly deprived of his property, there is no direct evidence of a demand for its return. This may be an accident; some of these arai may have been intended to secure the return of the property. But even if all such arai were simple ventings of the owners' hatred rather than attempts to recover property, a link between arai and flagitationes would still be feasible. They would still be the cognate Greek and Latin standard responses to the same situation.

If these arguments are correct, the genre arai fared in Roman literature in rather the same way as the komos. Some Roman examples of the genre were purely Greek in inspiration: for example, the *Dirae*, Ovid's *Ibis*, and Ovid *Amores* 1 12. In the last, no withholding of property is involved, but Ovid's writing-tablets, which have returned to him with news that his mistress cannot come to him, are cursed roundly. But the flagitationes proper, although also composed as members of the genre, are almost purely Roman.

The next example of possible ancient identification of a Roman genre with a Greek genre was, if it took place, an even more arbitrary procedure. Even the contexts of delivery are fairly dissimilar. The triumph was the most important single Roman socio-political event. Roman poets often refer to the triumph and describe triumphs at some length.[55] The description of the triumph (whether it be a real triumph or the imaginary triumph of a god, of the poet *qua* poet, or of the poet *qua* lover, or both) occurs, for example, at Virgil *Aeneid* 8 714-28; Propertius 2 14; 3 1 9ff.; Ovid *Amores* 1 2; 2 12; *Ars Amatoria* 1 213-28; *Tristia* 4 2; and also as the included genre (see ch.7) at Tibullus 1 7; Horace *Odes* 4 2; Propertius 3 4.

One's immediate thought is that Roman writers would have attempted to assimilate the Roman triumph-poem to the Greek *epinikion*; but apart from the laurel crown worn equally by triumphing generals and victors at the games there seem little to link the two genres, and Roman writers do not show any interest in such an identification. It may be that some references to Apollo and laurel crowns in triumph context are hints of an attempt to connect triumph-poems with some kind of *paean* – perhaps a victory *paean* (cf. Virgil *Aeneid* 7 720; Horace *Odes* 4 2 9, 46-7; Ovid *Tristia* 4 2 51, and Ovid *Ars Amatoria* 2 1 where '*io Paean*' replaces '*io Triumphe*'). But it is more probable that when the majority of Roman writers wrote triumph-poems, they imagined they were writing dithyrambs. The bulk of the evidence for this suggestion derives not from Roman triumph-poems but from the derivation of the word *triumphus* and from ancient beliefs about the nature and origin of the institution.[56] This evidence although bulky can be summed up briefly. The word *triumphus* derives ultimately from the Greek θρίαμβος; Romans at all periods were aware of this; the words θρίαμβος and διθύραμβος are, if not interchangeable, at least closely related; and finally Dionysus was believed in antiquity to have enjoyed the first triumph, after his victory over the Indians. Some confirmation that Roman writers did associate triumph-poems and dithyrambs may be derived from an examination of Horace *Odes* 4 2, although this ode may be alluding simultaneously to two different theories on the question (see above). In *Odes* 4 2 Horace is modestly asserting that Iulus Antonius and not himself has the poetic strength to sing of Augustus' triumph over the Sygambri. Horace makes it clear (1) that to treat such a theme is to imitate Pindar. His description of Pindar's style and work begins with an appreciation of Pindar's general poetic technique and then goes on to deal with various classes of Pindaric poems, *dithyrambs* (stanza 3), hymns, *paeans* and *encomia* (stanza 4), *epinikia* (stanza 5), *threnoi* (stanza 6). Not only do dithyrambs head this list but the general simile describing Pindaric style by comparison with a rushing river in 5-8 is interpreted through a related metaphor in relation only to dithyrambs in 11-12:

5 monte decurrens uelut amnis, imbres
    quem super notas aluere ripas,
    feruet immensusque ruit profundo
       Pindarus ore,
    laurea donandus Apollinari,
10 seu per audaces noua dithyrambos
    uerba deuoluit numerisque fertur
       lege solutis
    Horace *Odes* 4 2 5-12

Some further support for the notion that the Romans thought triumph-poems were dithyrambs comes from Roman triumph-poems themselves when they lay stress on Dionysiac elements which are quite out of keeping with the traditional Roman religious paraphernalia of the triumph (e.g. Tibullus 1 7, see pp. 167-8; Propertius 3 4 1, see p. 187; Ovid *Amores* 1 2 47-8, cp. *Ars Amatoria* 1 189-90).

The hypothesized Roman identification of triumph-poems and dithy-rambs, was, of course, just as shaky in factual terms as were the attempts of Alexandrian categorizors to decide what was a dithyramb and what was not.[57] Indeed the 'dithyrambs' with which the Romans were pre-sented by Alexandria can have helped just as little to stimulate the identi-fication, as they do to evidence its likelihood. The most that can be said to support a theory of such identification on the basis of surviving Greek 'dithyrambs' is that at least some of the Greek poems which may have been or were identified as dithyrambs in the Augustan Age did deal with a situation not too remote from the Roman triumph – a heroic deed, the coming of a victor, public rejoicing; for example, Bacchylides *Dithy-rambs* 17, 18, 20 (Snell), and Sophocles *Trachiniae* 205ff.

To sum up, Roman poets wrote ordinary hymns to Dionysus which they probably classified with a fair degree of accuracy as dithyrambs. One of these is Propertius 3 17, where the self-fulfilling undertaking[58] to sing of Bacchus,

> haec ego non humili referam memoranda coturno
> qualis Pindarico spiritus ore tonat.
>
> 39-40

with its reference to Pindar, leaves little doubt that Propertius thought he was writing a dithyramb. They also wrote triumph-poems, which they sometimes believed to belong to the same genre. The dithyramb is treated therefore in very much the same way at Rome as are the komos and arai.

4

Originality in the Use of Topoi

A writer working in accordance with generic patterns is in general
terms necessarily less original than a writer free from the restraints
of genre. He cannot, for example, draw his inspiration directly from
individual incidents and experiences in his own life but is confined to
the range of subjects proper to the genres, and within these genres
at least some of his material must be standard if his writings are to
be recognizable as belonging to specific genres. But even within the
framework of these constraints, certain types of originality are possible
and they were regarded as essential to good writing or speaking in
antiquity.

τίς γὰρ οὐκ οἶδε πλὴν τούτων, ὅτι τὸ μὲν τῶν γραμμάτων
ἀκινήτως ἔχει καὶ μένει κατὰ ταὐτόν, ὥστε τοῖς αὐτοῖς ἀεὶ
περὶ τῶν αὐτῶν χρώμενοι διατελοῦμεν, τὸ δὲ τῶν λόγων πᾶν
τοὐναντίον πέπονθεν· τὸ γὰρ ὑφ' ἑτέρου ῥηθὲν τῷ λέγοντι μετ'
ἐκεῖνον οὐχ ὁμοίως χρήσιμόν ἐστιν, ἀλλ' οὗτος εἶναι δοκεῖ τεχνι-
κώτατος, ὅστις ἂν ἀξίως μὲν λέγῃ τῶν πραγμάτων, μηδὲν δὲ τῶν
αὐτῶν τοῖς ἄλλοις εὑρίσκειν δύνηται. μέγιστον δὲ σημεῖον τῆς ἀνο-
μοιότητος αὐτῶν· τοὺς μὲν γὰρ λόγους οὐχ οἷόν τε καλῶς ἔχειν,
ἢν μὴ τῶν καιρῶν καὶ τοῦ πρεπόντως καὶ τοῦ καινῶς [ἔχειν]
μετάσχωσιν, τοῖς δὲ γράμμασιν οὐδενὸς τούτων προσεδέησεν.
Isocrates 13 12-13

πρὸς δὲ τούτοις εἰ μὲν μηδαμῶς ἄλλως οἷόν τ' ἦν δηλοῦν τὰς
αὐτὰς πράξεις ἀλλ' ἢ διὰ μιᾶς ἰδέας, εἶχεν ἄν τις ὑπολαβεῖν, ὡς
περίεργόν ἐστι τὸν αὐτὸν τρόπον ἐκείνοις λέγοντα πάλιν
ἐνοχλεῖν τοῖς ἀκούουσιν· ἐπειδὴ δ' οἱ λόγοι τοιαύτην ἔχουσι τὴν
φύσιν ὥσθ' οἷόν τ' εἶναι περὶ τῶν αὐτῶν πολλαχῶς ἐξηγήσασθαι,
καὶ τά τε μεγάλα ταπεινὰ ποιῆσαι καὶ τοῖς μικροῖς μέγεθος
περιθεῖναι, καὶ τά τε παλαιὰ καινῶς διελθεῖν καὶ περὶ τῶν
νεωστὶ γεγενημένων ἀρχαίως εἰπεῖν, οὐκέτι φευκτέον ταῦτ' ἐστί,
περὶ ὧν ἕτεροι πρότερον εἰρήκασιν, ἀλλ' ἄμεινον ἐκείνων εἰπεῖν
πειρατέον. αἱ μὲν γὰρ πράξεις αἱ προγεγενημέναι κοιναὶ πᾶσιν
ἡμῖν κατελείφθησαν, τὸ δ' ἐν καιρῷ ταύταις καταχρήσασθαι

καὶ τὰ προσήκοντα περὶ ἑκάστης ἐνθυμηθῆναι καὶ τοῖς ὀνόμασιν
εὖ διαθέσθαι τῶν εὖ φρονούντων ἴδιόν ἐστιν.

Isocrates 4 7-9

These passages are among many[1] which illustrate ancient insistence on
originality within generic composition, and some of the originality to be
found in generic examples can be discussed fruitfully in terms of distinctions made by Isocrates (see p. 100). Originality in generic composition can be treated under four categories, which together cover the
whole field: first, the novelty which consists in introducing into a generic
pattern topoi and notions not hitherto associated with it; second, the
individual writer's own choice, combination and arrangement of the
standard topoi of a particular genre; third, his alterations and modifica-
tions of single topoi; and fourth, the employment by a writer of the major
generic sophistications which are potentially applicable to all genres. The
use by ancient writers of the greater part of the last and most important
of these categories, which goes beyond topical originality, is the subject
of Chapters 5-9. In the present chapter I shall deal with the first three
kinds of originality, which all have to do with the employment of topoi.

At an early period the introduction of new material into a generic
pattern must often have involved the invention by the author of that
material. However, as the generic patterns became more elaborate and
as rhetorical training became more influential, the introduction of new
material into an example of a genre inevitably came to mean more and
more the use in an example of one genre of a topos associated with another genre. The ability of many topoi to move from one genre to another
is central to generic originality. The primary elements which differen-
tiate genres cannot of course behave in this way, but the secondary
elements, since they are not necessary constituents of genres, can move
freely between them.

A simple example of the ability of topoi to appear in several genres is
provided by the topos on friendship, the concept that willingness to
accompany a friend anywhere is a proof of friendship. This topos
appeared at Propertius 1 6 3-4 in a propemptikon (p. 4). It also appears,
for example, at Catullus 11 1-12 in a renuntiatio amoris, again in a propemptikon at Horace *Epode* 1 11-14, at *Odes* 2 6 1-4 in an epibaterion, at
Statius *Siluae* 5 1 127ff. in an epikedion. It is impossible to say in what
genre this topos originated, and its use is not confined to travel genres.
Because topoi can thus move from genre to genre, assignments to genres

must always be based not so much on secondary elements as on the logic of the situation. No quantity of secondary elements makes an example of a genre, although their presence is a welcome confirmation of an assignment based on primary elements. The introduction of new material into a generic pattern, whether or not this be considered as transference of that material from another genre, although constantly found in ancient literature, is not mentioned by Isocrates in the passages quoted above. This is probably because in these passages he begins to talk about composition at the point where the writer has already to hand all the material he might require.

The second and third categories of topical innovation, those to do with selection, combination, arrangement, and alteration of topoi, are summed up briefly by Isocrates in a later section of one of the works quoted above. Isocrates' summary, although open to the criticism of some inexactness, will form a good basis for discussion. The second category is described in these words:

τὸ δὲ τούτων ἐφ᾽ ἑκάστῳ τῶν πραγμάτων ἃς δεῖ προελέσθαι καὶ μῖξαι πρὸς ἀλλήλας καὶ τάξαι κατὰ τρόπον...
Isocrates 13 16

Isocrates' first point in the second category is that a writer must select from all the topoi available within a genre those which he wishes to use in a particular speech. Menander also holds selection to be of great importance, recommending it several times.[2] It may seem obvious that a writer must do this, since the length or nature of his work, or the character of his addressee, will demand that he abstain from some of the topoi. But neglect of the generic basis of ancient literature sometimes blinds scholars to the skilful selection which an author has made, and leads them to criticize him for faults which he has gone out of his way to avoid.

One excellent ancient poem rarely appreciated and notable for its selective use of topoi is Theocritus' *Idyll* 17.

’Εκ Διὸς ἀρχώμεσθα καὶ ἐς Δία λήγετε Μοῖσαι,
ἀθανάτων τὸν ἄριστον, ἐπὴν †ἀείδωμεν ἀοιδαῖς·
ἀνδρῶν δ᾽ αὖ Πτολεμαῖος ἐνὶ πρώτοισι λεγέσθω
καὶ πύματος καὶ μέσσος· ὃ γὰρ προφερέστατος ἀνδρῶν.
5 ἥρωες, τοὶ πρόσθεν ἀφ᾽ ἡμιθέων ἐγένοντο,
ῥέξαντες καλὰ ἔργα σοφῶν ἐκύρησαν ἀοιδῶν·

αὐτὰρ ἐγὼ Πτολεμαῖον ἐπιστάμενος καλὰ εἰπεῖν
ὑμνήσαιμ'· ὕμνοι δὲ καὶ ἀθανάτων γέρας αὐτῶν.
Ἴδαν ἐς πολύδενδρον ἀνὴρ ὑλατόμος ἐλθών
10 παπταίνει, παρεόντος ἄδην, πόθεν ἄρξεται ἔργου.
τί πρῶτον καταλέξω; ἐπεὶ πάρα μυρία εἰπεῖν
οἷσι θεοὶ τὸν ἄριστον ἐτίμησαν βασιλήων.
Ἐκ πατέρων οἷος μὲν ἔην τελέσαι μέγα ἔργον
Λαγείδας Πτολεμαῖος, ὅτε φρεσὶν ἐγκατάθοιτο
15 βουλάν, ἃν οὐκ ἄλλος ἀνὴρ οἷός τε νοῆσαι.
τῆνον καὶ μακάρεσσι πατὴρ ὁμότιμον ἔθηκεν
ἀθανάτοις καί οἱ χρύσεος θρόνος ἐν Διὸς οἴκῳ
δέδμηται· παρὰ δ' αὐτὸν Ἀλέξανδρος φίλα εἰδώς
ἑδριάει, Πέρσαισι βαρὺς θεὸς αἰολομίτρας.
20 ἀντία δ' Ἡρακλῆος ἕδρα κενταυροφόνοιο
ἵδρυται στερεοῖο τετυγμένα ἐξ ἀδάμαντος·
ἔνθα σὺν ἄλλοισιν θαλίας ἔχει Οὐρανίδῃσι,
χαίρων υἱωνῶν περιώσιον υἱωνοῖσιν,
ὅττι σφεων Κρονίδης μελέων ἐξείλετο γῆρας
25 ἀθάνατοι δὲ καλεῦνται ἑοὶ νέποδες γεγαῶτες.
ἄμφω γὰρ πρόγονός σφιν ὁ καρτερὸς Ἡρακλείδας
ἀμφότεροι δ' ἀριθμεῦνται ἐς ἔσχατον Ἡρακλῆα.
τῷ καὶ ἐπεὶ δαίτηθεν ἴοι κεκορημένος ἤδη
νέκταρος εὐόδμοιο φίλας ἐς δῶμ' ἀλόχοιο,
30 τῷ μὲν τόξον ἔδωκεν ὑπωλένιόν τε φαρέτραν,
τῷ δὲ σιδάρειον σκύταλον κεχαραγμένον ὄζοις·
οἱ δ' εἰς ἀμβρόσιον θάλαμον λευκοσφύρου Ἥβας
ὅπλα καὶ αὐτὸν ἄγουσι γενειήταν Διὸς υἱόν.
Οἵα δ' ἐν πινυταῖσι περικλειτὰ Βερενίκα
35 ἔπρεπε θηλυτέρῃς, ὄφελος μέγα γειναμένοισι.
τᾷ μὲν Κύπρον ἔχοισα Διώνας πότνια κούρα
κόλπον ἐς εὐώδη ῥαδινὰς ἐσεμάξατο χεῖρας·
τῷ οὔπω τινὰ φαντὶ ἀδεῖν τόσον ἀνδρὶ γυναικῶν
ὅσσον περ Πτολεμαῖος ἑὴν ἐφίλησεν ἄκοιτιν.
40 ἦ μὰν ἀντεφιλεῖτο πολὺ πλέον. ὧδέ κε παισί
θαρσήσας σφετέροισιν ἐπιτρέποι οἶκον ἅπαντα
ὁππότε κεν φιλέων βαίνῃ λέχος ἐς φιλεούσης·
ἀστόργου δὲ γυναικὸς ἐπ' ἀλλοτρίῳ νόος αἰεί,
ῥηίδιοι δὲ γοναί, τέκνα δ' οὐ ποτεοικότα πατρί.
45 κάλλει ἀριστεύουσα θεάων πότν' Ἀφροδίτα,

σοὶ τήνα μεμέλητο· σέθεν δ' ἕνεκεν Βερενίκα
εὐειδὴς 'Αχέροντα πολύστονον οὐκ ἐπέρασεν,
ἀλλά μιν ἁρπάξασα, πάροιθ' ἐπὶ νῆα κατελθεῖν
κυανέαν καὶ στυγνὸν ἀεὶ πορθμῆα καμόντων,
50 ἐς ναὸν κατέθηκας, ἑᾶς δ' ἀπεδάσσαο τιμᾶς.
πᾶσιν δ' ἤπιος ἥδε βροτοῖς μαλακοὺς μὲν ἔρωτας
προσπνείει, κούφας δὲ διδοῖ ποθέοντι μερίμνας.
'Αργεία κυάνοφρυ, σὺ λαοφόνον Διομήδεα
μισγομένα Τυδῆι τέκες, Καλυδωνίῳ ἀνδρί,
55 ἀλλὰ Θέτις βαθύκολπος ἀκοντιστὰν 'Αχιλῆα
Αἰακίδᾳ Πηλῆι· σὲ δ', αἰχμητὰ Πτολεμαῖε,
αἰχμητᾷ Πτολεμαίῳ ἀρίζηλος Βερενίκα.
καί σε Κόως ἀτίταλλε βρέφος νεογιλλὸν ἐόντα,
δεξαμένα παρὰ ματρὸς ὅτε πρώταν ἴδες ἀῶ.
60 ἔνθα γὰρ Εἰλείθυιαν ἐβώσατο λυσίζωνον
'Αντιγόνας θυγάτηρ βεβαρημένα ὠδίνεσσιν·
ἢ δέ οἱ εὐμενέοισα παρίστατο, κὰδ δ' ἄρα πάντων
νωδυνίαν κατέχευε μελῶν· ὃ δὲ πατρὶ ἐοικώς
παῖς ἀγαπητὸς ἔγεντο. Κόως δ' ὀλόλυξεν ἰδοῖσα,
65 φᾶ δὲ καθαπτομένα βρέφεος χείρεσσι φίλησιν·
'ὄλβιε κοῦρε γένοιο, τίοις δέ με τόσσον ὅσον περ
Δῆλον ἐτίμησεν κυανάμπυκα Φοῖβος 'Απόλλων·
ἐν δὲ μιᾷ τιμῇ Τρίοπον καταθεῖο κολώναν,
ἶσον Δωριέεσσι νέμων γέρας ἐγγὺς ἐοῦσιν·
70 ἶσον καὶ 'Ρήναιαν ἄναξ ἐφίλησεν 'Απόλλων.'
ὡς ἄρα νᾶσος ἔειπεν· ὃ δ' ὑψόθεν ἔκλαγε φωνᾷ
ἐς τρὶς ἀπὸ νεφέων μέγας αἰετός, αἴσιος ὄρνις.
Ζηνός που τόδε σᾶμα· Διὶ Κρονίωνι μέλοντι
αἰδοῖοι βασιλῆες, ὃ δ' ἔξοχος ὅν κε φιλήσῃ
75 γεινόμενον τὰ πρῶτα· πολὺς δέ οἱ ὄλβος ὀπαδεῖ,
πολλᾶς δὲ κρατέει γαίας, πολλᾶς δὲ θαλάσσας.
Μυρίαι ἄπειροί τε καὶ ἔθνεα μυρία φωτῶν
λήιον ἀλδήσκουσιν ὀφελλόμεναι Διὸς ὄμβρῳ,
ἀλλ' οὔτις τόσα φύει ὅσα χθαμαλὰ Αἴγυπτος,
80 Νεῖλος ἀναβλύζων διερὰν ὅτε βώλακα θρύπτει,
οὐδέ τις ἄστεα τόσσα βροτῶν ἔχει ἔργα δαέντων.
τρεῖς μεν οἱ πολίων ἑκατοντάδες ἐνδέδμηνται,
τρεῖς δ' ἄρα χιλιάδες τρισσαῖς ἐπὶ μυριάδεσσι,
δοιαὶ δὲ τριάδες, μετὰ δέ σφισιν ἐννεάδες τρεῖς·

85 τῶν πάντων Πτολεμαῖος ἀγήνωρ ἐμβασιλεύει.
    καὶ μὴν Φοινίκας ἀποτέμνεται Ἀρραβίας τε
    καὶ Συρίας Λιβύας τε κελαινῶν τ' Αἰθιοπήων·
    Παμφύλοισί τε πᾶσι καὶ αἰχμηταῖς Κιλίκεσσι
    σαμαίνει, Λυκίοις τε φιλοπτολέμοισί τε Καρσί
90 καὶ νάσοις Κυκλάδεσσιν, ἐπεί οἱ νᾶες ἄρισται
    πόντον ἐπιπλώοντι, θάλασσα δὲ πᾶσα καὶ αἶα
    καὶ ποταμοὶ κελάδοντες ἀνάσσονται Πτολεμαίῳ,
    πολλοὶ δ' ἱππῆες, πολλοὶ δέ μιν ἀσπιδιῶται
    χαλκῷ μαρμαίροντι σεσαγμένοι ἀμφαγέρονται.
95 Ὄλβῳ μὲν πάντας κε καταβρίθοι βασιλῆας·
    τόσσον ἐπ' ἆμαρ ἕκαστον ἐς ἀφνεὸν ἔρχεται οἶκον
    πάντοθε. λαοὶ δ' ἔργα περιστέλλουσιν ἕκηλοι·
    οὐ γάρ τις δηίων πολυκήτεα Νεῖλον ὑπερβάς
    πεζὸς ἐν ἀλλοτρίαισι βοὰν ἐστάσατο κώμαις,
100 οὐδέ τις αἰγιαλόνδε θοᾶς ἐξήλατο ναός
    θωρηχθεὶς ἐπὶ βουσὶν ἀνάρσιος Αἰγυπτίῃσιν·
    τοῖος ἀνὴρ πλατέεσσιν ἐνίδρυται πεδίοισι
    ξανθοκόμας Πτολεμαῖος, ἐπιστάμενος δόρυ πάλλειν,
    ᾧ ἐπίπαγχυ μέλει πατρώια πάντα φυλάσσειν
105 οἷ' ἀγαθῷ βασιλῆι, τὰ δὲ κτεατίζεται αὐτός.
    οὐ μὰν ἀχρεῖός γε δόμῳ ἐνὶ πίονι χρυσός
    μυρμάκων ἅτε πλοῦτος ἀεὶ κέχυται μογεόντων·
    ἀλλὰ πολὺν μὲν ἔχοντι θεῶν ἐρικυδέες οἶκοι
    αἰὲν ἀπαρχομένοιο σὺν ἄλλοισιν γεράεσσι,
110 πολλὸν δ' ἰφθίμοισι δεδώρηται βασιλεῦσι,
    πολλὸν δὲ πτολίεσσι, πολὺν δ' ἀγαθοῖσιν ἑταίροις.
    οὐδὲ Διωνύσου τις ἀνὴρ ἱεροὺς κατ' ἀγῶνας
    ἵκετ' ἐπιστάμενος λιγυρὰν ἀναμέλψαι ἀοιδάν,
    ᾧ οὐ δωτίναν ἀντάξιον ὤπασε τέχνας.
115 Μουσάων δ' ὑποφῆται ἀείδοντι Πτολεμαῖον
    ἀντ' εὐεργεσίης. τί δὲ κάλλιον ἀνδρί κεν εἴη
    ὀλβίῳ ἢ κλέος ἐσθλὸν ἐν ἀνθρώποισιν ἀρέσθαι;
    τοῦτο καὶ Ἀτρεΐδαισι μένει· τὰ δὲ μυρία τῆνα
    ὅσσα μέγαν Πριάμοιο δόμον κτεάτισσαν ἑλόντες
120 ἀέρι πᾳ κέκρυπται ὅθεν πάλιν οὐκέτι νόστος.
        Μοῦνος ὅδε προτέρων τε καὶ ὧν ἔτι θερμὰ κονία
    στειβομένα καθύπερθε ποδῶν ἐκμάσσεται ἴχνη
    ματρὶ φίλᾳ καὶ πατρὶ θυώδεας εἵσατο ναούς·

ἐν δ' αὐτοὺς χρυσῷ περικαλλέας ἠδ' ἐλέφαντι
125 ἵδρυται πάντεσσιν ἐπιχθονίοισιν ἀρωγούς.
πολλὰ δὲ πιανθέντα βοῶν ὅγε μηρία καίει
μησὶ περιπλομένοισιν ἐρευθομένων ἐπὶ βωμῶν,
αὐτός τ' ἰφθίμα τ' ἄλοχος, τᾶς οὔτις ἀρείων
νυμφίον ἐν μεγάροισι γυνὰ περιβάλλετ' ἀγοστῷ,
130 ἐκ θυμοῦ στέργοισα κασίγνητόν τε πόσιν τε.
ὧδε καὶ ἀθανάτων ἱερὸς γάμος ἐξετελέσθη
οὓς τέκετο κρείουσα ῾Ρέα βασιλῆας ᾿Ολύμπου·
ἓν δὲ λέχος στόρνυσιν ἰαύειν Ζηνὶ καὶ ῞Ηρῃ
χεῖρας φοιβήσασα μύροις ἔτι παρθένος ᾿Ιρις.
135 Χαῖρε, ἄναξ Πτολεμαῖε· σέθεν δ' ἐγὼ ἶσα καὶ ἄλλων
μνάσομαι ἡμιθέων, δοκέω δ' ἔπος οὐκ ἀπόβλητον
φθέγξομαι ἐσσομένοις· ἀρετήν γε μὲν ἐκ Διὸς αἰτεῦ.

Gow's assessment of this Idyll as 'stiff, conventional and sycophantic'[3] is a fairly representative view.[4]

Part of the failure to appreciate *Idyll* 17 is due to scholars not understanding or being unwilling to accept the avowedly encomiastic nature of much ancient literature. Everyone in antiquity knew that poets were paid to praise their patrons and no one concerned made any serious attempt to conceal this. Modern criticisms of ancient literature for its encomiastic content would have amused ancient writers and audiences. For a writer to be critical of his patron in a published work would have appeared to them as senseless and as self-damaging as would appear to us the action of a modern composer who, commissioned to write a symphony, thought to demonstrate his independence by producing a mass.[5]

A further cause of scholars' failure to esteem *Idyll* 17 is the misleading account usually given of its literary background. Gow expresses the normal view in three statements made in his introduction to *Idyll* 17, namely:

> The *Idyll* stands in Theocritus' work much closer to *Idyll* 16 than to anything else.
> *Idyll* 17 is framed on the pattern of a Homeric Hymn.
> *Idyll* 17 in fact resembles the Hymns of Callimachus more closely than it resembles *Idyll* 16, and with two of these, that to Zeus (*Hymn* 1) and that to Delos (*Hymn* 4), it has resemblances which cannot be wholly accidental.

No one could deny that *Idyll* 17 does have certain hymnic features and that Theocritus is deliberately trying to give it something of the flavour of a Homeric Hymn. But the real background of the idyll is rhetorical. It has long been realized that *Idyll* 17 has many of the features of the formal encomium. It is in fact an example of that specialized type of encomium which Menander calls *basilikos logos*.[6] The following demonstration of this fact is attempted not only because it allows Theocritus' masterly selectivity in his use of topoi in this idyll to be detected but also because the very close coincidences between Theocritus and Menander are a further useful indication of the general reliability of Menander as a witness for the state of the generic patterns many centuries before he lived.

Menander begins his account of the basilikos logos by defining his subject:

ὁ βασιλικὸς λόγος ἐγκώμιόν ἐστι βασιλέως

368 3

'The basilikos logos is an encomium of a king'[7]

Then after a warning about the subject-matter, namely that it must not in any way be open to question by the hearer,[8] he proceeds to detail the three sections of the proem. Menander's description of the proem of the basilikos logos corresponds with Theocritus 1-12.

For the first section of the proem Menander gives four alternative possibilities. The first three are not relevant here. Theocritus in 1-4 applies the fourth.

...ἢ ὅτι δύο τὰ μέγιστα τῶν ὑπαρχόντων ἐν τῷ βίῳ τῶν ἀνθρώ-
πων ἐστὶν εὐσέβεια περὶ τὸ θεῖον καὶ τιμὴ περὶ τὸν βασιλέα,
ἃ προσήκει καὶ θαυμάζειν καὶ ὑμνεῖν κατὰ δύναμιν....ὥσπερ
οὖν τὸ κρεῖττον ὕμνοις καὶ ἀρεταῖς ἱλασκόμεθα, οὕτω καὶ
βασιλέα λόγοις.

Menander 368 17-21, 369 5-7

'or that two of the most important things in life are piety towards the gods and honour for the king and that we must respect and extol the gods and the king to the limit of our ability. . . . So just as we placate the superior power of heaven with hymns and praise of his deeds and virtues so we placate the king with our speeches.'

Corresponding with Theocritus 5-8 is the second section of the Menandrian proem:

ὅταν αὐξήσεως ἕνεκα παραλαμβάνηται, λήψει [δὲ] δευτέρων

105

προοιμίων ἐννοίας ἢ ἀπὸ Ὁμήρου τῆς μεγαλοφωνίας, ὅτι
ταύτης μόνης ἐδεῖτο ἡ ὑπόθεσις, ἢ ἀπὸ Ὀρφέως τοῦ Καλλιόπης
ἢ ἀπὸ τῶν Μουσῶν αὐτῶν, ὅτι μόλις ἂν καὶ αὗται πρὸς
ἀξίαν τῆς ὑποθέσεως εἰπεῖν ἐδυνήθησαν, ὅμως δὲ οὐδὲν κωλύει
καὶ ἡμᾶς ἐγχειρῆσαι πρὸς δύναμιν.

Menander 369 7-13

'When, in order to make your speech more impressive you have a
second ⟨ section of your⟩ proem, you will get its material either from
the mighty voice of Homer, saying that his voice is needed for your undertaking and no other is sufficient, or from Orpheus, son of Kalliope,
or the Muses themselves, saying that even they could hardly have
spoken worthily of your subject, but however I can only do my best.'

The presence of this idea in the stereotyped rhetorical prescription of
Menander may indicate that Homeric language and stylistic devices
were considered to be especially relevant to the genre; this could explain
the superficial but undoubted resemblances of *Idyll* 17 to the Homeric
Hymns noted by commentators. Theocritus 9-12 corresponds with the
third section of Menander's proem.

ἡ τρίτη δὲ τοῦ προοιμίου ἔννοια, (καθόλου δὲ τούτου μέμνησο
τοῦ παραγγέλματος) προκαταρκτικὴ γενέσθω τῶν κεφαλαίων,
λοιπὸν ὡς διαποροῦντος τοῦ λέγοντος, ὅθεν χρὴ τὴν ἀρχὴν τῶν
ἐγκωμίων ποιήσασθαι.

Menander 369 13-17

'The third theme in the proem (and keep this precept in mind generally) should introduce the sections of the speech and should be that
the speaker does not know from what point to begin his encomia.'

The correspondence here is not only one of theme and position. Menander specifically instructs his students to make the same structural use
of the topos as is found in Theocritus; the topos functions as a link
passage, introducing the remainder of the basilikos logos.

Following his proem Menander moves on to three related subjects –
the country, race and family of the king being praised. The first two are
alternatives: if the king's country is not famous, his race may be praised;
but in fact neither need be treated.

ἐὰν δὲ μήτε ἡ πατρὶς μήτε τὸ ἔθνος τυγχάνῃ περίβλεπτον,
ἀφήσεις μὲν τοῦτο, θεωρήσεις δὲ πάλιν, πότερον ἔνδοξον αὐτοῦ
τὸ γένος ἢ οὔ.

Menander 370 9-11

'But if neither his country nor his race is famous, then you will have to lay aside this theme and consider in turn whether or not his family is distinguished.'

Theocritus treats neither Ptolemy's country nor his race but deals immediately with his family (13-57), a procedure fully envisaged in Menander's instructions, although the reason for their omission can hardly be that Theocritus considered them undistinguished (see p. 110). Menander considers several possibilities as regards the king's family. Two are that if it is famous it should be treated, if not, then the king should be supplied with divine ancestors (370 11ff.). Theocritus uses both techniques in 13-57: the Lagid dynasty is briefly eulogized, and their divine ancestor, Hercules, is introduced in the company of Ptolemy's father and of the somewhat ambiguous figure of Alexander the Great. Moreover, Theocritus also devoted a long passage to Ptolemy's mother Berenice (see p. 119).

Menander, after dealing with the king's family, proceeds to his birth. Theocritus, too, describes the birth of Ptolemy in his next section (52-77). Menander notes especially the importance of describing marvels accompanying the king's birth:

...εἴ τι σύμβολον γέγονε περὶ τὸν τόκον ἢ κατὰ γῆν ἢ κατ' οὐρανὸν ἢ κατὰ θάλασσαν...
    Menander 371 5-6
'... if any omen occurred at the time of the birth on land or in the heavens or in the sea, ⟨ put it in ⟩. . . . '

Theocritus obliges with Zeus' eagle (71-6). Menander advises comparison with the births of Romulus, Cyrus, etc. (371 6-10). Theocritus outdoes this in his comparison of the birth of Ptolemy with the birth of Apollo, implicit throughout the passage and explicit in the words of Cos (66-9). The clearly fabulous nature of the whole Cos passage is illustrated by a Menandrian instruction at this point:

κἂν μὲν ᾖ τι τοιοῦτον περὶ τὸν βασιλέα, ἐξέργασαι, ἐὰν δὲ οἷόν τε ᾖ πλάσαι καὶ ποιεῖν τοῦτο πιθανῶς, μὴ κατόκνει· δίδωσι γὰρ ἡ ὑπόθεσις διὰ τὸ τοὺς ἀκούοντας ἀνάγκην ἔχειν ἀβασανίστως δέχεσθαι τὰ ἐγκώμια.
    Menander 371 10-14
'If any marvel accompanied the birth of the king, recount it. But if it is possible to invent some such occurrence in a plausible way, do not

107

hesitate to do so. For your subject allows this, your audience being under constraint to accept the praises without putting them to the test.'

Following the birth of the king, Menander specifies two sections on the physical characteristics and upbringing of the child-king. It is possible that Theocritus has subsumed these two sections into his description of the birth, representing the child's physical characteristics in 63-4, and his upbringing in his reception and nursing by Cos (esp. 58-9, 65). But this notion need not be pressed. Theocritus' selectivity is prominent in this idyll and these points may have been deliberately suppressed (see pp. 110-11).

Following these sections Menander turns to the king's achievements, first in war and then in peace (372). At first sight it does not appear that Theocritus is following the same arrangement but is embarking on a description of Egypt and its subject territories (77-94). But, because of the recentness of the war in which many of these territories were gained, Theocritus' original readers probably read, and were meant to read these lines as a eulogy of Ptolemy's military prowess. This war had preserved Egypt from its enemies and increased its subject territories; thus the eulogy aptly culminates in a picture of the warlike Ptolemy surrounded by his mailed cavalry and footmen.

The king's deeds in war, under the heading of bravery, are followed in Menander by four further sections:
(i) a description of the king's deeds in peace, under the heading of the other three virtues
(ii) praise of his 'luck' ($\tau \acute{u} \chi \eta$)
(iii) a comparison of his reign with previous reigns
(iv) an epilogue.

In *Idyll* 17, 77-94 (warfare) are followed by a passage (95-103) which probably reflects in a general fashion the first of these sections, the king's deeds in peace. It emphasizes the peaceful and prosperous state of Egypt, protected as it is by Ptolemy. But throughout this passage and afterwards, the order of topoi in Theocritus and Menander is different, although the topoi themselves correspond to some extent.

Lines 95-103 correspond with Menander's 'deeds of the king in peace' in the same way as 77-94 correspond with 'the king's deeds in war': they detail the results of the deeds rather than the actual deeds. But they also overlap with some of the Menandrian epilogue material.

This is natural since epilogues often function as summaries of what has gone before (see pp.114-15). The Menandrian epilogue passage is:

...γεωργεῖται μετ' εἰρήνης ἡ γῆ, πλεῖται ἡ θάλασσα ἀκινδύνως
...οὐ δεδοίκαμεν βαρβάρους, οὐ πολεμίους, ὀχυρώτερον τοῖς
βασιλέως ὅπλοις τετειχίσμεθα ἢ τοῖς τείχεσιν αἱ πόλεις...
Menander 377 13-14, 15-17
'...the earth is farmed in peace, the sea sailed without danger...we are not afraid of barbarians or enemies. The king's weapons guard us more securely than cities are guarded by their walls....'

Moreover, Theocritus 104-5 appear to reflect the comparison recommended in:

ἥξεις δὲ ἐπὶ τὴν τελειοτάτην σύγκρισιν, ἀντεξετάζων τὴν αὐτοῦ
βασιλείαν πρὸς τὰς πρὸ αὐτοῦ βασιλείας, οὐ καθαιρῶν ἐκείνας·
ἄτεχνον γάρ, ἀλλὰ θαυμάζων μὲν ἐκείνας, τὸ δὲ τέλειον ἀποδιδοὺς
τῇ παρούσῃ.
Menander 376 31-377 2
'And you will come to the most comprehensive comparison and weigh up the king's rule against those of his predecessors, not attacking them – for that would be inappropriate – but awarding the palm to the present administration, while complimenting the former ones.'

Furthermore, Ptolemy's generosity to the gods (108-9) and his building of shrines to his deified parents, etc. (123-7), may correspond with an item of Menander's epilogue:

...εὐσέβεια δὲ ἡ περὶ τὸ θεῖον ηὔξηται, τιμαὶ δὲ κατὰ τὸ
προσῆκον ἑκάστοις νέμονται....
Menander 377 14-15
'...piety towards the gods has increased and honours are given to each as is fitting....'

The praise of Ptolemy's queen and of their marriage (128ff.) reflects a precept from the Menandrian 'deeds in peace' section:

εἰ δὲ ἐπ' ἀξίας εἴη καὶ τιμῆς μεγίστης ἡ βασιλίς, ἐρεῖς τι καὶ
κατὰ καιρὸν ἐνθάδε· ἣν θαυμάσας ἠγάπησε, ταύτην κοινωνὸν
τῆς ἑαυτοῦ βασιλείας πεποίηται, καὶ οὐδ' εἰ ἔστιν ἄλλο οἶδε
γυναικεῖον φῦλον.
Menander 376 9-13

'If the queen is in high repute and honour you will speak in suitable terms about her: ⟨you will say for example⟩ "The woman who excited his admiration and love he has made a partner in his kingdom and, as for other women, he does not know if they exist or not".'

The generic attribution allows Theocritus' originality in *Idyll* 17 to be detected. It is manifested to some extent in Theocritus' additions to, or elaborations of, the corpus of generic themes (see pp. 119-20). But the greater part of Theocritus' originality and literary merit is his careful and skilled selection of topoi from the generic corpus so as to create a dignified basilikos logos, suited to its addressee and yet free from servile adulation. Theocritus has omitted the following topics prescribed by Menander:

(i) the country, race, physical appearance and upbringing of Ptolemy (370ff.)

(ii) his personal military prowess (373-4)

(iii) his mental abilities (372, 374, 376)

(iv) his mildness to subjects, choice of deputies, his taxes and laws (375-376)

(v) his 'luck' (376)

(vi) his children (376)

(vii) the loyalty of his bodyguard (376)

Finally (viii) Theocritus has deliberately not treated Ptolemy's activities and qualities in accordance with the standard four-virtue division of Menander (374). That Theocritus knew of such a method of treating the virtues is guaranteed by the occurrence of the four-virtue division in earlier encomia.[9]

In each case a reason is forthcoming for Theocritus' omission.

(i) His failure to treat, or at any rate his indirect and mythologized treatment of Ptolemy's upbringing stems from the fact that Ptolemy was not his father's eldest son and legitimate successor (see below). Theocritus may have felt that concentration on Ptolemy's country and race was otiose since they were so well known or because the family was being given a full treatment; but it is more likely that he thought that mention of them might also direct his audience's minds to uncomfortable thoughts about the legitimacy of Ptolemy's claims to the throne. The suppression of these and other items which might embarrass Ptolemy is part of the procedure which differentiated encomium and apologia in antiquity and which led to such matters, with a few exceptions, being silently passed over in encomium.[10] Instead, Theocritus attempts to mythologize Ptolemy and his life and attributes, and so raise him to the level of a hero or demi-god.

(ii) In treating the character of Ptolemy, Theocritus shows very great discretion. He could not, as was standard, insert a section on Ptolemy's personal military prowess since Ptolemy was, in fact, a weak and somewhat effete man personally, and any attempt to fly in the face of this fact would have produced a credibility gap ($\tau\grave{o}$ $\dot{\alpha}\pi\acute{\iota}\theta\alpha\nu o\nu$) which according to Menander the writer of the basilikos logos must avoid at all costs (see above).

(iii) Conversely, Theocritus chooses not to praise Ptolemy's mental gifts directly, although these were not in dispute. His idea was probably that he could best represent Ptolemy favourably as a military man by avoiding excess. This meant not including praise of personal prowess and also avoiding praise of aspects of Ptolemy's character which might seem to detract from his ability in action, such as mental prowess. By avoiding these two Theocritus was able to create the vague, but impressive picture of a Homeric hero, the spearman guardian of Egypt surrounded by his armies (93-4, 102-3).

(iv) The omission of mildness, deputies, taxes, etc., is partly a further attempt not to detract from Ptolemy's martial glory and partly a reflection of the particular situation of the Macedonian kings of Egypt. Their subjects fell into two categories. The first was the privileged Greeks, who were favoured as regards taxation, upon whom Ptolemy depended for military and administrative support, and for whom this idyll was written. The second was the Egyptians, who were powerless, paid most of the taxes and would not read the idyll. Thus, the standard virtues of rulers in their dealings with their subjects were irrelevant in Ptolemy's case.

(v-vii) The omission of the king's 'luck' is not because the notion was not contemporary – the $\tau\acute{v}\chi\eta$ of Alexander had set the pattern – but probably because it was already closely associated with two other ideas omitted by Theocritus and classed by Menander as subheadings of 'luck', namely loyalty of bodyguards and the possession of children. Theocritus cannot mention Ptolemy's children because they were the children of Ptolemy not by the Arsinoe celebrated in *Idyll* 17 but by a previous wife (also called Arsinoe) who was then in exile in Upper Egypt following a charge of treason. The loyalty of Ptolemy's bodyguards cannot be included because of a revolt of Gallic mercenaries against Ptolemy in

274 B C.[11] The mercenaries who revolted were not, in fact, bodyguards, but the event was too recent for Theocritus to risk praising Ptolemy for the loyality of his hired troops. Since both these topics were by necessity excluded, Theocritus probably felt that to include the 'luck' without mentioning these two closely associated items would call attention to their absence. He therefore omitted the 'luck' altogether.

(viii) The omission of the four-virtue division is not political but poetic. Theocritus must have thought it too prosaic for his purposes.[12]

It may seem as if the selection described above, because reasons can be given for the omission of each item, was easy and obvious for Theocritus and that he was merely following the rhetorical rule for encomia, namely that the subject's deficiencies should be omitted as far as possible.[13] But a well-known characteristic of good literature is that it appears easy, natural and obvious. When we have such good evidence of Theocritus' critical approach to the generic pattern and of his careful and judicious selection of material, it is no longer possible to assent to any sweeping condemnation of *Idyll* 17.

The second point Isocrates made while discussing the selection and arrangement of topoi is that the writer should be skilled in their combination ($\mu\hat{\iota}\xi\alpha\iota$ $\pi\rho\grave{o}s$ $\dot{\alpha}\lambda\lambda\acute{\eta}\lambda\alpha s$). The apt juxtaposition of topoi and their introduction not as dead items of a list but as a living chain of linked ideas, performing structural as well as informational functions, is one of the most notable and widespread characteristics of the best classical literature. A brief example will suffice:

Dicamus bona uerba: uenit Natalis ad aras:
    quisquis ades, lingua, uir mulierque, faue.
urantur pia tura focis, urantur odores
    quos tener e terra diuite mittit Arabs.
5 ipse suos Genius adsit uisurus honores,
    cui decorent sanctas mollia serta comas.
illius puro destillent tempora nardo,
    atque satur libo sit madeatque mero,
adnuat et, Cornute, tibi, quodcumque rogabis.
10   en age (quid cessas? adnuit ille) roga.
auguror, uxoris fidos optabis amores:
    iam reor hoc ipsos edidicisse deos.
nec tibi malueris, totum quaecumque per orbem
    fortis arat ualido rusticus arua boue,

15 nec tibi, gemmarum quidquid felicibus Indis
      nascitur, Eoi qua maris unda rubet.
    uota cadunt: utinam strepitantibus aduolet alis
      flauaque coniugio uincula portet Amor,
    uincula quae maneant semper dum tarda senectus
20   inducat rugas inficiatque comas.
    haec ueniat, Natalis, auis prolemque ministret,
      ludat et ante tuos turba nouella pedes.
    Tibullus 2 2

This elegy is a genethliakon celebrating the birthday of Cornutus. The genre is well exemplified.[14] The method which Tibullus uses to combine some of the standard topoi is subtle and characteristic of his work. *Natalis* (the birthday itself) and *Amor* are both personified so that with the *Genius* they can function as principals in a series of three successive epiphanies of divine beings (1, 5, 17-18). Within the framework of the three epiphanies other topoi are used as links. The burning of incense and other fragrant substances is characteristic of birthdays and so follows the advent of *Natalis* (3-4). It immediately calls to mind, and so forms an apt introduction to, the *Genius* (5) to whom incense is characteristically offered on birthdays. After a description of the *Genius*, which further links itself with the incense topos by alluding to more offerings normally made to the *Genius*, nard, wine and honeycake (7-8), Tibullus turns easily to the wish which people in antiquity often made on their birthdays (9-10), using as an unstated connexion the fact that the *Genius* was the normal addressee of these wishes made on birthdays.[15] Cornutus' wish will be for the love of his wife (11-12). And so *Amor*, a standard feature of elegiac genethliaka, and associated with birthdays in real life, is introduced (17ff.), to be followed, again naturally, by a second mention of *Natalis* in the company of the generation topos so relevant to the cult of the *Genius* and to birthday celebrations (21-2).

    The outstanding excellence of this genethliakon is that each topos flows into the next as though it were the most natural thing in the world that it should do so, while at the same time the poem's 'ascending tricolon' structure carries it forward to its climax.

    Isocrates' third point, in his account of the selection, combination and arrangement of topoi (τάξαι κατὰ τρόπον), is that the speaker should know how to make apt alterations of the order in which the topoi are presented from the order in which they appear in the master pattern, or alternatively should know how to use the standard order in circumstances where it happened to be the best order.

The final sections of Theocritus *Idyll* 17 might appear to exemplify originality of this type in that, as was observed above, the order of the topoi of 95-134 diverges widely from the order of the Menandrian prescription for the basilikos logos. It is possible that Theocritus was employing an original order of presentation of material in this passage, but various factors make this uncertain. First, Theocritus employs two topoi found in earlier encomia, the king's wealth and generosity,[16] which are absent from the Menandrian prescription. This suggests that Theocritus may be following an older order, a suggestion which may be confirmed by the evidence of Horace *Odes* 4 5 17ff. *Odes* 4 5 is not a basilikos logos but a kletikon. But 17ff. of Horace *Odes* 4 5 contain a set of topoi which correspond with those from the Menandrian epilogue to the basilikos logos.[17] The reason for the correspondence is that the formula for the kletikon to a ruler includes praise of the ruler summoned (Menander 429) and, if the ruler is a king, his praises will naturally resemble the basilikos logos. But in the centre of these epilogue topoi occur the lines

> nullis polluitur casta domus stupris,
> mos et lex maculosum edomuit nefas,
> laudantur simili prole puerperae,
>   culpam poena premit comes.
> Horace *Odes* 4 5 21-4

which correspond with

> ὅτι διὰ βασιλέα σώφρονες μὲν οἱ γάμοι, γνήσιοι δὲ τοῖς πατράσιν
> οἱ παῖδες. . . .
> Menander 376 4-6

'Because of the king, marriages are pure and fathers have legitimate children. . . .'

In Menander this concept is found in the 'king's deeds in peace' section, under the heading of self-control. This might lead us to think that both Theocritus and Horace are simply following a different standard order from that of Menander. And the same may go for another Menandrian epilogue topos which Theocritus uses in his war passage (77-80).

> ὄμβροι γὰρ κατὰ καιρὸν καὶ θαλάσσης φοραὶ καὶ καρπῶν
> εὐφορίαι διὰ τὴν τοῦ βασιλέως δικαιοσύνην ἡμῖν εὐτυχοῦνται·

Menander 377 22-4 (cp. Homer *Odyssey* 19 110ff. and Stanford ad loc.)

'Because of the king's justice we have the good fortune to enjoy rain in due season and the produce of the sea and excellent harvests.'

Another factor which makes it impossible to say whether or not Theocritus is being original in his order is that epilogues are in any case often summaries of what has gone before. Safer examples of manipulation of the order of topoi by various authors can be discovered by analysis of four propemptika of a type mentioned on pp. 9-12 – Euripides *Helen* 1451ff.; Propertius 1 6; Statius *Siluae* 3 2; Paulinus *Carmina* 17. These are non-schetliastic propemptika which, because they are non-schetliastic, do not follow the Menandrian propemptikon prescription but have a logic of their own. The fact that we have no formula for the non-schetliastic propemptikon, and so do not know what order of subject-matter, if any, was orthodox, is no barrier to this discussion. The reasons for different orders and their effectiveness can still be discerned, and if one of the effective orders happens to be, unknown to us, the orthodox order, this is perfectly acceptable since the orthodox order of topoi can sometimes be the most effective one.

To help our analysis, we may categorize some of the material of these propemptika as follows:
(i) good wishes and divine help for outlined journey ending at destination
(ii) description of destination
(iii) speaker's wish to accompany/excuse for not doing so
(iv) reiteration of good wishes and divine help of (i)
In terms of these headings, the material of the four propemptika is arranged in these orders:

Euripides *Helen* 1451ff.	(i) (ii) (iii) (iv)
Propertius 1 6	– (iii) (ii) –
Statius *Siluae* 3 2	(i) (iii) (iv) (ii)
Paulinus *Carmina* 17	(ii) (i) (iii) (iv)

Naturally this table does not give a detailed or full analysis of the material of these propemptika; but it shows that different authors employ some of the larger divisions of content in markedly different order. In some cases the purpose of a particular order can be discerned.

An initial distinction must be made between Euripides *Helen* 1451ff.

and Paulinus *Carmina* 17 on one hand, and Propertius 1 6 and Statius *Siluae* 3 2 on the other. This distinction is not one which is found in the Menandrian account of the propemptikon, but it is nevertheless a genuine, ancient distinction, important for the genre, since a parallel concept occurs in Menander's accounts of the syntaktikon and epibaterion. The distinction is between propemptika addressed to persons going to their home and those addressed to persons going to another place. The propemptika of Euripides and Paulinus are both addressed to a person going home, and both share more or less the same order of the selected material. The one difference in order between them is easily explained. Euripides' chorus has no impulse whatsoever to urge Helen to stay in Egypt; therefore good wishes for her voyage take first place. Paulinus, although not urging Nicetas to stay, would be pleased if he did. By not putting the account of the voyage and concomitant good wishes first he shows a certain lack of enthusiasm for the voyage. In the case of Euripides it is also possible to discern something of the aptness of his order to his subject-matter and to the play as a whole. Prominent both in detail and position is the mention of Helen's home. Paulinus gives a similar prominence to Nicetas' home, although it is one of order only, since a description is lacking. The prominence of the home is dictated by the type of propemptikon which these two poems are. But Euripides' detailed lingering on Sparta and anticipation of Helen's arrival is also dramatically apt in a play whose theme is that Helen, far from being the adulterous betrayer of husband and country, is in fact a chaste, model wife who, through a combination of Paris' villainy and her own misfortune, has been absent from husband and country perforce.

The excuse/wish to accompany is in both poems weak, unemphatically placed, and employs the 'I wish I were a bird to accompany the addressee' topos.[18] It must be weak, because if the speaker were really to go with the addressee the speaker would be leaving his own home. In addition, if the speaker sounded too eager to leave his own home, this would clash with his acknowledgement that the addressee's desire to go home justified his wish to depart. Such a clash would weaken the importance of the very concept that leads to the absence of schetliasmos in propemptika like these.[19] Euripides so orders his material as to place the excuse in the least emphatic position in the ode and thus to reinforce the studied vagueness of the wish he puts in the mouth of his chorus. Were it not for the occurrence of the commonplace in the genre we would not even be sure that the chorus were wishing to be birds in order to accompany Helen or in order to carry to Sparta the news of Helen and Menelaus' impending return.

Both Paulinus and Euripides end with reiterated good wishes for their addressees' voyages, the prominent final position combining with the reiteration to set the tone of the propemptika. In Euripides' case these good wishes and invocations of the sea-gods to protect Helen and give her a good voyage are exploited in a dramatic master-stroke. For the sea-gods invoked in this final section of the propemptikon are none other than Castor and Pollux, the brothers of Helen, who are not only traditional protectors of travellers at sea but who will also appear *ex machina* at the end of the play to ensure that Helen leaves Egypt in peace and safety. It would appear from this example and from the final section of Sophocles' *Philoctetes* (see pp. 42-4) that a good dramatist will try to give the topoi of his generic example not only internal significance for that generic example but also external significance for other events within the drama.

The other two poems, Propertius 1 6 and *Siluae* 3 2, are non-schetliastic propemptika to persons leaving their native land, and the reason for the lack of schetliasmos in them is that these persons are both in a general sense, governors. The Statian order of material is likely *a priori* to be nearer to the orthodox order for this variant of the propemptikon, since Statius' normal generic practice is to stay close to the standard models of genres, in terms both of the topoi included and of the order in which they are presented. If this is so, it highlights what is in any case a peculiarity in the order of material in Propertius 1 6. This elegy begins with (iii) – the excuses of Propertius for not going. The prominence of this idea stresses Propertius' concern with the seeming affront to his patron which is implied in his refusal to accompany him to Asia. The encomiastic effect of beginning with excuses of this sort is heightened by Propertius' selection of topoi, which leads to the virtual absence of the topoi of (i) and (iv). This suggests Tullus' fearlessness and a presumption that due help will be his. The praise of Tullus is further swelled by the fact that the final and therefore emphatic block of topoi (ii) is the description of Tullus' triumphant role in Asia set off against Propertius' own wretched life at Rome.

After his comment on that selection, combination, and ordering of topoi of which the good speaker must be capable, Isocrates continues with a description of the alterations which the speaker must make to individual topoi:

> ...ἔτι δὲ τῶν καιρῶν μὴ διαμαρτεῖν ἀλλὰ καὶ τοῖς ἐνθυμήμασι πρεπόντως ὅλον τὸν λόγον καταποικῖλαι καὶ τοῖς ὀνόμασιν εὐρύθμως καὶ μουσικῶς εἰπεῖν...
>
> 13 16

This third category of originality in the use of topoi divides, as indeed Isocrates had divided it, into two distinct spheres – the intellectual (ἐνθυμήματα) and the verbal (ὀνόματα).

The latter, a field which corresponds roughly with the σχήματα λέξεως ('figures of speech') of developed rhetoric, is a large and important one and relevant to discussions of originality in generic composition;[20] but it is a field well enough understood, and by its nature falls outside the concern of this book, which sets out to treat not verbal matters but some of the intellectual and thematic aspects of ancient literature.

The former field, however, is of great relevance. It is related, although the relationship is inexact, to the σχήματα διανοίας ('figures of thought') of rhetoric. Such alterations are not, like the 'figures of speech', verbal matters, but affect the meaning of those examples of the topoi in which they occur. The 'figures of thought' of later rhetoric are the products of an over-diligent categorizing activity. This was sometimes so detailed and mechanical that paradoxically it caused confusion, or alleged confusion, between the two.[21] But the idea behind the 'figures of thought' is real and useful: if ancient thinkers ever discussed intellectual alterations to individual topoi they can only have done so by employing this notion. They would not, of course, have been concerned with the over-precisely categorized 'figures of thought' of developed rhetoric, but with earlier and simpler categories. The latter can be equated with the intellectual 'Gorgian' figures[22] which Plato dismisses in sarcastic terms, in contrast to Isocrates' serious description in the passage previously quoted (4 7-9):

> Τεισίαν δὲ Γοργίαν τε ἐάσομεν εὕδειν, οἳ πρὸ τῶν ἀληθῶν τὰ εἰκότα εἶδον ὡς τιμητέα μᾶλλον, τά τε αὖ σμικρὰ μεγάλα καὶ τὰ μεγάλα σμικρὰ φαίνεσθαι ποιοῦσιν διὰ ῥώμην λόγου, καινά τε ἀρχαίως τά τ' ἐναντία καινῶς, συντομίαν τε λόγων καὶ ἄπειρα μήκη περὶ πάντων ἀνηῦρον;
>
> Plato *Phaedrus* 267A-B

This summary is somewhat confused but several headings emerge which together cover the field:

macrologia, lengthy treatment magnifying the subject

brachylogia (*syntomia*), brief treatment minimizing the subject

innovation upon old subject-matter or, amounting to the same thing, introduction of new subject-matter under old guises

Macrologia. One type of macrologia used by Gorgias himself is mentioned by Aristotle:

καὶ ὃ ἔλεγε Γοργίας, ὅτι οὐχ ὑπολείπει αὐτὸν ὁ λόγος, τοῦτό ἐστιν· εἰ γὰρ Ἀχιλλέα λέγει, Πηλέα ἐπαινεῖ, εἶτα Αἰακόν, εἶτα τὸν θεόν, ὁμοίως δὲ καὶ ἀνδρίαν, ἢ τὰ καὶ τὰ ποιεῖ ἢ τοιόνδε ἐστίν.

Rhetoric 1418A

But macrologia as a means of generic originality covers more than this. It embraces many of the later 'figures of thought' in addition to the figure actually called macrologia. This is because many of these figures are simply means of amplifying upon, repeating, emphasizing, or magnifying a topos.

Theocritus *Idyll* 17 produces two excellent examples of macrologia. Both the king's mother and the king's wife are standard topics of the genre basilikos logos, the first in connexion with his birth and ancestry, the second in the 'deeds of the king in peace' passage. But Theocritus gives much greater prominence both to Berenice (Ptolemy's mother) and to Arsinoe (his wife) than the mother and wife of a king would normally receive in a basilikos logos. This prominence is reflected partly in the number of lines he assigns to the treatment of each of them – Berenice 34-57, Arsinoe 128-34.

Theocritus' macrologia in these cases is due to a particular problem he faced as eulogist of Ptolemy. Normally a poet's description of the paternity of the king he was praising would be in itself a statement of the legitimate hereditary right of that king to be king. But in the case of Ptolemy this was not so, since Ptolemy was not his father's eldest son: there were two older sons by a previous marriage, and this fact was the cue for Theocritus' treatment of the matter. By laying great stress on Ptolemy's mother, Berenice, and on her marriage with Ptolemy's father and the mutual love between them, he is attempting to strengthen his assertion of Ptolemy's right to be king by obscuring in the readers' minds Ptolemy's previous marriage and hence the rightful claims of sons of that marriage.

The prominence given to Arsinoe may be due partly to the Egyptian setting. By native Egyptian custom the Pharaoh's right to the throne derived from his position as husband to the female in line of matrilineal succession. But the natives were of little importance at this period. It is more likely that Theocritus gives Arsinoe such prominent treatment because he wishes to face up to the brother-sister marriage between Ptolemy and Arsinoe, a situation still slightly scandalous to Greek eyes, and to brazen out its embarrassment by comparing it to the marriage of Zeus and Hera. If this is so, we have a rare case of apologia rather than omission in an encomium (see above), the king's wife being so prominent, politically and generically, that her omission would have drawn attention to her. But probably the most important reason for Arsinoe's prominence is that, in Greek eyes, since she was Ptolemy's full sister, she was also regarded as being in line of patrilineal succession to their father; thus their marriage strengthened Ptolemy's claim to the throne.

Another interesting example of macrologia is to be found in Ovid *Amores* 2 11 9-32. In this propemptikon to Corinna these lines (twenty-four out of fifty-six) are devoted solely to the topos of attempted deterrence of the traveller by mention of the dangers of travel by sea.

Syntomia (brachylogia). The macrologia mentioned above in *Amores* 2 11 is made more prominent and its function is partly explained by the pronounced brachylogia of the rest of that poem. Lines 9-32 are preceded by:

> ecce fugit notumque torum sociosque Penates
> fallacisque uias ire Corinna parat.
>
> 7-8

Into these two lines several other schetliastic topoi are compressed – the love/friendship between speaker and traveller, their common experiences, the broken oaths of the traveller (*fallacis*), the traveller's departure from home and the anticipated dangers of the journey (the other meaning of *fallacis*). Brachylogia is again displayed in:

> at si uana ferunt uolucres mea dicta procellae,
> aequa tamen puppi sit Galatea tuae.
> uestrum crimen erit talis iactura puellae,
> Nereidesque deae Nereidumque pater.
> vade memor nostri, vento reditura secundo;
>
> 33-7

These lines represent the commonplace change of mind on the part of the propemptic speaker. Compare

ἐπειδὰν δὲ ἐπὶ τὸ λειπόμενον μέρος ἔλθῃς τῆς λαλιᾶς, σχετλιάσεις πάλιν ὡς βουληθεὶς πεῖσαι, εἶτα ἀποτυχών, καὶ ἐπάξεις λέγων· οὐκοῦν ἐπειδὴ δέδοκται καὶ νενίκημαι, φέρε δὴ καὶ τῇ βουλήσει συνδράμωμεν.

Menander 397 12-16
'When you come to the remaining section of the speech, you will complain as if you had actually wanted to persuade him and failed, and ⟨ subsequently ⟩ go on in your speech: "so, since you are resolved and I am defeated, come let us go along with your wish".'

In addition, 33 is the complaint of the would-be persuader who has failed, and 34 the good wishes for the traveller (cp. Propertius 1 8 17-18). Lines 34-6 are prayers for the traveller;[23] 34 and 36 introduce the sea-gods who are to favour the traveller;[24] 35 alludes covertly to the topos that the traveller is 'owed'[25] (here by the sea-gods); and 37 contains the formal injunction to go,[26] the 'remember me' topos,[27] and a hint at the 'good wind' topos (see p. 161).[28] Two reasons can be given for this combination of macrologia and brachylogia in *Amores* 2 11. First, Ovid is writing a fairly cynical and depersonalized propemptikon. He therefore compresses those schetliastic topoi which would normally carry the main weight of personalized material and expands the impersonal 'dangers of the sea' and 'attack on seafaring' topoi. Second, Ovid may have felt that a greater emphasis on personal schetliastic or good wish elements for Corinna's journey and stay abroad in the propemptikon proper was inappropriate since he was going on to anticipate Corinna's return and to describe the enjoyment he hoped for when this event took place (37-54, see. p. 161).

Such brachylogia, which like macrologia covers a whole group of the developed 'figures of thought', is just as important as macrologia as a means of originality in the use of topoi. Through it, and various 'figures of thought' which fall under it, topoi are reduced to mere hints and allusions. Just as in the case of macrologia the audience's pleasure lies in recognizing the same topoi in diverse forms and appreciating the author's skill in elaborating without causing tedium, so in brachylogia the audience derives its pleasure from recognizing entire topoi from hints and allusions.

Brachylogia is often, as in Ovid *Amores* 2 11, a technique used in concert with macrologia to emphasize certain topoi of a poem while minimizing others. Another example of this combined use is Catullus 9, a prosphonetikon to Veranius:

> Verani, omnibus e meis amicis
> antistans mihi milibus trecentis,
> uenistine domum ad tuos Penates
> fratresque unanimos anumque matrem?
> 5 uenisti. o mihi nuntii beati!
> uisam te incolumem audiamque Hiberum
> narrantem loca, facta, nationes,
> ut mos est tuus, applicansque collum
> iucundum os oculosque suauiabor.
> 10 o quantum est hominum beatiorum,
> quid me laetius est beatiusue?

The skeleton of this lyric consists of three expressions of affection for Veranius and of joy at his return (B3), expressions which form the poem's beginning (1-2), middle (5), and end (10-11), and so occupy all its emphatic points. Five lines thus contain macrologic versions of a single topos, or at most two topoi, if 1-2 are also a discreet variant of the 'preferred status of the welcomer' topos (B12), expressed indirectly out of consideration for Veranius' family. In the remaining six lines Catullus employs brachylogia to communicate a string of other topoi of the genre. These are the repeated verb of 'coming' (B1, 3 and 5), the fact that Veranius has come home (B5, 3), the welcoming family group besides the speaker (B17, 4), the dangers through which Veranius has come (B8, 7), unscathed (B7, 6), the place where he has been (B2, 6-7), the traveller's tales and a humorous hit at them (B13*, 7-8), Catullus and Veranius hugging and kissing (B4, 8-9). The effect of this artful brachylogia sandwiched between the three outbursts of affection is to produce an impression of complete spontaneity. The illusion is created that the poet is emotionally out of control and is simply blurting out his feelings for Veranius. In fact, under cover of this illusion, Catullus is supplying all the information the reader needs to understand the situation. In this way he has composed a highly sophisticated example of one of the more common ancient genres.

These two examples have shown brachylogia operating in concert with macrologia. Brachylogia can, however, occur in contexts where no macrologia is apparent. A good example of this, already treated on pp. 44-5, is Catullus 46 (syntaktikon).

Innovation. Between them, macrologia and brachylogia, which are easily comprehensible and exemplifiable, cover a large proportion of the alterations to individual topoi made by ancient writers in search of originality. The third category of Gorgian figures – innovation upon old subject-matter, or alternatively introduction of new subject-matter under old guises, is easy to understand but hard to define. In crude terms it amounts to altering the standard forms of topoi in such a way that the new forms remain recognizable as variants of the old. Two simple examples will speak here more clearly than pages of definition. Other examples occur throughout the book.

In the komos one topos is that the lover kisses his beloved's door or door-post, for example:

ἐλθὼν δ' οὐκ ἐβόησα, τίς ἢ τίνος, ἀλλ' ἐφίλησα
τὴν φλιήν· εἰ τοῦτ' ἔστ' ἀδίκημ', ἀδικῶ.
A.P. 12 118 5-6 (Callimachus)[29]

In the komastic scene at the beginning of Plautus' *Curculio*, the lover Phaedromus is enthusing about the silent functioning of the hinge on his beloved's door. His cynical slave Palinurus immediately quips '*quin das sauium?*' (94) – 'why don't you give it a kiss?' The joke depends on the audience recognizing the substitution of the hinge for the door or door-post.

In Propertius 1 6 3-4, one of the examples of the 'assertion of friendship' topos mentioned previously on p. 99, much of the topos is perfectly normal – a statement of willingness to accompany the friend, and two ends of the earth, the Rhipaean mountains in the north and Ethiopia in the south. But one aspect of it is abnormal: usually the man proclaiming friendship says 'I would accompany you *to* the ends of the earth'. This is what Propertius says in connexion with the Rhipaean mountains: over the Rhipaean mountains lies the Ocean so that, once they are passed, the traveller has come to the end of the earth.[30] In this case Propertius is therefore preserving the normal relationship between the components of subject-matter in the topos. But with the second end of the earth, Ethiopia, Propertius employs a further sophistication: he says that he will go with Tullus not *to* it, but *beyond* it. Propertius has therefore altered the logical relationship between himself and the ends of the earth. Propertius' alteration of the topos makes it deliberately paradoxical, and the oddity of the language of 4 (*ulterius* with accusative *domos* which, because it is unparalleled, has troubled commentators) is simply another illustration of the usefulness of a general principle for the interpretation of Propertius, namely that when Propertius is tortuous, involved or odd linguistically, this reflects a similar tortuousness and involution in his thought process.[31]

PART TWO

The Constructive Principles
of Genre

5

Inversion

Menander's dictum that there are many kinds of propemptikon has already been mentioned on p. 7. When Menander says this, he is not referring to differences caused by topical alterations of the sorts discussed in Chapter 4. As his explanation shows, he is talking about major differences which affect whole generic examples, and which are caused by alterations of the primary elements of the genre. The propemptikon is not the only genre to have several variants in this sense; they are found in most if not all genres. Although little is said in antiquity about the subject, the most esteemed ancient writers constantly alter the primary elements of genres in order to create such variants. We can therefore conclude that this activity was regarded as important and meritorious. Moreover, because it affects whole generic examples and not merely single topoi or groups of topoi, we may reasonably believe that the practice was considered to demonstrate an author's originality and ingenuity even more than did his variations of topoi.

But although alterations of the primary elements are part of artistic originality, some such alterations tend to recur in different examples of the same and different genres. It is convenient, therefore, for critical purposes, to recognize these recurrences and to collect them into groups. This categorization does not of course imply that authors necessarily had a similar set of clear and rigid categories consciously in mind when they composed; but the recurrence of standard types of innovation does imply knowledge of these compositional techniques on the part of the ancient authors employing them.

Some alterations of primary elements will be dealt with at length in Chapters 5-9. But before we begin to consider these, it is convenient to set aside two kinds of alteration to primary elements which will not be given lengthy treatment in this work. The first kind involves changes in the 'form' of generic examples. We have already seen examples of this: on p. 12 the reported, third person, past tense schetliasmos of Cynthia to Propertius (1 6 5-12) and the anticipated future schetliastic activity of Cynthia (1 6 13-18) were both said to be the equivalent of a present tense, direct first person schetliasmos; on p. 54, Sappho's propemptikon (*Fr.* 94 (LP)) was seen to be a narration of a past utterance in direct speech rather than a direct speech in the present; in addition, Sappho introduced a dialogue into the propemptikon instead of producing the normal monologue; we saw on p. 82 that various examples of the renuntiatio amoris are conditional and future rather than unconditional and present, and on p. 94 that Catullus 12 is a flagitatio in the form of a threat of flagitatio.

We shall see more similar examples: at 131-5 an epic propemptikon will be treated, which is split in two, a syntaktikon being inserted between the two halves (Virgil *Aeneid* 4 305-30, 365-89); on pp. 152-3. I shall point out the narrative frame in which Ovid's minor kletikon (*Amores* 1 13) is set; on pp. 153-7. I shall discuss major formal sophistications in three soteria (Propertius 2 28; [Tibullus] 3 10 = 4 4; Ovid *Amores* 2 13); we shall see, pp. 160-4 that in three cases (Ovid *Amores* 2 11 37-56, Statius *Siluae* 3 2 127-43 and Theocritus *Idyll* 7 63-72) a narrative of the traveller's anticipated arrival, rather than a present-tense speech, functions as a prosphonetikon; similarly, in Horace *Odes* 1 7, a future-tense epibateric speech replaces the normal present-tense speech (pp. 212-16), and in Sappho *Fr.* 5 (LP) a future prosphonetic speech does likewise (pp. 229-30).

Formal alterations such as these affect the meaning of whole generic examples. Sometimes they can usefully be distinguished from similar alterations which concern only single topoi. Of this latter category we have seen some cases: on pp. 27-30 we noted that in Theocritus *Idyll* 7 52-6 and *Idyll* 12 27-37 statement was substituted for wish, and in *Idyll* 12 10-21 wish for statement; similarly, Catullus 46 1-3 was recognized as containing statement where wish would have been normal (p. 44). In addition, on pp. 180-1, some topical formal sophistications in Horace *Odes* 3 14 will be treated. It would be idle to pretend, however, that a clear distinction can always be made between formal alterations of a generic and of a topical nature, although it is often useful to make it when possible. Formal alterations of the kind we have been discussing all involve changes in case, person, voice, tense or mood; they can be put in a single category because they are so describable in grammatical terms. Where they affect whole generic examples they are important generic sophistications.

The second sort of alteration in primary elements which will not be treated at length here is the omission of one, or more, of them. This is found when one, or more, of the primary elements occurs neither explicitly nor implicitly in a generic example. Cases of such omission were seen on p. 12, where we noted that Cynthia's propemptikon to Propertius (Propertius 1 6 5-18) consisted of a schetliasmos alone, and on p. 89, where it was suggested that Horace *Odes* 1 25 was a komos in which the komastic scene was not set but left to the reader's imagination; other such alterations of the primary elements by omission will be hypothesized, on p. 157 in Ovid *Amores* 2 13, and in Horace *Odes* 3 7 on p. 210. It will be apparent that alterations of the primary elements by omission are much more elusive and much more difficult to describe than formal alterations.

I hope to treat these two kinds of alterations at greater length and more systematically in a later work. In the remaining chapters of this book I shall discuss some of the alterations of the primary elements of generic examples which come about by addition to or transformation of part of the primary elements. Such 'constructive' alterations come about in many different ways. They can, however, be discussed for convenience under the heading of the five 'constructive principles' of genre to which the remaining chapters are devoted.

These 'constructive principles' do not cover all alterations of the primary elements of genres by addition or transformation. Some of these alterations are confined to single genres or groups of genres: for example, the alterations to travel genres produced when home or abroad is the traveller's destination or point of arrival. Such variations do not fall within the scope of the 'constructive principles of genre' even though they are of great interest. The 'constructive principles' are confined to variations which potentially could occur in any genre where their application would not be logically absurd. It must be re-emphasized at this point that the discussion of artistic originality under such headings is not an attempt to impugn the writers concerned; rather, it is an attempt to comprehend how these writers added to the expressive capacity of the genres by expanding the common ground between themselves and their readers in ways which the readers could continue to understand.

The constructive principles will be treated in order of ascending complexity. In these terms, the first constructive principle is 'inversion'. Every genre has a 'function', which is often to convey a communication of a certain character. For example, a propemptikon has the function of bidding an affectionate and encomiastic farewell, the prosphonetikon of bidding an affectionate and encomiastic welcome. Inversion takes place when, in an example of a genre, the normal function of the genre is replaced by a diametrically opposite function, while at the same time the

I

generic identity of that example remains clear. This clarity is achieved by the continued presence of some of the primary elements (for example, speaker, addressee,[1] and generic situation in normal form), and of at least some altered but recognizable secondary elements. Some of the cases already noted of the first constructive principle in action will clarify this definition.

Chapter 2 exemplified inversion in operation in three epideictic genres: syntaktikon, propemptikon, and epibaterion. In these cases the normal function of epideictic genres, namely to praise the addressee (object), was replaced by disparagement of the addressee. In Juvenal 3 (syntaktikon), Umbricius attacks Rome when he is leaving it instead of praising it. In Archilochus *Fr.* 79a(D)/Hipponax *Fr.* 115 (Masson), and in its derivative, Horace *Epode* 10, both propemptika, the departing travellers are treated with open hostility and derision rather than with the friendship and praise which it is the genre's normal function to display. Horace *Epode* 10 carries its inversion down to the level of individual topoi. The friendly propemptic speaker may emphasize the good omens which attend the departing traveller[2] and will probably wish for him good winds,[3] good stars,[4] a calm and safe voyage[5] and the help of the gods.[6] A friend of a traveller may promise a sacrifice to the gods in thanksgiving for his safety.[7] Horace inverts each of these ideas. His traveller Maevius departs with evil omens (1), Horace wishes for him bad winds (3-8), no good stars (9-10), rough seas (11ff.), heaven to be deaf to his prayers (18), shipwreck (19ff.), and finally promises the deified storm-winds a thank-offering if Maevius is wrecked (21-4).

Also in Chapter 2, a whole group of inversions of the genre epibaterion was treated in which the speakers, instead of expressing pleasure at their arrival and praise of the places at which they had arrived, took the opposite point of view. Therefore, in these epibateria, as in all epideictic genres, inversion amounted in general terms to a substitution of vituperation of the addressee (object) for encomium.

Inversion of the kind defined and exemplified above is built into the foundations of ancient rhetorical theory. Each of the three divisions of oratory is further divided into two parts: dicanic into accusation and defence, symbouleutic into protreptic and apotreptic, epideictic into encomium and vituperation; and each of these subdivisions is the 'inversion' of the other. Similarly, to take an example from the progymnasmata, the pair *anaskeue-kataskeue* are inversions of each other. In these cases the two 'inversions of the other' both have generic names in antiquity. In them the ancient generic nomenclature will be preserved throughout this book, and in discussing them the principle of inversion will not be invoked. The principle is simply a recognition that this basic rhetorical division applies throughout the whole generic field. Ancient rhetoricians gave names only where they were of practical use. It was convenient for them to have a name for the inversion of protreptic, but not for the inversion of the propemptikon, because apotreptic was a genre useful for a practising orator, while the inverse propemptikon was not. It is for this reason that Menander calls vituperation 'indivisible' (331 18). The result may be momentarily confusing, but it simply exemplifies the cardinal rule of ancient rhetorical theory, namely that distinctions are made not for logical but for practical reasons.

The remainder of this chapter will examine further examples of inversion. The first is a propemptikon:

305 dissimulare etiam sperasti, perfide, tantum
    posse nefas tacitusque mea decedere terra?
    nec te noster amor nec te data dextera quondam
    nec moritura tenet crudeli funere Dido?
    quin etiam hiberno moliris sidere classem
310 et mediis properas Aquilonibus ire per altum,
    crudelis? quid, si non arua aliena domosque
    ignotas peteres, et Troia antiqua maneret,
    Troia per undosum peteretur classibus aequor?
    mene fugis? per ego has lacrimas dextramque tuam te
315 (quando aliud mihi iam miserae nihil ipsa reliqui),
    per conubia nostra, per inceptos hymenaeos,
    si bene quid de te merui, fuit aut tibi quicquam
    dulce meum, miserere domus labentis et istam,
    oro, si quis adhuc precibus locus, exue mentem.
320 te propter Libycae gentes Nomadumque tyranni
    odere, infensi Tyrii; te propter eundem
    exstinctus pudor et, qua sola sidera adibam,
    fama prior. cui me moribundam deseris hospes
    (hoc solum nomen quoniam de coniuge restat)?
325 quid moror? an mea Pygmalion dum moenia frater
    destruat aut captam ducat Gaetulus Iarbas?
    saltem si qua mihi de te suscepta fuisset
    ante fugam suboles, si quis mihi paruulus aula

luderet Aeneas, qui te tamen ore referret,
330 non equidem omnino capta ac deserta uiderer.

　·　·　·　·　·

365 nec tibi diua parens generis nec Dardanus auctor,
perfide, sed duris genuit te cautibus horrens
Caucasus Hyrcanaeque admorunt ubera tigres.
nam quid dissimulo aut quae me ad maiora reseruo?
num fletu ingemuit nostro? num lumina flexit?
370 num lacrimas uictus dedit aut miseratus amantem est?
quae quibus anteferam? iam iam nec maxima Iuno
nec Saturnius haec oculis pater aspicit aequis.
nusquam tuta fides. eiectum litore, egentem
excepi et regni demens in parte locaui.
375 amissam classem, socios a morte reduxi
(heu furiis incensa feror!): nunc augur Apollo,
nunc Lyciae sortes, nunc et Ioue missus ab ipso
interpres diuum fert horrida iussa per auras.
scilicet is superis labor est, ea cura quietos
380 sollicitat. neque te teneo neque dicta refello:
i, sequere Italiam uentis, pete regna per undas.
spero, equidem mediis, si quid pia numina possunt,
supplicia hausurum scopulis et nomine Dido
saepe uocaturum. sequar atris ignibus absens
385 et, cum frigida mors anima seduxerit artus,
omnibus umbra locis adero. dabis, improbe, poenas.
audiam et haec Manis ueniet mihi fama sub imos.
    Virgil *Aeneid* 4 305-30, 365-87

This is a fuller inverse propemptikon than the two examples discussed above and it is spread over two separate speeches of Dido. The division into two separate speeches and the reiteration, at the beginning of the second, of the schetliasmos which occupies the whole of the first speech, are less strange than they might seem at first sight. Menander recommends a double schetliasmos: first the long schetliasmos of the first part of the propemptikon (396 3ff.), and then a second schetliasmos, that of the propemptic speaker who has wished to persuade and failed to do so. This second schetliasmos immediately precedes the change of mind and the beginning of the second non-schetliastic section of the propemptikon (397 12ff.). Menander's prescription is mirrored in Dido's words, except that Virgil has shown his originality by spreading her propemptikon over two speeches. Moreover, in its fullness Dido's inverse propemptikon exploits the intrinsic ambiguity of the schetliasmos of the standard deprecatory propemptikon. It will be remembered that the schetliasmos is a highly charged and emotional attempt to dissuade the addressee from departing. Although motivated by strong affection for the addressee, it may paradoxically show the speaker's extreme concern in the form of hostile-sounding accusations of perfidy and cruelty. Therefore, in the standard schetliastic propemptikon, when the schetliasmos is succeeded by the section containing good wishes and so forth, a change of mind on the part of the speaker and a new compliance with the wishes of the addressee are needed. Virgil exploits this apparent contradiction between schetliasmos and good wishes in the normal propemptikon in order to compose an inverse propemptikon which consists of three parts: first, a schetliasmos of normal type (305-30); then a second schetliasmos (365-380), which is much more bitter and much less informed by affection than the first, and which is probably longer than that envisaged by the generic formula; and finally, not the good wishes of the normal propemptikon but instead a set of evil wishes. These are linked to the two schetliasmoi, but not by an adversative relationship. Instead, they are fully consonant with the second, harsher schetliasmos, which has subtly prepared the way for the inverted, and therefore evil wishes of 381-7. In dramatic terms, the tone of the second schetliasmos is justified by its immediate precursor, the interposed speech of Aeneas (333-61), which attempts, in rejecting Dido's pleas, to answer points made by her in her first schetliasmos. Aeneas' speech only enrages Dido the more, and thus stimulates the second, harsher schetliasmos, which leads naturally into the evil wishes of the final lines of the propemptikon.

Some more detailed remarks about Dido's propemptikon may be in order. Dido's first speech, like her second, places itself firmly in the mainstream of the genre by announcing breach of faith as the principal topos of the schetliasmos[8] (*perfide* 305 cp. 366). This is amplified (306-8) and is alluded to again in 314ff. and 323-4. The rest of the speech, with the exception of 309-13, dwells on the other main Menandrian schetliastic topic, the solitary and miserable state in which the addressee will be leaving the speaker.[9]

Lines 309-13 are especially interesting in that generic considerations clarify a difficulty of interpretation. Aeneas is leaving in winter – the season of storms. This is a sign of extreme eagerness to leave, and thus is a target for special abuse on the part of Dido. Propertius speaks in similar fashion in his propemptikon to Cynthia of Cynthia's eagerness to leave him:

> an tibi sum gelida uilior Illyria?
> et tibi iam tanti, quicumque est, iste uidetur,
> ut sine me uento quolibet ire uelis?
> Propertius 1 8 2-4 (cp. 9ff.)

Dido reinforces her protest with a reference to that key concept in the travel genres, the distinction between home and abroad (311-13).[10] Dido is not saying here, as has sometimes been thought,[11] 'If Troy still stood, would you be going to Troy?' She is saying: 'You are going away in mid-winter at the height of the storms. What more could you do if it was not a strange land you were going to, if Troy still stood, if Troy was the destination of your voyage?'

This form of argument is common in antiquity,[12] and we should understand *si* with all the verbs in the sentence; compare, for example,

> quid, si praeripiat flauae Venus arma Mineruae,
> uentilet accensas flaua Minerua faces?
> Ovid *Amores* 1 1 7-8

> sed enim id metuere si nemo esset homo quem reueremur, quidquid luberet faceremus, ne sub solo imperio nostro in seruitute nostra essent.
> M. Porcius Cato *Pro Rhodiensibus* (*Oratorum Romanorum Fragmenta* ed. Malcovati 1) 164

It is this argument of Dido that leads Aeneas to say in his reply

> sed nunc Italiam magnam Gryneus Apollo,
> Italiam Lyciae iussere capessere sortes;
> hic amor, haec patria est.
> Virgil *Aeneid* 4 345-7

Dido has claimed that Troy is Aeneas' native land. 'No', he replies, 'Italy is my native land', and then produces the parallel *argumentum ad hominem* about Dido and Carthage (347-50). In this reply of Aeneas the repetition of *Italiam* (345-6) echoes the repetition of *Troia* (312-13) in Dido's attack on him.

Dido's second speech (365-87) begins with her second schetliasmos. She rejects Aeneas' final plea that he is departing against his will. We may contrast Sappho's treatment of the same plea in *Fr.* 94 (p. 55). Dido's second schetliasmos is one which shows little affection and much bitterness towards Aeneas. She denies his ancestry (365), accuses him in succession of perfidy (366), hardness of heart (365ff.), and ingratitude (373ff.), and refuses to accept his excuse that the gods have ordered him to depart (376ff.). At 380 the schetliasmos ends. Dido declares that she will not restrain Aeneas. Thus Dido gives, after a fashion, that assent prescribed by Menander (397 15-16); and the imperative *i* (381) signals that the final section of the propemptikon has begun. But no good wishes follow: Dido hopes that the gods will shipwreck Aeneas in mid-sea, just as Horace's final evil wish for Maevius in *Epode* 10 was shipwreck. Moreover, Dido declares that her vengeful ghost will follow Aeneas everywhere – a gruesome variant perhaps of the propemptic speaker's promise to keep the departing traveller always in mind.[13]

An easy but instructive example of inversion in another epideictic genre – the genethliakon[14] – is Ovid *Tristia* 3 13.

Ecce superuacuus (quid enim fuit utile gigni?)
    ad sua natalis tempora noster adest.
dure, quid ad miseros ueniebas exulis annos?
    debueras illis inposuisse modum.
5 si tibi cura mei, uel si pudor ullus inesset,
    non ultra patriam me sequerere meam,
quoque loco primum tibi sum male cognitus infans,
    illo temptasses ultimus esse mihi,
inque relinquendo, quod idem fecere sodales,
10 tu quoque dixisses tristis in urbe 'uale'.
quid tibi cum Ponto? num te quoque Caesaris ira
    extremam gelidi misit in orbis humum?
scilicet expectas soliti tibi moris honorem
    pendeat ex umeris uestis ut alba meis,
15 fumida cingatur florentibus ara coronis,
    micaque sollemni turis in igne sonet,
libaque dem proprie genitale notantia tempus,
    concipiamque bonas ore fauente preces.
non ita sum positus, nec sunt ea tempora nobis,
20 aduentu possim laetus ut esse tuo.
funeris ara mihi, ferali cincta cupresso,
    conuenit et structis flamma parata rogis.

nec dare tura libet nil exorantia diuos,
    in tantis subeunt nec bona uerba malis.
25 si tamen est aliquid nobis hac luce petendum,
    in loca ne redeas amplius ista, precor,
    dum me terrarum pars paene nouissima, Pontus,
    Euxinus falso nomine dictus, habet.

Normally the coming of a birthday was a very pleasant occasion in antiquity. The general shortness of life made the achievement of yet another year a subject of greater rejoicing for adults than a birthday would be today. The normal function of the genethliakon is to welcome the birthday in a manner which compliments the person whose birthday it is. Ovid, in exile at Tomis, expresses the unpleasantness of his situation and way of life by a conspicuous failure to show welcoming pleasure at the coming of his own birthday. In 1-12 he innovates upon the well-known saying 'better never to have been born, or to have died at birth ',[15] by declaring in macrologic terms 'better had I never been born, or that I had died on leaving Italy '. At 13ff. he begins to negate all the commonplace components of birthday celebrations, descriptions of which form the topoi of the normal genethliakon.[16] He will not wear fine clothes (13-14), wreath the altar with flowers (15), offer incense and honey-cakes to the *Genius* (16-17), or pray to the *Genius* while avoiding ill-omened words (18). Ovid then repeats the death motif of the beginning of the elegy and introduces material of a conspicuously ill-omened nature; more suitable for my situation, he says, is the funeral pyre with its cypress-wreath and with the torch standing by (21-2). A further refusal to conform with the normal birthday customs of offering incense and uttering words of good omen (23-4) leads to an apparent concession: he will make the customary birthday wish (25). But the concession is not real: it is only a device to introduce a wish for an end to his exile, which in view of the pessimistic tone of the whole poem amounts to yet another wish for death. Such wishes were totally opposed to the whole tenor of ancient thought about birthdays, which saw them as festivals of life to which death, even the death of a sacrificial animal, was utterly inappropriate.[17]

The effect of inverting the genethliakon in this manner is almost blasphemous. The inversion amounts to a complete assault on the religious concepts and ceremonies underlying ancient birthdays, particularly in as much as it involves the repeated introduction of death into the

136

birthday. Ovid's bold use of inversion in *Tristia* 3 13 is one of those many features which make his later work, for all its lack of surface attraction, even more powerful and just as ingenious as his earlier work. In categorizing *Tristia* 3 13 generically, it is not possible for us to speak of disparagement of the addressee, as we can do in most inversions of epideictic genres. This is principally because, in this genethliakon, speaker and addressee are one person (see p. 221). But, in the genre genethliakon, the due and proper performance of the birthday rites is so linked with encomium of the person whose birthday it is that the rejection of this makes *Tristia* 3 13 unmistakably an inverse genethliakon.

Inversion can also be found in the minor genres, which in antiquity may have been thought of as poor relations of the rhetorical genres (see p. 74). There is a specialized minor kletikon addressed to the dawn or to the morning star.[18] The normal form of this genre (normal in the generic sense, that it is not inverted, rather than in the sense of most frequently occurring) is an encomiastic invitation to dawn or the morning star to come. It is well exemplified in Martial 8 21 : in this epigram a set of reproaches, pleas and mythologized appeals are made to the dawn, asking it to come because the Emperor will then appear. Inversions of this genre are found at *A.P.* 5 172 (Meleager), 5 173 (Meleager), 5 223 (Macedonius), and in a fuller form at Ovid *Amores* 1 13. In these poems dawn or the morning star is addressed and the poet's wish is that day shall not come. The Ovidian example, an elaborate *jeu d'esprit* packed with ingenious argumentation and use of mythological material, compounds its humorous effect by adopting loosely and in parody the form of a kletic hymn (inverted), a form justified by the divinity of Aurora.

Completely non-rhetorical genres, in the sense defined in Chapter 3, can also be inverted. A kind of 'threat-prophecy' akin to the type treated there is the warning that the beloved, by breaking her oaths to the lover, that is by rejecting or neglecting him, will attract the vengeance of the gods upon her perjury (e.g. Propertius 1 15). The inversion of the 'gloating over fulfilment' of this kind of 'threat-prophecy' can be found, for example, at Horace *Odes* 2 8 and Ovid *Amores* 3 3. The latter poem includes a witty section (13-22) in which Ovid explains that, although the gods have not punished his mistress for her perjuries, they have punished him by giving him ophthalmia because she broke an oath she had sworn by his eyes.

Other examples of inversion treated later are: Tibullus 1 6 15-42 (p. 174); Propertius 2 16 (pp. 206-8); Horace *Odes* 3 7 (pp. 209-11).

6

Reaction

The subject-matter of the genres consists of reproductions of events from real or imaginary human lives. The boundaries of the genres are natural in that they accord with the divisions human beings make of their experience. But life is a continuum and these divisions are, in a sense, arbitrary; and generic divisions too are, in the same sense, arbitrary. In epic and drama this is not noticeable. These forms of literature imitate large sections of life; and the generic examples which are part of an epic or play are integrated by temporal and causal links to a context imitating a life background. But, outside epic and drama, generic examples lack this background.

The principle of reaction describes one way in which the material of a particular example of a genre can be enlarged so as to give the impression that the example is set against an imaginary life background. When reaction occurs, new material is introduced and the primary elements of the genre are accordingly altered. To allow the new material to be introduced, the writer makes the speaker or addressee of the genre 'react' to the generic situation or speech. Such a reaction creates a 'dramatic' temporal and causal sequence not found in the generic formula and so appears to link the generic example to its imaginary life context.[1]

Reaction is not foreign to rhetorical theory. In his account of the schetliastic propemptikon Menander prescribes just such a reaction. The propemptic speaker utters a schetliasmos which has as its main sentiment 'do not go' and then proceeds to a final section, the burden of which is 'good luck with your journey'. In this final section he is reacting to the failure of his schetliasmos, and this reaction is dramatic, involving time sequence and cause-effect sequence. Reaction then, like inversion, is recognized by rhetorical theory. But just as the principle of inversion was invoked only when its applications went beyond rhetorical theory, so the principle of reaction will not be invoked when reactions are prescribed in generic formulae, but only when they are innovations upon a generic formula.

A reaction by the speaker always involves to some extent a change of mind on his part. The example of the genre in which this occurs begins like any other example of that genre. Then, at some point within the example, the feelings of the speaker change and take a different, although not necessarily completely contrary turn. This change can be caused by an internal conflict of mind, or by some action or, more usually, by some failure to act on the part of the addressee. Change of mind caused by internal conflict occurs six times among those examples of renuntiatio amoris mentioned on p. 80; in Theocritus *Idyll* 30; *A.P.* 5 184 (Meleager); Horace *Odes* 3 26; Propertius 2 5; Ovid *Amores* 3 11; *A.P.* 12 201 (Strato). From a psychological point of view, it is natural that changes of mind should occur frequently in this genre; a person renouncing love or a beloved is, both in real life and in literary renuntiationes (see p. 82), liable to be in a state of mental conflict.

Scholars' failure to understand the commonness of the phenomenon in classical literature in general, and in this genre in particular, has sometimes led to the printing of Ovid *Amores* 3 11 as two separate poems.[2] The unity of the poem, assured by generic considerations, is even further strengthened by the verbal and conceptual correspondences between the two sections (distinguished below as A and B) into which it has erroneously been divided. These correspondences are:

1. The change of mind is not unheralded in A. There Ovid is not single-minded: he admits *dolor* (7); he also alludes to Catullus 8 11 in '*perfer et obdura*' (7), a quotation which anticipates and reinforces B's

luctantur pectusque leue in contraria tendunt
    hac amor, hac odium

33-4

– another Catullan allusion (to Catullus 85).

2. A. multa diuque tuli; uitiis patientia uicta est (1)
   B. me miserum, uitiis plus ualet illa suis (44)
3. A. turpia quid referam uanae mendacia linguae
      et periuratos in mea damna deos (21-2)
   B. parce per o lecti socialia iura, per omnes
      qui dant fallendos se tibi saepe deos (45-6)
4. A. iam mea uotiua puppis redimita corona (29)
   B. et uideor uoti nescius esse mei (40)
5. A. iam mea uotiua puppis redimita corona

lenta tumescentes aequoris audit aquas (29-30)
(where Ovid imagines that his ship is coming
into harbour)
B. lintea dem potius uentisque ferentibus utar
et quam, si nolim, cogar amare, uelim (51-2)
(where in contrast Ovid imagines his ship as setting
sail from harbour)
A similar change of mind caused by internal conflict, but occurring at a
different point within the generic pattern and in a much more sophisticated way, can be seen in Horace's first *Epode*:

Ibis Liburnis inter alta nauium,
amice, propugnacula,
paratus omne Caesaris periculum
subire, Maecenas, tuo.
5   quid nos, quibus te uita si superstite
iucunda, si contra, grauis?
utrumne iussi persequemur otium,
non dulce, ni tecum simul,
an hunc laborem, mente laturi decet
10   qua ferre non mollis uiros?
feremus et te uel per Alpium iuga
inhospitalem et Caucasum
uel Occidentis usque ad ultimum sinum
forti sequemur pectore.
15   roges, tuum labore quid iuuem meo,
imbellis ac firmus parum?
comes minore sum futurus in metu,
qui maior absentis habet;
ut adsidens implumibus pullis auis
20   serpentium allapsus timet
magis relictis, non, ut adsit, auxili
latura plus praesentibus.
libenter hoc et omne militabitur
bellum in tuae spem gratiae,
25   non ut iuuencis illigata pluribus
aratra nitantur mea,
pecusue Calabris ante sidus feruidum
Lucana mutet pascuis,

neque ut superni uilla candens Tusculi
30 Circaea tangat moenia.
    satis superque me benignitas tua
        ditauit: haud parauero,
    quod aut auarus ut Chremes terra premam,
        discinctus aut perdam nepos.

This epode begins as though it is going to be a standard excusatory
propemptikon. Maecenas is a governor in the broad sense and is intending to depart with Octavianus' fleet (1-4). Horace stresses his own
friendly feelings towards Maecenas: he addresses him as *amice* (2); if
Maecenas lives, life is sweet for Horace, if Maecenas dies, it is not (5-6) –
the same sentiment as is often expressed by the 'half-soul' topos in
propemptika.[3] So far the propemptikon has declared its generic identity
from the very first word, *ibis*,[4] and has kept within the normal run of
propemptic topoi. Then Horace produces a complication of great interest.
He could have produced in this non-schetliastic propemptikon a change
of mind on the part of the propemptic speaker (himself) parallel to the
regular change of mind which occurs in a schetliastic propemptikon.
Just as the schetliastic speaker changes his mind from opposition to
concurrence with the traveller's departure, so Horace could have
changed his mind from excusatory unwillingness to accompany Maecenas to willingness. But, in order to enhance the encomiastic effect of
his propemptikon, Horace does not even put up the straw image of a
self-excusing refusal to accompany Maecenas so as to knock it down with
a change of mind. He merely hints at the possibility of his remaining
behind (7), and at what his excuse would have been had he decided to do
so (*iussi*, 7, another compliment), before going straight into the reaction.
The reaction has thus been transformed from a reversal of a previous
decision into a straight answer to a question putting forward two alternative possible decisions: to stay behind or to accompany Maecenas.

    The rest of the epode consists in a working out of this decision. It
begins with the topos on friendship (11-14), but the topos is used in an
original and striking way. Normally it is in hypothetical form: 'I am
your friend and therefore would accompany you anywhere'. But
Horace uses it in a factual form: 'I will accompany you anywhere'; and
this makes the topos relevant to the situation in hand, where Horace is
stating that he will in fact accompany Maecenas. What follows next is
an interesting example of how, when a writer uses a sophisticated and

abnormal form of a genre, the standard topoi of the normal form may remain standard in substance but be used in new and interesting ways. The contents of 15-16 would normally constitute one or all of the excuses of the speaker of the excusatory propemptikon for not accompanying the governor (cp. Propertius 1 6 25ff., esp. 29-30; Statius *Siluae* 3 2 90ff.). Horace instead uses the topos as further evidence of his friendship for Maecenas and as a further means of emphasizing the difference between himself, the unwarlike poet, and Maecenas; for in *Epode* 1 Maecenas is being characterized and praised as a man of war (1-4, 10), just as Tullus is so represented and praised in Propertius 1 6.

The last section of *Epode* 1 (23ff.) is of multiple interest. Its generic function is to handle one propemptic topic – the motive for departure.[5] The excellent motives are usually those of the addressee, since he is usually the only person departing. In *Epode* 1 the motives of the addressee are treated in 3-4. But Horace, the speaker in *Epode* 1, is departing also; and although there is no question here of a propemptikon to himself – for in terms of the division of epideictic genres this is an impossibility – Horace does deal with his own motive for departure. His motive, he says, is not wealth but friendship. Wealth was traditionally associated with war in antiquity (cp. Tibullus 1 1); Horace deliberately separates the two here.[6] He has several purposes in so doing: he wishes to echo and amplify the first rendering of the topos in relation to Maecenas (3-4, where Maecenas' motive for departure is *his* friendship for Octavianus); he also wants to praise Maecenas further in another statement of his own affection for him; and he wants to stress the sincerity of his own feelings for Maecenas.

Finally, 23ff. are connected with the purpose of *Epode* 1 in relation to the other epodes. *Epode* 1 is the prologue to a book of epodes and so will necessarily have the functions of a prologue, its main function being programmatic, to display Horace as an epodic poet. In effect this means representing Horace as the Roman Archilochus. It does so by the common device of giving an account of his life.[7] This is not the primitive life of the passionate, poor and proud soldier Archilochus, with his intense loves, hates and friendships, but a civilized and more sophisticated equivalent. It is the life of a poet, not over-wealthy but not motivated by greed, prepared to go off to war when duty and friendship calls, with a command of the vocabulary of affection and vituperation (33-4). The secondary prologue function of 23ff. is dedicatory. The address to Maecenas at 4 is a dedication of the book of epodes to him,[8] and Horace returns to Maecenas in his role as dedicatee in this last section of the epode. Horace denies that he goes to war to seek riches; what he wants, he says, is the favour of Maecenas. This clearly alludes to Horace's poet-patron relationship with Maecenas, and the allusion reinforces the dedication at the beginning of the poem. Lines 31-2 amplify the point: Horace does not need to seek wealth, because Maecenas' generosity has enriched him sufficiently. The propemptikon to Maecenas therefore fulfils the functions of a prologue as well as being a highly sophisticated and characteristically Horatian example of generic composition.[9]

A reaction on the part of the speaker caused by the lack of response of the addressee is found in two Theocritean komoi. The first of these is the song of Polyphemus in *Idyll* 11:

Ὦ λευκὰ Γαλάτεια, τί τὸν φιλέοντ' ἀποβάλλῃ,
20 λευκοτέρα πακτᾶς ποτιδεῖν, ἀπαλωτέρα ἀρνός,
μόσχω γαυροτέρα, φιαρωτέρα ὄμφακος ὠμᾶς;
φοιτῇς δ' αὖθ' οὕτως ὄκκα γλυκὺς ὕπνος ἔχῃ με,
οἴχῃ δ' εὐθὺς ἰοῖσ' ὄκκα γλυκὺς ὕπνος ἀνῇ με,
φεύγεις δ' ὥσπερ ὄις πολιὸν λύκον ἀθρήσασα;
25 ἠράσθην μὲν ἔγωγε τεοῦς, κόρα, ἁνίκα πρᾶτον
ἦνθες ἐμᾷ σὺν ματρὶ θέλοισ' ὑακίνθινα φύλλα
ἐξ ὄρεος δρέψασθαι, ἐγὼ δ' ὁδὸν ἁγεμόνευον.
παύσασθαι δ' ἐσιδών τυ καὶ ὕστερον οὐδ' ἔτι πα νῦν
ἐκ τήνω δύναμαι· τὶν δ' οὐ μέλει, οὐ μὰ Δί' οὐδέν.
30 γινώσκω, χαρίεσσα κόρα, τίνος οὔνεκα φεύγεις·
οὔνεκά μοι λασία μὲν ὀφρὺς ἐπὶ παντὶ μετώπῳ
ἐξ ὠτὸς τέταται ποτὶ θώτερον ὣς μία μακρά,
εἷς δ' ὀφθαλμὸς ὕπεστι, πλατεῖα δὲ ῥὶς ἐπὶ χείλει.
ἀλλ' οὗτος τοιοῦτος ἐὼν βοτὰ χίλια βόσκω,
35 κἠκ τούτων τὸ κράτιστον ἀμελγόμενος γάλα πίνω·
τυρὸς δ' οὐ λείπει μ' οὔτ' ἐν θέρει οὔτ' ἐν ὀπώρᾳ,
οὐ χειμῶνος ἄκρω· ταρσοὶ δ' ὑπεραχθέες αἰεί.
συρίσδεν δ' ὡς οὔτις ἐπίσταμαι ὧδε Κυκλώπων,
τίν, τὸ φίλον γλυκύμαλον, ἁμᾷ κἠμαυτὸν ἀείδων
40 πολλάκι νυκτὸς ἀωρί. τράφω δέ τοι ἔνδεκα νεβρώς,
πάσας μαννοφόρως, καὶ σκύμνως τέσσαρας ἄρκτων.
ἀλλ' ἀφίκευσο ποθ' ἁμέ, καὶ ἐξεῖς οὐδὲν ἔλασσον,
τὰν γλαυκὰν δὲ θάλασσαν ἔα ποτὶ χέρσον ὀρεχθεῖν·
ἄδιον ἐν τὠντρῳ παρ' ἐμὶν τὰν νύκτα διαξεῖς.

45 ἐντὶ δάφναι τηνεί, ἐντὶ ῥαδιναὶ κυπάρισσοι,
ἔστι μέλας κισσός, ἔστ' ἄμπελος ἁ γλυκύκαρπος,
ἔστι ψυχρὸν ὕδωρ, τό μοι ἁ πολυδένδρεος Αἴτνα
λευκᾶς ἐκ χιόνος ποτὸν ἀμβρόσιον προΐητι.
τίς κα τῶνδε θάλασσαν ἔχειν καὶ κύμαθ' ἕλοιτο;
50 αἱ δέ τοι αὐτὸς ἐγὼν δοκέω λασιώτερος ἦμεν,
ἐντὶ δρυὸς ξύλα μοι καὶ ὑπὸ σποδῷ ἀκάματον πῦρ·
καιόμενος δ' ὑπὸ τεῦς καὶ τὰν ψυχὰν ἀνεχοίμαν
καὶ τὸν ἕν' ὀφθαλμόν, τῶ μοι γλυκερώτερον οὐδέν.
ὤμοι ὅτ' οὐκ ἔτεκέν μ' ἁ μάτηρ βράγχι' ἔχοντα,
55 ὡς κατέδυν ποτὶ τὶν καὶ τὰν χέρα τεῦς ἐφίλησα,
αἰ μὴ τὸ στόμα λῇς, ἔφερον δέ τοι ἢ κρίνα λευκά
ἢ μάκων' ἁπαλὰν ἐρυθρὰ πλαταγώνι' ἔχοισαν·
ἀλλὰ τὰ μὲν θέρεος, τὰ δὲ γίνεται ἐν χειμῶνι,
ὥστ' οὔ κά τοι ταῦτα φέρειν ἅμα πάντ' ἐδυνάθην.
60 νῦν μάν, ὦ κόριον, νῦν αὐτίκα νεῖν γε μαθεῦμαι,
αἴ κά τις σὺν ναῒ πλέων ξένος ὧδ' ἀφίκηται,
ὡς εἰδῶ τί ποχ' ἁδὺ κατοικεῖν τὸν βυθὸν ὕμμιν.
ἐξένθοις, Γαλάτεια, καὶ ἐξενθοῖσα λάθοιο,
ὥσπερ ἐγὼ νῦν ὧδε καθήμενος, οἴκαδ' ἀπενθεῖν·
65 ποιμαίνειν δ' ἐθέλοις σὺν ἐμὶν ἅμα καὶ γάλ' ἀμέλγειν
καὶ τυρὸν πᾶξαι τάμισον δριμεῖαν ἐνεῖσα.
ἁ μάτηρ ἀδικεῖ με μόνα, καὶ μέμφομαι αὐτᾷ·
οὐδὲν πήποχ' ὅλως ποτὶ τὶν φίλον εἶπεν ὑπέρ μευ,
καὶ ταῦτ' ἆμαρ ἐπ' ἆμαρ ὁρεῦσά με λεπτύνοντα.
70 φασῶ τὰν κεφαλὰν καὶ τὼς πόδας ἀμφοτέρως μευ
σφύσδειν, ὡς ἀνιαθῇ ἐπεὶ κἠγὼν ἀνιῶμαι.
ὦ Κύκλωψ Κύκλωψ, πᾷ τὰς φρένας ἐκπεπότασαι;
αἴ κ' ἐνθὼν ταλάρως τε πλέκοις καὶ θαλλὸν ἀμάσας
ταῖς ἄρνεσσι φέροις, τάχα κα πολὺ μᾶλλον ἔχοις νῶν.
75 τὰν παρεοῖσαν ἄμελγε· τί τὸν φεύγοντα διώκεις;
εὑρησεῖς Γαλάτειαν ἴσως καὶ καλλίον' ἄλλαν.
πολλαὶ συμπαίσδεν με κόραι τὰν νύκτα κέλονται,
κιχλίζοντι δὲ πᾶσαι, ἐπεί κ' αὐταῖς ὑπακούσω.
δῆλον ὅτ' ἐν τᾷ γᾷ κἠγών τις φαίνομαι ἦμεν.

Theocritus *Idyll* 11 19-79

That the song of Polyphemus is a komos is not at once obvious but
requires demonstration. A characteristic literary practice of Theocritus

is to entertain his sophisticated urban audience by transferring the habits of townspeople to a rustic environment; he writes idylls in which his rustic characters act out countrified variants of town situations. An accepted example of this practice is *Idyll* 3, another Theocritean komos and recognized as such by scholars. In *Idyll* 3 the goatherd approaches the cave in which his rustic mistress Amaryllis lives, and there goes through a country equivalent of the rigmarole of threats and pleas characteristic of the urban komos. Another adaptation of urban behaviour to the country occurs in *Idyll* 10, which has been treated in this respect elsewhere.[10]

In the passage under discussion, the song of Polyphemus in *Idyll* 11, the same urban practice is being adapted as in *Idyll* 3 – the komos. In *Idyll* 3 the new location of the komos was the bucolic countryside of Theocritus' 'contemporary' poetic imagination and the speaker was a mortal goatherd; but in *Idyll* 11 the new location is the ancient Homeric landscape of Sicily where the komast, the Cyclops Polyphemus, is a monstrous primitive shepherd. The degree of adaptation required is consequently greater. In *Idyll* 3 the goatherd could approach his mistress's cave just as the urban komast approached the house of the courtesan. In *Idyll* 11 the scene must be a different one. Galatea, the sea-nymph beloved of Polyphemus, lived in, and took refuge in the sea; so Polyphemus, when he comes to sing his song to her, comes to the sea-shore and sings there (14). The sea-shore therefore is his mistress's threshold. The urban komast went to his mistress' door in the evening or at night (cp. *Idyll* 2 118). Polyphemus sleeps at night (22-3) and sings from dawn (15) to dusk (12). Interestingly enough, the goatherd komast in *Idyll* 3 also comes to his mistress by day. This is perhaps a realistic touch in both cases, differentiating the late reveller of the city from the busier countryman. The normal komast wants to be admitted to his mistress's house; Polyphemus cannot ask this. He wishes he could enter the sea and so come to her; but he knows that, having no gills, he could not survive under water; so his wish is not a real one. Instead, he asks Galatea to come out (42, 63). But this may be only a minor adaptation; other komasts ask their mistresses to come out;[11] this may therefore be almost as normal as asking for admission.

Two possible inconsistencies in *Idyll* 11 might show Theocritus slipping from country to urban patterns of thought. First, Polyphemus is represented as piping and singing of Galatea in the dead of night (38-9), although his singing time was, at an earlier point in the song, linked with the daytime (see above). Second, Galatea is asked (42ff.) to come out of the sea during the day and spend the night with Polyphemus in his cave, because his cave is pleasanter than the sea. But we have already been told (22-3) that Galatea comes to Polyphemus as soon as he falls asleep and leaves as soon as he wakes. But (*pace* Gow) Polyphemus is probably referring to his dreams; and in any case such small points are too elusive to form the basis for any conclusions.

As well as the general circumstances of Polyphemus' song outlined above, many correspondences in theme between *Idyll* 3 and *Idyll* 11 argue for the identification of Polyphemus' song as a komos:

1. The komast's remarks on his own appearance:

ἦ ῥά γέ τοι σιμὸς καταφαίνομαι ἐγγύθεν ἦμεν,
νύμφα, καὶ προγένειος ;
    Idyll 3 8-9 (cp. *Idyll* 11 30-3)

2. The gifts the komast is keeping for his mistress:

ἠνίδε τοι δέκα μᾶλα φέρω· τηνῶθε καθεῖλον
ὧ μ᾽ ἐκέλευ καθελεῖν τύ, καὶ αὔριον ἄλλα τοι οἰσῶ.
. . . . .
ἦ μάν τοι λευκὰν διδυματόκον αἶγα φυλάσσω
    Idyll 3 10-11, 34 (cp. *Idyll* 11 40-1)

3. The komast wishes he was another living thing so as to reach his mistress:

αἴθε γενοίμαν
ἁ βομβεῦσα μέλισσα καὶ ἐς τεὸν ἄντρον ἱκοίμαν
    Idyll 3 12-13 (cp. *Idyll* 11 54-5)

4. The intensity of the komast's love and the girl's cruelty:

νῦν ἔγνων τὸν Ἔρωτα· βαρὺς θεός· ἦ ῥα λεαίνας
μαζὸν ἐθήλαζεν, δρυμῷ τέ νιν ἔτραφε μάτηρ,
ὅς με κατασμύχων καὶ ἐς ὀστίον ἄχρις ἰάπτει.
    Idyll 3 15-17, see 18 (cp. *Idyll* 11 25ff., 52-3, 10-11, 15-16)

5. The komast's wish for kisses:

ὦ τὸ καλὸν ποθορεῦσα, τὸ πᾶν λίθος, ὦ κυάνοφρυ
νύμφα, πρόσπτυξαί με τὸν αἰπόλον ὥς τυ φιλήσω.
ἔστι καὶ ἐν κενεοῖσι φιλήμασιν ἁδέα τέρψις.
    Idyll 3 18-20 (cp. *Idyll* 11 55-6)

6. The komast brings flowers:

τὸν στέφανον τῖλαί με κατ' αὐτίκα λεπτὰ ποησεῖς,
τόν τοι ἐγών, 'Αμαρυλλὶ φίλα, κισσοῖο φυλάσσω,
ἀμπλέξας καλύκεσσι καὶ εὐόδμοισι σελίνοις.
Idyll 3 21-3 (cp. *Idyll* 11 56-7)

7. The komast's aches and pains:

ἀλγέω τὰν κεφαλάν, τὶν δ' οὐ μέλει.
Idyll 3 52 (cp. *Idyll* 11 70-1)

I have quoted extensively from *Idyll* 3 because the best evidence that one idyll of Theocritus is a komos is provided by another idyll which certainly is. That reaction occurs in Polyphemus' song is easier to show. Polyphemus, like the goatherd of *Idyll* 3, tries every appeal he knows and then desists from appeals. But the goatherd, having abandoned verbal attempts to gain his end, resorts to a variant of the 'lying down to sleep at the door'.[12] This is a further non-verbal attempt to win the sympathy of his mistress and so to gain his end after all. Polyphemus, however, abruptly abandons the whole project. He decides that he has been foolish, and that common sense requires him to go back to work, and to enjoy the favours of one of the girls who invite him to do so, rather than continue to pursue the unwilling Galatea. The sea-nymph may not want him, but he is a great man on the land (72-9).

If *Idyll* 11 consisted simply of the song of Polyphemus without introduction or tail-piece we might well think that this final section of the song was another and subtler effort to win Galatea's favours.[13] But the story and song of Polyphemus are introduced by Theocritus (7ff.) to illustrate to Nicias the dictum that the Muses alone can cure love (1ff.). Polyphemus was mad with love for Galatea; everything else was nothing in comparison; but he found the cure: the song which he was singing on the rock and which Theocritus records (17-18). At the end of the song (80-1) we are told again that by singing it Polyphemus cured himself. Theocritus must therefore show the cure occurring within the song. Had Polyphemus behaved like a normal komast Nicias might well have been unable to see how the Cyclops was helped by singing. The change of mind is therefore both required and guaranteed by the use to which Theocritus puts the song of Polyphemus. The second Theocritean komos displaying a change of mind (*Idyll* 7 96-127) will be discussed in this and other respects on pp. 202-4.

A final example of a change of mind on the part of the speaker caused by the lack of response of the addressee may be treated here briefly, since the poem in which it is found has already been mentioned (p. 93). Catullus 42 (flagitatio) proceeds in normal fashion up to 20. Then with deadly humour the poem continues:

> sed nil proficimus, nihil mouetur.
> mutanda est ratio modusque uobis,
> siquid proficere amplius potestis:
> 'pudica et proba, redde codicillos'.
>
> 21-4

The speaker changes his mind, since he or rather his proxies (p. 217) have had no effect on the addressee; and the flagitatio alters course and attempts to obtain the return of the notebooks by honorific addresses.

It may be that reaction on the part of the addressee is found less often than reaction on the part of the speaker. If so, the reason will be that reaction on the part of the speaker can easily be shown in non-dramatic and non-narrative poetry without the need to introduce into it a dramatic or narrative form. On the other hand it is very much harder, although not impossible, to show reaction on the part of the addressee in non-dramatic poetry without introducing into it a dramatic or narrative form. When reaction on the part of the addressee does occur, it may well be less likely to consist of a change of mind than does a reaction on the part of the speaker. In the case of the speaker some kind of change of mind is almost the only possible indication that a reaction has taken place. For the addressee a wider choice of reaction is open without obscuring the fact that a reaction has taken place.

Reaction on the part of the addressee occurs both as a change of mind and without the introduction of a dramatic element in Propertius 1 8 (propemptikon):

> Tune igitur demens, nec te mea cura moratur?
>   an tibi sum gelida uilior Illyria?
> et tibi iam tanti, quicumque est, iste uidetur,
>   ut sine me uento quolibet ire uelis?
> 5 tune audire potes uesani murmura ponti
>   fortis, et in dura naue iacere potes?
> tu pedibus teneris positas fulcire pruinas,
>   tu potes insolitas, Cynthia, ferre niues?

o utinam hibernae duplicentur tempora brumae,
10   et sit iners tardis nauita Vergiliis,
nec tibi Tyrrhena soluatur funis harena,
neue inimica meas eleuet aura preces!
atque ego non uideam talis subsidere uentos,
cum tibi prouectas auferat unda ratis,
15 et me defixum uacua patiatur in ora
crudelem infesta saepe uocare manu!
sed quocumque modo de me, periura, mereris,
sit Galatea tuae non aliena uiae:
ut te, felici praeuecta Ceraunia remo,
20   accipiat placidis Oricos aequoribus.
nam me non ullae poterunt corrumpere, de te
quin ego, uita, tuo limine uerba querar;
nec me deficiet nautas rogitare citatos
'Dicite, quo portu clausa puella mea est?',
25 et dicam 'Licet Atraciis considat in oris,
et licet Hylleis, illa futura mea est.'
hic erat! hic iurata manet! rumpantur iniqui!
uicimus: assiduas non tulit illa preces.
falsa licet cupidus deponat gaudia liuor:
30   destitit ire nouas Cynthia nostra uias.
illi carus ego et per me carissima Roma
dicitur, et sine me dulcia regna negat.
illa uel angusto mecum requiescere lecto
et quocumque modo maluit esse mea,
35 quam sibi dotatae regnum uetus Hippodamiae,
et quas Elis opes ante pararat equis.
quamuis magna daret, quamuis maiora daturus,
non tamen illa meos fugit auara sinus.
hanc ego non auro, non Indis flectere conchis,
40   sed potui blandi carminis obsequio.
sunt igitur Musae, neque amanti tardus Apollo,
quis ego fretus amo: Cynthia rara mea est!
nunc mihi summa licet contingere sidera plantis:
siue dies seu nox uenerit, illa mea est!
45 nec mihi riualis certos subducit amores:
ista meam norit gloria canitiem.

This elegy, like Ovid *Amores* 3 11, has sometimes been bisected by scholars who did not take into account the reaction which occurs in it. Propertius contrives to introduce a reaction on the part of the addressee without dramatizing the elegy. He does so by making the speaker react in his turn to a change of mind on the part of the addressee: the speaker's reaction is to describe and praise this change of mind. Propertius 1 8 begins as a standard schetliastic propemptikon. Propertius, as propemptic speaker, urges Cynthia not to depart in a schetliasmos of sixteen lines, in which he rings the changes on the usual topoi: the love between them (1);[14] her destination (2);[15] her motive for departure, a rival (3-4);[16] the dangers and discomforts of the voyage and of the place Cynthia is going to (5-8);[17] may Cynthia not be able to sail because of the adverse season, winds, etc. (11-14);[18] Propertius abandoned and alone (15);[19] Cynthia's cruelty (16).[20] Propertius then produces the normal second schetliasmos and change of mind (17-18) found in the Menandrian model and discussed above (pp. 132-3), emphasizing in the second schetliasmos (17) the 'oaths-perjury' topos.[21] In 17-26 good wishes for Cynthia's journey[22] are followed by encomiastic declarations of Propertius' abiding love for her.[23] The sea-goddess Galatea, relevant to this voyage not only as a sea-goddess and as Galaneia the goddess of calm, but also as the mother of Illyrios,[24] is to protect Cynthia (18).[25] Cynthia is to escape the dangers of Acroceraunia; she is to be brought to harbour safely at Oricos (20).[26] Propertius in the meantime will keep her constantly in mind (21-6), the other side of the 'remember me' topos and itself a propemptic commonplace.[27] Propertius will keep hoping for her return to his love (26).[28]

It is after 26 that some editors have divided the poem. No such division is needed: all that is happening is that a further change of mind, not part of the standard formula for the schetliastic propemptikon, takes place. What makes this second change of mind so interesting is that it is primarily a change of mind not on the part of the speaker (as in Horace *Epode* 1) but on the part of the addressee, although the sentiments of the speaker are naturally changed in their turn (see p. 151). Cynthia's change of mind is perfectly natural. The purpose of the schetliasmos of the propemptikon is to persuade the departing traveller not to go. In this propemptikon we are shown a case where the schetliasmos is successful. Cynthia, won over by the propemptikon of Propertius (28), changes her mind: she decides not to go. The effectiveness of a propemptikon in persuading someone not to go is paralleled within Propertius' own work by the effectiveness of Cynthia's schetliastic propemptikon to

Propertius himself in 1 6 5-18 (see p. 13). As a result of Cynthia's change of mind between 26 and 27 of 1 8, Propertius himself alters his sentiments at 27. He turns from schetliasmos followed by resigned good wishes, and so forth, to exultation (27-30). The word *uicimus* (28) is probably used consciously by Propertius as the active form of the same verb as is used passively (νενίκημαι) by Menander (397 15) to signal the final abandonment of schetliasmos. This exultation is taken up again in 41 and continues to the end of the elegy. It mingles Propertius' claims to literary and to erotic distinction in a way which is characteristic of elegiac poets, but which is especially relevant in this place because it is Propertius' poetic schetliasmos (1-17) which has succeeded in dissuading Cynthia. This fact gives substance to Propertius' commonplace claims that the gods of poetry, the Muses and Apollo, are efficacious in his case (39-42). Between these two outbursts of joy, 31-40 treat for the second time within the poem that standard propemptic topos, the motivations of the departing traveller.

Propertius differentiates his two treatments of this topos in a witty manner. In the schetliasmos Propertius suppressed Cynthia's real motives for departure. In 1-8 he propounded the choice open to Cynthia in narrow terms: he tried to convey to her that staying at home meant safety and his own love, and that going away meant icy Illyria, a dangerous voyage and another man, who is passed over in a contemptuous allusion. This brief and derogatory mention of the attractions available to Cynthia if she is willing to abandon Propertius, and the concomitant suppression of her real motives for wanting to go, are of course very much in place from a practical point of view. The schetliasmos seeks to persuade the departing traveller not to go; naturally, therefore, the attractions of going are minimized and the dangers maximized. Naturally, too, the propemptic speaker does not in these circumstances insult the traveller by suggesting that she is motivated by meretricious greed in wanting to go.

However, once Cynthia has made up her mind to stay, Propertius can deliberately, and with equal aptness, answer his first treatment of her motives and the attractions of travel with a second much more explicit and contrasting treatment. Cynthia had been offered wealth in abundance to induce her to depart and had been paid heavily already (37). We know from Propertius 2 16 that the rival who wanted to take Cynthia away was a magistrate going out to govern a province and, although this is not specifically stated in 1 8, it is made clear that Cynthia would have occupied a privileged position had she gone abroad (35-7).

Finally, although her destination is stated within the schetliasmos to be Illyria (2), the second treatment of her motives suggests that she was really being asked to go to Greece (35-6). It is impossible to say whether the two physically contiguous provinces were also politically connected at this time, or whether it is simply that Cynthia, as mistress of the governor of Illyria, would have been able to spend most of her time in Greece. At all events Cynthia's real motives for thinking of departing can be brought into the open by Propertius now that Cynthia has decided not to go, since at this point they constitute not a censure of Cynthia for greed but an encomium of her for not yielding to greed. Bisection of the elegy not only does little justice to the constructive principle which allows temporal progress and causality within a single poem through reaction, but also destroys the value of 31-40 as a further commentary on 1ff. and so as an example of true Propertian irony.

A case where dramatization occurs, and where the reaction of the addressee is other than a change of mind, is Theocritus *Idyll* 6 6-41, which will be treated at greater length on pp. 193-5. Lines 6-19 – the song of Daphnis – are in content a normal komastic speech. In Damoitas' song (21-40) Theocritus brings about something always inherently possible in the komastic situation. This possibility is that the addressee of the komos, the reluctant beloved, will answer the lover's pleas by making explicit and verbal that rejection of the lover which is usually implicit and non-verbal – the non-opening of the door and non-appearance of the beloved. The same reaction also occurs in the genre komos at Aristaenetus *Epistles* 2 20.

Similar to this is the reaction introduced along with a narrative element by Ovid into *Amores* 1 13. In this inverse kletikon (see p. 137), Ovid, employing a formal sophistication, gives his speech a narrative frame. He prefaces his address to Aurora with two lines of narrative scene-setting:

Iam super oceanum uenit a seniore marito
    flaua pruinoso quae uehit axe diem
    1-2

He then launches into forty-four lines of appeals to dawn not to come. At 47 he returns to narrative:

iurgia finieram. scires audisse; rubebat,
    nec tamen adsueto tardius orta dies.
    47-8

In these he uses narrative to tell us in a witty way something always and obviously implicit in the situation, namely that dawn did not respond to his appeals.

We must now distinguish between reaction and a formal sophistication which resembles it in effect. This is the rearrangement of the topoi of a normally static, unitemporal genre so as to create an internal time sequence and causal sequence without alteration of any kind to the primary elements. Because the primary elements are unaffected, no constructive principle is involved. The phenomenon can be found in Propertius 2 28 (soteria). Scholars who have not understood what is involved have cut up this elegy and transposed 33-4. No such expedients are necessary. The elegy begins with a long prayer made by Propertius to Jupiter (1-46). Within this prayer, which is imagined as being made while Cynthia lies seriously ill, information is given about the illness and its possible causes. In it also, in characteristic Propertian fashion, Cynthia, who is of course the logical addressee of the elegy (see p. 178) is directly addressed (9-32). It is this address to Cynthia which has brought about the transpositions of 33-4. Even if it were true that at 33 Propertius, who has been addressing Cynthia for over twenty lines, without warning suddenly turns back to Jupiter and addresses him not by name but by the second person pronoun only, this would still not be a good reason for transposing the lines. Such sudden transitions are part and parcel of Propertius' style,[29] and in this very elegy a less striking but similar transition occurs in 11-14. Lines 11-12 are an address to Cynthia, while 13 addresses the whole class of *formosae*, and 14 goes back to Cynthia, named only by second person pronoun. But the truth of the matter is that the reappearance of Jupiter in 33 is not unheralded. The line before his supposed sudden reappearance is '*et deus et durus uertitur ipse dies*'. The *deus* cannot be any other than Jupiter, particularly in view of Propertius' etymological allusion in *dies* to the archaic *Diespiter* = Jupiter.

This prayer to Jupiter continues to 46. At 35-40 a brief touch of despair leads Propertius to declare that he will live and die with Cynthia, before he makes a final petition to Jupiter (41), followed by a vow of thank-offerings (*soteria*) to be performed by himself and Cynthia (43-6).

At 47 Propertius begins a second prayer, this time to Persephone and Pluto. After this second prayer ends at 58 the phenomenon under discussion occurs: within the poem a lapse of time and a cause-effect sequence are found. From the time of Cynthia's illness and the prayers for her recovery, Propertius transports himself to the time of her recovery: in 59-60 Cynthia is cured. She must make offerings to Diana and to Isis and – a light touch – pay the ten nights of love vowed to Propertius (see p. 156).

Appreciation of the unusual nature of this soteria is not obscured by our lack of a rhetorical formula for the genre soteria. The fact that the soteria is eucharistic and presupposes a cure implies that the illness and cure will normally be narrated in examples of the genre as past occurrences. Thus the logic of the soteria guarantees that the dramatic representation of illness, prayer and recovery found in Propertius 2 28 is an abnormal and sophisticated mode of handling the generic material. Further confirmation of this derives from the fact that other eucharistic genres usually function in similar fashion. Additionally, our lack of a rhetorical prescription for the soteria is partly compensated for by the survival of the long Statian soteria for Rutilius Gallicus (*Siluae* 1 4). Statius certainly introduces into this soteria a species of ring-composition not likely to have been found in the rhetorical prescription:

A^1 (1-37) Rejoicing and thanksgiving over Gallicus' cure, with an invocation of Gallicus to inspire Statius' own thanksgiving.

B^1 (38-57) General concern, prayers, etc. over Gallicus' illness.

C^1 (58-68) Apollo urges Aesculapius to join him in curing Gallicus.

D (69-93) Encomium of Gallicus.

C^2 (94-114) Apollo and Aesculapius cure Gallicus.

B^2 (115-22) Statius' own concern, prayers over Gallicus' illness amidst the general concern.

A^2 (123-31) Rejoicing and thanksgiving over Gallicus' cure, including Statius' own thanksgiving.

Doubtless, Statius is also making other innovations: such elegant devices as the request for inspiration to his addressee Gallicus, instead of to a Muse, and the placing of the encomium of Gallicus in Apollo's mouth rather than in his own.[30] However, the general relationship between other Statian examples of genres and their known rhetorical prescriptions suggests that at least the material of *Siluae* 1 4, if not its treatment, is close to the material of the rhetorical prescription for soteria.

In his unusual and dramatic soteria (2 28) Propertius is not unique. Another soteria, [Tibullus] 3 10 = 4 4, has the same structure and something of the same emotional flavour. Like Propertius 2 28 it has sometimes suffered an unnecessary transposition (of 21-2):

Huc ades et tenerae morbos expelle puellae,
   huc ades, intonsa Phoebe superbe coma.
crede mihi, propera: nec te iam, Phoebe, pigebit
   formosae medicas applicuisse manus.
5 effice ne macies pallentes occupet artus,
   neu notet informis candida membra color,
et quodcumque mali est et quidquid triste timemus,
   in pelagus rapidis euehat amnis aquis.
sancte, ueni, tecumque feras, quicumque sapores,
10   quicumque et cantus corpora fessa leuant:
neu iuuenem torque, metuit qui fata puellae
   uotaque pro domina uix numeranda facit.
interdum uouet, interdum, quod langueat illa,
   dicit in aeternos aspera uerba deos.
15 pone metum, Cerinthe; deus non laedit amantes.
   tu modo semper ama: salua puella tibi est.
at nunc tota tua est, te solum candida secum
   cogitat, et frustra credula turba sedet.
Phoebe, faue: laus magna tibi tribuetur in uno
20   corpore seruato restituisse duos.
nil opus est fletu: lacrimis erit aptius uti,
   si quando fuerit tristior illa tibi.
iam celeber, iam laetus eris, cum debita reddet
   certatim sanctis laetus uterque focis.
25 tunc te felicem dicet pia turba deorum,
   optabunt artes et sibi quisque tuas.

When this soteria begins, Sulpicia is ill and a prayer is made for help from Phoebus (1-14, cp. Propertius praying to Jupiter for Cynthia). The prayer contains a description of Sulpicia's illness, as does Propertius' prayer of Cynthia's illness. In the last four lines of the prayer we are told of Sulpicia's lover Cerinthus, his concern for her and his vows for her recovery, as well as his reproaches to the gods when her illness takes a turn for the worse. At 15 the same dramatic lapse of time and cause-effect sequence can be detected as in Propertius 2 28. The prayer for Sulpicia has been heard, she is cured (16), and in 15-18 Cerinthus is told this joyful news. In 19-20 Phoebus is again invoked and is asked to favour the lovers, since by curing Sulpicia he has restored both to life. Compare '*uiuam si uiuet; si cadet illa cadam*' (Propertius 2 28 42).

As the speaker has turned suddenly from Cerinthus to Phoebus and back again, so he now once more addresses Cerinthus at 21. Just as at 15 Cerinthus has been told not to worry about Sulpicia's illness, so at 21 he is told not to weep but to save his tears for any future occasion when Sulpicia will reject his advances. His immediate prospects are joyful (23-6): the pair will pay their soteria to the gods and Cerinthus will be envied for his fortune in love[31] by the crowds at the temples. This soteria is lighter than that of Propertius, but both are shot through with love-motifs and both end on an erotic note, the ending of the soteria for Sulpicia being an excellent argument for retaining the *et mihi* of the M S S at Propertius 2 28 62, with its erotic implications.

Sulpicia's thank-offerings are paid to the god who has saved her, Phoebus, and this is as it should be. But the end of Propertius 2 28 is puzzling in this respect. Propertius has prayed to Jupiter, Persephone and Pluto for Cynthia's recovery. Cynthia is now to pay her thank-offerings to Diana, Isis and Propertius. To identify Diana (Hecate) with Persephone would be possible; it would also be possible to identify Isis with Persephone.[32] But although identifications of this sort would have been plausible if they had yielded different equivalents for Diana and Isis, the fact that they yield the same equivalent is their condemnation. It appears that something is happening here similar to what occurs in Tibullus 1 3 23ff. There, Delia, we are told, had prayed to Isis for Tibullus' safety abroad. Tibullus, now in danger abroad, himself prays to Isis; but Delia, not Tibullus, will pay the vows made by Tibullus to Isis (29-32). Tibullus immediately goes on to mention his Roman *Penates* and *Lar*. The implication is that Romans, although in danger they may pray to foreign deities, like to have as little to do with them as possible. However, they recognize that foreigners, such as elegiac mistresses, will have recourse to these deities.

In these terms Propertius 2 28 can be interpreted as follows. Propertius prays to Jupiter, Persephone and Pluto, all good Roman gods; he even imagines Cynthia as making thank-offerings to Jupiter. Cynthia, we presume, prays to Diana and Isis. When settlement becomes due, Propertius forgets that Cynthia was supposed to sacrifice to Jupiter, represents her as repaying only the deities to whom she has prayed, and so as sacrificing to Isis (a goddess favoured by courtesans and also a goddess of health, see p. 157), and to Diana, another goddess of women and of healing. Cynthia is to give Propertius ten nights as a reward for his prayers to Jupiter and the other Roman gods, and possibly to compensate him for his payment of vows to these gods.

On this interpretation the prayers to the two goddesses are perfectly explicable. It is interesting, however, that in *Amores* 2 13, a poem in which Ovid prays for the recovery of his mistress from sickness following an abortion, Ovid addresses Isis and Ilithyia (Diana as goddess of childbirth). This elegy is an account of Corinna's sickness (1-6), with prayers for her recovery to the two goddesses (7-22); it ends with promises of soteria (23-6), and an erotic note comparable to that of Propertius and Pseudo-Tibullus – a request to Corinna to be more amenable to Ovid in the future (27-8). Moreover, it contains the 'two lives' topos (cp. Propertius and Pseudo-Tibullus above):

> huc adhibe uultus et in una parce duobus;
> nam uitam dominae tu dabis, illa mihi.
>
> 15-16

It is more than possible that Ovid meant this elegy to be understood as a dramatized soteria of the same sort as those of Propertius and Pseudo-Tibullus, the concluding cure being omitted in accordance with the principle of omission discussed on pp. 128-9. The similar material and structure of Propertius 2 28 and Ovid *Amores* 2 13 suggest a further possibility about Isis and Diana in Propertius 2 28. Unwanted pregnancies and abortions are an occupational hazard of prostitutes. When Ovid prays on Corinna's behalf to Isis as a goddess of women, childbirth, and healing,[33] and to Diana as Ilithyia, his prayers may be the traditional responses of lovers to this plight of their mistresses.[34] And although Cynthia's illness is not due to an abortion, Propertius may have been partly influenced to select Isis and Diana as the recipients of Cynthia's thanks because they were the usual deities addressed on behalf of prostitutes ill after an abortion.

I have found the formal sophistication described above only in examples of the soteria. This may be so for several reasons: some generic formulae already contain dramatic sequences of time and cause-effect; in other genres they would be inappropriate; moreover, the constructive principles of genre, especially reaction and inclusion (as well as the absorption of other generic examples, see p. 89), produce dramatic effects. The formal sophistication analysed may not, therefore, be required in most genres, although there may well be examples of it in genres other than the soteria.

7

Inclusion

The greatest obstacle to the formulation of a framework within which generic composition can be examined has always been the fact that material from different genres can be found within the boundaries of single poems which are not epics or dramas. This has produced the belief that in many cases the assignment of poems to single genres is impossible, or even that ancient authors were not clear about generic distinctions. The phenomenon has sometimes been described as the 'mixing of genres'.

I should prefer to avoid this term, since it could carry two false implications: when material from different genres is found in one poem, it is inextricably and arbitrarily intermingled; and no one genre has primacy of place within the 'mixture'. In fact, when material from different genres occurs in the same poem, the topoi from the different genres are not intermingled, but kept separate; and material from one of the genres seems to be of greater importance than that from the other(s). The material of greater importance may, but need not necessarily, occupy more space than that of the other genre(s). It will, in terms of the total impact, function, and significance of the poem, show itself to be paramount in importance, and so make it clear that the genre to which it belongs is the 'overall' genre. We might anticipate that cases would often arise where it was difficult to discern the overall genre; but in practice this is rarely difficult.

There are several ways in which material from one genre can be found in a poem where the predominant material belongs to another genre or – a different but analogous case – to another example of the same genre. It may be that within an example of one genre there occurs a fleeting reference or allusion to another genre or to another example of the same genre. In Roman elegy, for example, it is a common practice for poets to allude in many genres to the komos.[1] Such fleeting allusions are usually, but not always, of little generic significance, although they may be innovations on the topical level.

Another circumstance in which material of one genre may be found within an example of another is when progymnasmata are absorbed

158

within an example of another genre. As we saw on pp. 88-90, it appears that some minor genres which are not rhetorical progymnasmata nevertheless behave like them. When progymnasmata and other minor genres are absorbed, their function is subordinated to that of the genre absorbing them, but they may still form a distinct and noticeable section of the poem.

The final mode whereby material from one genre can be found within an example of another is 'inclusion'. Inclusion like absorption occurs when, in addition to the overall generic example, another example of the same or of another genre is found within a single poem or speech. The difference is that, in inclusion, the included generic example is not treated like a progymnasma, but fully retains its own generic identity and function, which are related to those of the including genre. As was pointed out in Chapter 3, it is impossible to make a clear distinction in all cases between the absorption of progymnasmata and inclusion. But the value of the distinction, where it can be made, was upheld, because two different levels of originality are involved and because the primary elements are altered by inclusion though not by absorption.

We begin with some cases where the included example belongs to a different genre from the overall genre. Ovid *Amores* 2 11 and Statius *Siluae* 3 2 are both propemptika; at the end of each a prosphonetikon is included. The propemptic examples in the two poems are first-person, present-tense speeches; the prosphonetic examples are narrated anticipations of future returns. These 'formal', grammatically describable differences do not affect generic assignments; they are common and have already been treated in Chapter 5.

The inclusion of prosphonetika within propemptika has an interesting connexion with the Menandrian propemptic prescriptions. In Menander's account of the propemptika addressed to men, there is no hint of any anticipation or description of the return of the departing traveller; moreover, most examples of the genre do not touch on this subject. However, in his treatise on hymns, Menander discusses what he calls the 'apopemptic hymn'. This is a propemptic hymn addressed to one of the migratory gods of Greek religion. At the end of his description of the apopemptic (propemptic) hymn, Menander prescribes the following topos:

ἀνάγκη δὲ γίνεσθαι καὶ τὴν εὐχὴν ἐπὶ ἐπανόδῳ καὶ ἐπιδημίᾳ δευτέρᾳ.
336 21-2

'It is also necessary that a prayer should be made ⟨to the god⟩ asking him to come back and stay again in your country.'

The propemptic hymn is just as much a propemptikon as any other kind. So we can say that this is a rhetorical prescription of a topos anticipating or wishing for the return of the addressee of a propemptikon. The departure of a god was part of an automatic cycle of departures and returns connected with recurrent festivals. The mechanical certainty of the god's return may have meant that an anticipation of return was standard in the hymnic propemptikon.

But although Menander does not prescribe this topos for propemptika to men, whose return was not so certain, it is likely to have been used fairly frequently. It occurs in a secular propemptikon at Aristophanes *Equites* 500ff., and there may be a hint of it at Propertius 1 8 26. Moreover, the frequency of inclusions of prosphonetika within propemptika itself argues for the presence of a topical anticipation of return in the formula for the secular propemptikon. It may be then that the inclusion of a prosphonetikon within propemptikon is a substitute for a topical allusion to the return in the propemptic formula.

Ovid *Amores* 2 11 begins as an orthodox schetliastic propemptikon. The schetliasmos ends at 33 to be followed by good wishes at 34. In the middle of 37 Ovid transforms the good wishes into a prayerful anticipation of Corinna's return, which constitutes an included prosphonetikon:

> uade memor nostri, uento reditura secundo;
> > impleat illa tuos fortior aura sinus.
> tum mare in haec magnus proclinet litora Nereus,
> 40   huc uenti spectent, huc agat aestus aquas.
> > ipsa roges, Zephyri ueniant in lintea soli,
> > > ipsa tua moueas turgida uela manu.
> primus ego aspiciam notam de litore puppim
> > et dicam 'nostros aduehit illa deos!'
> 45 excipiamque umeris et multa sine ordine carpam
> > oscula; pro reditu uictima uota cadet,
> inque tori formam molles sternentur harenae
> > et cumulus mensae quilibet esse potest.
> illic adposito narrabis multa Lyaeo,
> 50   paene sit ut mediis obruta nauis aquis,
> > dumque ad me properas, neque iniquae tempora noctis
> > > nec te praecipites extimuisse Notos.

omnia pro ueris credam, sint ficta licebit:
cur ego non uotis blandiar ipse meis?
55 haec mihi quam primum caelo nitidissimus alto
Lucifer admisso tempora portet equo.
Ovid *Amores* 2 11 37-56

Lines 37-42 are a link-passage of a kind sometimes found connecting overall and included genres, and by its nature difficult to explain as part of either generic pattern. The concept of the favourable but strong winds and sea which are to direct Corinna's ship is introduced, as the word *fortior* (38) makes clear, to allude to the theme of 33-4 (*procellae, aequa Galatea, puppi*), just as *Nereus* (39) echoes *Nereidesque deae Nereidumque pater* (36). But it is also a device to fill the gap between Corinna's departure and her arrival home by applying to her return voyage topoi normally applied to the outward voyage of the departing traveller addressed in the propemptikon. Such material is not usually found in the prosphonetikon because the prosphonetic addressee is generally, though not always, safely arrived, making it unnecessary for the welcomer to pray for his safe journey home. On the other hand prayer for the safe return of the prosphonetic addressee, in a prosphonetikon also set in the future, can be found at Sappho *Fr.* 5 (LP) (see p. 229). It would appear that Ovid is arriving at a similar device in a similar anticipated future prosphonetikon independently of the direct influence of Sappho, and is thinking of his procedure in terms of grafting altered propemptic topoi on to the beginning of his prosphonetikon. This is perhaps a common procedure (see below). The explicitness of his device is almost an open boast of his generic skill; *ipsa roges*, etc. (41), an amplification which transfers the wish to the addressee, is the final touch.

At 43 the familiar prosphonetic topoi begin: Ovid will be first to welcome Corinna – the topos of the priority of the welcomer (B12, 43, cp. 51 Corinna's hurrying back to Ovid); Ovid will embrace and kiss Corinna (B4, 45-6); a votive (B15) sacrificial offering will be made (B16) for her safe return (B1, 46); there will be a *cena aduenticia* (welcoming banquet) on the sand to celebrate her return (B18, 47-8); wine will be drunk (49); Corinna will tell her traveller's tales (49-52); and Ovid will believe them even if they are untrue (B13*, 53) – the topos of the humorous hit at the traveller's tales; there is a hint of lovemaking (B19, 54); finally, 55-6 reiterate the prayer already made by the subjunctives of 38ff. Line 44, as well as being complimentary to

L

Corinna, may also possibly show a consciousness on Ovid's part that what he is doing, namely praying for and anticipating the return of the propemptic addressee, was something very often done when the addressee was divine (see above).

Statius *Siluae* 3 2 is an excusatory not a schetliastic propemptikon; but like some other non-schetliastic propemptika it also contrives to hint at schetliasmos without making it explicit.[2] After good wishes, implicit schetliasmos, and excuses, *Siluae* 3 2 goes on at 101 with a prayer to Isis, lasting until 126. In this prayer Statius does something characteristic of his poetic technique: he combines the description of the places the propemptic addressee Celer will visit[3] with a prayer for Celer's safety additional to the prayers of 1ff.[4] At 127 a four-line passage introducing the included prosphonetikon begins:

> ergo erit illa dies qua te maiora daturus
> Caesar ab emerito iubeat decedere bello.
> at nos hoc iterum stantes in litore uastos
> 130 cernemus fluctus aliasque rogabimus auras.
> o tum quantus ego aut quanta uotiua movebo
> plectra lyra! cum me magna ceruice ligatum
> attolles umeris atque in mea pectora primum
> incumbes e puppe nouus, seruataque reddes
> 135 colloquia inque uicem medios narrabimus annos;
> tu rapidum Euphraten et regia Bactra sacrasque
> antiquae Babylonis opes et Zeugma, Latinae
> pacis iter; quam dulce nemus florentis Idymes,
> quo pretiosa Tyros rubeat, quo purpura fuco
> 140 Sidoniis iterata cadis, ubi germine primum
> candida felices sudent opobalsama uirgae:
> ast ego, deuictis dederim quae busta Pelasgis
> quaeue laboratas claudat mihi pagina Thebas.
>   Statius *Siluae* 3 2 127-43

In this prosphonetikon, it is Statius alone, the welcomer, who prays for winds to bring Celer home (130) and not also, as in Ovid, the returning traveller. But Statius is just as self-conscious as Ovid about the unusual use to which the wind topos is being put (*alias auras* 130). Statius will pay his vows for Celer's safe return (B 15, 16) but his payment will be not a sacrificial victim: it will be – good Statian touch – a song, something more fitting for a poet (131-2).[5] Statius and Celer will embrace

162

(B4) and Statius will be the first to receive this mark of Celer's affection (B12, 132-4); Celer will tell his traveller's tales (B13) and Statius will also narrate his stay-at-home doings (B14, 135ff.). There is no humour at the expense of Celer's traveller's tales: Celer was an important man and *Siluae* 3 2 is a formal poem, so that humour at Celer's expense would be out of place. Instead, the adventures of Celer are treated with respect (B9). Encomiastic details are piled one on another – *pacis iter* (138) and the precious substances of 138ff. fulfil the same function as Propertius 1 6 31ff., that of suggesting the addressee's strength and power. Finally Statius introduces a variation on the topos of a humorous remark about the traveller's tales in such a way as further to enhance his encomium of Celer. The humorous remarks are made not about Celer's tales but about Statius's narrative of his own doings in the years Celer has been away. Celer the man of war has been described, like Tullus in Propertius 1 6, as being in peace abroad. This home-peace/abroad-warfare paradox is now intensified by a description of Statius the man of peace as being at war at home. The convention that an author can describe himself as doing what he is writing about[6] is invoked by Statius to allow him to laugh at his own doings. These he describes in 142 in grandiose and bellicose terms, not as writing but as fighting heroic wars, before going on to explain the joke and advertise his epic poem, the *Thebaid*, in the final line of the poem (143). Thus the humorous topos is worked in a novel fashion into the prosphonetikon and Celer's repute is further increased by it.

A third example of the inclusion in a propemptikon of a prosphonetikon occurs in Theocritus *Idyll* 7:

> κἠγὼ τῆνο κατ᾽ ἆμαρ ἀνήτινον ἢ ῥοδόεντα
> ἢ καὶ λευκοΐων στέφανον περὶ κρατὶ φυλάσσων
> 65 τὸν Πτελεατικὸν οἶνον ἀπὸ κρατῆρος ἀφυξῶ
> πὰρ πυρὶ κεκλιμένος, κύαμον δέ τις ἐν πυρὶ φρυξεῖ.
> χἀ στιβὰς ἐσσεῖται πεπυκασμένα ἔστ᾽ ἐπὶ πᾶχυν
> κνύζᾳ τ᾽ ἀσφοδέλῳ τε πολυγνάμπτῳ τε σελίνῳ.
> καὶ πίομαι μαλακῶς μεμναμένος Ἀγεάνακτος
> 70 αὐταῖς ἐν κυλίκεσσι καὶ ἐς τρύγα χεῖλος ἐρείδων.
> αὐλησεῦντι δέ μοι δύο ποιμένες, εἷς μὲν Ἀχαρνεύς,
> εἷς δὲ Λυκωπίτας· ὁ δὲ Τίτυρος ἐγγύθεν ᾀσεῖ.

Theocritus *Idyll* 7 63-72

Here, however, the included prosphonetikon has to do not, as was the case in Ovid *Amores* 2 11 and Statius *Siluae* 3 2, with the return of the departing traveller but with the safe arrival of the departing traveller at his destination. In normal propemptika the speaker escorts the traveller in his imagination all the way to his destination and safe arrival in harbour.[7] In Theocritus *Idyll* 7 52ff. the speaker Lycidas does much more. He enhances the topical description of safe arrival at harbour by declaring that when the traveller Ageanax arrives at his destination he (Lycidas), who will still be at the place where he is delivering the propemptikon, will celebrate that arrival with a banquet. It was a normal part of the prosphonetic process among Greeks as well as Romans to hold a banquet to celebrate the arrival of a returning traveller (B 18).[8] Usually, the returning traveller was the guest of honour at this banquet, although it was not strictly necessary that he be present at all.[9] But Theocritus' concept is unique – a 'welcoming banquet', held at the place the traveller has left, to celebrate not his return but his arrival at his destination. Moreover, the concept involves an impossibility: in antiquity communications were such that Lycidas on Cos could not know of the safe arrival of Ageanax at Mytilene on the very same day (63) as Ageanax arrived there.

This impossibility, as well as the oddity of the included prosphonetikon, is part of a deliberate design of Theocritus to convey a state of mind of the propemptic speaker Lycidas, which is not altogether dissimilar to that of the lover of *Idyll* 12 (see p. 30). Theocritus begins his presentation of the unusual psychological state of the lover at 52, where Lycidas' propemptikon starts not with the normal unconditional propemptic good wishes, but with conditional good wishes amounting to mild intimidation.[10] At 53, as an antidote to this suggestion of intimidation, the good wishes are extended to include wishes for a good voyage at a bad sailing time. This is not only an implied schetliasmos, hinting at the unhappiness at the speaker of the prospective departure of the addressee, but also a clumsy and ill-omened way for a propemptic well-wisher to speak. The tension seen here between Lycidas' desire, on the one hand to press his advantage and on the other not to seem a poor and mercenary lover, is increased by his suppressed unhappiness and produces the further oddity of the unusual and impossible 'welcoming banquet'.

These are some examples of the inclusion of prosphonetika within propemptika. A further such case is treated on pp. 198ff. (Propertius 3 12, cp. the treatment of Propertius 3 4 in the same chapter). The propemptikon can include examples of genres other than the prosphonetikon:

for example, Horace *Odes* 3 27 includes an inverse epibaterion (34-75) (see p. 67), and Sappho *Fr.* 94 (LP) includes a syntaktikon (see p. 54). The propemptikon, since it is a frequently exemplified travel genre, will for this reason, and because sophisticated writers wished to enliven its familiar material, provide a good many cases of inclusion. But other travel genres have a similar capacity to include: Tibullus 1 3, treated previously in Chapters 1 and 2, begins with the propemptikon of Tibullus to Messalla, when Tibullus, owing to illness, has had to stay behind at Corcyra and cannot accompany Messalla further (1-3). But the elegy as a whole is an inverse epibaterion expressing Tibullus' lack of pleasure at finding himself in Corcyra, the initial propemptikon to Messalla being included. Similarly, Juvenal 3 is an inverse syntaktikon, including at its beginning a propemptikon (see. p. 47). So too on a different scale the *hodoiporikon* of Rutilius Namatianus begins with an included syntaktikon (see p. 48).

Inclusions of kindred genres are found outside the travel genres.

> Hunc cecinere diem Parcae fatalia nentes
>> stamina, non ulli dissoluenda deo:
> hunc fore, Aquitanas posset qui fundere gentes,
>> quem tremeret forti milite uictus Atax.
> 5 euenere: nouos pubes Romana triumphos
>> uidit et euinctos bracchia capta duces:
> at te uictrices lauros, Messalla, gerentem
>> portabat nitidis currus eburnus equis.
> non sine me est tibi partus honos: Tarbella Pyrene
> 10 testis et Oceani litora Santonici,
> testis Arar Rhodanusque celer magnusque Garunna,
>> Carnutis et flaui caerula lympha Liger.
> an te, Cydne, canam, tacitis qui leniter undis
>> caeruleus placidis per uada serpis aquis,
> 15 quantus et aetherio contingens uertice nubes
>> frigidus intonsos Taurus alat Cilicas?
> quid referam ut uolitet crebras intacta per urbes
>> alba Palaestino sancta columba Syro,
> utque maris uastum prospectet turribus aequor
> 20 prima ratem uentis credere docta Tyros,
> qualis et, arentes cum findit Sirius agros,
>> fertilis aestiua Nilus abundet aqua?

Nile pater, quanam possim te dicere causa
    aut quibus in terris occuluisse caput?
25 te propter nullos tellus tua postulat imbres,
    arida nec pluuio supplicat herba Ioui.
te canit atque suum pubes miratur Osirim
    barbara, Memphiten plangere docta bouem.
primus aratra manu sollerti fecit Osiris
30   et teneram ferro sollicitauit humum,
primus inexpertae commisit semina terrae
    pomaque non notis legit ab arboribus.
hic docuit teneram palis adiungere uitem,
    hic uiridem dura caedere falce comam:
35 illi iucundos primum matura sapores
    expressa incultis uua dedit pedibus.
ille liquor docuit uoces inflectere cantu,
    mouit et ad certos nescia membra modos:
Bacchus et agricolae magno confecta labore
40   pectora tristitiae dissoluenda dedit:
Bacchus et adflictis requiem mortalibus adfert,
    crura licet dura compede pulsa sonent.
non tibi sunt tristes curae nec luctus, Osiri,
    sed chorus et cantus et leuis aptus amor,
45 sed uarii flores et frons redimita corymbis,
    fusa sed ad teneros lutea palla pedes
et Tyriae uestes et dulcis tibia cantu
    et leuis occultis conscia cista sacris.
huc ades et Genium ludis centumque choreis
50   concelebra et multo tempora funde mero:
illius et nitido stillent unguenta capillo,
    et capite et collo mollia serta gerat.
sic uenias hodierne: tibi dem turis honores,
    liba et Mopsopio dulcia melle feram.
55 at tibi succrescat proles quae facta parentis
    augeat et circa stet ueneranda senem.
nec taceat monumenta uiae, quem Tuscula tellus
    candidaque antiquo detinet Alba Lare.
namque opibus congesta tuis hic glarea dura
60   sternitur, hic apta iungitur arte silex.
te canet agricola, a magna cum uenerit urbe

serus, inoffensum rettuleritque pedem.
at tu, Natalis multos celebrande per annos,
candidior semper candidiorque ueni.
    Tibullus 1 7

Tibullus 1 7 is a genethliakon which includes a triumph-poem. The two genres are akin in that both celebrate a happy event of a semi-religious nature concerned with a single individual and occurring on a single day. The generic description of Tibullus 1 7 may contribute towards the understanding of its unity and meaning, since it is one of those Tibullan elegies scholars have sometimes thought rambling, digressive and un-organised.

The first couplet identifies the overall genre genethliakon. The *dies* prophesied by the *Parcae* at Messalla's birth must be the birthday which is now being celebrated, since the threads they weave are primarily the threads of time allotted to Messalla. That the *dies* is Messalla's birthday and not the day of his triumph is confirmed at 6, where it is revealed that Messalla's triumph has already taken place in the past, whereas the birthday is in the present.

Tibullus uses the prophecy of the *Parcae* to identify in 3-4 the addressee of the poem, Messalla, as the person whose birthday it is. The *Parcae* also ease the transposition from the genethliakon to the included triumph-poem in the second couplet, since both the birthday and the feats which won Messalla his triumph are prophesied by the *Parcae*.[11] The triumph-poem continues from these conquests of Messalla with a brief description of the actual triumphal procession (5-8). At 9-10 a notable sophistication allows Tibullus to reintroduce the theme of Messalla's conquests. It is a commonplace in several genres that the speaker should state how he stands in relation to the addressee;[12] one of these genres is the triumph-poem. The purpose of this topos is encomiastic. The normal form of the topos in the triumph-poem seems to be to dissociate the poet from the triumphing general by stating that the former has been living at home in security and peace while the latter has been ensuring this security and peace by winning his triumph abroad at the wars.

praeda sit haec illis, quorum meruere labores:
    me sit erit Sacra plaudere posse Via.
    Propertius 3 4 21-2 (cp. 15ff.)[13]

This is a device whereby the poet displays personal modesty and praises the general by a contrast with himself – a mere applauding spectator. Tibullus, however, treats the topos in the opposite way: he stresses his association with Messalla[14] by stating that he was a soldier in Messalla's army (9). The implication of this statement is that Tibullus has been a witness of Messalla's great deeds and is therefore a reliable source. We may compare the proverb *Pluris est oculatus testis unus quam auriti decem* (Plautus *Truculentus* 490).[15] The encomiastic implication of 9 also allows Tibullus to reintroduce a more detailed account of the conquests which have won Messalla a triumph, a piece of commendable structural invention. Messalla's warfare has covered terrain from Aquitania to Egypt and is described in 9-22. His arrival in Egypt calls forth a hymn to the Nile, which is identified with Osiris, who is in turn identified with Bacchus (23-50).

Perhaps it is not useful to ask whether this hymn is part of the triumph-poem or of the genethliakon, since the hymn may be partly or wholly a link-passage (see above). On the other hand the hymn is long and structurally important. We can therefore conjecture that it reflects the associations between Bacchus, triumphs, and dithyrambs discussed on pp. 95-7, and thus forms part of the triumph-poem. Indeed, if Tibullus was trying to equate his triumph-poem with a dithyramb, he could not have done so more clearly than by invoking Bacchus at such length at this important point in the elegy. But at the same time, whatever the hymn is or is part of, it forms an excellent transitional passage between triumph-poem and genethliakon. Both triumphs and birthdays were religious occasions. The identifications Nile-Osiris-Bacchus not only demonstrate Tibullus' Alexandrian learning and allow him to move from Egypt back to Messalla's birthday celebrations; they also allow the centre of this elegy to be occupied by a deity equally important in triumph-poems and genethliaka. In genethliaka Bacchus is the god of wine and so of social enjoyment; he is also the actual wine whose pouring to the *Genius* is the central feature of birthday celebrations.

Lines 50-6 briefly treat several genethliac topoi:[16] wine is offered to the *Genius* (50), perfumes are poured over him (51), garlands are placed on his head and neck (52); he is invoked (53) and given incense and honey-cakes (53-4); and his role as a begetting force is emphasized (55-6). At 57 Tibullus unifies the two themes of the poem further by exploiting this topos of generation. Messalla's progeny will *augere facta parentis*. The mention of Messalla's great deeds allows Tibullus to insert easily into the genethliakon six lines (57-62) dealing with the beneficial results of the victories for which Messalla triumphed: the road built by him out of the spoils of victory, in accordance with the custom that a triumphing general used part of his spoils to perform public works.

The insertion of a vignette, in which a farmer praises Messalla's road, allows Tibullus to allude to the triumph-poem before closing with a final genethliac topos – the wish for many years of life for Messalla (63-4).[17]

Another kind of inclusion occurs when one example of a genre includes another example of the same genre. The included example is usually, though not necessarily, a member of a different variant of the genre. This kind of inclusion occurs in Theocritus *Idyll* 14.

ΑΙΣΧΙΝΑΣ, ΘΥΩΝΙΧΟΣ

ΑΙ. Χαίρειν πολλὰ τὸν ἄνδρα Θυώνιχον. ΘΥ. ἄλλα τοιαῦτα
Αἰσχίνᾳ. ὡς χρόνιος. ΑΙ. χρόνιος. ΘΥ. τί δέ τοι τὸ μέλημα;
ΑΙ. πράσσομες οὐχ ὡς λῷστα, Θυώνιχε. ΘΥ. ταῦτ᾽ ἄρα
                    λεπτός,
χὠ μύσταξ πολὺς οὗτος, ἀυσταλέοι δὲ κίκιννοι.
5 τοιοῦτος πρώαν τις ἀφίκετο Πυθαγορικτάς,
ὠχρὸς κἀνυπόδητος· Ἀθαναῖος δ᾽ ἔφατ᾽ ἦμεν.
ΑΙ. ἤρατο μὰν καὶ τῆνος; ΘΥ. ἐμὶν δοκεῖ, ὀπτῶ ἀλεύρω.
ΑΙ. παίσδεις, ὠγάθ᾽, ἔχων· ἐμὲ δ᾽ ἁ χαρίεσσα Κυνίσκα
ὑβρίσδει· λασῶ δὲ μανείς ποκα, θρὶξ ἀνὰ μέσσον.
10 ΘΥ. τοιοῦτος μὲν ἀεὶ τύ, φίλ᾽ Αἰσχίνα, ἀσυχᾷ ὀξύς,
πάντ᾽ ἐθέλων κατὰ καιρόν· ὅμως δ᾽ εἶπον τί τὸ καινόν.
ΑΙ. Ὡργεῖος κἠγὼν καὶ ὁ Θεσσαλὸς ἱπποδιώκτας
Ἄγις καὶ Κλεύνικος ἐπίνομες ὁ στρατιώτας
ἐν χώρῳ παρ᾽ ἐμίν. δύο μὲν κατέκοψα νεοσσώς
15 θηλάζοντά τε χοῖρον, ἀνῷξα δὲ Βίβλινον αὐτοῖς
εὐώδη τετόρων ἐτέων σχεδὸν ὡς ἀπὸ λανῶ·
βολβός τις, κοχλίας, ἐξαιρέθη· ἧς πότος ἁδύς.
ἤδη δὲ προϊόντος ἔδοξ᾽ ἐπιχεῖσθαι ἄκρατον
ὧτινος ἤθελ᾽ ἕκαστος· ἔδει μόνον ὧτινος εἰπεῖν.
20 ἀμὲς μὲν φωνεῦντες ἐπίνομες, ὡς ἐδέδοκτο·
ἁ δ᾽ οὐδὲν παρεόντος ἐμεῦ. τίν᾽ ἔχειν με δοκεῖς νῶν;
'οὐ φθεγξῇ; λύκον εἶδες;' ἔπαιξέ τις. 'ὡς σοφός' εἶπεν,
κἠφλέγετ᾽· εὐμαρέως κεν ἀπ᾽ αὐτᾶς καὶ λύχνον ἄψας.
ἔστι Λύκος, Λύκος ἐστί, Λάβα τῶ γείτονος υἱός,

25 εὐμάκης, ἀπαλός, πολλοῖς δοκέων καλὸς ἦμεν·
τούτῳ τὸν κλύμενον κατεφρύγετο τῆνον ἔρωτα.
χἀμὶν τοῦτο δι' ὠτὸς ἔγεντό ποχ' ἀσυχᾷ οὕτως·
οὐ μὰν ἐξήταξα, μάταν εἰς ἄνδρα γενειῶν.
ἤδη δ' ὦν πόσιος τοὶ τέσσαρες ἐν βάθει ἦμες,
30 χὠ Λαρισαῖος 'τὸν ἐμὸν Λύκον' ᾆδεν ἀπ' ἀρχᾶς,
Θεσσαλικόν τι μέλισμα, κακαὶ φρένες· ἁ δὲ Κυνίσκα
ἔκλαεν ἐξαπίνας θαλερώτερον ἢ παρὰ ματρί
παρθένος ἑξαετὴς κόλπῳ ἐπιθυμήσασα.
τᾶμος ἐγώ, τὸν ἴσαις τύ, Θυώνιχε, πὺξ ἐπὶ κόρρας
35 ἤλασα, κἄλλαν αὖθις. ἀνειρύσασα δὲ πέπλως
ἔξω ἀποίχετο θᾶσσον. 'ἐμὸν κακόν, οὔ τοι ἀρέσκω;
ἄλλος τοι γλυκίων ὑποκόλπιος; ἄλλον ἰοῖσα
θάλπε φίλον. τήνῳ τεὰ δάκρυα; μᾶλα ῥεόντω.'
μάστακα δοῖσα τέκνοισιν ὑπωροφίοισι χελιδών
40 ἄψορρον ταχινὰ πέτεται βίον ἄλλον ἀγείρειν·
ὠκυτέρα μαλακᾶς ἀπὸ δίφρακος ἔπτετο τήνα
ἰθὺ δι' ἀμφιθύρω καὶ δικλίδος, ᾇ πόδες ἆγον.
αἰνός θην λέγεταί τις 'ἔβα ποκὰ ταῦρος ἀν' ὕλαν'.
εἴκατι· ταὶ δ' ὀκτώ, ταὶ δ' ἐννέα, ταὶ δὲ δέκ' ἄλλαι·
45 σάμερον ἑνδεκάτα· ποτίθες δύο, καὶ δύο μῆνες
ἐξ ὦ ἀπ' ἀλλάλων· οὐδ' εἰ Θρᾳκιστὶ κέκαρμαι
οἶδε. Λύκος νῦν πάντα, Λύκῳ καὶ νυκτὸς ἀνῷκται·
ἄμμες δ' οὔτε λόγω τινὸς ἄξιοι οὔτ' ἀριθμητοί,
δύστανοι Μεγαρῆες ἀτιμοτάτᾳ ἐνὶ μοίρᾳ.
50 κεἰ μὲν ἀποστέρξαιμι, τὰ πάντα κεν ἐς δέον ἔρποι.
νῦν δὲ πόθεν; μῦς, φαντί, Θυώνιχε, γεύμεθα πίσσας·
χὤτι τὸ φάρμακόν ἐστιν ἀμηχανέοντος ἔρωτος
οὐκ οἶδα· πλὰν Σῖμος, ὁ τᾶς ἐπιχάλκω ἐρασθείς,
ἐκπλεύσας ὑγιὴς ἐπανῆνθ', ἐμὸς ἁλικιώτας.
55 πλευσεῦμαι κἠγὼν διαπόντιος· οὔτε κάκιστος
οὔτε πρᾶτος ἴσως, ὁμαλὸς δέ τις ὁ στρατιώτας.
ΘΥ. ὤφελε μὲν χωρεῖν κατὰ νῶν τεὸν ὦν ἐπεθύμεις,
Αἰσχίνα. εἰ δ' οὕτως ἄρα τοι δοκεῖ ὥστ' ἀποδαμεῖν,
μισθοδότας Πτολεμαῖος ἐλευθέρῳ οἷος ἄριστος.
60 ΑΙ. τἆλλα δ' ἀνὴρ ποῖός τις; ΘΥ. ...τοισιν ἄριστος·
εὐγνώμων, φιλόμουσος, ἐρωτικός, εἰς ἄκρον ἁδύς,
εἰδὼς τὸν φιλέοντα, τὸν οὐ φιλέοντ' ἔτι μᾶλλον,
πολλοῖς πολλὰ διδούς, αἰτεύμενος οὐκ ἀνανεύων,

οἷα χρὴ βασιλῆ'· αἰτεῖν δὲ δεῖ οὐκ ἐπὶ παντί,
65 Αἰσχίνα. ὥστ' εἴ τοι κατὰ δεξιὸν ὦμον ἀρέσκει
λῶπος ἄκρον περονᾶσθαι, ἐπ' ἀμφοτέροις δὲ βεβακώς
τολμασεῖς ἐπιόντα μένειν θρασὺν ἀσπιδιώταν,
ᾇ τάχος εἰς Αἴγυπτον. ἀπὸ κροτάφων πελόμεσθα
πάντες γηραλέοι, καὶ ἐπισχερὼ ἐς γένυν ἕρπει
70 λευκαίνων ὁ χρόνος· ποιεῖν τι δεῖ ᾆς γόνυ χλωρόν.

This idyll as a whole belongs to the genre 'symptoms of love'. But 12-42 are an example of the same genre as the overall example. In the overall example (1-11 and 43-70), Thyonichus, the non-lover, interrogates Aeschinas, the lover, about certain characteristic symptoms of love which the latter is displaying, thinness, unkempt hair and moustache, pallor (2-6).[18] Aeschinas explains that he is in love with Cynisca, who is treating him badly, and that he is likely to go mad as a result of this (8-9). The included example (12-42) functions within the overall example as an explanation of how and why Cynisca began to treat Aeschinas badly. Once the origin of their breach has been explained, Aeschinas reverts at 43 to the overall example, with further description of his own sad state. He follows this with the notion that he will go overseas, a commonplace cure for love,[19] and become a soldier. Thyonichus praises Aeschinas' proposal and suggests Ptolemy as a good employer for a mercenary soldier.

In the overall genre the questioner Thyonichus is not an *irrisor amoris* ('mocker of love') in the crudest sense, as the questioner sometimes is in these circumstances – compare, for example, Theocritus *Idyll* 10; but he is not a fellow-lover of the addressee either. And there are hints of scorn at love, and amusement at the lover's plight in some of Thyonichus' remarks to Aeschinas: the humorous comparison of Aeschinas to a pale, barefoot Pythagorean philosopher (5-6); the subsequent joke at Aeschinas' expense, when Aeschinas failed in his love-sickness to realize that Thyonichus was being humorous in his comparison of him to a Pythagorean (7). That there is some bite in this humour is confirmed by the slight huffiness of Aeschinas' reaction to it (8).

These hints do add up to a characterization of Aeschinas as a more subtle, more sophisticated 'mocker of love' than, for example, Milon in *Idyll* 10. Thus Thyonichus does not attack Cynisca, although sometimes the questioner in this genre does attack the beloved. Theocritus was probably intending Aeschinas' own attacks on Cynisca within the in-cluded generic example to take the place of the topos of an attack on the beloved in the overall example, an interesting reversal of role for the lover in this genre (see also below). But on the other hand Thyonichus agrees with the suggestion Aeschinas makes in the overall generic ex-ample about how he can stop loving Cynisca. This indicates that he agrees with Aeschinas' strictures on Cynisca.

In the included example (12-42) the roles of questioner and lover are switched. Whereas in the overall example Aeschinas was the lover who answered the questions and Cynisca was the beloved about whom the questions were asked, in the included example Aeschinas is the ques-tioner, Cynisca the lover, and the beloved another man called Lykos. The tension and variation involved in this role-switching is intentional on the part of Theocritus. Naturally Aeschinas cannot function as an outright 'mocker of love' in the included example, since he is also the lover in the overall example; but in it he does have some hard things to say about Cynisca, the lover (36-8), as well as punching her on the head (34-5) and resolving to give up love (53-5). Moreover, when talking afterwards to Thyonichus, he does make a vicious attack on Cynisca's beloved, Lykos. Lykos is soft and he is thought by many people to be good-looking, a sarcastic remark, as the confirmatory sarcasm of the next line shows.[20] Thus the questioner in the overall example acts, albeit in a muted and subtle fashion, as a 'mocker of love', but does not attack the beloved; while on the other hand the questioner in the included example attacks the beloved and the lover, although he is not a 'mocker of love' at all but is himself the lover in the overall example. The inter-play between overall and included examples in this respect is a notable demonstration of Theocritus' generic skill. Theocritus exploits the fact that there are two different standard interrogators within the genre, a non-lover *irrisor amoris* and a fellow-lover, and he presents both in the one idyll in a paradoxical and contrasted way.

The included example of the genre 'symptoms of love' also has another generic function. It confirms the generic identity of the overall example and indicates the original setting of the genre, the symposium.[21] As in *Idyll* 10, another example of the genre (see below), and as in some other Theocritean komoi, the setting of the included example of *Idyll* 14 has been transferred from town to country, and again, as in *Idyll* 10, the transference is emphasized in small equivalences. In *Idyll* 14, the symposium is deliberately characterized as a country symposium.

The simple country food (14-17) is meant to contrast implicitly with finer town fare. Country boorishness is further contrasted with town refinement in the singing of a Thessalian song (30-1), and in the violent behaviour of Aeschinas (34-5). But whereas in *Idyll* 10 the transference is from town symposium to country hayfield, in *Idyll* 14 the transference is from town symposium to country symposium and so to a much closer approximation to the original context of the genre. Moreover, the people at the country symposium are represented as toasting their beloveds by name. Such toasting was one of the two symposiastic practices (the other being the playing of cottabus to the accompaniment of the beloved's name) which may have constituted the origin or original occasion of the genre. Whichever of the two practices did in fact produce the genre, it appears that Theocritus is implying that it was toasting.

The purpose of this close approximation of setting between the included example of the genre and the urban generic origin is fairly clear. The overall example of *Idyll* 14, like *Idyll* 10, occurs in a context far removed from the original urban symposiastic context of the genre. In *Idyll* 10 Theocritus trusts to detailed country correspondences with the original urban symposiastic context, and also to repetition (see below), to identify for his readers the genre within which he was working. Here in *Idyll* 14 he uses a different device. He includes in the overall generic example, which lacks any setting reminiscent of the urban symposium, another example of the same genre that is much closer to the original context of the genre than the overall example. Thus he signifies indirectly the generic identity of the overall example.

The same kind of inclusion can be found in Tibullus 1 6, although here the genre involved is erotodidaxis. A. L. Wheeler noted that the same and different erotic teachers can give different kinds of erotic instruction.[22] There are of course overlaps between the different kinds of instruction and the stock figures are not consistent in what they teach; but the following kinds of erotic teaching and teachers are worth distinguishing:

1. Instruction aimed at promoting a non-mercenary successful mutual love between a pair of lovers and given by a love-god, courtesan, experienced lover, or poet in the role of 'teacher of love'.

2. Instruction aimed at enabling the mistress to deceive her husband, or the man keeping her, or the poet's rivals, and so to confer her favours on the poet, and given by a poet as 'teacher of love'.

3. Instruction directed towards influencing the beloved to extract

money and presents from as many lovers as possible simultaneously to the detriment of impoverished, sincere, lovers of single beloveds like the elegiac poet. This instruction is given by a bawd or courtesan. In Tibullus 1 6 complex use is made of the different kinds of erotic teachers and teaching. The main body of the poem (15-86) is made up of four sets of erotic precepts together with, in some cases, the circumstances of their delivery:

(i) 15-42. Tibullus instructs the man keeping Delia to guard her from Tibullus' rivals or to give her to Tibullus to guard(!) This is an inversion of type 2 which amounts to type 1.

(ii) 43-56. The priestess of Bellona[23] prescribes fidelity for Delia and warns off Tibullus' rivals (type 1).

(iii) 57-72. Delia's mother is to instruct Delia in fidelity to Tibullus (type 1).

(iv) 73-86. Tibullus himself instructs Delia in fidelity to him and warns her of the penalties of infidelity (type 1).

It will be seen that these four sets of precepts are all basically of the same kind and that together they constitute a single body of erotodidaxis (see below). Their fourfold division is brought about partially by a substitution of addressee, that is where Tibullus instructs the man keeping Delia (i), and partially by the substitution of speakers in the parts where the priestess of Bellona and Delia's mother act for, and are substituted for Tibullus ((ii) and (iii)). Such substitutions of speaker and addressee will be treated in Chapters 8 and 9.

Preceding this example of erotodidaxis and following on the scene-setting of 1-4 is an included example of another type of erotodidaxis (5-14) in which Tibullus remembers how he gave Delia erotic instructions of a different sort to enable her to deceive the man keeping her (type 2). Delia is now following these instructions in order to deceive Tibullus himself. This inclusion is of course a piece of deadly irony, since it explains Tibullus' present plight and his need to give Delia quite different erotic instructions, this time instructions to be faithful to himself (type 1). Because the elegy begins with an included example of type 2 erotodidaxis, in consequence the first set of the erotic precepts which make up the type 1 erotodidaxis of the overall generic example consists of type 2 erotodidaxis, inverted so as to amount to type 1 erotodidaxis. This juxtaposition has considerable humorous effect (esp. 34ff.). The elegy as a whole exemplifies a peculiarly Tibullan mode of generic composition.

A further case of the inclusion within one example of a genre of a different variant of the same genre has already been mentioned on pp. 12-13. This is Propertius 1 6, where the overall example is Propertius' excusatory propemptikon to Tullus and the included example is Cynthia's schetliastic propemptikon to Propertius (5-18). The nature of 5-18 seems to be specified in 11 where *querelae*, like *questus* in Statius *Siluae* 3 2 90 (cf. 78), probably represents schetliasmos. Another such inclusion occurring in Horace *Odes* 3 7 is treated on pp. 209-11. As was noted above, it appears that an included example of the same genre as the overall genre is generally an example of a different variant of the same genre. But cases in which the same variant is found in both overall and included examples do seem to occur. Propertius 3 9, which exemplifies this situation, will be treated on p. 224. Another case is Horace *Odes* 1 25, already discussed on pp.88-9, where an overall komos includes another komos of the same variant.

It is convenient to end this chapter by mentioning two phenomena which might appear to be cases of inclusion but are not so. The first is exemplified in Theocritus *Idyll* 10 ('symptoms of love'), where the same generic material is worked through twice. There, 21-58 repeat the same themes as occurred in 1-20.[24] This cannot be classified as inclusion: speaker, addressee, and situation are all identical, and neither treatment of the generic material is more important than the other. Neither then can be said to include the other; one is simply a continuation of the other. The phenomenon is therefore nothing more than a highly stylized form of macrologia; it does not involve a constructive principle of genre since it does not alter or enlarge upon the primary elements. This is not to say that it is unimportant from a literary point of view. It allows Theocritus to obtain a thematic symmetry in *Idyll* 10, and it also helps Theocritus' readers to identify the genre of the poem. Just as in *Idyll* 14 Theocritus helped the reader to understand that the overall example belonged to the genre 'symptoms of love' by including a variant of this genre in a context much closer to the original generic situation, so in *Idyll* 10, as well as providing equivalent details in the country context to those normally found in the symposium, Theocritus has also assisted his readers by going through the same generic pattern twice.

A similar example, not of a twofold but of a fourfold repetition of the generic material, has already been seen in this chapter in Tibullus 1 6 (erotodidaxis). Here the poet's motive is not to ease identification of the genre, which is obvious, but to represent a psychological state in which Tibullus is so desperately eager to make Delia faithful to him that he will approach in turn the man keeping her, the goddess Bellona and her priestess, Delia's mother and Delia herself, hoping that the cumulative effect of these appeals and intercessions will achieve his purpose.

The second phenomenon (or phenomena) is when two or more themes, speakers, addressees, or speaker and addressee, are treated in combination or, in the case of speakers or addressees, have interests that are identified. Such occurrences, whether they involve a treatment of the different themes, speakers or addressees, in different sections of a poem, or whether the different themes are treated together, do not in themselves necessarily involve inclusion. Where inclusion is not otherwise demonstrable, such occurrences will fall under the constructive principles to be discussed in Chapters 8 and 9.

8

Speaker-variation

Up to this point, constructive principles dealing with subject-matter
have been introduced; now two further principles will be put forward
which concern the speaker and the addressee. By dividing the constructive principles in this way, we are following a division made by Aristotle
in a different context:

> σύγκειται μὲν γὰρ ἐκ τριῶν ὁ λόγος, ἔκ τε τοῦ λέγοντος καὶ
> περὶ οὗ λέγει καὶ πρὸς ὅν, καὶ τὸ τέλος πρὸς τοῦτόν ἐστι, λέγω
> δὲ τὸν ἀκροατήν.

Aristotle *Rhetoric* 1358A-B

Similar remarks occur in a discussion of proems in the same work (1415
A7), and they exemplify an ancient way of thinking about a speech or
part of a speech.[1]

In this and the following chapter we shall be studying cases where
there is some variation in the speaker/subject or addressee/object of
a generic example. From now on speaker will be understood to include
subject, and addressee to include object. To help us arrive at generic
distinctions in these matters, variation will be judged with reference to
artificial norms – common denominators of the speakers and addressees
of examples of all genres. We will now define the standard (common
denominator) speaker in such a way that examples of speaker-variation
can be treated systematically in this chapter as divergences from the
various characteristics of the standard speaker.

The standard speaker is a human being as opposed to a god or an
animal; he is distinct from the addressee; he is not a substitute speaker
but is himself the generic protagonist. In the public sphere, being the
generic protagonist means not speaking wholly or partly on behalf of,
or instead of, or with reference to the state; to do so would mean that
the state was the real generic protagonist. The standard speaker is not,
in other words, a public orator, or a speaker in some other public role,
or a chorus. In the private sphere, being the generic protagonist means
not speaking wholly or partly on behalf of, or with reference to, or in
place of another human being; for then that human being would be the

generic protagonist. Furthermore, the standard speaker does not employ a substitute speaker, that is, he does not have someone or something to speak on his behalf or instead of him; nor is he a joint speaker; and finally he stands in a certain status relationship with the addressee.

Where variation in the speaker has gone so far that in a particular generic example the standard speaker has been replaced by another, we shall speak of the standard speaker as the 'logical' speaker of that generic example in contrast to the 'actual' speaker, who is the substitute or vicarious speaker. Where the logical speaker is also the actual speaker of a particular example, he will simply be referred to as 'the speaker'. The same conventions will be observed in Chapter 9 when a substitute or vicarious addressee occurs.

We shall now examine variations from most aspects of the norm. Cases where the speaker and the addressee are not distinct, and matters concerning their relative status, will be treated in Chapter 9; in this way we shall acknowledge the fact that in ancient literature the addressee is more important than the speaker. In Chapters 8 and 9 care will be taken to distinguish apostrophe from genuine address: apostrophe is simply a topical sophistication; but genuine address makes the person addressed a principal in the generic situation. In both chapters also, more interesting variations will be treated at length, less interesting ones briefly.

Non-Human Speakers. A case in which the speaker is divine occurs in Virgil, *Aeneid* 1 65-75 (*euktikon*). A prayer is normally uttered by a human being and addressed to a god. But gods also sometimes need to make requests of one another, and when they do they can, as here, employ the prayer form. Virgil has made admirably sophisticated use of the possibilities inherent in this situation. Juno, a goddess of great power, is asking a favour of an inferior deity, Aeolus, who is, however, in a position to give or withhold this favour. Juno employs prayer style: *namque*, etc., 65 = δύνασαι γάρ, and it is followed by explanation of circumstances (67-8), request (69-70), and offer of reward (71-5). This fairly humble prayer, in which Juno does not recite her own services to Aeolus, as the genre would have permitted her, is counterpointed and supplemented with beautiful discretion in Aeolus' reply. He readily agrees to her request and continues with the reasons:

> tu mihi quodcumque hoc regni, tu sceptra Iouemque
> concilias, tu das epulis accumbere diuum

nimborumque facis tempestatumque potentem.

78-80

In these lines *du-stil* in asyndeton is used to echo and amplify the formulaic aspects of Juno's prayer. Aeolus graciously mentions in his agreement to Juno's request those former services of Juno to himself which Juno could have mentioned in her prayer, but with equal graciousness omitted to do so.[2]

Moschus I (*"Ἔρως Δραπέτης*, 'public advertisement') is another example of this sophistication. Advertisements are normally posted or publicized by men; but in this poem the goddess of love is the advertiser and she offers rewards suited to her personality. Much of the humour of the piece derives from the identity of the advertiser. In the 'public advertisement' the addressee is the person or thing advertised and not the potential finder or the general public. The addressee of Moschus I is therefore also a god, the runaway Eros, who is treated like a normal runaway human slave with yet more humorous results. The latter sophistication falls under the principle of addressee-variation (see p. 218). An animal is speaker in Homer *Iliad* 19 408-17, where Achilles' horse Xanthos utters a prophecy (cf. 420).

Substitute Speakers. A common type of substitute speaker acting on behalf of the state is the public orator, an everyday figure in the ancient world. He speaks on behalf of the city as well as, or rather than, on his own behalf. This may be because, in symbouleutic speeches, he is permitted as a citizen by the laws of the state to urge a public course of action upon the whole community; or it may be because, in epideictic and sometimes in dicanic speeches, he has been formally appointed by the state to speak on behalf of the whole community. There are many surviving and recognized examples of such speeches: Isocrates, Demosthenes, Cicero, and other orators and rhetoricians provide real speeches of public orators; Homer, the dramatic poets, Thucydides, and others provide imaginary ones.

Such public speeches, both real and imaginary, are well understood. However, when lyric and elegiac poets take upon themselves the role of the public orator, what they are doing is sometimes not fully appreciated. An example in which a lyric poet imagines himself to be a public orator is Horace *Odes* 3 14, where Horace utters a prosphonetikon welcoming Augustus home from Spain:

Herculis ritu modo dictus, o plebs,
morte uenalem petiisse laurum

Caesar Hispana repetit penatis
　　uictor ab ora.
5　unico gaudens mulier marito
　　prodeat iustis operata diuis,
　　et soror clari ducis et decorae
　　　　supplice uitta
　　uirginum matres iuuenumque nuper
10　sospitum. uos, o pueri et puellae
　　non uirum expertae, male nominatis
　　　　parcite uerbis.
　　hic dies uere mihi festus atras
　　eximet curas; ego nec tumultum
15　nec mori per uim metuam tenente
　　　　Caesare terras.
　　i pete unguentum, puer, et coronas
　　et cadum Marsi memorem duelli,
　　Spartacum si qua potuit uagantem
20　　fallere testa.
　　dic et argutae properet Neaerae
　　murreum nodo cohibere crinem;
　　si per inuisum mora ianitorem
　　　　fiet, abito.
25　lenit albescens animos capillus
　　litium et rixae cupidos proteruae;
　　non ego hoc ferrem calidus iuuenta
　　　　consule Planco.
　　　　Horace *Odes* 3 14

Horace's role as public orator is not entailed by Augustus' public office –
a man in public life could perfectly well be celebrated by a poet speaking
in his own private capacity.[3] What makes Horace's position clear right
at the beginning of the ode is his apostrophe of the Roman people (1).
They, like the girls and boys of the welcoming chorus (10-11), are not
substitute or joint addressees. It is Augustus who is the sole addressee of
the ode; he is the generic protagonist whose return the prosphonetikon
treats. The Roman people and the boys' and girls' chorus are apostro-
phized in the first section of the poem, much of which consists of mandata
(5-12). The apostrophe and the mandata are balanced later in the ode
by other mandata to a slave (17-24). The address to the slave is also

apostrophe and the slave is no more an addressee of the prosphonetikon than are the Roman people or the boys and girls. Horace, by introducing his own personal slave, is indicating that he is withdrawing from his public role. In the same way, the initial apostrophe showed that the prosphonetikon was imagined as publicly delivered by Horace in a public capacity.

By describing Augustus rather than addressing him directly, Horace displays reverence and so enhances the status of the Emperor.[4] He further demonstrates his own public capacity by describing the welcoming group (B17) under the guise of giving them instructions on the parts they are to play in the official welcome. The boldness of his commands to the wife of the Emperor (5-6), to his sister (7), to the married women of Rome (7ff.), and to the chorus (10ff.), can only be explained on the hypothesis that Horace is a public orator. Within the highly public utterance of the first three stanzas Horace includes in brachylogia many standard prosphonetic topoi: the statement of return (B1, *repetit* 3); the place where the returning traveller has been, namely Spain (B2, 3); the emphasis on home (B5, *penatis* 3); the danger the traveller has experienced (B8, *morte* 2); and his achievements (B9, *laurum* 2).

The saviour god of prosphonetika (B6) is at first sight absent; but instead of this topical and so anticipated saviour-god, Augustus himself is compared to the celebrated saviour-god Hercules. Hercules was also a demigod promoted to full deity after his good work on earth, Spain and the West included. In underlining the parallel between Augustus' and Hercules' activities in Spain, Horace is alluding to Augustus' predetermined, posthumous deification. Any possible tinge of blasphemy is counterbalanced in 6ff., where Livia and the rest sacrifice to the gods (B16) who have earned this honour by bringing Augustus home safe (B6). The expanded treatment of these topoi in stanzas two and three contrasts with the brachylogia of stanza one. But it should be said that Horace also introduces into stanzas two and three another topos of the genre, a welcoming group (B17) representing both Augustus' family and the state; the macrologia there is accordingly not over-pronounced.

Naturally, as befits both the importance of the persons involved in the welcome scene and also the public role of Horace, there are no tears, embraces (B4), or explicit priorities of affection (B12) in stanzas one to three;[5] in stanza two, however, Horace states Livia's affection for Augustus in a dignified way, and her appearance at the head of the welcoming group implies priority of affection (B12).

Scholars have often remarked on the difference between the tone of the first three stanzas of this ode and the last three. The transitional stanza four gives a clue to Horace's intentions. One group of topoi of the prosphonetikon to a governor expresses the joy and security of the city to which the governor has come (B 11):[6] stanza four begins to express the sentiments of Rome at the return of Augustus. Horace exploits his role as a public spokesman by conveying the joy and security of Rome in the form of a personal statement. He knows that this will be accepted as an expression of general feeling, since the public orator has feelings representative of the city as a whole.

In this transitional fourth stanza, the sentiments Horace expresses can easily be imagined to be general – freedom from care and from fear of violent death because of the security provided by Caesar's rule. But in the final three stanzas Horace allows personal statement to become even more personal: we have instructions to Horace's slave to prepare a banquet, orders to fetch the courtesan Neaera, and a Horatian reminiscence of Philippi. Nevertheless, the banquet of these stanzas reflects the topical 'welcoming banquet' of the genre (B 18), and the erotic hint about Neaera echoes the erotic element sometimes found in prosphonetika (B 19). Naturally Horace could not associate such activities with Augustus: this would have been unseemly; but he can introduce them in this indirect fashion in connexion with himself. In this way he introduces into the ode the generic topoi involving personal feeling which public considerations have suppressed in stanzas one to three.

The device Horace employs in this ode – apparent retreat from public matters to private considerations – is one which may well have been taught in the rhetorical schools and which is employed by public speakers in symbouleutic and epideictic speeches. It can be found, for example, at the end of Demosthenes *Orationes* 4, 10, and 16, and of Cicero's Second Philippic, and very prominently at the close of Libanius *Orationes* 14, 15, and 17. In each of these cases the public orator concludes by referring to something connected with his private life. In doing so he is not diminishing his public role; he is attempting to demonstrate the sincerity of his speeches in the public field by showing that he is also involved in what he is saying as a private individual. Here, then, Horace is showing that his welcome to Augustus is really heartfelt because he is celebrating it not only in his public capacity but also in his private life.

However, those parts of stanzas four to seven which refer to public matters should not be forgotten, since they continue to remind the reader that even in these stanzas Horace is still the public orator, representative and typical of the citizenry. The security he feels in stanza four alludes back to the concept of Hercules the saviour (1) and the young men *sospitum* (10). In the same way the *tumultus* and *uis* of stanza four look forward to those very public experiences, the Social War (18), the uprising of Spartacus (19-20), and the battle of Philippi (27-8). These latter public reminiscences about law, order and peace are not out of place in the last three stanzas : they come in the midst of sober preparations for an orderly, not a drunken celebratory banquet; and the courtesan is to be summoned quietly and peacefully, not in a riotous komastic manner. The enjoyments are those of ordinary, decent citizens, who, as long as Augustus is alive, can go about them without fear. Horace is not alone in having learnt the lesson of Philippi.[7]

The encomiastic method adopted by Horace in *Odes* 3 14 is at once the antithesis of the 'small voice in the crowd' topos and a synthesis of this and its opposite attitude. Here Horace does not do what he did at *Odes* 4 2 45ff., where he characterized himself as a small voice in the crowd and followed this characterization with his own humble sacrifice of thanks. Nor, like Propertius at 3 4 15ff., does he depict himself as a humble love-poet in the crowd, girl on arm, secure through the valour of his opposite – the soldier. Horace here steps first into the limelight and speaks for the whole of Rome; then, without ever actually abandoning his public role, he gradually retires from it, so that the partial guise of a private personality can give more potency to his public welcome.

It is sometimes easier for a poet to make it clear that he is imagining himself to be a public orator speaking for the state if he takes upon himself not the general role of public orator, but another more specific role associated with public speech. A poem employing this device is Horace *Epode* 16 (protreptic). Scholars have realized that in this long poem Horace has a public role and is addressing a political assembly ; but there is no agreement on the precise nature either of the role or of the assembly.[8] In fact, Horace tells us what the role is in fairly clear terms : he refers to himself as *me uate* in the last line. *Vates* means both 'poet' and 'prophet', and the ambiguity of the term is doubtless deliberate. If Fraenkel was correct in thinking that Horace was obliged to take steps to avoid the social censure that a freedman's son might incur by appearing to make a public proposal to a Roman assembly, the meaning 'poet' would relieve him of this stricture.

But the other meaning (prophet) is paramount. The role of prophet is of great importance throughout, and *me uate* is no afterthought: the whole epode is full of sacral material suited to such a speaker. The situation unfolded in 1-8 is interpreted in 9 in a way characteristic of such personages, that is, in terms of the moral degeneracy and religious accursedness of the Roman people. The *uates* proceeds in 10-14 to prophesy the destruction of Rome; he proposes emigration (17ff.); he states that the omens for sailing are good (23-4); he not only suggests that an oath be taken never to return to Rome but actually dictates the terms of the oath (25ff.). These specifically sacral actions which the *uates* performs explain how he comes to be making the proposal, since public policy in antiquity was directed only by priests and prophets when important religious considerations were involved.

The role Horace has chosen in *Epode* 16 has much to do with one notable feature of the poem: although some of his language suggests the technical terminology of public assemblies, the body he is addressing cannot be identified with any particular Roman assembly. What seems to be happening is this: Horace, perhaps faithful to the spirit of his Archilochan model, is thinking about a long tradition of emigrations, both total and partial, in the Greek and Roman world. *Epode* 16 presents concepts found in many ancient accounts of migrations: a disaster, interpretation of it as a sign of divine anger, and an oracle or other sacral advice proposing emigration as a solution.[9] Not all emigrations involved all these factors; but they are all well attested, together and apart. One of the most interesting emigrations which did involve a prophet is the colonization of Thurii as a Panhellenic colony under the auspices of Athens in 443 BC. The prophet Lampon was not only one of the founders of Thurii but also made proposals in the Athenian assembly about the project.[10] We can see that within the whole tradition of emigrations, both Greek and Italian, Horace was thinking more about Greek examples: in 17-18 he refers by name to the Phocaeans, who emigrated in a body from Phocaea, *c.* 545 BC, rather than submit to Persian conquest. Moreover, the oath Horace proposes for the Romans (25-6) is an amplified version of the oath recorded by Herodotus as having been sworn by the emigrating Phocaeans.[11] In these circumstances it is hardly surprising that Horace should have deliberately left the nature of the assembly he is addressing unclear; he wanted his audience to think not of any particular Roman body but rather of a body non-existent at Rome – an imaginary equivalent of the whole citizen body which would normally have decided questions of emigration in Greek cities.

In *Epode* 16, a public protreptic, Horace felt it necessary to assume the role of prophet in order to make his position clear. This fact may highlight a difference between Greek and Roman political life: in Greece a man could address assemblies and be appointed a public orator on grounds of oratorical merit or of common sense as well as of political importance; in Rome political importance was the one qualification. This may explain why Horace, the as yet little-known poet, felt it necessary to adopt a specific role in *Epode* 16: he was trying not so much to escape social censure as to represent himself adequately as a public speaker.

Perhaps Propertius, whose normal image was very far from a public orator, felt it even more necessary to adopt another sacral role, that of augur, when addressing a propemptikon to the Roman army (and perhaps also to Augustus) in a public capacity.

> Arma deus Caesar dites meditatur ad Indos,
>   et freta gemmiferi findere classe maris.
> magna, uiri, merces: parat ultima terra triumphos;
>   Tigris et Euphrates sub tua iura fluent;
> 5 sera, sed Ausoniis ueniet prouincia uirgis;
>   assuescent Latio Partha tropaea Ioui.
> ite agite, expertae bello date lintea prorae
>   et solitum armigeri ducite munus equi!
> omina fausta cano. Crassos clademque piate!
> 10   ite et Romanae consulite historiae!
> Mars pater, et sacrae fatalia lumina Vestae,
>   ante meos obitus sit precor illa dies,
> qua uideam spoliis oneratos Caesaris axis,
>   ad uulgi plausus saepe resistere equos,
> 15 inque sinu carae nixus spectare puellae
>   incipiam et titulis oppida capta legam,
> tela fugacis equi et bracati militis arcus,
>   et subter captos arma sedere duces!
> ipsa tuam serua prolem, Venus: hoc sit in aeuum,
> 20   cernis ab Aenea quod superesse caput.
> praeda sit haec illis, quorum meruere labores:
>   me sat erit Sacra plaudere posse Via.
> Propertius 3 4

In addition to the difficulty of his own normal personal image, Propertius faced a further problem caused by the epideictic character of the propemptikon. This prevented Propertius from adopting the guise of a Greek symbouleutic speaker, a guise easier to adopt than that of a public epideictic orator, because the former was self-appointed, the latter appointed by the state.

The role of augur is a natural one for a propemptic speaker. In the early Republic a great variety of actions were preceded at Rome by the taking of auspices.[12] Even in the Augustan age private journeys could be preceded by consideration of omens;[13] and for public departures the taking of auspices and the procural of good omens was considered of great importance. No one had forgotten Crassus' ill-omened departure for the East in 55 B C and the disaster which followed.[14] Indeed, Propertius 3 4 9 contrasts Crassus' ill-omened departure with the well-omened departure of the army of Augustus.

Propertius 3 4 naturally contains no schetliasmos. The Roman army is going abroad on public duty and so is in the same category as a governor. The propemptikon is therefore addressed by an inferior to a superior and so is characterized by encomium (see Chapters 1 and 9). The Roman motives for departure[15] – wealth, military glory and territorial expansion – are stated with unabashed admiration (1-6). The tone of the propemptikon is totally and directly encomiastic: the gaining of wealth and *deus Caesar* are placed in a single line (1); the idea of Roman conquest is linked with Jupiter (3-6), and it is cast in the sacral form of prophecy. This, as well as being appropriate to Propertius' augural role, consecrates Roman aggression as the will of destiny.

The remainder of the propemptic material is also subtly adapted to Propertius' theme and his character as augur. The command or injunction to go,[16] typical of the propemptikon, is repeated in 7 and 10, and in 7-10 the Roman army is commanded simultaneously to be successful and to perform the sacred task of expiating Crassus' defeat. In these lines, too, Propertius declares that the omens are good – the specific task of the augur (9). The prayers for the army which follow are not to the gods of journeys but – a much more apt touch – to the Roman war-god Mars and to the flame of Vesta, the heart and symbol of Rome on whose behalf the expedition is being mounted.

At line 12 Propertius does something well paralleled in the propemptikon.[17] He begins an included anticipation of the return of the propemptic addressee, in this case the Roman army. The way in which the included genre is introduced is typical: prayers turn out to be for the return,[18] instead of for the outward journey. But it should be noted that

Propertius' prayers contrive to unite the two functions, since they are prayers for a triumph, which implies success abroad as well as a safe return. What is outstanding is that the included example is not a prosphonetikon but a triumph-poem. In this, Propertius is innovating further upon the common habit of writing examples of travel genres which include examples of other travel genres: his propemptikon includes a member of a non-travel genre. At the same time Propertius is enhancing his propemptic good wishes for the army by anticipating the form of return relevant to a successful army, namely the triumph. He seeks to relate the triumph-poem to the propemptikon by stressing those aspects of the former which are contiguous to elements of the public prosphonetikon (cp. Horace *Odes* 3 14); in this way he attempts to make the substitution of the one for the other appear natural.

We cannot, of course, argue from this inclusion that Propertius believed the triumph-poem to be a specialized form of prosphonetikon, and not a dithyramb. Such a hypothesis would conflict with the dithyrambic evidence discussed in Chapter 3; and in any case most Roman triumph-poems are quite unlike prosphonetika. Furthermore, Propertius in 3 4 1-2 appears to be urging the dithyrambic connexions of the triumph-poem by beginning his propemptikon with an unmistakable allusion to Bacchus. The link Propertius makes between *deus Caesar* and the Indians would inevitably have suggested Bacchus to an ancient audience. This fact also explains what otherwise might have seemed over obvious flattery of Augustus; for to suggest a connexion between Augustus and Bacchus, who like Hercules (cp. Horace *Odes* 3 14) was a great benefactor of man and like him had won god-head for his benefactions, was to link deification of Augustus with a concept respectable in philosophic circles. At 19-20 Propertius seems once more to be handling propemptic material when he makes a prayer to Venus like that made to Mars and Vesta at 11ff.; and we might feel that a genuine intermingling of the topoi of two genres is occurring here rather than an inclusion. But the prayers to all three gods are simply hinges on which the triumph material is introduced and it is impossible to attach such hinges to either genre exclusively.[19]

Two problems remain concerning this elegy: first the place of Augustus in it, and second the apparent return of Propertius to a private role in the latter part of the elegy (15ff.). Augustus occupies the three places of honour in Propertius 3 4: the beginning (1), the middle (13) and the end (19-20); and yet it is never clear whether Augustus is setting out with the army. The reason for this obscurity is, I believe, that Augustus was already in the East awaiting the arrival of the army Propertius describes as leaving Rome. The date of 3 4 is uncertain, but Book 3 as a whole appears to have been written within the years 25 to 20 BC and probably within the years 24 to 21 BC.[20] Augustus was in Asia from 23 to 19 BC. If Augustus was abroad when 3 4 was written, as seems likely, Propertius was in a delicate position: he could not represent Augustus as leading his army from Rome since this would have been manifestly untrue; on the other hand he would not wish to stress Augustus' absence. So he probably obfuscated the matter by representing Augustus as leading his army eastwards, although not specifically from Rome (1).

The address to the army (3), like the apostrophe *o plebs* in Horace *Odes* 3 14 1, makes it clear that Propertius is speaking in a public capacity. It is of course different from the Horatian apostrophe: the Roman people there were not true addressees; but the army here is the logical and actual addressee, since it is leaving for the East. As well as showing Propertius to be a public speaker, the address to the Roman army also helps to cover up the deliberate silence about Augustus' whereabouts. In the second half of the poem Propertius concentrates on Augustus' triumphal return, because in this context he can represent Augustus as leading the army. In all these ways the encomiastic significance of the propemptikon is extended to Augustus, although he is not a joint addressee of the propemptikon but only of the included triumph-poem.

The second problem – the apparent inconsistency between the augur of the first part of 3 4 and the elegiac lover-poet of the second – can be treated partly in the same terms as the parallel Horatian problem in *Odes* 3 14. The sincerity of Propertius' rejoicing at Augustus' triumph is displayed by his private celebratory behaviour, and he can introduce this material without infringing the rules for making public speeches. In the case of both Horace and Propertius a poetic motive is also visible. The poets, although adopting the roles of public speakers, intend their readers to remain fully aware that a lyric poem and elegy are being composed. There is no attempt to hoodwink the reader into thinking that they are listening to a real public orator. The return to a more characteristic pose at the end of both poems, with the lyric poet at a banquet and the elegiac poet with his girl-friend, is partly an acknowledgement that the works are lyric and elegiac poems imagined as public speeches and not mimicries of public speeches. In addition, in the case of

Propertius, the augur role is found only in the propemptic section and the elegiac lover role only in the triumph-poem. In antiquity sacral personages were only clerical when performing their sacred functions. The augur going through a solemn ritual at one moment would normally be behaving like everyone else the next. If he were a member of the college of augurs, the proper body to supply an official for a public event like the departure of an army, he would not be a full-time professional but someone who had another profession and also practised public augury. So there is no real inconsistency. The augur functions in propemptic circumstances but not at triumphs. If he is also an elegiac love-poet, he may be in the streets at a triumph with his girl in tow, contrasting implicitly and encomiastically his own erotic idleness with the valour of men of war[21] – and perhaps even making the contrast explicit, as does Propertius in 21-2.

It should not be assumed that the role of augur always gives the poet adopting it the status of a public orator. In *Odes* 3 27 Horace delivers a propemptikon in this role (*auspex*) but retains the persona of a private citizen. It is worth quoting and discussing the propemptic section here because other aspects of *Odes* 3 27 have already been treated in chapter 2 (see pp. 67ff.).

Impios parrae recinentis omen
ducat et praegnas canis aut ab agro
raua decurrens lupa Lanuuino
    fetaque uulpes:
5 rumpat et serpens iter institutum
si per obliquum similis sagittae
terruit mannos: ego cui timebo
    prouidus auspex,
antequam stantis repetat paludes
10 imbrium diuina auis imminentum,
oscinem coruum prece suscitabo
    solis ab ortu.
sis licet felix ubicumque mauis,
et memor nostri, Galatea, uiuas,
15 teque nec laeuus uetet ire picus
    nec uaga cornix.
sed uides quanto trepidet tumultu
pronus Orion. ego quid sit ater

Hadriae noui sinus et quid albus
20   peccet Iapyx.
hostium uxores puerique caecos
sentiant motus orientis Austri et
aequoris nigri fremitum et trementis
      uerbere ripas.
25 sic et Europe niueum doloso
credidit tauro latus et scatentem
beluis pontum mediasque fraudes
      palluit audax.
nuper in pratis studiosa florum et
30 debitae Nymphis opifex coronae,
nocte sublustri nihil astra praeter
      uidit et undas.
quae simul centum tetigit potentem
oppidis Creten . . .
      Horace *Odes* 3 27 1-34

Besides the interest of the augur (*auspex*) role adopted by Horace, *Odes*
3 27 is also generically interesting in another way. It is one of those
propemptika where no explicit schetliasmos occurs but where one is
indirectly implied.[22]

Horace can adopt the augural role for two reasons: private citizens
setting off on a journey could have auspices taken on their behalf just as
could public men; and a private citizen who felt a calling to augury
could set up as a private augur without public appointment.[23] Horace
does not become a public orator by adopting the role; but he does become
consciously more self-important. This contrasts amusingly with the
matter on hand – the departure of Galatea with another lover (see
below), a situation parallel to that of Propertius 1 8, where the poet is
being abandoned by his mistress for a preferred rival. Horace keeps his
dignity partly through his role and its concomitants, pompous augural
language and the apparatus of omen-mongering. The augural content
of the first four stanzas is an amplification of the good wishes for a fair
voyage normally directed towards the propemptic addressee.[24] In this
ode the departing traveller is called Galatea. This is a joking allusion to
the fact that Galatea is sometimes one of the sea-gods asked to protect
the traveller in a propemptikon.[25] It is also a warning that the propemptikon is not completely serious. In 13-14, Horace adds general good wishes

and the 'remember me' topos.[26] The continued augural pronouncements terminate in the sixth stanza in a second *apopompe* (banishment of evil) parallel to that of the first two stanzas.

It is in stanzas five and six that the significance of Horace's oddly negative way of making good wishes becomes clear. There it becomes apparent that the seemingly non-schetliastic good wishes cloak an implicit schetliasmos to which Horace's role as augur adds authority. The good wishes are for the most part negations of the deterrent topoi of schetliasmoi – bad weather, a bad time of year, storms[27] – rather than simple wishes for good weather, and so forth. Horace's real disapproval of Galatea's journey is all the more effectively expressed by his pretence at suppressing it: the bad omens which Horace speaks of, however much they are discounted, are all the more menacing in the mouth of an augur, the recognized authority on such matters.

The implicit schetliasmos is continued in the myth of Europa: stanza eight, in glancing back at Europa's activities at home, employs the topos of picking flowers in a peaceful land setting; with this may be compared the topos of gathering stones and shells on the shore used at Ovid *Amores* 2 11 13-14 in a propemptic schetliasmos. Europa's sufferings on her sea-trip are described (stanza seven): she has the topical pallor of the storm-tossed and has visions of sea-monsters.[28] Her lamentations for her lost native land are long and vivid (34-66). All this is indirectly applicable as a prophecy to Galatea, and it strengthens the implicit schetliasmos previously addressed to her, since Europa has been introduced as a parallel to Galatea (25). At 66 Venus enters the ode: she consoles Europa with the information that Europa is the wife of Jupiter, that all is well, and that Europa will give her name to a continent. On one level these words of Venus are intended to be relevant to Galatea, and to convey the same explicit sentiments as the first section of the ode. Just as Horace explicitly wished Galatea well at the beginning of the ode, so her analogue Europa has a happy outcome to her voyage at the end of the ode. Horace also intends by the Europa-Galatea equation to inform the reader that Galatea too is going abroad with a lover, and that Horace himself is her rejected ex-lover. But the comparison falters, as Horace must have intended it to falter: neither part of Venus' consolation to Europa applies in substance to Galatea; she will not name a continent nor is she the wife of Jupiter. We must be meant to reflect that the device which Horace uses to provide a happy ending for Europa cannot apply at all to Galatea. So Horace's use of the Europa myth is intended to suggest that same blend of explicit good-willed acceptance of Galatea's departure and implicit doubts and non-acceptance which manifested itself in the first six stanzas. *Odes* 3 27 is therefore Horace's characteristically subtle treatment of that favourite contemporary subject, the propemptikon to the departing mistress. Both in generic and thematic terms, it shows a poetic mastery of a different and higher order from that of Propertius and Ovid.

A chorus acting on behalf of the community is often the speaker of hymns of various kinds. Sappho *Fr.* 2 (LP) is such a kletic hymn, summoning Aphrodite to a cult-epiphany in her temple on a public religious occasion.[29] With this we may contrast Sappho *Fr.* 1 (LP), likewise a kletic hymn to Aphrodite, but one spoken by Sappho, in a purely private capacity. I believe that many choric poems have not been recognized as such because of failure to understand the ancient convention that choruses can give themselves instructions and that these instructions are in many cases self-fulfilling. Examples of unrecognized choric poems are Callimachus' Hymns (especially 2, 5, and 6), Catullus 61, and Horace *Odes* 4 6. I have argued elsewhere that the last of these and also Horace *Odes* 1 21 are choric hymns, and that Horace *Odes* 1 2 is a paean imagined as being uttered by a chorus.[30]

A vicarious or substitute speaker can sometimes speak on behalf of another human being who is the real protagonist of the generic example. Two short kletic hymns show this in its simplest form:

Ἁ Κύπρον, ἅ τε Κύθηρα, καὶ ἃ Μίλητον ἐποιχνεῖς,
καὶ καλὸν Συρίης ἱπποκρότου δάπεδον,
ἔλθοις ἵλαος Καλλιστίῳ, ἣ τὸν ἐραστὴν
οὐδέ ποτ᾽ οἰκείων ὦσεν ἀπὸ προθύρων.
A.P. 12 131 (Posidippus)

O Venus, regina Cnidi Paphique,
sperne dilectam Cypron et uocantis
ture te multo Glycerae decoram
    transfer in aedem.
5 feruidus tecum puer et solutis
Gratiae zonis properentque Nymphae
et parum comis sine te Iuuentas
    Mercuriusque.
Horace *Odes* 1 30

In each case the poet summons Aphrodite (Venus) to come to a courtesan. In Posidippus' epigram the summoning of Aphrodite to help Kallistion is followed by a statement that Kallistion has never refused a lover. This juxtaposition carries the implication that Posidippus himself has benefited from Kallistion's generosity and so provides a reason – gratitude – for Posidippus' action in making the vicarious summons. Horace has a different purpose discussed elsewhere.[31]

A vicarious speaker in a more complex poem occurs in Theocritus *Idyll* 6 6-40.

ΔΑΦΝΙΣ

βάλλει τοι, Πολύφαμε, τὸ ποίμνιον ἁ Γαλάτεια
μάλοισιν, δυσέρωτα καὶ αἰπόλον ἄνδρα καλεῦσα·
καὶ τύ νιν οὐ ποθόρησθα, τάλαν τάλαν, ἀλλὰ κάθησαι
ἁδέα συρίσδων. πάλιν ἅδ᾽, ἴδε, τὰν κύνα βάλλει,
10 ἅ τοι τᾶν ὀίων ἕπεται σκοπός· ἁ δὲ βαΰσδει
εἰς ἅλα δερκομένα, τὰ δέ νιν καλὰ κύματα φαίνει
ἅσυχα καχλάζοντος ἐπ᾽ αἰγιαλοῖο θέοισαν.
φράζεο μὴ τᾶς παιδὸς ἐπὶ κνάμαισιν ὀρούσῃ
ἐξ ἁλὸς ἐρχομένας, κατὰ δὲ χρόα καλὸν ἀμύξῃ.
15 ἁ δὲ καὶ αὐτόθε τοι διαθρύπτεται· ὡς ἀπ᾽ ἀκάνθας
ταὶ καπυραὶ χαῖται, τὸ καλὸν θέρος ἁνίκα φρύγει,
καὶ φεύγει φιλέοντα καὶ οὐ φιλέοντα διώκει,
καὶ τὸν ἀπὸ γραμμᾶς κινεῖ λίθον· ἦ γὰρ ἔρωτι
πολλάκις, ὦ Πολύφαμε, τὰ μὴ καλὰ καλὰ πέφανται.
20 —Τῷ δ᾽ ἐπὶ Δαμοίτας ἀνεβάλλετο καὶ τάδ᾽ ἄειδεν.

ΔΑΜΟΙΤΑΣ

εἶδον, ναὶ τὸν Πᾶνα, τὸ ποίμνιον ἁνίκ᾽ ἔβαλλε,
κοὔ μ᾽ ἔλαθ᾽, οὐ τὸν ἐμὸν τὸν ἕνα γλυκύν, ᾧ ποθορῶμι
ἐς τέλος (αὐτὰρ ὁ μάντις ὁ Τήλεμος ἔχθρ᾽ ἀγορεύων
ἐχθρὰ φέροι ποτὶ οἶκον ὅπως τεκέεσσι φυλάσσοι)·
25 ἀλλὰ καὶ αὐτὸς ἐγὼ κνίζων πάλιν οὐ ποθόρημι,
ἀλλ᾽ ἄλλαν τινὰ φαμὶ γυναῖκ᾽ ἔχεν· ἁ δ᾽ ἀίοισα
ζαλοῖ μ᾽, ὦ Παιάν, καὶ τάκεται, ἐκ δὲ θαλάσσας
οἰστρεῖ παπταίνοισα ποτ᾽ ἄντρα τε καὶ ποτὶ ποίμνας.
σίξα δ᾽ ὑλακτεῖν νιν καὶ τᾷ κυνί· καὶ γὰρ ὅκ᾽ ἤρων,
30 αὐτᾶς ἐκνυζεῖτο ποτ᾽ ἰσχία ῥύγχος ἔχοισα.
ταῦτα δ᾽ ἴσως ἐσορεῦσα ποεῦντά με πολλάκι πεμψεῖ
ἄγγελον. αὐτὰρ ἐγὼ κλᾳξῶ θύρας ἔστε κ᾽ ὀμόσσῃ

αὐτά μοι στορεσεῖν καλὰ δέμνια τᾶσδ' ἐπὶ νάσω·
καὶ γάρ θην οὐδ' εἶδος ἔχω κακὸν ὥς με λέγοντι.
35 ἦ γὰρ πρᾶν ἐς πόντον ἐσέβλεπον, ἦς δὲ γαλάνα,
καὶ καλὰ μὲν τὰ γένεια, καλὰ δέ μευ ἀ μία κώρα,
ὡς παρ' ἐμὶν κέκριται, κατεφαίνετο, τῶν δέ τ' ὀδόντων
λευκοτέραν αὐγὰν Παρίας ὑπέφαινε λίθοιο.
ὡς μὴ βασκανθῶ δὲ τρὶς εἰς ἐμὸν ἔπτυσα κόλπον·
40 ταῦτα γὰρ ἀ γραία με Κοτυτταρὶς ἐξεδίδαξε.

The latter half of this komos (21-40, the song of Damoitas) has already been mentioned in Chapter 6 as an example of reaction. In this second song Polyphemus, who is the beloved and the komastic addressee, is allowed to make explicit the normal and usually implicit rejection by the beloved of the komast's pleas. One might have expected that, just as Damoitas' song is the direct speech of Polyphemus the beloved, Daphnis' song (6-19) would be the direct speech of the komast Galatea; but this is not the case. Instead, Daphnis acts as actual speaker on behalf of Galatea, the logical speaker, and narrates her komastic actions to Polyphemus. A clear and uncontrovertible indication that a komos is in progress is not given until 32, but hints are already provided by the setting of 6ff. – another town to country transference – and by various komastic topoi: Galatea's reproaches of Polyphemus,[32] Galatea's apple-throwing (6ff.),[33] and the comparison of her to a parched thistledown (15-16).[34] Finally, the dog which tries to prevent Galatea coming on land (13-14) may be meant to conjure up the idea of a house watchdog – compare *Idyll* 11 19-79 (komos), where the shore is the threshold separating Polyphemus and Galatea.

Besides the pleasure of generic ingenuity in itself for author and reader, two other reasons can be surmised for Theocritus' use of reaction and speaker-variation in *Idyll* 6 6-40. The first is mythological. In *Idyll* 11, where Theocritus showed Polyphemus, as komast, finally reversing his attitude and abandoning Galatea, he was probably inventing a myth to suit the real situation of his dedicatee Nicias. But in *Idyll* 6 Theocritus appears to have been thinking in terms of the common myth, according to which Polyphemus eventually won the love of Galatea and had children by her.[35] In order to show that this is what he is thinking of, and in order to make the unsuccessful komos of Galatea consonant with the eventual fruition of their love, Theocritus sets the komos of Galatea not in her mouth but in that of Daphnis. He thereby softens the effect of

Polyphemus' refusal, since it is not a direct one. Moreover, Theocritus employs reaction: he makes Polyphemus refuse Galatea's suit explicitly. But, at the same time, the refusal is qualified so as to imply the ultimate success of Galatea's komos: Polyphemus stipulates complete surrender on Galatea's part before he will love her (32-3); because he has the upper hand, this qualification implies that she will surrender to him completely.

The second reason for these sophistications is that the typical Theocritean tension created by them echoes the agonistic situation in which the two cowherds Daphnis and Damoitas sing their two songs (1-5 and 42-6). They sing in competition; but their competition is friendly, the songs are evenly matched (46), and the two competitors end with kisses and exchange of gifts (42-3). Theocritus makes it clear that this echo is intentional when he gives the specific information that of the two cowherds Damoitas is the older (3) and the lover – it is he who kisses in 42 – and Daphnis the younger (3) and the beloved (42); for the idyll is being paradoxical in showing Galatea as lover pursuing Polyphemus the beloved. That Polyphemus is really the lover playing the part of the beloved for tactical reasons, and that his love for Galatea is still strong and will come to fruition, is not concealed (esp. 32-3). The true situation of Polyphemus and Galatea, and its anticipated happy ending, are hinted at by the allotment and nature of the two songs and by what follows them. Daphnis the beloved delivers the komos on behalf of Galatea, and Damoitas the lover sings the qualified refusal of Polyphemus. The two songs are judged equal, and are the prelude to the love-making of the bucolic singers.

A simpler yet no less subtle example of a vicarious speaker can be found in Horace *Odes* 1 36. In its topical content this is a fairly standard prosphonetikon: Numida has returned safe (B7, 4); the gods responsible for his safe return (B6, 3) must be rewarded by the sacrifice (B16, 1-2) previously vowed to them (B15, *debito* 2); Numida has come from Spain (B2, 4); he is now distributing kisses (B4) to the welcoming group (B17, 5-6) and Lamia has the preferred place among the welcomers (B12, 6-7); the day is a lucky one (10) – a declaration which is an expression of joy (B11); the sacrifice will be part of a welcoming banquet, accompanied by drinking (B18) and by erotic activity centring on Numida, the returned traveller (B19, 18ff.). All this is so simple and normal that the one unusual feature of the ode might easily go unnoticed: Horace, the actual speaker, does not appear in the welcoming group. The logical speaker is Lamia and the emphasis which the welcomer usually puts on himself, and the primacy he gives himself, have therefore been transferred to Lamia. Similarly the account of the previous shared experiences of speaker and traveller – a topos of travel genres – deals with those of Lamia and Numida:

> actae non alio rege puertiae
> mutataeque simul togae.
> 8-9

Horace, then, is purely a vicarious speaker acting on behalf of Lamia. The purpose of this sophistication, besides its intrinsic literary ingenuity, is to enable the poet to confer praise on two people simultaneously, since the direct encomiastic effect of *Odes* 1 36 extends not only to Numida the returning traveller, which is normal, but also to Lamia the welcomer.

It may be objected that Theocritus *Idyll* 6 6-40 and Horace *Odes* 1 36 are quite different from *A.P.* 12 131 (Posidippus) and Horace *Odes* 1 30. The two kletic hymns, it might be argued, are genuine tripersonal examples. But in Theocritus *Idyll* 6 6-40 and Horace *Odes* 1 36 we have normal bipersonal examples, which are narrated rather than composed in the form of speeches. The sophistication would thus be formal rather than constructive. This objection can be rebutted for *Idyll* 6 6-40 and *Odes* 1 36 by the consideration that in them the actual speakers are not lay-figures but genuinely impinge on the generic examples. In the succeeding song of Damoitas in *Idyll* 6, Polyphemus speaks directly to his komastic lover, Galatea, without interposition of another person. This forces us to be aware that, in the speech of Daphnis, Galatea has not spoken directly as actual speaker, although she is the logical speaker, but that another speaker has taken her part. Daphnis is not merely narrator: the reader is meant to appreciate the interplay between the loves of Galatea-Polyphemus and Daphnis-Damoitas, and Daphnis' taking of Galatea's part is an important indication of this interplay with a real effect on the meaning of the idyll as a whole. Theocritus alludes at 32 to his own sophistication in 6-19. He makes Polyphemus speak not of Galatea herself coming in person to him to capitulate, but of her sending a messenger. The notion of such a vicarious speaker is found elsewhere in komastic circumstances and may be due to the commonness of go-betweens (often slaves) in ancient society.

In Horace *Odes* 1 36 the situation must also be considered genuinely tripersonal. Lyric poems are always the utterance of a strong *ego*-figure speaker and never of a lay-figure. This *ego*-figure may be the poet in his lyric persona, or a chorus, or the chorus-leader, or an amalgam.[36] *Odes* 1 36 is tripersonal because, although Horace explicitly refrains from exposing himself or his own personal interest, as lyric poet he remains implicitly prominent as the *ego*-figure speaker. He welcomes Numida on behalf of Lamia rather than simply telling us how Lamia welcomed Numida; while at the same time he does this in a studiedly impersonal way. It is the intentional contrast between the readers' expectation about the prosphonetic speaker and Horace's deliberate non-fulfilment of it which stresses Lamia the logical speaker so heavily. As in Theocritus *Idyll* 6 6-40, the meaning of *Odes* 1 36, in terms of the persons involved, is altered by Horace's device, so that a constructive and not a formal sophistication is present.

Another example of a vicarious speaker, in a situation which is tripersonal in the same way as the kletic hymns discussed above, is to be found in Propertius 3 12 (propemptikon):

> Postume, plorantem potuisti linquere Gallam,
> > miles et Augusti fortia signa sequi?
> tantine ulla fuit spoliati gloria Parthi,
> > ne faceres Galla multa rogante tua?
> 5 si fas est, omnes pariter pereatis auari,
> > et quisquis fido praetulit arma toro!
> tu tamen iniecta tectus, uesane, lacerna
> > potabis galea fessus Araxis aquam.
> illa quidem interea fama tabescet inani,
> 10 haec tua ne uirtus fiat amara tibi,
> neue tua Medae laetentur caede sagittae,
> > ferreus aurato neu cataphractus equo,
> neue aliquid de te flendum referatur in urna:
> > sic redeunt, illis qui cecidere locis.
> 15 ter quater in casta felix, o Postume, Galla!
> > moribus his alia coniuge dignus eras.
> quid faciet nullo munita puella timore,
> > cum sit luxuriae Roma magistra suae?
> sed securus eas: Gallam non munera uincent,
> 20 duritiaeque tuae non erit illa memor.
> nam quocumque die saluum te fata remittent,
> > pendebit collo Galla pudica tuo.

Postumus alter erit miranda coniuge Vlixes:
  non illi longae tot nocuere morae,
25 castra decem annorum, et Ciconum mons Ismara, Calpe,
  exustaeque tuae mox, Polypheme, genae,
  et Circae fraudes, lotosque herbaeque tenaces,
  Scyllaque et alternas scissa Charybdis aquas,
  Lampeties Ithacis ueribus mugisse iuuencos
30 (pauerat hos Phoebo filia Lampetie),
  et thalamum Aeaeae flentis fugisse puellae,
  totque hiemis noctes totque natasse dies,
  nigrantisque domos animarum intrasse silentum,
  Sirenum surdo remige adisse lacus,
35 et ueteres arcus leto renouasse procorum,
  errorisque sui sic statuisse modum.
  nec frustra, quia casta domi persederat uxor.
  uincit Penelopes Aelia Galla fidem.
  Propertius 3 12

In this propemptikon, which like Sappho *Fr.* 94 (LP) and Horace *Odes* 1 3 is delivered after the departure of the addressee, Propertius addresses Postumus on behalf of Postumus' wife Galla. Propertius was probably a relative of Postumus, a fact which explains on one level why Propertius felt he had a right to utter a propemptikon to Postumus on behalf of Galla. On another level the justification and effect of the sophistication involve literary considerations. First, this is a schetliastic propemptikon to a person who has already departed, a deliberate illogicality justifiable perhaps if the person on whose behalf the schetliasmos is being delivered is the traveller's wife. Second, Postumus is a soldier going off to the wars, and therefore is in the same class as a governor (cp. Propertius 1 6) or the Roman army (cp. Propertius 3 4). In normal circumstances Propertius would have been unable to deliver an explicitly schetliastic propemptikon to a superior addressee like this man. However, by speaking not on his own behalf but on behalf of Postumus' wife, Propertius is able to contrast Postumus' aims and reasons for departure, not with any hurt feelings of his own but with the softer and more justifiable emotions of Galla. In this way Propertius obtains a standpoint from which he is able to utter a schetliastic propemptikon to a person of Postumus' status.

The device is an important generic sophistication: it allows the encomiastic ethos of the non-schetliastic propemptikon to a superior to be maintained. This is because the feminine appeals and sufferings of Galla, which constitute the schetliasmos, highlight Postumus' ability to resist them and so emphasize his manly virtue – emphasize which complements other encomia of his valour in this elegy. Similarly the fears of Galla (9-14) for Postumus' safety are an indirect way of complimenting the fearlessness of Postumus in the midst of his dangers. Propertius' function as vicarious speaker is also to eulogize Postumus by implicitly comparing Postumus with himself, an unwarlike and unmanly elegiac poet. Propertius' skill as an eulogist extends to such subtle concealments of the encomiastic purpose as the attacks on Postumus at 5, where the traditional hostile association of war and avarice is trotted out in febrile and deliberately unconvincing tones. Because he is a third party, Propertius is able to combine indirect praise of Postumus, through expression of his own and Galla's anti-war sentiments, with open praise of military life, of Augustus and of Postumus as a man of war (1-2, 10).

Therefore, in technical terms, lines 1-14, although subtly encomiastic, constitute the schetliasmos of this propemptikon: they deal with the tears, fears and pleas of Galla, attack Postumus' motives for going,[37] and mention travails and dangers[38] (with a brief hint of an itinerary, 7-12).[39] It is not apparent at first sight whether 15-18 form part of the schetliasmos or not. But the conventional verbal signals that the schetliasmos is at an end, and that the encomiastic good-wish section is beginning, occur at 19 – the combination of adversative conjunction, injunction to go,[40] and good-wish,[41] namely *sed, securus, eas*; therefore 15-18 belong to the schetliasmos. They are apparently a macrologic variant of the schetliastic oaths-fidelity topos.[42] Galla has been and will be faithful to Postumus; Postumus, because of his infidelity – which in this case means his departure – deserves not the faithful Galla but a different sort of wife. But the element of open encomium may already have begun to intrude itself at 15 to provide a transition to the good-wish encomium section proper.

At 19 schetliasmos has ended and the good-wish section of the propemptikon begins. Lines 19-20, as well as signalling and reiterating Galla's fidelity, exemplify a variant of the 'remember me' topos so characteristic of this post-schetliastic section of the propemptikon as to be a propemptic topos in its own right.[43] It is not the addressee Postumus who is told to keep Galla in mind; instead, Propertius declares that Galla, on whose behalf the propemptikon is being uttered, will not keep in mind Postumus' cruelty (*duritia*) – a word which may represent the Menandrian second schetliasmos; she will rather, one presumes, keep Postumus himself in mind. This topos emphasizes the function of the second half of this propemptikon. In the schetliasmos Propertius was eager to imply, in contrast to what he says explicitly, nothing but praise of Postumus; he may then have felt that, in the elegy as a whole, Galla was in some danger of appearing to be a whining and unrealistic girl, no fit wife for a soldier of Augustus. In order to counteract this tendency Propertius first restates Galla's chastity in 19-22; he then goes on to devote the whole of the second half of the propemptikon to a macrologic treatment of this same theme, by means of a long comparison of Postumus to Ulysses and hence of Galla to Penelope.

This comparison has the advantage of justifying Galla entirely: it shows, by comparing her to the paragon of wives, that her feelings for Postumus are the natural feelings of a good wife rather than, as they might otherwise have seemed, mere emotional outpourings. In addition, although it concentrates on the theme of Galla's chastity, it nevertheless appears to keep Postumus in the foreground. This appearance is maintained by a list of the doings of Odysseus (Postumus) rather than those of Penelope (Galla). Thus, the theme of the first half of the propemptikon is in fact the virtues of Postumus, and of the second half the chastity of Galla. But Propertius has so modulated these themes that the propemptikon can paradoxically retain a normal appearance: it gives the impression that the first half, the schetliasmos, is concentrating on the grief of Galla and the second half on the virtues of Postumus.

In spite of the utility of the Postumus-Odysseus comparison, it is not immediately clear why Propertius should want to devote twelve lines out of thirty-eight in this propemptikon to a summary of the *Odyssey*. A generic approach provides some assistance: at 21 Propertius begins to envisage Postumus' return, and this subject continues until the end of the elegy; thus, in this as in other propemptika, a prosphonetikon is included. Only a few prosphonetic topoi occur in simple form – Postumus' return (B1, 21), in safety (B7, 21), through divine assistance (B6, *fata* 21), and the embraces of Galla (B4, 22). But these are enough to indicate the function of the *Odyssey* summary: it replaces the normal traveller's tales of the prosphonetikon (B13); since Postumus equals Odysseus, he will, it is implied, have many exciting and brave deeds to tell. We could further surmise that this prosphonetic material is a partial substitute for the absent itinerary of the good-wish section of the propemptikon; another partial substitute is 7-12, where the propemptic schetliasmos contains allusions to Postumus' journeys.

The fact that the summary of the *Odyssey* can be interpreted in these ways explains its presence in the elegy in one sense. In another sense we can still ask why Propertius did not simply describe Postumus' route, achievements, and so forth. In spite of the convention of humorous hits at the traveller's tales, the *Odyssey* summary is not meant to have a humorous effect. Although the comparison of the pair to Penelope and Odysseus might appear odd to us, the generic substructure of the elegy and the commonness of such heroic comparisons guarantee Propertius' seriousness. It is possible that Postumus was not of high military rank at this period;[44] in this case Propertius may have preferred the certain encomiastic effect of a vague, heroic comparison to the dangers of a truthful but anticlimactic, prophetic description of Postumus at war, or of an exaggerated description liable to meet with disbelief. Alternatively this propemptikon may have been written after Postumus' return from a peaceful tour of duty abroad or from an unsuccessful expedition. But this is simply guesswork.

What can, however, be noted relevantly and with certainty is this: in the most important of the Homeric passages from which the generic material of the prosphonetikon was originally drawn, the homecoming of Odysseus (*Odyssey* 23 205-350), Odysseus himself, when he tells his traveller's tales, does so in the form of a summary of the *Odyssey*. The Propertian *Odyssey* summary is part therefore of the identification of Postumus with Odysseus in that Odysseus' traveller's tales, as told by him on his return home, are set down in place of those Postumus will tell on his return home. Moreover, the summary also functions as a reference to the generic identity of the included prosphonetikon.

We have seen in Theocritus *Idyll* 6 6-40 a substitute actual speaker in a komos which contains a reaction on the part of the addressee. We shall now examine another Theocritean komos in which a reaction, in the form of a change of mind, is urged upon, or even assumed on behalf of the logical speaker by the actual, substitute speaker.

Σιμιχίδᾳ μὲν "Ερωτες ἐπέπταρον· ἦ γὰρ ὁ δειλός
τόσσον ἐρᾷ Μυρτοῦς ὅσον εἴαρος αἶγες ἔρανται.
"Ωρατος δ' ὁ τὰ πάντα φιλαίτατος ἀνέρι τήνῳ
παιδὸς ὑπὸ σπλάγχνοισιν ἔχει πόθον. οἶδεν "Αριστις,
100 ἐσθλὸς ἀνήρ, μέγ' ἄριστος, ὃν οὐδέ κεν αὐτὸς ἀείδειν

Φοῖβος σὺν φόρμιγγι παρὰ τριπόδεσσι μεγαίροι,
ὡς ἐκ παιδὸς Ἄρατος ὑπ᾽ ὀστίον αἴθετ᾽ ἔρωτι.
τόν μοι, Πάν, Ὁμόλας ἐρατὸν πέδον ὅστε λέλογχας,
ἄκλητον τήνοιο φίλας ἐς χεῖρας ἐρείσαις,
105 εἴτ᾽ ἔστ᾽ ἄρα Φιλῖνος ὁ μαλθακὸς εἴτε τις ἄλλος.
κεἰ μὲν ταῦτ᾽ ἔρδοις, ὦ Πὰν φίλε, μήτι τυ παῖδες
Ἀρκαδικοὶ σκίλλαισιν ὑπὸ πλευράς τε καὶ ὤμως
τανίκα μαστίζοιεν ὅτε κρέα τυτθὰ παρείη·
εἰ δ᾽ ἄλλως νεύσαις, κατὰ μὲν χρόα πάντ᾽ ὀνύχεσσι
110 δακνόμενος κνάσαιο καὶ ἐν κνίδαισι καθεύδοις·
εἴης δ᾽ Ἠδωνῶν μὲν ἐν ὤρεσι χείματι μέσσῳ
Ἕβρον πὰρ ποταμὸν τετραμμένος ἐγγύθεν Ἄρκτω,
ἐν δὲ θέρει πυμάτοισι παρ᾽ Αἰθιόπεσσι νομεύοις
πέτρᾳ ὗπο Βλεμύων, ὅθεν οὐκέτι Νεῖλος ὁρατός.
115 ὔμμες δ᾽ Ὑετίδος καὶ Βυβλίδος ἁδὺ λιπόντες
νᾶμα καὶ Οἰκοῦντα, ξανθᾶς ἕδος αἰπὺ Διώνας,
ὦ μάλοισιν Ἔρωτες ἐρευθομένοισιν ὁμοῖοι,
βάλλετέ μοι τόξοισι τὸν ἱμερόεντα Φιλῖνον,
βάλλετ᾽, ἐπεὶ τὸν ξεῖνον ὁ δύσμορος οὐκ ἐλεεῖ μευ.
120 καὶ δὴ μὰν ἀπίοιο πεπαίτερος, αἱ δὲ γυναῖκες,
"αἰαῖ", φαντί, "Φιλῖνε, τό τοι καλὸν ἄνθος ἀπορρεῖ".
μηκέτι τοι φρουρέωμες ἐπὶ προθύροισιν, Ἄρατε,
μηδὲ πόδας τρίβωμες· ὁ δ᾽ ὄρθριος ἄλλον ἀλέκτωρ
κοκκύσδων νάρκαισιν ἀνιαραῖσι διδοίη·
125 εἷς δ᾽ ἀπὸ τᾶσδε, φέριστε, Μόλων ἄγχοιτο παλαίστρας.
ἄμμιν δ᾽ ἀσυχία τε μέλοι, γραία τε παρείη
ἄτις ἐπιφθύζοισα τὰ μὴ καλὰ νόσφιν ἐρύκοι.᾽
Theocritus *Idyll* 7 96-127

That this song is a komos is not completely clear until 122-4;[45] but the komastic references in these lines are clear beyond doubt. The watch at the door[46] of Philinus by Aratus and also, as one presumes from the plural verbs of 122-3, by his friend and companion Simichidas, their walking up and down,[47] dawn coming upon them with its bird-cries while they are still at the door[48] — these are unmistakable, and reveal the genre of the whole song to be a komos. Lines 122-4 allow identification of other komastic topoi in the rest of the song: the topical threat to the beloved that his beauty is fading,[49] put partly and cleverly into the mouth not of the komast but of women, the natural competitors of a beautiful boy (120-1); the resort to a witch by the lover in the hope of getting rid of his love by magical means (126-7);[50] the attack on the lover's rival (125);[51] and the pitilessness of the beloved (119).[52] The prayers to Pan and the Cupids to bring Aratus' beloved to him are also topical in that they are substitutes for the normal pleas of the lover to the beloved.

What is unusual about this komos is that, as in Theocritus *Idyll* 6 6ff., the komast himself does not speak; the speaker is someone else, Simichidas, who speaks vicariously on behalf of the komast. This sophistication is more easily comprehensible here than in *Idyll* 6; komasts were often accompanied by friends or slaves,[53] and it is not unnatural that one of these attendants should speak on the komast's behalf; but the reason why the bucolic character Daphnis speaks on behalf of Galatea is at first more difficult to understand.

As well as having a substitute speaker, the komos also exemplifies reaction. This takes the form of change of mind on the part of the vicarious speaker which leads him to an exhortation that both vicarious speaker and logical speaker should together abandon the komos. Speaker-variation is employed so that the change of mind can be put in the mouth of Simichidas in order to imply that Aratus himself has not necessarily abandoned his love of Philinus. The substitution of prayers to the gods for pleas to Philinus is also connected with the change of mind in the komos. Although Philinus is the logical addressee of the komos, he is not the actual addressee. The gods are actual addressees (see p. 226); therefore Philinus does not reject direct pleas; the gods reject them or at most Philinus rejects indirect pleas. The fact that Philinus does not reject direct pleas further hints that Aratus is not necessarily involved in the change of mind. At the same time the pleas to the gods imply that the change of mind is sensible as far as Simichidas is concerned, because the highest powers operative in the matter – Pan the bucolic god and patron of countrymen and therefore patron of the characters of *Idyll* 7, and also the gods of love themselves – have been invoked by Simichidas without result.

The result of these generic sophistications is a literary artefact whose subtlety is increased by the withholding of the information that the song is a komos until near its end – in fact up to the change of mind. It is also a clear delineation of a psychological contrast between Aratus, unable to commit himself to the abandonment of his love for Philinus, and his friend Simichidas, able and willing to make such a decision for Aratus, but at the same time paradoxically himself hopelessly in love with someone else Myrto (96-7). Moreover, the pathos of the situation is enhanced by the fact that Simichidas, in advising Aratus to abandon an unsuccessful and harmful love, is doing what in antiquity was considered to be the duty of a friend in such circumstances,[54] while at the same time he is in need of such advice himself.

Two more small but clever touches in the prayers (103-19) may be mentioned: the rough threats to Pan not only produce bucolic credibility, but also contrast with the more humble and pleasing attitude of Simichidas towards the Cupids, a difference of approach which shows a realistic view of which gods have power to affect the issue. Moreover, the threats to Pan, should he not act on behalf of Aratus the lover, reflect in exaggeratedly humorous terms and so amplify the commonplace sufferings of unsuccessful komastic lovers. Pan is threatened with stripes (106ff.), biting and scratching (109-10), sleeping rough on nettles, that is, sleeplessness (110), excessive cold (111-12), and excessive heat (113-14). These are fit punishments for a god who neglects the komastic sufferings of Aratus – the heat of love (102), his rough nights at the door and weary feet (122-3), the chill of dawn (124).

In Propertius 2 16 we have yet another kind of substitute speaker:

> Praetor ab Illyricis uenit modo, Cynthia, terris,
>   maxima praeda tibi, maxima cura mihi.
> non potuit saxo uitam posuisse Cerauno?
>   a, Neptune, tibi qualia dona darem!
> 5 nunc sine me plena fiunt conuiuia mensa,
>   nunc sine me tota ianua nocte patet.
> quare, si sapis, oblatas ne desere messis
>   et stolidum pleno uellere carpe pecus;
> deinde, ubi consumpto restabit munere pauper,
> 10   dic alias iterum nauiget Illyrias!
> Cynthia non sequitur fascis nec curat honores,
>   semper amatorum ponderat una sinus.
> at tu nunc nostro, Venus, o succurre dolori,
>   rumpat ut assiduis membra libidinibus!
> 15 ergo muneribus quiuis mercatur amorem?
>   Iuppiter, indigna merce puella perit.
> semper in Oceanum mittit me quaerere gemmas,
>   et iubet ex ipsa tollere dona Tyro.

atque utinam Romae nemo esset diues, et ipse
20   straminea posset dux habitare casa!
numquam uenales essent ad munus amicae,
    atque una fieret cana puella domo;
numquam septenas noctes seiuncta cubares,
    candida tam foedo bracchia fusa uiro;
25 non quia peccarim (testor te), sed quia uulgo
    formosis leuitas semper amica fuit.
barbarus exclusis agitat uestigia lumbis –
    et subito felix nunc mea regna tenet!
aspice quid donis Eriphyla inuenit amaris,
30   arserit et quantis nupta Creusa malis.
nullane sedabit nostros iniuria fletus?
    an dolor hic uitiis nescit abesse tuis?
tot iam abiere dies, cum me nec cura theatri
    nec tetigit Campi, nec mea mensa iuuat.
35 at pudeat certe, pudeat! – nisi forte, quod aiunt,
    turpis amor surdis auribus esse solet.
cerne ducem, modo fremitu compleuit inani
    Actia damnatis aequora militibus:
hunc infamis amor uersis dare terga carinis
40   iussit et extremo quaerere in orbe fugam.
Caesaris haec uirtus et gloria Caesaris haec est:
    illa, qua uicit, condidit arma manu.
sed quascumque tibi uestis, quoscumque smaragdos,
    quosue dedit flauo lumine chrysolithos,
45 haec uideam rapidas in uanum ferre procellas:
    quae tibi terra, uelim, quae tibi fiat aqua.
non semper placidus periuros ridet amantis
    Iuppiter et surda neglegit aure preces.
uidistis toto sonitus percurrere caelo,
50   fulminaque aetheria desiluisse domo:
non haec Pleiades faciunt neque aquosus Orion,
    nec sic de nihilo fulminis ira cadit;
periuras tunc ille solet punire puellas,
    deceptus quoniam fleuit et ipse deus.
55 quare ne tibi sit tanti Sidonia uestis,
    ut timeas, quotiens nubilus Auster erit.
    Propertius 2 16

This elegy is an inverse prosphonetikon. Its logical addressee is that same praetor who in 1 8 was inviting Cynthia to accompany him abroad. He has now returned to Rome and is once more trying, apparently with success, to oust Propertius from Cynthia's affections. The prosphonetikon Propertius addresses to him expresses an inversion of the normal prosphonetic sentiments. But Propertius is not uttering the elegy from an independent standpoint: he is speaking with reference to Cynthia. His position is very like that of Simichidas in the latter part of his song in Theocritus *Idyll* 7. After the reaction has occurred in that komos, Simichidas is simultaneously trying to act for Aratus by abandoning the komos and trying to influence him to share his own viewpoint with, as is implied, dubious prospects of success. So in 2 16 Propertius is at once trying to speak for Cynthia in offering the praetor a non-welcome and trying to influence her not to welcome the praetor. Propertius' effort is both pathetic and paradoxical, since it is too late: Cynthia has already received the praetor (5ff., 23ff.). The result is that, although Propertius can be said to be a substitute speaker and to be acting on behalf of Cynthia, he cannot simply be said to be acting in her interests. Rather, he is acting in what he and not necessarily she considers to be Cynthia's interests and against the generic function of the prosphonetikon, so as to produce an inversion of that genre.

It will be seen that many degrees and types of implication in the function and subject-matter of the genres can be found in the substitute speakers in the examples so far treated. This ranges from (apparently) very little in the case of Horace *Odes* 1 36, to a little in Theocritus *Idyll* 6 6-40, to a fair amount in the case of the two kletic hymns, in Propertius 3 12 and Theocritus *Idyll* 7 96ff., to a great deal here in Propertius 2 16.

In the first few lines of 2 16 Propertius briefly handles many of the standard prosphonetic topoi, inverting them where this is suitable. Line 1 announces the return of the praetor (B1, *uenit*), states where he has come from (B2), and introduces as an interested party, Cynthia, who should be regarded as the logical speaker of the poem. Line 2 specifies the diverse nature of the concerns of the poet and Cynthia in what turns out to be both a forewarning of the more specific inversions to come and a programmatic anticipation of the two major themes of the elegy (see below). In 3-6 the inversion becomes open and apparent. Normally the prosphonetic speaker announces the safety of the returned traveller (B7), in spite of the dangers the traveller has experienced (B8), and rejoices in this safety (B 11). Propertius announces the praetor's safety by implication in 3, but at the same time, instead of rejoicing in it, wishes that the praetor had perished at Acroceraunia, the most dangerous part of the voyage from Epirus to Italy. Similarly, where most prosphonetika describe the paying vows to the gods for the safe return of the person being welcomed (B 6, 16), Propertius (4) says that he would be making great sacrifices to the sea-god Neptune if the praetor had perished. At 5 a 'welcoming banquet' for the praetor (B 18) is being held. A 'welcoming banquet' did not have to be held immediately on the traveller's return (see Plutarch *Moralia* 678C); in this case the praetor has been back for seven days (23). Propertius is no joyful participant at this celebration; instead he is excluded and the erotic aspect of the banquet (B 19) is in full swing in 6, with the praetor and not Propertius enjoying Cynthia.

The first six lines thus constitute a clear announcement of the genre of 2 16. This is necessary as a prelude to the presentation of subtle variations and amplifications of standard topoi; the mode of generic presentation is reminiscent of Theocritus *Idyll* 12, another example of the same genre. The remainder of 2 16 is for the most part made up of macrologic reiterations of two topoi. The first is the notion of the praetor as spoil for Cynthia (7-12, 15-32, 43-55). The specific provision of gifts to Cynthia by the praetor is emphasized at 7-12, 21-2, 29-30, 43-4. This theme is amplified first with rhetorical 'vituperation of wealth' material (15ff.): there Propertius blames wealth among other things for Cynthia's corruption by the praetor. It is also filled out with warnings to Cynthia that the punishment of perjury will fall on her (47ff.).[55] The second recurrent topos of the rest of the poem is the notion of the praetor as source of concern to Propertius; this is expressed specifically in 13-14 and 31-6, as well as colouring the whole elegy.

Both these reiterated topoi are anticipated in 2; in addition, they are in various senses inversions of normal prosphonetic topoi. Returning travellers normally brought back for their friends or loved ones small gifts from abroad, which were treasured for their sentimental rather than their intrinsic value.[56] Naturally we do not find mention of these gifts in prosphonetic speeches. It is because such gifts were given but are not mentioned in friendly prosphonetika that Propertius places so much emphasis on them in this inverse prosphonetikon. His purpose is to cast total doubt on Cynthia's motives for welcoming the praetor, and to insult the praetor as someone welcome only for his money. Propertius constantly stresses something connected with the return of travellers but normally

passed over in tactful silence. The inversion, in this sense, of a prosphonetic topos is a master stroke. It is combined with an instruction to
Cynthia that, when she has fleeced the praetor, she should tell him to be
off on his travels again (9-10). This expresses an attitude very far from
that of the friendly prosphonetic speaker, whose last wish was that the
returned traveller should once more depart.

Propertius' concern is the inversion of the normal prosphonetic
speaker's repeated exclamations and manifestations of pleasure at the
arrival of the traveller. Just as the friendly prosphonetic speaker tells,
sometimes at length, of the pleasant effects on him of the arrival (B11),
so Propertius tells how the coming of the praetor has soured his whole
life. The themes of spoil and concern could also be said to be interlinked
in that both are, in a sense, inversions of B11 – the joys and benefits
conferred on the welcomer by the arrival of the traveller. Cynthia the
logical speaker will get money, and by implication nothing else; Propertius the actual and substitute speaker will experience concern, the
inversion of joy.

Propertius in 2 16 spoke against the aspirations of the praetor, the
logical addressee of the prosphonetikon. This was because, as substitute
speaker, he was acting on behalf of the logical speaker Cynthia, although
what he said was contrary to her temporary desires. Horace in *Odes* 3 7
employs a slightly different sophistication: as substitute speaker he
acts against the aspirations of the logical speaker and in the long-term
interests of the addressee.

> Quid fles, Asterie, quem tibi candidi
> primo restituent uere Fauonii
>   Thyna merce beatum,
>   constantis iuuenem fide
>
> 5 Gygen? ille Notis actus ad Oricum
> post insana Caprae sidera frigidas
>   noctes non sine multis
>   insomnis lacrimis agit.
>
> atqui sollicitae nuntius hospitae,
> 10 suspirare Chloen et miseram tuis
>   dicens ignibus uri,
>   temptat mille uafer modis.
>
> ut Proetum mulier perfida credulum
> falsis impulerit criminibus nimis

15   casto Bellerophontae
          maturare necem refert:
       narrat paene datum Pelea Tartaro,
       Magnessam Hippolyten dum fugit abstinens;
          et peccare docentis
20   fallax historias monet.
       frustra: nam scopulis surdior Icari
       uoces audit adhuc integer. at tibi
          ne uicinus Enipeus
             plus iusto placeat caue;
25   quamuis non alius flectere equum sciens
       aeque conspicitur gramine Martio,
          nec quisquam citus aeque
             Tusco denatat alueo.
       prima nocte domum claude neque in uias
30   sub cantu querulae despice tibiae,
          et te saepe uocanti
             duram difficilis mane.
       Horace *Odes* 3 7

The result is that apparent impossibility, an inverse komos. It comes
about in the following way: Enipeus is attempting by komastic means to
gain the love of Asterie. Horace speaks as a substitute for Enipeus; but
instead of speaking to persuade Asterie to admit the komast Enipeus (as
the substitute speaker Simichidas in Theocritus *Idyll* 7 96ff. at first
tries to persuade Philinus to admit Aratus), he inverts the function of
the komos: he speaks to persuade Asterie not to admit Enipeus. Horace
specifies the genre in a few selected topoi delayed until the last stanza.
Asterie is told to shut up her house at nightfall, that is to close the door
(29), and not to look out; *despicere* (30) is the Latin equivalent of
παρακύπτειν (peep out), which is the characteristic behaviour of
komastic beloveds likely to open the door to komasts.[57] Enipeus will be
playing his *tibiae*, musical instruments frequently being part of the
accoutrements of komasts.[58] Enipeus will often call Asterie *dura*, as
komasts often attack their beloveds' cruelty,[59] but she is to remain unwilling (32). The komastic nature of this scene is unmistakable and the
retention of it until the end of the ode compounds the generic humour of
the apparently impossible inversion.

    o   *209*

Horace means us to look back from the last stanza to other komastic material in the rest of the ode, as does Theocritus in some of the Theocritean komoi previously discussed.[60] At 23 Enipeus is first mentioned. Horace asks Asterie not to favour Enipeus more than is right, even though he is a fine horseman and swimmer. When Horace talks about Enipeus' athletic prowess he is alluding to his good looks, the connexion between athletics and good looks being commonplace in antiquity.[61] In thus advising Asterie not to be swayed by Enipeus' good looks, Horace is inverting a standard komastic topos: the komast's use of his good looks as an argument for admission.[62]

In 5-22 Horace has employed the principle of inclusion; these lines are an example of another variant of the same genre (komos) to which the ode as a whole belongs. The included example is of an ordinary, not of an inverse komos. The use Horace makes of the included normal komos shows how skilled he was in handling generic sophistications. His injunctions to Asterie that she should not yield to Enipeus' komos are prefaced by a description of an analogous situation in which Asterie's husband Gyges, who is a merchant and abroad, is the object of an unsuccessful komos made on behalf of his foreign hostess Chloe. Chloe sends a messenger to Gyges to convey her feelings for him. We may compare Theocritus *Idyll* 6 31-2 for another messenger who speaks as a go-between on behalf of a woman in a komastic situation. The messenger tells Gyges that Chloe is in love with him and on fire for him, attempts his virtue in a thousand ways, and uses myths to try to persuade him to be unfaithful to Asterie and to yield to Chloe (13ff.). This included komos omits much of the komastic situation and relies upon the proximity of the overall example to clarify its generic identity in the eyes of the reader.[63]

It is noticeable in Horace *Odes* 3 7 that there is a substitute speaker in the included komos as well as in the overall komos. In the included komos the messenger urges Gyges the beloved to yield to the komast Chloe, as in contrast Horace in the overall komos is a substitute speaker urging the beloved Asterie not to yield to the komast Enipeus. The parallelism between the two situations goes even further: Chloe is Gyges' hostess, Enipeus is Asterie's neighbour; both thus have ready access to the objects of their komoi. Just as Horace tells Asterie a story about Gyges to persuade her not to yield to Enipeus, so the messenger tells Gyges myths to induce him to yield to Chloe. Moreover, the myths told by the messenger to Gyges present contexts identical with his own, in which women are in love with their guests. The myths also present to Gyges the hidden threat of a fate similar to that of the virtuous Bellerophon and Peleus, comparisons which give Gyges a heroic stature. In the same way Horace's tale to Asterie about her husband Gyges not only reminds her of his chastity, but also stimulates her to refuse Enipeus by showing her that Gyges is refusing Chloe in a context identical in every respect with Asterie's own situation, except that Gyges is also incurring personal danger by his refusal.

To round off this discussion, an example may be added where the use of a vicarious speaker is justified within the poem by a declaration of total identity of interest[64] between the actual substitute speaker and the logical subject (Horace *Odes* 1 7 – epibaterion).

> Laudabunt alii claram Rhodon aut Mytilenen
>   aut Epheson bimarisque Corinthi
> moenia uel Baccho Thebas uel Apolline Delphos
>   insignis aut Thessala Tempe:
> 5 sunt quibus unum opus est intactae Palladis urbem
>   carmine perpetuo celebrare et
> undique decerptam fronti praeponere oliuam:
>   plurimus in Iunonis honorem
> aptum dicet equis Argos ditisque Mycenas:
> 10   me nec tam patiens Lacedaemon
> nec tam Larisae percussit campus opimae,
>   quam domus Albuneae resonantis
> et praeceps Anio ac Tiburni lucus et uda
>   mobilibus pomaria riuis.
> 15 albus ut obscuro deterget nubila caelo
>   saepe Notus neque parturit imbris
> perpetuo, sic tu sapiens finire memento
>   tristitiam uitaeque labores
> molli, Plance, mero, seu te fulgentia signis
> 20   castra tenent seu densa tenebit
> Tiburis umbra tui. Teucer Salamina patremque
>   cum fugeret, tamen uda Lyaeo
> tempora populea fertur uinxisse corona,
>   sic tristis adfatus amicos:
> 25 'quo nos cumque feret melior fortuna parente,
>   ibimus, o socii comitesque.

nil desperandum Teucro duce et auspice Teucro;
  certus enim promisit Apollo
ambiguam tellure noua Salamina futuram.
30   o fortes peioraque passi
  mecum saepe uiri, nunc uino pellite curas;
    cras ingens iterabimus aequor.'

It should of course be observed that the device of a substitute speaker is one means whereby in a lyric example of a genre the logical speaker can be anyone different from the actual *ego*-figure speaker of lyrics.[65] The generic identification of *Odes* 1 7 goes some way towards solving old problems connected with it. At first sight the ode does not seem to have any obvious unity of theme but to fall into three sections, the priamel (1ff.), the central portion (15ff.), and the myth of Teucer (21ff.). Generic identification is rendered more difficult by the occurrence in the ode of two major sophistications. First, the epibateric situation is placed in the future (*tenebit* 20) not, as is normal, in the present – a formal sophistication (pp. 127-8). Second, Horace makes himself a substitute speaker for Munatius. *Odes* 1 7 is that type of epibaterion which is usually uttered by the returning traveller on arrival at his native city (Menander 382 10ff.). Horace places himself in the position of substitute speaker, Munatius being the logical speaker. This latter device, as well as having the technical justification mentioned above, allows Munatius' feelings to be expressed in an indirect and therefore dignified way. In order to explain it, Horace stresses the identity of interest which allows him to interpret and express Munatius' feelings vicariously: Horace loves Tibur so much (10ff.) that he can understand and describe how Munatius, whose home was Tibur (20-1), will feel on his return there.

The rhetorical account of the contents of this type of epibaterion (Menander 382ff.) does much to illuminate the subject-matter of *Odes* 1 7.[66] Menander's prescription can be summarized as follows:
(i) The returner's affection for his native city expressed in many ways including the following:

ἄλλοι μὲν γὰρ ἄλλοις χαίρουσιν, οἱ μὲν ἵπποις, οἱ δὲ ὅπλοις,
ἐγὼ δὲ ἀγαπῶ τὴν ἐμαυτοῦ πατρίδα καὶ νομίζω μηδὲν διαφέρειν
τὴν περὶ ταύτην ἐπιθυμίαν τῆς περὶ τὴν ἀκτῖνα, ἣν ὁ ἥλιος ἐξ
ὠκεανοῦ ἐκτείνει φανείς·
  Menander 382 19-23

'Some like one thing, some another: some horses, some weapons; I love my country and I believe that my desire for it is as great as my desire for the beam that the risen sun extends from the sea.'

(ii) Praise of the founder of the city.
(iii) A description of the city's physical features.
(iv) A description of the city's development(?) (ἀνατροφή).
(v) A description of the character of the inhabitants.
(vi) A description of the actions of the inhabitants in terms of the four virtue division, embroidered by comparisons.
(vii) A general comparison of the city with others.
(viii) Epilogue – the city and its buildings.
No epibaterion of return to one's home country, even a long prose oration, could be expected to include all this material in great detail. A poetic epibaterion, especially one written by Horace, would be expected to be brief and to shed some items. Horace *Odes* 1 7 appears to employ material from sections (i), (ii), (iii), (v), and (vii).

The priamel with which the ode begins (1-14) is an amplified equivalent of the priamel found in the generic prescription and fulfils the same function of indicating preference for the homeland. In the prescription the homeland is compared to other objects of desire, in the ode to other towns. Comparison of one's own homeland with other towns was conventional in rhetoric and later on in the epibateric prescription such comparisons are prescribed. The elaborate priamel at the beginning of *Odes* 1 7 therefore embraces topoi from (vii) as well as (i).

Interwoven into the final stage of this long priamel are topoi from (ii) and (iii), namely praise of one of the founders of Tibur, Tiburnus, and of the prehistoric native nymph Albunea, combined with descriptions of celebrated natural features of Tibur (12-14). The description of natural features continues in *densa umbra* (21) and the praise of the city's ancient history in the allusive reference to Hercules, the patron god of Tibur, within the myth (23).

The myth appears to belong to section (v) of the generic prescription, and the clue which points to this is non-generic and structural. The myth and the priamel are passages balanced in length, sited in counterposition at the end and at the beginning of the poem respectively, and together contrasting with the short central portion of the ode, which relates to Munatius. In the priamel a number of Greek towns are mentioned which are celebrated in one way or another, and these towns preface the introduction of the Italian Tibur to which they are com-

pared to their disadvantage. Within the myth the Greek Teucer goes
into exile in Cyprus, the place of his exile becoming for him a new home
named after his old home, Salamis. This Greek myth highlights a celebrated and parallel feature of the Italian Tibur, that it was a pleasant
place of exile for Romans in early times; Livy, for example, records that
it gave refuge to M. Claudius (5 58) and C. Matienus (43 2). Other
towns near Rome, such as Praeneste, Ardea and Lavinium, also received
early exiles (Livy 2 2; 5 29; 5 43); but Tibur, perhaps because of its
great scenic beauty, seems to have become regarded as the prototype for
a place of exile. Ovid, when himself an exile in Tomis, ends a catalogue
of earlier fellow exiles with:

> uenit ad Adrastum Tydeus Calydone fugatus,
>> et Teucrum Veneri grata recepit humus.
> quid referam ueteres Romanae gentis, apud quos
>> exulibus tellus ultima Tibur erat?
> Ovid *Epistulae ex Ponto* 1 5 79-82

The fact that Teucer occurs last in Ovid's list of exiles and that he and his
Cypriot place of exile immediately precede Tibur may well be an accident
and unrelated to Horace *Odes* 1 7. But the whole passage (*Epistulae ex
Ponto* 1 5 61ff.) shows what Tibur meant to Augustans in the context of
exile. Tibur then, as a standard and pleasant place of exile, corresponds
with the new Salamis of the Teucer myth. In generic terms, therefore,
the myth belongs to section (v) of the generic prescription because it
tells of the character of the inhabitants of Tibur, revealing that they are
hospitable people who offer strangers in exile their own city as a home-
from-home. This welcome, of course, consisted in part of the full citizen
rights which the early Roman exiles received in their nearby refuge.[67]
We may compare part of this section of Menander's prescription:

> ἐρεῖς οὖν ὅτι πρὸς τοὺς ξένους φιλάνθρωπος, ὅτι πρὸς τὰ
> συμβόλαια νόμιμος, ὅτι μεθ' ὁμονοίας συνοικοῦσιν ἀλλήλοις,
> καὶ ὅτι ὁποῖοι πρὸς ἀλλήλους, τοιοῦτοι καὶ πρὸς τοὺς ἔξωθεν.
> Menander 384 22-5
> 'You will say therefore that the city is kind to strangers, that it is
> law-abiding in keeping treaties, that its people live together in har-
> mony and that they treat foreigners as they treat one another.'

But the myth also says something about Munatius Plancus, who was
not being exiled but was a native of Tibur returning to his homeland.

It is able to do so because Teucer's place of exile was the homonymous Salamis in Cyprus, which became in reality as well as in name Teucer's second homeland. Horace underlines the relevance of the myth to Munatius by taking pains to associate Munatius and Teucer in his depiction of them both as care-worn and banishing their cares with wine (14ff., 21ff.). The significance of all this is that Tibur, the town so kindly to exiles, will give an even greater welcome to its own son Munatius.

The above explanation of the meaning of the Teucer myth is offered as an explanation of the exoteric meaning. The complementary esoteric meaning of the myth, that is the meaning as Munatius and Roman readers politically aware would have seen it, is well expressed in a recent modification of Kumaniecki's theory (see Williams 83-5, 763-4). This interpretation is that Horace is consoling Munatius for the death in 43 BC of his brother Plautius Plancus in circumstances in which Munatius was unable to help him, by referring discreetly to Teucer who had lost a brother in similar circumstances. The most valid objection to this notion has always been not that Horace's allusion would have been tactless but that it was an esoteric connexion unintelligible outside a small circle; the ordinary reader would have been left wondering what the connexion was between Tiber and Teucer. The exile hypothesis put forward above, if correct, disposes of this objection, and it is now possible to turn the accusation of tactlessness[68] and ask if it would not have been crass stupidity on Horace's part to recount the Teucer legend in a poem addressed to Munatius Plancus had he not intended an acceptable allusion to Plautius Plancus. We may compare another Horatian passage where a similar double (esoteric and exoteric) significance is intended. This is *Epode* 14 9-14, where Bathyllus was for most readers Anacreon's boyfriend and for the informed few the Bathyllus of Maecenas. There is one further link between Tibur, exile, and Plautius Plancus worth mentioning briefly, although no conclusion can be drawn from it. According to a celebrated legend,[69] in the year 311 BC the flute-players of Rome, incensed at restrictions on their conduct, went into voluntary exile at Tibur in a body. Ovid, probably writing from exile in Tomis and telling this story in *Fasti* 6, again takes occasion to comment on Tibur as a place of exile:

> exilio mutant Urbem Tiburque recedunt,
>   exilium quodam tempore Tibur erat!
> 665-6

The censors at the time, who were responsible for the restrictions, were Appius Claudius Caecus and C. Plautius Venox. Religious life suffered at Rome and eventually the flute-players were tricked into returning. C. Plautius Venox was probably believed to have connived at their return by providing them with masks. That Plautius Venox was or was thought to be a relative of the Plautii of Tibur, and that the memory of these events was still green in Horace's day, is shown by coins of L. Plautius Plancus, the brother of Munatius Plancus, issued *c.* 45 BC, which carry representations of masks.[70]

A poem where an animal is the actual speaker and a human being is the logical speaker is Callimachus *Epigram* 5 (Pf.) (*anathematikon*). The dedicator is the logical speaker in a dedicatory poem. But sometimes, as here, the dedication is put into the mouth of the thing dedicated, in this case a conch, which recounts its life history prior to being dedicated. We may compare Catullus 4, where the ship being dedicated behaves in a similar fashion.

Objects also sometimes function as actual speakers in cases where a human speaker is the logical speaker. Although in most funerary epigrams an unidentified human is the speaker, in some the tomb itself speaks, for example *A.P.* 7 82 (Anon.), 91 [Diogenes Laertius]. Another example is Propertius 1 16 (komos). The door frequented by a komast is the actual speaker at the beginning (1-16) and the end (45-8) of this elegy. The central section is the speech of the komast. The door is speaking in the interests of the logical addressee, the beloved, and against those of the logical speaker, the komast. In Propertius 1 16 there are therefore joint speakers, the door – an object – which is substitute actual speaker of part of the elegy (cp. Horace in *Odes* 5 7), and the komast, the logical human speaker of the komos, who is also actual speaker of part of it. The significance of these sophistications will be treated in Chapter 9 where a further application of a constructive principle in the elegy, the address to the door in 17-44, will be discussed.

Speakers Employing Substitutes. The logical speaker of the genre employs a substitute speaker in two short Catullan lyrics (11, 42). In 11 (renuntiatio amoris) Catullus, instead of delivering his rejection directly to Lesbia, tells Furius and Aurelius to give her a message renouncing his love. The purpose of this device is partly to express Catullus' psychological state and partly to insult all concerned – Furius, Aurelius, and Lesbia. Catullus' mood of renunciation is such that he cannot even bear to speak to Lesbia directly, but seeks to separate himself still further from her by

216

means of interposed persons. These persons are enemies of Catullus: this is clear elsewhere in Catullus' work and is made clear here.[71] The contrast between the trivial nature of Catullus' request to Furius and Aurelius and the long and inflated topos on friendship (1-14) shows Catullus' lack of sincerity in his declaration of Furius' and Aurelius' friendship for him. Catullus is insulting these enemies of his by making them his lackeys in such a sordid matter, by accompanying his request with such open and exaggerated insincerity, and finally by couching the message in obscene terms (*moechis* 17, *ilia rumpens* 20). Such language, although at home in Catullus' *iambi* (vituperative poetry), is designedly out of place in this lyric; it is meant to clash with the language of the first four stanzas and of the last stanza, and it is put into the mouths of Furius and Aurelius as an insult to them. Lesbia is insulted not only by having this language directed towards her but by having such foul characters as Furius and Aurelius employed as messengers to her.

In Catullus 42 (flagitatio) Catullus appoints his verses (*hendecasyllabi*) as substitute speakers. This is an altogether more light-hearted effort: the purpose of the substitute speakers is partly to supply for Catullus the necessary crowd of witnesses and, if possible, fellow participants in the flagitatio; it is also partly to soften the reaction (change of mind) which occurs in 21 (see p. 148). It is easier for Catullus to introduce this change of mind if the worst preceding insults against the addressee can by a convenient fiction be put not into his own mouth but into those of the verses. The effect of separating logical speaker and addressee by interposing a substituted speaker can also be observed here.

Joint Speakers. These are perhaps not a very common phenomenon. They have been found (p. 174) in Tibullus 1 6 (erotodidaxis). In this elegy, along with Tibullus himself (1-42, 73-86), there is a substitute speaker in Tibullus' interest, the priestess of Bellona (43-56), and a substitute speaker employed by Tibullus, Delia's mother (57-72).[72] In Propertius 1 16 (komos) the door speaks (1-16, 45-8) as well as the komast (17-48, see pp. 230-1).

9

Addressee-variation

The standard addressee can be defined for the purposes of this chapter in more or less the same terms as the standard speaker was defined in Chapter 8. The standard addressee is human rather than a god, animal, thing or collective body; he is distinct from the addressee; he is not a substitute addressee, that is he neither acts for the state when the state is the real generic protagonist nor does he function as addressee partly or wholly on behalf of or in place of the appropriate human generic protagonist. He is not a joint addressee and he stands in a certain status relationship with the speaker.

We can now treat examples of addressee-variation as divergences from the various characteristics of the standard addressee.

Non-human Addressees. In hymns and prayers a divine addressee is the norm and so, in these specialized examples of various genres, a divine addressee should not be considered a generic sophistication. But cases do arise where a god is addressee in a context where a human addressee is usual: Moschus I is one;[1] here the object Eros is divine, where a human object would be normal. Such cases involve generic originality and are significant. However, the real oddity in this area (which does not easily fit into the framework proposed) is when a human being is given godlike attributes and addressed in hymns and prayers. This is honorific; it occurs, for example, in the prosphonetic hymn to Demeter and to a more prominent addressee, the human Demetrius Poliorketes (preserved at Athenaeus *Deipnosophistae* 253 D-F), and in the paean in honour of T. Flamininus (Powell, *Collectanea Alexandrina* p. 173).

An animal as object is common in funerary poems, where the death of an animal is in question rather than the death of a human: for example Catullus 3, and the other cases cited by C. J. Fordyce ad loc.

A thing (or a collective body) as addressee is exemplified in a limited sense by Horace *Odes* 1 14:

O nauis, referent in mare te noui
fluctus! o quid agis? fortiter occupa

portum! nonne uides ut
nudum remigio latus,

5 et malus celeri saucius Africo,
antennaeque gemant, ac sine funibus
uix durare carinae
possint imperiosius

aequor? non tibi sunt integra lintea,
10 non di quos iterum pressa uoces malo.
quamuis Pontica pinus,
siluae filia nobilis,

iactes et genus et nomen inutile,
nil pictis timidus nauita puppibus
15 fidit. tu, nisi uentis
debes ludibrium, caue.

nuper sollicitum quae mihi taedium,
nunc desiderium curaque non leuis,
interfusa nitentis
20 uites aequora Cycladas.

The ship represents allegorically the state,[2] so that the ship-state is the logical as well as the actual addressee. The ode is a propemptikon of the commonest type.[3] Stanzas one to four contain schetliasmos which employs as deterrents propemptic topoi concerned with the dangers of the sea – bad winds, bad seas, the terrified sailor (cp., e.g. Ovid *Amores* 2 11).[4] Another propemptic topos is an amusing variant of the commonplace on 'owing' which Horace knew (15-16).[5]

Stanza five is not easy to understand in any terms, generic or nongeneric. From the generic point of view the main difficulty is this: up to 16 we clearly have schetliasmos; in 19-20 we have good wishes for the ship's journey; but it is by no means clear where the schetliasmos ends and the second part of the propemptikon begins. The apparent lack of the usual verbal signals indicating this is puzzling, since an ancient audience depended on such signals as much as we do.

There is one way of approaching stanza five which allows us to discern in it the verbal signals required. On accepted interpretations *nuper*, etc. (17), refers to those previous occasions when the ship was at sea and when it was storm-damaged (1ff.), and *nunc*, etc., (18) to the ship's present position. It is true that *nunc* refers to the latter subject; *desiderium* is an emotion normally felt for someone or something once possessed and not at the moment possessed. For Horace to call the ship his *desiderium* in 18 accords with the picture of it already setting out (1ff.) and with the implication of *uites* (20), namely that the ship is under way. For the language we may compare the πόθοι (longings) and προμηθία (anxiety) of Ismene for her absent father (Sophocles *Oedipus Coloneus* 332, 334). Since *desiderium* has this significance and since 18 therefore refers to the ship's being under way with Horace's blessing, 18 is part of the second, affectionate good wishes / encomium section of the propemptikon.

It is also true that 17 refers to Horace's feelings about the past voyages of the ship. The ship's situation in *Odes* 1 14 is precisely paralleled by part of a speech of Iolaus in Euripides *Heracleidae*.

> ὦ τέκν', ἔοιγμεν ναυτίλοισιν, οἵτινες
> χειμῶνος ἐκφυγόντες ἄγριον μένος
> ἐς χεῖρα γῇ συνῆψαν, εἶτα χερσόθεν
> 430 πνοιαῖσιν ἠλάθησαν ἐς πόντον πάλιν.
> οὕτω δὲ χἠμεῖς τῆσδ' ἀπωθούμεσθα γῆς
> ἤδη πρὸς ἀκταῖς ὄντες ὡς σεσῳσμένοι.
> 427-32

But 17 has another function within the generic layout of the ode. It will be remembered that Menander instructed his propemptic speaker to utter a full schetliasmos and then another, presumably very brief, schetliasmos, before going on with his good wishes. The second schetliasmos is that of a speaker who supposedly has wished to persuade the traveller to remain, but has failed to persuade him. Line 17 represents in Horace *Odes* 1 14 this second schetliasmos prescribed by Menander and found elsewhere in literary propemptika. *Sollicitum taedium* is presumably *taedium sollicitudinis* (being weary of feeling anxious) (cp. *taedium curarum*),[6] and so a good description of the effect of absence on someone feeling affection for the absentee.[7] The propemptic speaker who has wished to persuade and failed to do so can therefore use these words appropriately as his second schetliasmos. If this suggestion is correct, the ode does contain verbal signals that the schetliasmos is over. Lines 17-18 are not then repetitious emotionalism, but through the contrast between *nuper* and *nunc* they accord with the Menandrian pattern of second schetliasmos followed by change of mind and affectionate good wishes.

One further generic feature of *Odes* 1 14 calls for comment: the ship-state is a superior addressee. Yet Horace employs schetliasmos towards it and, when his schetliasmos is over, expresses affection rather than encomium. Thus he treats a superior addressee in a fashion normally reserved for an equal addressee (see p. 9 and below, p. 235ff.). We must not be overmechanical in such distinctions, but Horace is clearly achieving a major sophistication in this matter. By using schetliasmos and displaying affection in highly personal terms Horace is demonstrating his love of his country in a much more affecting way than could have been achieved by encomium. He is also justifying the fact that he ventures to comment on affairs of state. Just as in *Epode* 16 he established his right to advise the state by his adoption of a prophetic role, so here he first allegorizes the state as a ship, a device which places him in the tradition of Alcaeus, and then represents himself as a 'lover of the city', a self-portrait which allows him to speak freely without attracting censure.[8]

A better example of a thing as addressee is Horace *Odes* 3 21. In this ode a wine-jar is given the attributes of a god in a hymn-parody. Epibateria and syntaktika sometimes have the land as their addressee. This is usually a *polis*, which is a body of men. But sometimes, as in Sophocles *Philoctetes* 1452-71, the physical land itself is the addressee, for Lemnos was then unpopulated. In Propertius 3 23 the lost writing-tablets are the object.

A collective body is frequently addressed: many dicanic, symbouleutic, and public epideictic orations are directed to the people of a state as a whole or to a collective section of them. Propertius 3 4 is addressed to such a collective section – the Roman army (see pp. 185ff.).

Conflation of Speaker and Addressee. In the infrequent cases where speaker and addressee are not distinct, the logical addressee functions also as actual speaker. One example of this, Ovid *Tristia* 3 13, has already been treated on pp. 135ff. This is an extraordinary poem in other ways: it is an inverse genethliakon, something which was very rare in antiquity; and it was composed by an exile. Because there was no one else to write about his birthday, Ovid himself treated the subject and thus increased the pathos of the elegy. The bipersonality of genres is such a strong tradition that Ovid addresses his personified birthday, which is thus the actual and substitute addressee. The birthday is probably to be considered as analogous to a god in this role (cp. Tibullus 2 2).

As usual Horace has exploited the possibilities of this sophistication to their fullest:

> Cur me querelis exanimas tuis?
> nec dis amicum est nec mihi te prius
>   obire, Maecenas, mearum
>   grande decus columenque rerum.
> 5 a! te meae si partem animae rapit
> maturior uis, quid moror altera,
>   nec carus aeque nec superstes
>   integer? ille dies utramque
> ducet ruinam. non ego perfidum
> 10 dixi sacramentum: ibimus, ibimus,
>   utcumque praecedes, supremum
>   carpere iter comites parati.
> me nec Chimaerae spiritus igneae
> nec, si resurgat, centimanus Gyas
> 15   diuellet umquam: sic potenti
>   Iustitiae placitumque Parcis.
> seu Libra seu me Scorpios aspicit
> formidulosus, pars uiolentior
>   natalis horae, seu tyrannus
> 20   Hesperiae Capricornus undae,
> utrumque nostrum incredibili modo
> consentit astrum: te Iouis impio
>   tutela Saturno refulgens
>   eripuit uolucrisque Fati
> 25 tardauit alas, cum populus frequens
> laetum theatris ter crepuit sonum:
>   me truncus illapsus cerebro
>   sustulerat, nisi Faunus ictum
> dextra levasset, Mercurialium
> 30 custos uirorum. reddere uictimas
>   aedemque uotiuam memento:
>   nos humilem feriemus agnam.
>   Horace *Odes* 2 17

There is a convention, common in many genres, that the speaker identifies his own interest with that of the addressee: in Catullus 1 (anathematikon), the author, in dedicating his book to Cornelius Nepos, tries to make it appear that he and Nepos are writers of a kind;[9] in Statius *Siluae* 1 4 115-22 (soteria) the poet declares that his interests and those of Rutilius Gallicus are linked; we have already discussed Horace *Odes* 1 7 in this connexion, on p. 212. These examples of the convention are of course encomiastic in purpose, and are meant to show the sincerity of the poet's feelings. We must observe a distinction between these examples and *Odes* 2 17: Catullus 1 is a dedication to Nepos but not also to Catullus; *Siluae* 1 4 is a soteria for Gallicus but not also for Statius; Horace *Odes* 1 7 is an epibaterion of Plancus but not also of Horace. However, in Odes 2 17, Horace composed simultaneously a soteria for Maecenas' recovery from illness and for his own preservation from an accident. The interest of the two is identified, but the identification differs from those mentioned above. The actual and logical speaker of the soteria for Maecenas is Horace; the actual speaker and logical addressee of the soteria for Horace is Horace himself.

The generic identity of *Odes* 2 17 deserves closer scrutiny, since it shows Horace's characteristic selectivity in the use of topoi. This, as often, means that the genre only becomes clear at the end of the poem: at 22ff. we are informed that Horace and Maecenas have both been saved by divine help,[10] that Maecenas' recovery produced public demonstrations of joy,[11] and that both must offer *soteria* suited to their status,[12] Maecenas by offering cattle and a temple, Horace by offering a lamb. These clearly soteric topoi are preceded by a long passage (stanzas one to five) in which Horace declares, with many affirmations of affection for Maecenas, that he and Maecenas will die together, neither preceding the other; this passage is a specific statement of association of interest. In a sense Horace produces a hysteron-proteron arrangement of material: he does not initially state Maecenas' recovery from sickness and his own preservation from accident, and then subsequently introduce, as a conclusion drawn from this coincidence, his own association of interest with Maecenas. Instead he makes the joint recovery/safety of Maecenas and himself act as a subsequent example and proof of their initially stated association of interest. Furthermore, to enliven this initial statement Horace introduces it in the form of a question referring to an imaginary event (1). This line has sometimes been understood as illustrative of Maecenas' hypochondria which is known from other sources. Quite apart from the improbability that Horace would proclaim to the world such a fault in his patron, it is unwise to ignore the conventional element in such questions at the beginning of poems.[13] We can with no more security give a biographical interpretation to *Odes* 2 17 1 than interpret Propertius 1 22 1-2 literally:

Qualis et unde genus, qui sint mihi, Tulle, Penates,
    quaeris pro nostra semper amicitia.

If Tullus, a man from Perugia (3f.), did not know that his protégé Propertius was from neighbouring Assisi, he was stupid as well as importunate.[14]

It might be asked why Horace, in order to enliven the ode, imagined this situation which has given rise to biographical misinterpretation. The reason is probably that Horace wished to affect reluctance to identify with a greater man. This encomiastic implication is obtained by the fiction that it is Maecenas who has taken the initiative in identifying with Horace. The poet's humility in identifying himself with the addressee is seen also in Statius *Siluae* 1 4 115-22 and in Catullus 1. In his first poem Catullus not only diminishes the importance of his own work in comparison with that of Nepos but also represents Nepos as having taken the initiative in liking Catullus' work. So here Horace represents Maecenas as taking the initiative in expressing an identity of interest with himself. This tendency on Horace's part is confirmed later: in 9-10, where Horace represents himself as swearing an oath of fidelity to Maecenas but not the reverse (a designation of Maecenas' superior status); and in the thank-offerings of the last stanza, where Maecenas, as befits the superior, makes splendid offerings which contrast with Horace's humble lamb.

Stanzas one to five of *Odes* 2 17 are not merely a statement of identity of interest: they are that specific kind of statement of identity of interest relevant to the soteria. Another example of the genre sums up these stanzas of Horace in one line: '*uiuam si uiuet; si cadet illa, cadam*' (Propertius 2 28 42). The same topos occurs in two other soteria, at [Tibullus] 3 10 = 4 4 19-20 and Ovid *Amores* 2 13 15-16 (see p. 157). It is the special relevance of this kind of statement to the soteria that encourages Horace to expand it and make it the theme which the joint safety of himself and Maecenas exemplifies.

No inclusion occurs in Horace *Odes* 2 17. A poem where identification of interest is made by means of inclusion is Propertius 3 9, a *recusatio* addressed by Propertius to Maecenas. Rejecting the idea of writing epic, Propertius identifies his interests with those of Maecenas in 21-34, an included recusatio which describes how Maecenas has rejected the political power, and so forth, offered to him by Augustus (cp. also 47).

Substitute Addressees. Examples of substitute addressees acting on behalf of the state must be few and specialized, for instance, in replies to ambassadors. A simple example where an addressee is substitute for a human generic protagonist is Ovid *Amores* 1 6. Here in a komos the komast addresses not the beloved but the doorkeeper, although naturally the komast's real interest is in the beloved who is the logical addressee in komoi. By writing a komos in which the doorkeeper and not the beloved is addressed, Ovid contrives to create the impression that the doorkeeper and not the beloved is the main barrier to the komast's entry. Hence, as well as constructing an interesting variant upon the normal generic pattern, Ovid is able to depict a novel dramatic situation in which the beloved is in no way responsible for the exclusion of the lover. She can therefore be represented in favourable terms throughout, the blame and accusations, which in normal komoi come the way of the beloved, being transferred to the doorkeeper.

Within the framework of this sophistication the komastic topoi occur, sometimes in their simplest form, sometimes adapted in amusing ways to suit the vicarious addressee. The topoi which occur in their simpler form are treated by Copley.[15] Among the amusingly adapted topoi may be noted:

1. The komast claims admission on the grounds of services done to the doorkeeper, not to the beloved.[16] The erotic services to the beloved described in love-poetry have to do with the fact that he or she is the beloved. But Ovid's substitute services are linked with the doorkeeper's servile state. The komast has saved the doorkeeper from a beating (19-20) and has shielded him – from other punishment? (43-4). Copley also notes this extended use of the komastic topos.

2. The komast, instead of tempting the beloved with gifts,[17] tempts the doorkeeper with the hope of freedom (25-6).

3. The komast, instead of imagining his beloved as sleeping with a rival,[18] imagines the doorkeeper as occupied with his girl-friend (45-6).

4. The komast's reproaches of cruelty, falling not on the beloved but on the doorkeeper, are made by comparing his hardness to that of the door he keeps (62), and by saying that he ought to have been a prison warder (63-4).

In this case, the use of a substitute addressee is not consequent upon the employment of another constructive principle in the same poem; it can sometimes be such a consequence. Some poems treated in Chapter 8 exemplify this phenomenon: in Propertius 2 16, Cynthia is the logical speaker; but when Propertius introduces himself as substitute speaker in order to try to ensure the praetor's non-welcome, he addresses the elegy not directly to the logical addressee the praetor, but to Cynthia, who from logical speaker is converted into a substitute addressee. Something similar occurs in Theocritus *Idyll* 7 96-127, where Aratus, the logical speaker of the komos, is converted into a joint substitute addressee (122-7). In Horace *Odes* 1 7 Plancus, the logical speaker, is similarly converted into a substitute addressee.

Sometimes a god functions as substitute addressee for a human protagonist. The origin of this sophistication is either that the normal generic formula includes a partial topical address to a god, or that such addresses are possible as variants created by formal alterations in single topoi. This topical address to a god is then expanded so that the whole example or a large section of it is so constituted. The meaning of the example and the primary elements are thereby positively affected so that a constructive principle is involved. A god acting as substitute addressee has been seen in this chapter in Ovid *Tristia* 3 13 (p. 221) and a substitute divine addressee as a joint addressee has been seen on p. 155 in [Tibullus] 3 10 = 4 4. Gods were joint substitute addressees in Theocritus *Idyll* 7 96ff. (p. 203).

Other examples are provided by two Sapphic fragments, *Fr.* 17 (LP), a propemptikon, and *Fr.* 5 (LP), a prosphonetikon. These two examples are early, are addressed to gods throughout, and belong to genres which also have examples in hymnic form with gods as their addressees. This might suggest that the hymnic form is ancestor of these two Sapphic lyrics. Such a conclusion would, I believe, be incorrect: the existence of such Sapphic examples as these would imply the prior existence of examples of the same genres addressed directly to men, even if we did not (as we do) have such surviving examples in Homer.

> πλάσιον δή μ' [
> πότνι' "Ηρα, σὰ χ[
> τὰν ἀράταν 'Ατ[ρεΐδαι
> τοι βασίληες·
> 5 ἐκτελέσσαντες μ[
> πρῶτα μὲν πὲρ "Ι[λιον

τυίδ' ἀπορμάθεν[τες
οὐκ ἐδύναντο,
πρὶν σὲ καὶ Δί' ἀντ[ίαον κάλεσσαι
10 καὶ Θυώνας ἰμε[ρόεντα παῖδα·
νῦν δὲ κ[ἄμοι
κὰτ τὸ πάλ[αιον.
ἄγνα καὶ κα[
    [π]αρθ[εν
15 [ἀ]μφὶ σ[
    (3 lines missing)
ἔμμενα[ι
20 [?]ραπικέ[σθαι].
    Sappho *Fr.* 17 (LP)

Near to me . . .
lady Hera, your beautiful . . .
you to whom to the Atreidae prayed . . .
the kings.
5 They when they come to the end of . . .
first around Ilion . . .
when they had voyaged here . . .
They could not
before praying to you and Zeus Antiaos
10 and the charming son of Thyone
and now for me too . . .
in accordance with your age-old practice
the holy and . . . things . . .
maiden . . .
15 around . . .
    (3 lines missing)
to be
20 . . . to arrive . . .

In *Fr.* 17 instead of addressing the departing girl directly (cf. 13) and
wishing her a good voyage and a safe arrival (20?), Sappho addresses the
goddess Hera, asking her to perform for the girl the same services as she
and other deities once performed for the Greek fleet on its way to Troy,
namely to help her departure and ensure her arrival.[19] If, as seems likely,
Hera alone is invoked in the prayer for the girl, and not the other deities,
this is to distinguish the lesser, the girl's case, from the greater, that of

227

the Greek army; it is also because Hera alone is the appropriate divinity in the girl's case. We cannot be certain why this is so, but we may conjecture that she is about to be married and that she is departing in the company of or to go to her future husband. Employing as she does a prayer-form for her propemptikon, Sappho follows up the summons of 1-2 with another typical prayer feature – the appeal to the god to do something for his suppliant on the analogy of some good deed he did before either for the same suppliant or for another suppliant in a parallel situation.[20] In prayers the appeal by analogy functions both as a compliment to the god and as a reminder that the action requested by his present petitioner is within the god's competence. By means of this prayer Sappho and the girl, who is the logical addressee of the propemptikon, are lifted into the realm of the Homeric heroes and linked not only with epic mythology, but with important local Lesbian cults. Another effect of directing the propemptikon to a substitute divine addressee is to give distinction to the relationship between Sappho and the departing girl, whatever this may be. It is not clear whether the details of the myth are meant to correspond with anything in the contemporary reality; it may be that Sappho's purposes were sufficiently achieved by the general similarity in the two situations.

Κύπρι καὶ] Νηρήιδες ἀβλάβη[ν μοι
τὸν κασί]γνητον δ[ό]τε τυίδ' ἴκεσθα[ι
κὤσσα ϝ]ῳ θύμῳ κε θέλῃ γένεσθαι
.....τε]λέσθην,
5 ὄσσα δὲ πρ]όσθ' ἄμβροτε πάντα λῦσα[ι
καὶ φίλοισ]ι ϝοῖσι χάραν γένεσθαι
.......ἔ]χθροισι, γένοιτο δ' ἄμμι
.......]ηδ' εἶς·
τὰν κασιγ]νήταν δὲ θέλοι πόησθαι
10   ]τίμας, [ὀν]ίαν δὲ λύγραν
         ]οτοισι π[ά]ροιθ' ἀχεύων
         ].να
         ].εισαΐω[ν] τὸ κέγχρω
         ]λεπαγ[..(.)]αι πολίταν
15   ]λλως[...]νηκε δ' αὖτ' οὐ
         ]κρω[]
         ]οναικ[ ]εο[ ].ι

].. [.]ν· σὺ [δὲ] Κύπ[ρ(.)].. [.. (.)]να
]θεμ[έν] α κάκαν [
20   ]ι.

Sappho *Fr.* 5 (LP)
Cypris and Nereids, grant
that my brother come here unharmed
grant too that what he wishes in his heart
... be fulfilled
5 and grant that he make good his former failings
and that he be a joy to his friends and kinsfolk
... to his enemies and may there be to us
... no ...
and may he wish to give his sister
10 ... honour and as for that miserable anguish
... he was formerly suffering
(6 fragmentary lines)
18 and may you, Cypris, ...
... putting aside that evil ...

In *Fr.* 5,[21] a prosphonetikon of which the logical addressee is Sappho's
brother Charaxus, the actual and substitute addressees are the goddesses Aphrodite and the Nereids. These are highly appropriate substitute addressees for a traveller returning, like Charaxus, by sea from
Egypt to Lesbos. The Nereids are sea-goddesses who had a cult in Lesbos,
and sea-goddesses are often asked to provide safe journeys for travellers
by sea. Aphrodite has multiple relevance: she is an important Lesbian
deity, has links with the Nereids, is also herself a sea-goddess and is the
goddess of love. This last relevance is connected with Charaxus' attachment to the courtesan Doricha (see Sappho *Fr.* 15 (b), (LP) Herodotus
2, 134-5).

The effect of an address to gods rather than to the logical human
addressee in *Fr.* 5, is very different from the effect of the same device in
Fr. 17. The Nereids are introduced to make it clear that Charaxus will
have a sea-voyage in front of him. Aphrodite is the more important
addressee: it is she who has the power to secure implementation of
Sappho's pleas, for as the goddess of love she can release Charaxus from
his unfortunate attachment to Doricha (18-19?). Furthermore, under
the guise of an address to this important Lesbian goddess, who has
control over sexual activities, Sappho can give Charaxus sound advice

about how to bring his sexual life into conformity with the moral, familial and social obligations of a member of this community.

With the exception of its substitute addressees and its setting in the future rather than the present tense as is normal – a formal sophistication – the material of *Fr.* 5 is fairly conventional; but it does show some subtle variation on the standard forms of prosphonetic topoi: Charaxus is to come home (B5) (2, 7ff., 14?), safe (B7) (1); all of his desires are to be fulfilled (3-4) – a wish which expresses Sappho's feelings of affection for her brother (B3); Charaxus is to make up for his previous offences, presumably against his kin (5). The last sentiment is a variation upon the prosphonetic topoi that the returning traveller has, simply by his absence, brought misery upon the welcomer and others, but by his return has compensated them for this misery, or indeed overcompensated them (B10, 11). Charaxus is to be a joy to his kinsfolk and friends (B17), as returning travellers are to the whole welcoming group (6); the wish is polarized (7) and then generalized further (8). At 9-10 Sappho requests special honorific treatment at Charaxus' hands, a reflection of the normal primacy of the welcomer in prosphonetika (B12). In the rest of the third stanza Sappho may perhaps repeat, with reference to herself only, the sentiments previously expressed by her at 6ff. with reference to the whole welcoming group. The adaptation of standard topoi described above is such that Charaxus is accused of having caused the welcoming group, including Sappho, not the harm which the traveller is customarily accused of causing, that is, simply being absent, but other and positive harm. We do not know at what point in the poem the nature of this harm, namely his expenditures on and infatuation for the harlot Doricha, was revealed.

It is not often that an animal acts as substitute addressee. [Erinna's] propemptikon quoted by Athenaeus, *Deipnosophistae* 283D, appears to be an example. It is addressed to a *pompilos*, an erotic creature[22] and therefore a suitable substitute addressee of a propemptikon composed by a lover for a departing beloved. A fairly simple example of a thing acting as substitute addressee occurs in Propertius 1 16 17-44 (komos) where instead of addressing his beloved the komast addresses the door. The address to the door can be viewed in several ways. It is, along with the use of the door as substitute speaker in the rest of the elegy, a Roman feature within this komos, since emphasis on and concern with the door is a distinctly Roman contribution to the genre. In 1 16 Propertius stresses the Roman nature of the scene in other ways too (1-4). Second, the address to the door over twenty-seven lines is an extension of fleeting addresses to the door sometimes found in komoi when the komast's emotion leads him into the pathetic fallacy. Third, various interesting tensions are obtained by the use of door and komast as joint speakers in different parts of the elegy, and of the door as addressee in one section. The door represents itself in its own narration as a virtuous being struggling with the problem of an immoral mistress, unable to protect her from the consequences of her own viciousness, and subject to constant torment from the komast and his fellows. In his own eyes, however, the komast is a poor soul harried by the door, a being even more cruel than its mistress, standing pitilessly as it does between himself and her. The unyielding door is in this way implicitly compared with the mistress who would, so the komast thinks, be sympathetic to him if only his pleas could reach her (27ff.). So within a single short poem, two contrasting views of door, komast, and mistress are shown. Partial use of the door as substitute addressee with somewhat similar effect is found at Tibullus 1 2 7-14 (komos).

Another more complex poem, where an object is vicarious addressee, is Horace *Odes* 1 3, a propemptikon where the ship which has carried Virgil off on his voyage to Greece is addressed instead of the departed traveller, Virgil himself.

> Sic te diua potens Cypri,
> sic fratres Helenae, lucida sidera,
> uentorumque regat pater
> obstrictis aliis praeter Iapyga,
> 5   nauis, quae tibi creditum
> debes Vergilium, finibus Atticis
> reddas incolumem precor,
> et serues animae dimidium meae.
> illi robur et aes triplex
> 10 circa pectus erat, qui fragilem truci
> commisit pelago ratem
> primus, nec timuit praecipitem Africum
> decertantem Aquilonibus
> nec tristis Hyadas nec rabiem Noti,
> 15   quo non arbiter Hadriae
> maior, tollere seu ponere uult freta.
> quem mortis timuit gradum,

qui siccis oculis monstra natantia,
    qui uidit mare turbidum et
20 infamis scopulos Acroceraunia?
    nequiquam deus abscidit
    prudens Oceano dissociabili
      terras, si tamen impiae
    non tangenda rates transiliunt uada.
25   audax omnia perpeti
    gens humana ruit per uetitum nefas.
    audax Iapeti genus
    ignem fraude mala gentibus intulit.
    post ignem aetheria domo
30 subductum macies et noua febrium
      terris incubuit cohors,
    semotique prius tarda necessitas
      leti corripuit gradum.
    expertus uacuum Daedalus aera
35   pennis non homini datis:
    perrupit Acheronta Herculeus labor.
    nil mortalibus ardui est:
    caelum ipsum petimus stultitia neque
    per nostrum patimur scelus
40 iracunda Iouem ponere fulmina.
    Horace *Odes* 1 3

This ode is difficult to understand and it has often been felt to be lacking in poetic merit. Most recently Nisbet-Hubbard have condemned *Odes* 1 3 in strong terms. It is 'an accomplished piece of versification but little more', which shows 'none of [Horace's] usual tact and charm' but rather 'trite and unseasonable moralising', and lacks 'the Horatian virtues of brevity and incisiveness'.[23] No explanation of the meaning of a poem can compel anyone to like it; but it may remove false grounds for criticism. Already in this century G. L. Hendrickson and J. P. Elder have pointed the way to a just assessment of *Odes* 1 3 as an encomium of Virgil.[24] I wish to add a generic assessment of it which supports their views.

Horace could easily have written a propemptikon to Virgil displaying obvious tact, charm, brevity, and so forth; it would have been either schetliastic, and so openly affectionate, or excusatory, and equally affectionate but more deferential. Instead he has written a non-schetliastic, non-excusatory propemptikon which is striving after an impersonal tone. Horace has increased the oddity of his propemptikon by going on to employ one sophistication upon another: the propemptikon is for a traveller who has already gone; it is addressed not to him but to the ship as substitute addressee; finally the encomiastic section of the propemptikon contains an implicit schetliasmos.[25] Such devices are not the work of an immature poet or one lacking his normal poetic resources: by not doing what we would have expected him to do, Horace is trying to express something out of the ordinary.

Horace's main reason for refusing to write a schetliastic propemptikon for Virgil was that he wished to pay him the compliment of treating him as a superior (see p. 9 and p. 221). Although poetry is not mentioned in the ode, readers knowing who Horace and Virgil were could be expected to think of their relative status in poetic terms. In his implicit schetliasmos Horace pays Virgil a second compliment. This can best be understood by reference to Statius *Siluae* 3 2, the value of which as a commentary on Horace *Odes* 1 3 is well known. The thematic coincidences between the two poems are too great, even when the generic community of material is taken into account, for anything but direct imitation to be involved.[26] Statius in characteristic fashion expands where Horace has been brief, includes extra topoi where Horace has selected and omitted, and makes the purpose of each topos explicit where Horace has left it implicit. The 'attack on seafaring' of *Odes* 1 3 9ff., with its references to the impiety and wickedness of the first sailor and his analogues (21ff., 25-6, 28, 38ff.), is explained by the parallel Statian material. There the impiety of seafaring (62) and analogous activities is a celebration of the 'audacious courage' (64) of the first and therefore of all subsequent sailors, including the addressee of Statius' propemptikon. The encomiastic method employed both by Statius and by Horace is familiar: the sincerity of the author's encomium is proved by its being conveyed under the guise of an attack on the addressee. No excuses occur in *Odes* 1 3 (even though it is addressed to a superior) because they would have blunted the effect of this simulated attack.

Horace has further underlined his encomiastic purposes by emphasizing strongly the boldness of the first sailor (9ff.), his freedom from fear of death (17), and his steadfastness in the face of danger (18). These characteristics may be contrasted with the imagined fear of some addressees of schetliastic propemptika (Propertius 1 8 5-6; Ovid *Amores*

233

2 11 27ff.) and of Maevius, addressee of Horace's inverse propemptikon (*Epode* 10 15ff.). Horace has also made the voyage of the first sailor appear to be the same voyage as is being undertaken by Virgil: the first sailor, like Virgil, will apparently be sailing on the Adriatic (15), and like him he will see Acroceraunia (20).

It may be objected that some of the Horatian (and indeed Statian) material conflicts with this interpretation, especially the emphasis throughout the 'attack on seafaring' upon the evil effects of the actions of the first sailor and his analogues. It is true that there is such an emphasis; but an examination of these evil effects reveals Horace's intention. The first sailor suffered evil winds, sea-monsters and dangerous rocks; he was not afraid of death (17). Prometheus' gift eventually brought swifter death to men (30-3); Daedalus' daring brought Icarus' death (implied 34-5). Hercules attacked death directly (36), but in fact in the long run his effort was in vain; the giants were killed by the thunderbolts of Jupiter (40). The main effect of man's 'audacious courage' then is death. But this is not a real attack on Virgil: it increases the praise of his courage, for it is courage which looks death in the face. Moreover, its main function is to be informative not about Virgil but about Horace's feelings: the emphasis on death reveals Horace's own deep-seated fears and throws light on another feature of the 'attack on seafaring'. Statius refers to his attack as *questus* (cf. *iusta queror* (78) and *sed merui questus* (90)), that is, schetliasmos (cp. *querelae* Propertius 1 6 11). Statius, therefore, thought of this section of his propemptikon to Maecius Celer not as the open schetliasmos aimed at persuading the traveller not to go, but as an indirect schetliasmos, displaying affection for Celer by revealing Statius' fears for his safety, fears contrasted encomiastically with Celer's lack of fear.

Horace uses the 'attack on seafaring' in exactly the same way. In a propemptikon to a superior he cannot employ an open schetliasmos; so he conveys his suppressed feelings in this tense and vivid way. In contrast to Statius *Siluae* 3 2, where the speaker's fears for the traveller and affection for him are stated, in Horace *Odes* 1 3 the same feelings are given brooding and implicit dramatic expression in this, Horace's, self-portrait of a man in conflict with his own emotions.[27] The effect is not charming – Horatian odes can have other virtues – but it is highly tactful, employs conventional moralizing in an unusual and highly relevant way, and through its reticence, its selectivity in the use of topoi, and its implicit mode of conveying information, displays admirable brevity and incisiveness. Horace placed the ode in its important position in his first collection, not only because of Virgil's literary importance and his own close friendship with him but also because the ode demonstrates Horace's ability to handle an important genre in a masterly and very unusual way.

Virgil's importance as a poet and the generic excellence of *Odes* 1 3 explain its position in the three books published together. But if this is felt to be an insufficient explanation, it may be worth while to repeat a suggestion about a further significance which the ode could have had within Horace's literary circle, even though by its nature this suggestion is quite unprovable. By 23 BC, when the odes were collected, Virgil's *Aeneid* was well under way. Virgil visited Greece in 19 BC when the *Aeneid* was in its final stages;[28] this was part of an intended journey to Greece and Asia, lasting three years, to gain local colour for the *Aeneid*. Virgil cut his trip short, returned to Italy and died there in the same year. The language of Donatus' account might be taken to imply that his visit to Greece was decided upon in 19 BC. But Virgil was the kind of man who was already at the age of fifty-two planning the philosophic studies of his old age, so it is more likely that he had contemplated the trip to Greece and Asia a long time before he embarked on it.

In ancient poetry, and not least in Augustan poetry, sailing was one of the commonest metaphors for writing poetry;[29] in this imagery major sea voyages were the composition of epics.[30] In 25 BC at the latest, Propertius paid a long and explicit tribute to Virgil, which shows knowledge not only of the contents of the *Aeneid* but also of the exact form of its opening lines.[31] It is at least possible that Horace also wanted to pay some tribute to the forthcoming *Aeneid*, and chose to do so not in Propertius' explicit fashion but indirectly in this highly encomiastic propemptikon. On this interpretation, the composition of the *Aeneid* would be represented in allegorical terms as that sea-journey which Virgil intended to make when he came to put the final touch to his epic. It may be relevant that *Odes* 1 14, the other propemptikon addressed to a ship in Horace's *Odes*, is also allegorical. If this suggestion has any plausibility, it would also remove from the biography of Virgil the otherwise unattested earlier trip to Greece supposedly evidenced by *Odes* 1 3.

Joint Addressees. In addition to other cases mentioned above (pp. 226, 230), joint addressees can be found in Tibullus 1 2 (komos).

The Relative Status of Speaker and Addressee. Menander declares that when a propemptic speaker is superior to the addressee the propemptic speech will be characterized mainly by advice, that when the speaker is inferior the principal characteristic of the speech will be encomium, and that when the two are equal affection will dominate what is expressed (see p. 9). These distinctions are applicable within many genres as well as the propemptikon. The nature of ancient literature and the importance that it attaches to the addressee would suggest that the standard status-relationship between speaker and addressee ought to be the one in which the speaker is inferior, the addressee being superior, and that other relationships should be treated as divergences from this norm. But it is not worth making an issue of this point: I shall simply produce interesting cases of each relationship without being concerned about which is the norm and which are divergences.

When it is said that in cases where the speaker is superior, with the result that the addressee is inferior, advice will predominate, this should not be understood to mean that advice is found only in situations where the speaker is superior: Sappho's brother Charaxus is not her inferior in *Fr.* 5 (LP) and yet he receives advice there (see p. 230). There are in fact other definable situations where advice is possible;[32] but where we know that the status of the speaker is higher than that of the addressee, it is always worth while to look for symbouleutic material. Conversely symbouleutic material in an example of a genre should suggest the question about relative status, although it should not dictate an answer. Since the concept of the addressee as an inferior is not familiar, I shall exemplify it at length in the case of Propertius 2 19, which through an understanding of the concept, can be assigned to the genre propemptikon.

> Etsi me inuito discedis, Cynthia, Roma,
>   laetor quod sine me deuia rura coles.
> nullus erit castis iuuenis corruptor in agris,
>   qui te blanditiis non sinat esse probam;
> 5 nulla neque ante tuas orietur rixa fenestras,
>   nec tibi clamatae somnus amarus erit.
> sola eris et solos spectabis, Cynthia, montis
>   et pecus et finis pauperis agricolae.
> illic te nulli poterunt corrumpere ludi,
> 10   fanaque peccatis plurima causa tuis.
> illic assidue tauros spectabis arantis,
>   et uitem docta ponere falce comas;

atque ibi rara feres inculto tura sacello,
    haedus ubi agrestis corruet ante focos;
15 protinus et nuda choreas imitabere sura;
    omnia ab externo sint modo tuta uiro.
ipse ego uenabor: iam nunc me sacra Dianae
    suscipere et Veneris ponere uota iuuat.
incipiam captare feras et reddere pinu
20   cornua et audaces ipse monere canis;
non tamen ut uastos ausim temptare leones
    aut celer agrestis comminus ire sues.
haec igitur mihi sit lepores audacia mollis
    excipere et structo figere auem calamo,
25 qua formosa suo Clitumnus flumina luco
    integit, et niueos abluit unda boues.
tu quotiens aliquid conabere, uita, memento
    uenturum paucis me tibi Luciferis.
hic me nec solae poterunt auertere siluae,
30   nec uaga muscosis flumina fusa iugis,
quin ego in assidua mutem tua nomina lingua:
    absenti nemo non nocuisse uelit.
Propertius 2 19

Most propemptika are addressed to persons departing by sea; but this
is simply because most ancient journeys were sea-voyages. There is no
hard and fast rule about this matter; indeed one portion of Menander's
prescription (398 29ff.) provides for journeys by land. The virtual
absence of a schetliasmos from this elegy need not trouble us either:
schetliasmoi are characteristic of, although not logically essential to or
necessarily confined to the propemptikon of equal to equal.

The conceptual and topical basis of the elegy is as follows: after a hint
of a schetliasmos (1) Propertius gives his approval to Cynthia's departure[33] from Rome in the first two lines, which also intimate that the situation is propemptic, in that Cynthia is leaving Rome, is going to the
countryside,[34] and is being addressed at her departure by Propertius.
Into 2-16 (ostensibly a set of moralistic explanations of why Propertius
approves of Cynthia's choice of destination), Propertius works a description of Cynthia's future activities in the countryside. He is thus
combining a macrologic account of the commonplace description of the
traveller's journey[35] with advice. With one exception treated below,

2-16 do not contain commands or recommendations in as many words, unless the second person future indicatives in 7-8 and 11ff. be interpreted as polite imperatives; but this interpretation is difficult in view of the intermingled third person futures in 3ff. and 9-10, which cannot be so understood. Nevertheless, Propertius' approval of these future activities of Cynthia, and the moralizing, sententious and yet personal nature of his reasons for approving of them, amount to an implication that this is how he advises Cynthia to behave. As though to confirm that this is what the whole passage signifies, Propertius does go so far as to give Cynthia a permission in 15 upon a condition laid down in 16, and thus resorts to open recommendation.

The situation which Propertius is portraying in these lines is worth contrasting with that of Propertius 1 8, a propemptikon of equal to equal. There Cynthia was preparing to depart with another lover, Propertius' rival; here she is not only departing alone but going to a place where, notwithstanding later apprehensions on Propertius' part (27), the moral climate and general environment will, so Propertius hopes, give her no opportunity to find another lover. Naturally this does not mean that Propertius' position in 2 19 is universally characteristic of the superior speaker of an erotic propemptikon. Indeed, one of the ironies of Horace *Odes* 3 27 is that, although adopting the would-be superior role of augur and abstaining from direct schetliasmos, Horace is in exactly the same situation as Propertius in 1 8, and is using a symbouleutic ethos to cloak an implied schetliasmos.

At 17 Propertius turns to his own doings. It is conventional that the propemptic speaker should do this. In Menander the topos is part of the schetliasmos, and the speaker emphasizes the solitary life he will lead in the wilderness far from human society (397 4ff. cf. p. 16). It is interesting to observe the clever adaptation Propertius has made of this topos. Menander's schetliastic speaker is reacting to the 'treachery' of the departing traveller by seeking refuge in the wilderness far from man; and indeed hunting in the woods, which is the Propertian version of the topos and which is possibly also a reminiscence of Cornelius Gallus' propemptikon to Lycoris,[36] can sometimes be an antidote to love.[37] Propertius uses the idea in a different way altogether: he represents himself as hunting not because he is love-lorn, but to complete that pair of balanced vignettes around which the poem is built. In one the elegiac mistress is described with all her characteristic fickleness, and is set in the cultivated and tame countryside to which elegiac lovers always wanted to translate their mistresses; this almost amounts to a Tibullan bucolic fantasy. In the other Propertius sketches the elegiac lover in the wild part of the countryside but able only to hunt small tame beasts, loving and constant to Cynthia, a fulfilled Acontius.

At 27 the propemptikon reaches its climax: Propertius apprehends some possibility of danger (cp. 32) to his position as Cynthia's lover, even in the supposedly safe surroundings he has approved for her. He begins as though he is about to express a variant of the 'remember me' topos:[38] 'whenever you think of being unfaithful think of me' (27-8). But he transforms this into an expression of a reaction. He announces that he will join Cynthia soon, which is his reaction to the generic situation so far expressed. It is hard to know whether to call this a change of mind on Propertius' part; but it is certainly a decision not even hinted at in the preceding lines. In some ways it is like Horace's 'change of mind' in his first epode (cp. p. 141). Hard on the heels of this reaction Propertius compensates for the abortiveness of the direct expression of the 'remember me' topos by producing a kindred propemptic topos which runs its full course.[39] In the interval before joining Cynthia he will keep her in mind constantly by speaking her name repeatedly.

The last line of the elegy conveys a motif which has been present in more or less suppressed form throughout the whole of it, namely Propertius' fear of Cynthia being unfaithful to him. The suppressed permeance of this theme is part of Propertius' clever exploitation of his readers' expectations of a propemptikon to a departing mistress. They would expect a propemptikon such as Propertius 1 8 or Horace *Odes* 3 27, that is, one written to a mistress departing with another lover. On one level Propertius had disappointed his readers: Cynthia is departing alone to a place where she will find no other lover; but on another level he has fulfilled his audience's expectation by representing himself as nevertheless afraid that she may contrive to be unfaithful. The tension thus created is focused by the use of relative status in the elegy. The matter of the superior's moralizing advice is really his own fear of losing his superior position.

Examples of such superiority on the part of the speaker can be observed in other genres too. For example, in the 'symptoms of love',[40] cases of equality between speaker and addressee, that is, where the speaker is a lover like the addressee, differ in tone and content from cases where the speaker is a non-lover, whether a 'mocker of love' or not, and therefore a superior. Gentle, friendly and sympathetic questioning and comment indicate the equality relationship of fellow lovers; on the other hand the extent to which the speaker is uncomprehending and unsympathetic, and comments on the matter in a harsh, ironic and symbouleutic fashion, reflects fairly well the extent to which the speaker is being represented as a superior.

Examples of inferiority on the part of the speaker are sometimes easy enough to detect: for example, in propemptika like Propertius 1 6 or 3 4, or in a prosphonetikon like Horace *Odes* 3 14, where the addressee has an important public position. But in other genres the distinction between equality and inferiority on the part of the speaker is not quite as obvious. Such a genre is the specialized minor type of kletikon usually known as uocatio ad cenam.[41] Four clear examples addressed to superiors are *A.P.* 11 44 (Philodemus); Horace *Odes* 1 20; *Epistles* 1 5; Sidonius Apollinaris *Carmina* 17:

> Αὔριον εἰς λιτήν σε καλιάδα, φίλτατε Πείσων,
> ἐξ ἐνάτης ἕλκει μουσοφιλὴς ἕταρος,
> εἰκάδα δειπνίζων ἐνιαύσιον· εἰ δ' ἀπολείψεις
> οὔθατα καὶ Βρομίου χιογενῆ πρόποσιν,
> 5 ἀλλ' ἑτάρους ὄψει παναληθέας, ἀλλ' ἐπακούσῃ
> Φαιήκων γαίης πουλὺ μελιχρότερα·
> ἢν δέ ποτε στρέψῃς καὶ ἐς ἡμέας ὄμματα, Πείσων,
> ἄξομεν ἐκ λιτῆς εἰκάδα πιοτέρην.
> *A.P.* 11 44 (Philodemus)

This epigram expresses affection for Piso, but his superiority is stated explicitly. He is a wealthy man (3-4), wealth being usually regarded as a credit to its possessor and conferring a superior status; and Philodemus is imposing on him by inviting him away from his expensive food to a poor man's table (2). Piso is invited on the promise of good company and good talk, an encomiastic touch suggesting that Piso, like a true Epicurean, will be content with the poor food of a humble but happy celebration of Epicurus' birthday. Finally, Piso's role as Philodemus' patron rounds off the epigram (7-8).

> Vile potabis modicis Sabinum
> cantharis, Graeca quod ego ipse testa
> conditum leui, datus in theatro
>   cum tibi plausus,

5 care Maecenas eques, ut paterni
   fluminis ripae simul et iocosa
   redderet laudes tibi Vaticani
       montis imago.

   Caecubum et prelo domitam Caleno
10 tu bibes uuam: mea nec Falernae
   temperant uites neque Formiani
       pocula colles.
   Horace *Odes* 1 20

In this example Maecenas' superiority is demonstrated in two ways.
First, Horace apologetically contrasts his own poverty with Maecenas'
wealth at the beginning and at the end of the poem. Second, the core of
the poem, which is sandwiched between the two apologetic invitations,
is a reminiscence of a public demonstration in Maecenas' favour. The
link between the two encomiastic ideas is a proof of Horace's sincerity
as an encomiast. When Maecenas was applauded in the theatre Horace
laid down a wine to commemorate the event; he now invites Maecenas
to drink it with him. The humble Horace's poor commemorative wine
is a proof of the sincerity of his feelings for Maecenas, since it shows
that Maecenas' public success had an effect on Horace's private life.[42]
Horace *Epistles* 1 5 is a more elaborate invitation to Torquatus. Here
the superior addressee is not invited directly and unconditionally with
the polite future of invitation as is normal:

   Si potes Archiacis conuiua recumbere lectis
   nec modica cenare times holus omne patella,
   supremo te sole domi, Torquate, manebo.
   uina bibes iterum Tauro diffusa palustris
   inter Minturnas Sinuessanumque Petrinum.
   Horace *Epistles* 1 5 1-5

The invitation is conditional and at first oblique, the *si* clauses being
placed at the beginning and conveying an apology for the meanness of
Horace's furniture and the poverty of his food and china. Only in 4
does Horace use the future of invitation and then with respect to his
wine, in which he does appear to take some pride, simply because of its
association with Torquatus' family.[43] All this is encomiastic and emphasizes Horace's hesitation in offering an invitation to a wealthy and important man. Having established without any doubt their relative status,

Horace indulges in a mock display of independence and sturdy pride in 6: '*si melius quid habes, arcesse uel imperium fer*'. But this is a pale shadow of what passes between equals in this genre (see below, p. 243), and simply serves, along with other jests and impertinences (15, 19, 29, 30-1), to combine flattery of Torquatus' occupation and importance with that appearance of free speech which in itself was meant to be a further compliment to Torquatus' liberality and willingness to be frankly treated by his inferiors. These flattering audacities are in keeping with the rest of the poem: the setting of the supper at a time of day when an active, respectable Roman might reasonably dine (3); the careful moral and political defence of the celebration (9ff.); Horace's humour at his own expense (13-14); the concern shown that all shall be in order for Torquatus (7, 21ff.); the choice of other guests with Torquatus in mind (24ff.); the extension of the invitation to friends Torquatus may care to bring along (28ff.); and the emphasis throughout the epistle on Torquatus's busy and important legal activities. All these things create an aura of compliment and encomium suited to the superiority of the addressee.

Sidonius *Carmina* 17 is fairly conventional although Christianized: the addressee Ommatius will make the event lucky by coming; Sidonius has no fine furniture, plate, food or wine, as Ommatius by implication has, but Sidonius begs him to come; Christ will supply all, Christ to whom Sidonius owes Ommatius' kindness, which has given Sidonius a second home.

One encomiastic feature of all these poems is that in none of them is the superior addressee asked to bring anything as a contribution to the feast. The nearest any of them come to being asked to contribute is Horace *Epistles* 1 5 6, where the request is conditional, and in fact is not a genuine request but simply a piece of mock independence on Horace's part. The importance of not asking for a contribution is that in antiquity meals and drinking parties were of different kinds. They could be pure contribution feasts where, although one person might be nominal host, the guests contributed equally in cash or kind. Alternatively they could be of the sort where the host provided most of the first course and the bulk of the second, the guests contributing only small delicacies to the second dessert course.[44] Or lastly they could be occasions when the host provided everything and the guests nothing.

In antiquity, as now, the paradoxical social injustice prevailed that rich people were given free meals, which they did not need, by the poor, while poor people, even if guests of their fellows, had to pay for what they got. This is why invitations to superiors are to free meals, while those to equals are often to contribution feasts of one sort or another. Two such invitations will close this chapter: they are addressed by equal to equal and can be contrasted with those invitations from inferiors to their superiors discussed above. The first is humorous, relying for its humour partly on an exaggeration of the reasonable demand a host might make on his socially equal friend for a contribution.

> Cenabis bene, mi Fabulle, apud me
> paucis, si tibi di fauent, diebus,
> si tecum attuleris bonam atque magnam
> cenam, non sine candida puella
> 5 et uino et sale et omnibus cachinnis.
> haec si, inquam, attuleris, uenuste noster,
> cenabis bene; nam tui Catulli
> plenus sacculus est aranearum.
> sed contra accipies meros amores
> 10 seu quid suauius elegantiusue est:
> nam unguentum dabo, quod meae puellae
> donarunt Veneres Cupidinesque
> quod tu cum olfacies, deos rogabis
> totum ut te faciant, Fabulle, nasum.
> Catullus 13

This invitation purports in its opening words (1) to be a genuine invitation to hospitality. But when Catullus the host specifies Fabullus the guest's contribution, he asks Fabullus to provide the whole meal and almost all its accoutrements. Fabullus has to bring food, wine, a girl, and even salt (a pun, of course, but in its material sense something the poorest household had). Moreover, Fabullus must bring witty talk (contrast Philodemus 6). What Catullus offers is pure affection (9, compare Philodemus 5) and *unguentum* (perfumed ointment) (11-12). This latter offering at first seems generous because of the expense of perfumed ointment, but it turns out that it belongs to Lesbia, not Catullus, before the invitation dissolves into further humour at Fabullus' expense (13-14). Catullus demonstrates his own and Fabullus' friendship in many ways and the equality of the pair is manifest throughout. Good humoured freedom of speech[45] at Fabullus' expense parallels jokes made by Catullus at his own expense. The idea of the host asking for almost everything to be contributed by the guest is a delightful touch.

The second invitation between equals is that controversial ode of Horace (4 12) in which Virgil is addressed. It has often been doubted that the addressee of this ode is the author of the *Aeneid*, on the grounds that Horace would not have demanded a contribution from Virgil the poet (14ff.), would not have rebuked him for his 'greed for gain' (25), and would not have spoken of him as 'a dependent of young noblemen' (15).[46] Such doubts are a misunderstanding of the purpose of the ode. Unlike *Odes* 1 3, which treats Virgil as a superior, *Odes* 4 12 is meant to express the friendship of Horace for Virgil as an equal. It should be read in the same spirit as Catullus 13. It is a parody of the invitation to the rich and busy superior which reveals itself as such by its excessive demands on the guest, demands all the more outrageous because a real invitation to a superior would not ask anything from him. Horace is asking Virgil for nard (a perfumed ointment) and offering wine. Nard (17) was valuable in antiquity while wine in general was not. It is hard to resist the conclusion that Horace was, like Catullus, asking for more than a just contribution, especially as the spring topoi at the beginning of the ode hint at the time when last year's wine first becomes ready for drinking and so suggest that Horace is offering Virgil new and hence very cheap wine.[47] If this is so, 'put aside your greed for gain' (25) takes on a new complexion. Horace, like Catullus, is making a joke at his own expense as well as or even more than at the expense of the addressee. He accuses Virgil of meanness and being over-interested in money; we may compare this to 'give up your trivial expectations and your struggles for riches' (*Epistles* 1 5 8) addressed to Torquatus, a genuine rich superior, where although the riches are those of Torquatus' legal clients and not his own, the trend is the same. But all the time Horace is actually demonstrating comic greed and meanness on his own part by demanding an overgenerous compensation before he will give Virgil a cheap drink (15-16, 21ff.). The same double-edged freedom of speech is present in the gibe about Virgil being a dependent of young noblemen. This was not something dishonourable in antiquity. Horace himself was a dependent of a man who, if he could not claim to be a Roman noble, claimed the next best thing: to be a noble in his own part of Italy and to be the descendant of Etruscan royalty. But the description is also meant to tease Virgil further by providing evidence for Horace's belief that Virgil can afford to make this over-generous contribution to their little feast; it may also hint at Horace's mock envy of Virgil for this ability. Even if Virgil and Horace were as pompous as they are sometimes painted, the conventions of genre were there to save them from themselves. *Odes* 4. 12 reads throughout as a friendly, teasing invitation from one friend to another of equal status.

NOTES AND REFERENCES
Book titles are given in full except in
the case of commentaries and standard
reference works.

CHAPTER ONE
1. The first book of Propertius' elegies
is dedicated to Tullus by the
apostrophe at 1 1 9. For similar
Propertian and contemporary
dedications cp., e.g. Prop. 2 1 17,
Tib. 1 1 53, Hor. *O.* 1 1 1; 2 1 14.
2. For this topos see p. 99.
3. See also pp. 123 f.
4. Cp. also Tib. 1 7 9 ff. and 1 10.
5. This and other details of interpretation in Prop. 1 6 will be treated
elsewhere.
6. See Copley 145, n. 6.
7. I intend to treat the question of
exclusion in a future work.
8. For the propemptikon see Jäger
and N-H1, 40 ff. with the works
cited there.
9. 'Tibulls erste Elegie' (11) *RhM* 65
(1910) 24. Jäger (21) does not
appreciate the value of the assignment.
10. E.g. Paulin. *Carm.* 17 is type 2
and non-schetliastic. See pp. 11 f.,
155 ff.
11. E.g. Hor. *O.* 1 14 is type 3 but
schetliastic. See pp. 219 ff.
12. 396 26 ff.; 397 21 ff.
13. 395 8-10.
14. See, e.g. pp. 236 ff., for a type 1
literary propemptikon.
15. See above, n. 5.
16. See pp. 38 f., 41 ff., 61 ff., 71, 73 f.,
116 f., 134, 180 ff., 185 ff.
17. The 'excuse' in Hor. *Epod.* 1 7-8
is expressed in a more sophisticated
fashion than in the others. See
pp. 141 f.
18. See pp. 127 f.
19. Cp. also St. *Sil.* 3 2 78, 90.
20. See p. 57.
21. Cp., e.g. Prop. 1 8 15, Virg. *Aen.*
4 365 ff.
22. For motives for departure cp., e.g.
love: Prop. 1 8; Hor. *O.* 3 27;

Himer. *Or.* 12 33 (negated);
friendship: e.g. Hor. *Epod.* 1;
home: e.g. Hom. *Od.* 5 203 ff.;
Paulin. *Carm.* 17 5-6; Menander
396 8 ff.; *money* (negated): Hor.
Epod. 1; Prop. 1.8; *cultured
tourism*: Himer. *Or.* 12 33; 13
4(?); Cinna (*F.P.L.* ed. Morel,
pp. 87 f.) (negated).
23. Cp. Prop. 1 8 8-9 and see F. Cairns
'Notes on Propertius 1 8'
(forthcoming).
24. pp. 128 f.
25. For such macrologia see pp. 119 f.
26. This part of Menander's type 2
prescription can be used to illustrate Propertius' type 3 example,
since both variants contain eulogy
at this point.
27. See D. R. Shackleton Bailey *Pro-
pertiana* (Cambridge 1956) p. 271
on *tua aetas* (21).
28. Menander in this section of his
propemptikon prescription recommends praise of the addressee in
terms of the standard four-virtue
division (397 21 ff.). We might
be tempted to understand Prop.
1 6 20 as an oblique reference to
justice, 1 6 21 to self-control, and
1 6 22 to bravery (see also 1 6 1),
were it not hard to see wisdom
in 1 6 19 and were this approach
not in any case probably over-
mechanical.
29. For the 'remember me' topos cp.,
e.g. Sapph. *Fr.* 94 (LP) 7 f.; Tib.
1 3 2; Hor. *O.* 3 27 14; Ov. *Am.*
2 11 37; Paulin. *Carm.* 17 9;
Menander 398 26 ff. It is not, of
course, necessary that topoi should
occur in examples in the same
order as in the generic formula
(see pp. 40, 108 f., 113 ff.),
although such conformity is of
interest when found.
30. E.g. Sapph. *Fr.* 94 (LP); Hor. *O.*
1 3; 3 27; St. *Sil.* 3 2.
31. *Textgeschichte der griechischen
Bukoliker* (Berlin 1906) p. 171. The
present work was in press when G.

Giangrande's article 'Theocritus' Twelfth and Fourth Idylls: a study in Hellenistic irony' *Quad. Urbin.* 12 (1971) 95 ff., was published. This valuable paper expounds *Idyll* 12 as an 'epibaterion'.

32.Introduction to *Id.* 12 (vol. II, p. 221).

33.E.*g*. Libanius' Prosphonetikos to Julian (*Or.* 13) and *Frr.* 13, 33 (Foerster); Menander 414-18.

34.E.*g*. Doxopater, ed. Walz, *Rhetores Graeci* vol. II, 415 5; Ps.-Dion. Hal., ed. Usener-Radermacher, vol. VI², pp. 272 ff.

35.Menander 378 ff.

36.Cp. also Cat. 9 1 f, a variant of this topos.

37.See p. 164.

38.In accordance with the principle of addressee-variation (see pp. 218 ff.) and a 'formal' sophistication (see pp. 127 f.).

39.Cp., e.*g*. the announcement of impending departure or injunction to go in the propemptikon, and the door or threshold in the komos.

40.16 23; 17 41.

41.See Fraenkel on *Ag.* 899 ff.

42.*Ag.* p. 410.

43.Pp. 127 f.

44.E.*g*. Theogn. 1 691 f.; Arist. *Eq.* 498 ff.; Hor. *O.* 1 3 1 ff.; 3 27 13 ff; Prop. 1 8 19 ff; Ov. *Am.* 2 11 34.

45.See, e.*g*. on Lacedaemon, Leutsch-Schneidewin *C.P.G.* vol. II p. 479; on Thessaly, e.*g*. Athen. *Deip.* 418D; on Amyclae, Otto *Sprich-wörter, s.v.*

46.See Otto *Sprichwörter, s.v. Sparta.*

CHAPTER TWO

1.See G. Kennedy 'The ancient dispute over rhetoric in Homer' *AJPh* 78 (1957) 23 ff.

2.*Artium Scriptores* (Vienna 1951) A 2-4, pp. 3-10.

3.See W. Arend *Die Typischen Scenen bei Homer* (Problemata 7 Berlin 1933).

4.See pp. 38 ff. and below, n. 27.

5.See Burgess, *passim*, and esp. 92 f., 166 ff.

6.Hom. *Od.* 13 38 ff.

7.Hom. *Il.* 24 725 ff. Priam is a slip on Menander's part: in fact Andromache, Hecuba and Helen utter the laments.

8.5.

9.See, e.*g*. Menander 333 9 ff., 334 28 ff., 336 11 f., 437 20 f.

10.The following further syntaktika will not be analysed in the present discussion, although the common-place nature of the generic topoi is sometimes confirmed by reference to them: Eur. *Hec.* 445-83; *Phoen.* 625-35; Prop. 3 21; Virg. *Aen.* 4 333-61. I hope to treat of some of these in a future work.

11.E.*g*. Greg. Naz. *Or.* 42.

12.See pp. 40 f. and below, n. 27.

13.On combination of topoi see ch. 4.

14.But see Cat. 46, treated on pp. 44 f.

15.See, e.*g*. Thuc. 7 77.

16.Cp., e.*g*. Hom. *Od.* 13 39; Solon *Fr.* 7 (19) D 3 f., 5.

17.*As an excuse for going home:* e.*g*. Hom. *Od.* 13 42 f.; *as left behind:* e.*g*. Eur. *Phoen.* 632; Cat. 46 9 ff.; Prop. 3 21 15; *as accompanying:* Prop. 3 21 11.

18.E.*g*. Eur. *Phoen.* 630; *Hec.* 448 f.; Tib. 1 10 13; Virg. *Aen.* 4 340 ff.; Prop. 3 21 1.

19.See N-H1 on *O.* 1 4, and pp. 244 f. on Hor. *O.* 4 12.

20.The adaptation of topoi to indivi-dual addressees is prescribed by Menander (*passim*) and practised in all branches of ancient literature.

21.See above, n. 18.

22.See, e.*g*. Plaut. *Merc.* 865; Tib. 1 3 33 f.; Liv. 40 52 4.; and see G. Radke *Die Götter Altitaliens* (Münster 1965) *s.v. Lares.*

23.Cp. Theoc. *Id.* 10, discussed on p. 175.

24.See also pp. 129 ff.

25.Cp. Menander 431 25 f. But the propemptic speaker can equally well say 'remember me' or 'I will remember you'; so this syntaktic case may not be as striking as it might seem at first. See pp. 135, 150, 199, 239, and ch. 5, n. 13.

26.Cp. Eur. *Phoen.* 633 ff.; Menander 433 12 f.

27.But we may note in passing the syntaktikon of Odysseus to Alcinous and the Phaeacians (treated above) and *Il.* 3 428-36, an inverse prosphonetikon – see ch. 5. The latter passage was brought to my notice by Mr J. G. Howie.

28.Cp., e.*g.* *imperative* (with good wishes*): Arist. *Eq.* 498*; Ov. *Am.* 3 11 37; *future*: Hor. *Epod.* 1 1; Tib. 1 3 1; Prop. 1 6 34*; Paulin. *Carm.* 17 17 f.; *subjunctive*: Hom. *Od.* 15 128*; Theogn. 1 691*.

29.See ch. 1, n. 29.

30.Affection is always implied in the genre (see pp. 8-9). For explicit statements of it, see, e.g. [Erinna] ap. Athen. *Deip.* 283D; *A.P.* 12 52 1-2 (Meleager); Hor. *Epod.* 1 5 f.; *O.* 1 3 7 f.

31.For fictional assumptions that the addressee requires or wishes to be told something, see A. Ramminger *Motivgeschichtliche Studien zu Catulls Basiagedichten* (Diss. Tübingen 1937) pp. 7 ff.

32.See p. 16 and ch. 1, n. 30.

33.E.g. Prop. 1 6 5-18; 1 8 1-17.

34.For a similar attack on an oath-breaking comrade see Alcaeus *Fr.* 129 (LP) 21 ff.

35.On this fragment see D. L. Page *Sappho & Alcaeus* (Oxford 1955) pp. 198 ff. I have assumed that line 16 begins a new poem – though this is not essential to the discussion – and I have accepted Page's general interpretation of the sense of lines 26 f.

36.See Menander 377 ff., and pp. 212 ff.

37.See pp. 129 ff.

38.On this poem see also pp. 189 ff.

39.Cp., e.g. Cat. 63 59 ff.; Ov. *Tr.* 3 1 (esp. 33 ff.); 4 2.

CHAPTER THREE

1.See ch. 2, n. 5.

2.For these and other rhetorical sources and examples mentioned below see W. Kroll, art. 'Rhetorik' R-E Suppl. 7 pp. 1039-1138.

3.See W. R. Smyth 'Interpretationes Propertianae' *CQ* 43 (1949) 121 f.; F. Cairns *CR* NS19 (1969) 131 ff.

4.But see pp. 72 f., 84 on the possibility of specialized symbouleutic genres.

5.See, e.g. on eucharistic genres, pp. 73 f.

6.'Propertius as Praeceptor Amoris' *CPh* 5 (1910) 28 ff.; 'Erotic teaching in Roman elegy and the Greek sources' Part 1, 440 ff.; Part 2, 6 (1911) 56 ff.

7.E.g. Arist. *Av.* 716; Dio Chry. *Or.* 13 36; 35 2.

8.See also A. A. Day *The Origins of Latin Elegy* (Oxford 1938) p. 92, n. 1.

9.I owe to Mr Alex Hardie the assignment of Hor. *O.* 2 17 to the genre soteria.

10.For the equivalence between addressee and object see pp. 127 f., 177.

11.See LS *s.v.* For εὐχαριστηρία, see, e.g. Polyb. 5 14 8; Schol. Pind. *Pyth.* 7 9.

12.For examples see Gerber-Greef *Lexicon Taciteum* (repr. Hildesheim 1962) *s.v.* grates and, e.g. Plin. *Paneg.* 1 6; Ausonius' and Paulinus of Pella's *Eucharistica*; titles of *Paneg. Lat.* 11 (3), 8 (5).

13.A few Roman examples are: Cat. 49; Mart. 8 49; St. *Sil.* 4 2; Claud. *Carm. Min.* 14 (82); Sidon. *Carm.* 16; Martial and Statius are thanking the Emperor Domitian.

14.See N-H1, 244 ff; Williams 7 ff., 103 ff.

15.See G. Kennedy *The Art of Per-*

suasion in Greece (London 1963) pp. 270 ff.

16. See ch. 1, n. 7.

17. 'Drei Gedichte des Properz' *RhM* 69 (1914) 393 ff. See also F. Cairns 'Theocritus Idyll 10' *Hermes* 98 (1970) 38 ff.

18. See Bruns *Fontes Iuris Romani* (7 ed. Tübingen 1909) pp. 361 f., and F. Cairns 'Propertius 2 29A' *CQ* 21 (1971) 455 ff.

19. E.g. (besides the obvious literary manifestos) Prop. 2 13 and 2 30 (see L. P. Wilkinson, 'The continuity of Propertius 2 13' *CR* NS 16 (1966) 141 ff. and F. Cairns 'Propertius 2 30A and B' *CQ* 21 (1971) 204 ff.

20. For an analogous convention see F. Cairns 'Catullus 1' *Mnemosyne* 22 (1969) 153 ff.

21. For these themes see W. Kroll *Studien zum Verständnis der römischen Literatur* (Stuttgart 1924) ch. 2 and Cairns, op. cit. (above, n. 20).

22. See Wilkinson, op. cit. (above, n. 19) p. 143.

23. *cera* codd. *serta* edd. The correctness of the MSS reading has been established by Shackleton Bailey, op. cit. (ch. 1, n. 27) pp. 244 f.

24. Theophr. *H.P.* 5 4 5.

25. See Kroll, op. cit. (above, n. 21).

26. E.g. Cat. 12 13 f. For the sentimental value of a gift cp. also, e.g. Ov. *Her.* 17 71 ; Mart. 9 99.

27. The appearance of the word *aurum* in both passages may be noted.

28. On ancient friendship see, e.g. Williams 408.

29. This example is recovered from the text of Himerius.

30. K. Quinn 'Horace as a love poet. A reading of *Odes* 1, 5' *Arion* 2 (1963) 68 f., quoted and criticized by D. West *Reading Horace* (Edinburgh 1967) pp. 105 ff.

31. See ch. 2, n. 5.

32. In the scholion the word is found

in adjectival form. Classical dawn poems of several genres are assembled without generic distinction in *Eos* ed. A. T. Hatto (The Hague 1965) pp. 255 ff., 271 ff. The work collects dawn poetry of all languages and epochs.

33. See N-H1, 189.

34. For a parody of the 'gloating over fulfilment' of a different sort of prophecy see Ov. *Am.* 1 14.

35. For another possible example with an even more fleeting allusion to the komos see *A.P.* 5 92 (Rufinus).

36. See Jacoby, op. cit. (above, n. 17).

37. But see N-H1, 289 ff. for a different view of this ode.

38. *angiportus* = στενωπός, a feature of some komoi, e.g. Aristaen. *Ep.* 2 4 ; 2 19 ; Lucian *Bis Acc.* 31.

39. See, e.g. Prop. 3 6 21 f. and P. Pierrugues *Glossarium Eroticum Linguae Latinae* (repr. Amsterdam 1965) svv. *lupa, lupanar, meretrix, scortum*, etc.

40. See Copley, *passim*.

41. On the title mandata and on the genre mandata morituri (below, pp. 90 f.) see, e.g. Gerber-Greef, op. cit. (ch. 3, n. 12) s.v. *mando*. For the title epistaltikon see Proclus *Chrestomathia* 34.

42. For such mandata see N-H1 on *O.* 1 38, whose genre is mandata.

43. On this genre see W. Kese *Untersuchungen zu Epikedion und Consolatio in der römischen Dichtung* (Diss. Göttingen 1950).

44. Op. cit. (above, n. 19).

45. On questions relating to the addressee see ch. 9.

46. The conclusion of this section may throw some light on the problem about the soteria mentioned pp. 73 f.

47. See Copley, Chs. 3 ff.

48. See F. Cairns 'Five "Religious" Odes of Horace' *AJPh* 92 (1971) 433 ff.

49. 'Italische Volksjustiz' *RhM* 56 (1901) 1 ff.

50. E.g. Cat. 12 ; 25 ; Ov. *Am.* 3 449 f. ;

Petron. *Sat.* 92 ; Tac. *Hist.* 1 5 3 (an extended sense).

51.See op. cit. (above n.49).

52.*Flagitare* however originally means 'to disgrace' not 'to demand' – see op. cit. (above, n.49).

53.For another possible item of arai literature see *Collectanea Alexandrina* ed. J. U. Powell (Oxford 1925) p.28 – the editor's comments on the *Chiliades* of Euphorion in his introduction to Euphorion.

54.E.g. Plaut. *Pseud.* 357. In other cases quoted by Usener, op cit. (above, n.49), '*dicta*' is understood.

55.On triumph poems see K. Galinsky 'The triumph theme in the Augustan elegy', *WS* NS3 (1969) 75ff.

56.See H. S. Versnel *Triumphus* (Leiden 1970) *passim*.

57.On such matters see A. E. Harvey 'The classification of Greek lyric poetry' *CQ* NS5 (1955) 157ff., and R. Pfeiffer *History of Classical Scholarship* (Oxford 1968) pp. 183 ff.

58.For self-fulfilling undertakings see W. J. Slater 'Futures in Pindar' *CQ* 19 (1969) 86ff. ; N-H1, 254.

CHAPTER FOUR

1.For these see Burgess 101ff., 106.

2.E.g. 369 27ff. ; 370 9ff., 409 14ff.

3.Introduction to *Id.* 17, p.325.

4.But for an excellent treatment of the literary context of *Id.* 17 and a fair assessment of its merits see W. Meinke *Untersuchungen zu den Enkomiastischen Gedichten Theokrits* (Diss. Kiel 1965) pp. 87ff.

5.For a good account of ancient thought about encomium see Burgess 113ff.

6.The assignment was by Burgess 130, 171 (but with inaccurate concomitants).

7.In Menander's period of course one of the Roman Emperors.

8.On the distinction between encomium and apologia see below, p. 120 and Burgess 118.

9.For these see G. Fraustadt *Encomiorum in litteris Graecis usque ad Romanam aetatem historia* (Diss. Leipzig 1909), e.g. pp. 54f., 62f., 68.

10.See above, n. 8.

11.Cf. Callim. *H.*4 187ff. ; Paus. 1 7 2.

12.Cp. ch. 1, n.28.

13.See above, n.8.

14.See, e.g. Burgess 142ff. ; F. Muecke *Tibullus Book I: Critical Essays on Selected Poems* (B. Phil. thesis, Oxford 1970) pp. 66ff. ; F. Cairns 'Propertius 3 10 and Roman Birthdays' *Hermes* 99 (1971) 150ff.

15.In the case of women the Genius is replaced by the Juno (Natalis).

16.See Fraustadt, op. cit. (above, n.9), e.g. pp. 43, 55, 62.

17.See Kiessling-Heinze, ad loc.

18.Cp. *A.P.* 12 52 5f. (Meleager).

19.Since Nicetas is also a governor (in the sense that he is a bishop), and since he is going to rule his diocese, schetliasmos addressed to him would be doubly unusual.

20.For treatises on this subject see W. Kroll, op. cit. (ch. 3, n.2).

21.See, e.g., *Ad Herennium* ed. H. Caplan (Loeb Class. Libr. 1954) intr. pp. ixff.

22.See G. Kennedy, op. cit. (ch. 3, n. 15) pp. 64ff.

23.Cp., e.g. Theogn. 1 692 ; Eur. *Hel.* 1457ff., 1495ff. ; Hor. *O.* 1 3 1ff. ; Prop. 1 8 18 ; St. *Sil.* 3 2 8ff., 39ff., 101ff.

24.See above, n.23.

25.Cp., e.g. Hor. *O.* 1 3 5f. ; 1 14 16 (?) ; St. *Sil.* 3 2 5f.

26.See ch. 2, n.28.

27.See ch. 1, n.29.

28.Cp., e.g. Eur. *Hel.* 1455f., 1503f. ; Theoc. *Id.* 7 57f. ; *A.P.* 12 52 1f. (Meleager) ; Hor. *O.* 1 3 3f. ; St. *Sil.* 3 2 42ff.

29.Also e.g. at [Theoc.] *Id.* 23 17f. and see Copley 155, n.32.

30.See ch. 1, n.5.

31.See ch. 1, n.5.

CHAPTER FIVE

1.But see chs. 8-9 for possible additional speaker/addressee variations.

2.Cp., e.g. Hor. *O.* 3 27 1ff., 15f. For ancient practice see D. Wachsmuth *ΠΟΜΠΙΜΟΣ Ο ΔΑΙΜΩΝ* (Diss. Berlin 1967) pp. 177ff.

3.See ch. 4, n.28.

4.E.g. Eur. Hel. 1498ff. (?); Cinna *F.P.L.* ed. Morel, pp. 87f. *Fr.* 2; Hor. *O.* 1 3 2; St. *Sil.* 3 2 8ff., and (in varied forms) Theoc. *Id.* 7 53f.; Hor. *O.* 3 27 17ff.

5.See ch. 4, nn. 23, 28.

6.See ch. 4, n.23.

7.This notion does not appear in any other propemptikon known to me, but such vows are a topos of the prosphonetikon (B 15, cp. B 16) and are known as part of propemptic activity in ancient life – see op. cit. above, n.2, pp. 131ff.

8.See p. 57.

9.Cp., e.g. Sapph. *Fr.* 94 1f.; Prop. 1 8 1ff.; St. *Sil.* 3 2 78ff.; Himer. *Or.* 10 16; Menander 397 2ff.

10.For this distinction in the travel genres see general index, *s.v. abroad.*

11.See, e.g. Pease, ad. loc. The interpretation supported below was proposed by Palmer on Ov. *Her.* 7 53.

12.See, e.g. Heyne-Wagner on Virg. *Ecl.* 5 9 and, e.g. Ov. *Tr.* 2 497f.; Ov. *A.A.* 3 197f.; Sen. *Controv.* 3 *Praef.* 14.

13.E.g. Prop. 1 8 21ff.; St. *Sil.* 3 2 99f.; Paulin. *Carm.* 17 2ff.

14.On this genre see ch. 4, n.14.

15.For examples see Theogn. 1 425ff. and Young ad loc.

16.For these topoi see ch. 4, n.14.

17.See ch. 4, n.14.

18.See ch. 3, n.32.

CHAPTER SIX

1.Naturally, there are cases where the distinction between inclusion and reaction could give rise to argument. For example, reaction taking the form of change of mind might be thought to resemble inclusion of an 'inverse' member of the genre, or an inversion (e.g. Dido's propemptikon to Aeneas) could resemble an ordinary member of a genre with reaction. But the simpler view of such cases is usually discernible and preferable.

2.For current views see Williams 506ff., and (against unity) E. J. Kenney *O.C.T.*, Praef. p. x.

3.On the topos see N-H1, 48.

4.See ch. 2, n.28.

5.See ch. 1, n.22.

6.Cp. the parallel paradox at Hor. *O.* 3 2 1ff.

7.Cp. Tib. 1 1 and Prop. 1 1, where two versions of the life of an elegiac poet fulfil programmatic functions.

8.See ch. 1, n.1.

9.Prologue and epilogue do not appear to be genres in the sense in which the word is used in this book.

10.Cairns, op. cit. (ch. 3, n.17).

11.E.g. Plaut. *Curc.* 1-164; Aristaen. *Ep.* 2 4 and (most important) Eupolis *Fr.* 139K. It may be worth adding to the other arguments for regarding the Cyclops' song as komastic the fact that Lucian (*D. Mar.* 1 290) names and describes Polyphemus as Galatea's komast. The common denominator between Theocritus and Lucian may be mime.

12.Cp., e.g. Plat. *Symp.* 183A; Arist. *Ecl.* 962; *PTeb.* 2(d); *A.P.* 12 72 (Meleager); Copley 154, n.19.

13.Cp. the discussion of *Idyll* 6, pp. 194f.

14.See ch. 2, n.30.

15.Cp. Hom. *Od.* 15 128f.; Eur. *Hel.* 1469ff.; Theoc. *Id.* 7 52, 61f.; *A.P.* 12 52 6 (Meleager);

Hor. *Epod.* 1 1 f.; *O.* 1 3 6; St. *Sil.*
3 2 49, 101 ff.; Menander 399, 8 f.
16.See ch. 1, n. 22.
17.Cp. Hom. *Od.* 5 206 ff.; Theoc.
Id. 7 53 f.; Hor. *Epod.* 1 3 f.;
O. 1 3 9 ff.; *O.* 3 27 17 ff.; Ov.
Am. 2 119 ff.; St. *Sil.* 3 2 61 ff.
18.Cp. Prop. 1 6 17.
19.See ch. 5, n. 9.
20.Cp., e.g. Prop. 1 6 10, 18; Virg.
Aen. 4 365 ff.
21.See p. 57.
22.See ch. 1, n. 44.
23.See ch. 2, n. 30.
24.App. *Ill.* 2.
25.See ch. 4, n. 23.
26.Cp., e.g. Hom. *Od.* 15 128 f.; Eur.
Hel. 1469 f.; Theoc. *Id.* 7 61 f.;
Hor. *O.* 1 3 6; St. *Sil.* 3 2 48 f.;
Paulin. *Carm.* 17 188; Menander
399 8 f.
27.See ch. 2, n. 25; ch. 5, n. 13.
28.Perhaps a variant of the propemptic wish for the traveller's
return – but see pp. 159 ff.
29.See H. Tränkle *Die Sprachkunst
des Properz und die Tradition der
lateinischen Dichtersprache* (Wies-
baden 1960) pp. 147 ff.
30.Cp. similar Statian innovations in
the propemptikon (*Sil.* 3 2) in a
genre where direct comparison
with Menander's prescription is
possible – see pp. 162-3.
31.For *felix* as an erotic *t.t.* see R.
Pichon *Index Verborum Amatorium
apud Latinos Elegiarum Scriptores*
(repr. Hildesheim 1966) *s.v.*
32.For this latter identification see
J. G. Griffiths *Plutarch De Iside et
Osiride* (Cardiff 1970) general
index, *s.v. Persephassa.*
33.See R. Meyer *Die Bedeutung
Aegyptens in der lateinischen Literatur der vorchristlichen Zeit*
(Diss. Zürich 1961) index, *s.v.
Isis.*
34.On abortion see Brandt on Ov.
Am. p. 217.

CHAPTER SEVEN
1.See Copley, ch. 5.
2.Cp. e.g. Sapph. *Fr.* 94 (LP); Prop.
1 6; Hor. *O.* 1 3; 2 27.
3.See ch. 6, n. 15.
4.See ch. 4, n. 23.
5.For the contrast / comparison between song and sacrificial offering
see Callim. *Aet.* 1 24 f.; and
Pfeiffer, ad loc.
6.Cp., e.g. Thuc. 1 5 2; Moschus
3 82; Virg. *Ecl.* 6 46, 62; Hor. *Sat.*
1 10 36; 2 5 41; Prop. 2 30 19 ff.;
St. *Sil.* 2 7 77.
7.See ch. 6, n. 26.
8.See Plut. *Mor.* 678c, and N-H1,
401 f.
9.Cp. Hor. *O.* 3 14, treated on
pp. 182 f.
10.See pp. 27 f.
11.A penetrating analysis of these
lines and of Tib. 1 7 as a whole is
contained in F. Muecke, op. cit.
(ch. 4, n. 14) pp. 66 ff.
12.E.g. in the epithalamium (see
Menander 399 23 ff.) and the
soteria (cp. St. *Sil.* 1 4 115 ff.).
13.Hor. *O.* 4 2 45 ff.; Ov. *Tr.* 4 2 57 ff.
Cp. St. *Sil.* 1 4 115 ff. for the
soteria.
14.Cp. Menander 399 23 ff. for the
epithalamium.
15.See Otto *Sprichwörter, s.v. oculus*
10.
16.For these see op. cit. (ch. 4, n. 14).
17.Cp., e.g. Ov. *Tr.* 5 5 23 f.; Tib.
2 2 19 f.; Ov. *Tr.* 3 13 (negated).
18.*pallor*: see Enk on Prop. 1 1 22;
thinness: Theoc. *Id.* 2 89 f.; Prop.
1 5 22; 2 22 21; Ov. *Am.* 1 6 5;
2 10 23; *Her.* 11 27 f.; *unkempt-
ness*: Ov. *Her.* 13 31; *Ep. Sapph.
ad Phaon.* 73 ff.
19.Cp., e.g. Prop. 1 1 29; 3 21 1 f.;
Ov. *Rem. Am.* 213 ff.
20.See Gow, ad loc.
21.See ch. 3, n. 17.
22.See ch. 3, n. 6.
23.Bellona, originally the Roman war
goddess, was identified with the
Asiatic goddess Ma whose temple

was served by sacred prostitutes. This presumably explains the role of the priestess of Bellona here. See Kl.-Pauly, *s.v. Ma.*
24.See Cairns, op. cit. (ch. 3, n. 17).

CHAPTER EIGHT
1.See also, e.g. *Ad. Herenn.* 3 6 11.
2.See Williams 139 f.
3.E.g. Tullus in Prop. 1 6 and Maecius Celer in St. *Sil.* 3 2.
4.For such formal sophistications see pp. 127-8.
5.Contrast the tasteless and tactless *Consolatio ad Liviam* (*P.L.M.* I, v) 31 f.
6.This is equivalent to (B11) in prosphonetika to private individuals – cp. Menander 378 20 ff.; 381 15 ff.
7.Cp., e.g. pp. 185 ff. on Prop. 3 4 and Hor. *O.* 4 5 29 ff.
8.See E. Fraenkel *Horace* (Oxford 1957) pp. 42 ff. for discussions of *Epode* 16.
9.Some of the evidence on emigrations (including the *ver sacrum*) is conveniently summarised by R. G. Lewis 'Appian B.C.1, 49, 214 δεκατεύοντες: Rome's New Tribes 90–87 BC'. *Athenaeum* 46 (1968) 286 ff.
10.See Schol. Arist. *Nub.* 331.
11.1 165.
12.See Cicero *De Divinatione*, ed. Pease, index, *s.v. auspicia.*
13.For a contemporary elegiac example see Tib. 1 3 10 ff. and K. F. Smith, ad loc.
14.See Pease on *De Divinatione* 1 29.
15.See ch. 1, n. 22.
16.See ch. 2, n. 28.
17.See pp. 159 ff.
18.Cp., e.g. Ov. *Am.* 2 11 and St. *Sil.* 3 2, treated on pp. 161-2.
19.See pp. 161 ff.
20.See *Propertius* Book 3, ed. Camps, introd. p. 1.
21.See pp. 13 ff. for discussion of this topos.
22.See ch. 1, n. 30.
23.See above, n. 12.

24.See ch. 1, n. 44; ch. 4, n. 28; ch. 5, n. 4.
25.See ch. 4, n. 24, for the topos of sea gods' help to the departing traveller. Galatea also occurs in propemptika at Prop. 1 8 18 and (as Galaneia) at Eur. *Hel.* 1457 ff.
26.See ch. 1, n. 29.
27.See ch. 4, n. 28; ch. 5, n. 4; ch. 4, n. 23.
28.For *pallor* cp. Hor. *Epod.* 10 16; Ov. *Am.* 2 11 28; for *sea monsters* cp. Hor. *O.* 1 3 18.
29.See ch. 3, n. 48.
30.See ch. 3, n. 48 and F. Cairns 'Horace Odes 1 2' *Eranos* 69 (1971) 68 ff.
31.See ch. 3, n. 48.
32.See Copley 149, nn. 44-7; 154, n. 25.
33.For apples as a komastic gift cp., e.g. Theoc. *Id.* 2 120; *Id.* 3 10.
34.For burning in another Theocritean komos cp. *Id.* 7 102 and see also Copley 149, n. 37. On the house dog as a bane of lovers (below) see Owen on Ov. *Tr.* 2 459.
35.See R-E, *s.v. Galateia.*
36.See Slater, op. cit. (ch. 3, n. 58). I agree with N-H1, introd. p. xxiv, n. 2, that Hor. *O.* 3 12 is an address to Neobule. The status of Alc. *Fr.* 111 (LP) cannot be determined and Hor. *O.* 1 28 cannot, in view of its many difficulties, be taken account of here.
37.See ch. 1, n. 22.
38.See ch. 6, n. 17.
39.See, e.g. Cinna *F.P.L.* ed. Morel, pp. 87 f.; Prop. 1 6 31 ff.; 1 8 19 ff.; St. *Sil.* 3 2 86 ff., 103 ff. and ch. 6, nn. 15, 26.
40.See ch. 2, n. 28.
41.See ch. 1, n. 44.
42.See p. 57.
43.See ch. 5, n. 13, pp. 135, 150, 239.
44.If, as seems probable, Postumus is C. Propertius Postumus (*P.I.R.* P754) whose career contains no military offices, then one of two alternatives seems likely. Either he

took part in this expedition before his entry into the vigintivirate, in which case he would have had the low rank of military tribune, or he accompanied the expedition later in his career as a civilian. The latter interpretation would equally well explain Propertius' embarrassment.

45.For similar delays in komastic identification cp., e.g. Theoc. *Id.* 6 6ff.; Tib. 1 2; Hor. *O.* 3 7.

46.See ch. 6, n.12.

47.Cp., e.g. Tib. 1 5 7ff.; Ov. *Tr.* 2 459f.

48.*dawn*: see, e.g. Hor. *O.* 3 10 5ff.; Prop. 2 9 41; Ov. *Am.* 1 6 65f.; Copley 170, n.19; *birds*: e.g. Prop. 1 16 46; Ov. *Am.* 1 6 66.

49.See Copley 150, n.53; 155, n.33.

50.See Copley 164, n.16, where he is perhaps over-sceptical about the relevance of the topos to the komos.

51.Cp., e.g. Tib. 1 5 69ff.; Ov. *Am.* 3 15 11ff.

52.See above, n.32.

53.*friends*: e.g. Powell *Collectanea Alexandrina* pp.181f.; Plut. *Mor.* 772f-773a; Aristaen. *Ep.* 2 19 – see Headlam-Knox on Herodas 2 34ff.; *slaves*: Xen. *Symp.* 2 1; *PTeb.* 2 (d); Plaut. *Curc.* 1-164; for *flute-girls* see Headlam-Knox, loc. cit.

54.Cp. Prop. 1 4, 5 and many examples of the genre 'symptoms of love'.

55.For perjury and its consequences (or lack of them) cp. Prop. 1 15, Ov. *Am.* 3 3, and their commentators.

56.Cf. Theoc. *Id.* 28; Plaut. *Amph.* 760ff.; *Merc.* 399; *Truc.* 529ff. Cp. also gifts sent from abroad, e.g. Cat. 12, 25.

57.Cp. Arist. *Eccl.* 924; Theoc. *Id.* 3 7; *PTeb.* 2(d)9; Luc. *Bis Acc.* 31; Aristaen. *Ep.* 2 4 (προκύπτω).

58.See Copley 145, n.10.

59.See above, n.32.

60.See above, n.45 and pp.194f., 202ff.

61.See E. N. Gardiner *Athletics of the Ancient World* (Oxford 1930) pp.66, 71, 102.

62.Theoc. *Id.* 2 124-5; *Id.* 3 8-9; *Id.* 11 31ff; *Id.* 6 34ff. (negated). Cp. Aristaen. *Ep.* 2 19.

63.Cp. Prop. 1 6 where the overall propemptikon of Propertius to Tullus clarified the generic identity of the curtailed included propemptikon of Cynthia to Propertius (see pp.12-14). For the reverse procedure – included generic example clarifying the generic identity of the overall example – see pp.88f. on Hor. *O.* 1 25, and pp.171ff. on Theoc. *Id.* 14.

64.See also pp.222f. But note that Horace is not himself also a logical epibateric speaker here.

65.See above, n.36.

66.There are of course numerous literary epibateria whose testimony is not required here.

67.See T. Mommsen *Römisches Staatsrecht* (Leipzig 1887) vol.III, pp.48f. The connexion between Tibur and exile was noted but not exploited by F. R. Bliss 'The Plancus Ode' *TAPhA* 91(1960) 45.

68.With West, op. cit. (ch. 3, n.30) p.116.

69.The evidence is collected by T. R. S. Broughton *The Magistrates of the Roman Republic* (New York 1951) vol. I, p.160.

70.See Bömer on Ov. *Fast.* 6 663, 685.

71.For a recent expression of the contrary view see T. E. Kinsey 'Catullus 11', *Latomus* 24 (1965) 537ff.

72.The line references here are to sections, not just speeches.

CHAPTER NINE

1.See pp.76ff., 179.

2.See N-H1, 179f.

3.But for controversies of this question see Jäger 29 and for general literature on the ode see N-H1, 178ff.

4.See ch. 6, n.17.

5.See ch. 4, n.25.

6.See LS, *s.v. taedium*.

7.Cp. Arist. *Eq.* 612. For another temporal contrast between *taedium* and *desiderium* cp. *futuri desiderio laborat, praesentium taedio* (Sen. *De Brev. Vit.* 7 8).

8.Schetliasmos, although in our eyes partly composed of advice, was probably not so considered in antiquity. In *O.* 1 14 therefore, Horace's words would have been regarded as complaints and not as counsel.

9.See op. cit., ch. 3, n. 20.

10.Cp. [Tib.] 3 10 = 4 4; Prop. 2 28; St. *Sil.* 1 4 58 ff., 94 ff.

11.Cp. St. *Sil.* 1 4 9 ff., 115 f.

12.Cp. [Tib.] 3 10 = 4 4 23 f.; Prop. 2 28 60 ff.; St. *Sil.* 1 4 127 ff.

13.See Ramminger, loc. cit. (ch. 2, n. 31) and, in connexion with Horace and Maecenas, cp. Hor. *Epod.* 14 5.

14.It is also notable that Prop. 1 21 immediately precedes this question.

15.125-34.

16.See Copley 170, n. 21.

17.Cp., e.g. Theoc. *Id.* 2 120; *Id.* 3 10; *Id.* 6 6 f.; *Id.* 11 40 f.

18.Cp., e.g. *A.P.* 5 213 (Posidippus); Tib. 1 2; 5 17 f., 47 f., cp. Hor. *O.* 3 10 15 f.; Copley 52 ff.

19.For this interpretation see R. Merkelbach 'Sappho und ihr Kreis' *Philologus* 101 (1957) 23 ff.

20.See H. Meyer *Hymnische Stilelemente in der frühgriechische Dichtung* (Diss. Würzburg 1933) general index, *s.v. hypomnese*.

21.For the background to this poem see D. L. Page, op. cit. (ch. 2, n. 35) pp. 46 ff.

22.See Athen. *Deip.* 282F, and for a possible implication 284D.

23.N-HI, 44 f.

24.For references see N-HI, 40.

25.See ch. 1, n. 30.

26.For details see N-HI.

27.Theocritean portrayals of this emotion (e.g. *Id.* 12) may be compared.

28.See Donat. *Vit. Virg.* 35. The theory that, in *O.* 1 3, the voyage symbolises the Aeneid, is expounded at greater length in C. W. Lockyer Jr 'Horace's Propemptikon and Virgil's Voyage' *CW* 61 (1967) 42 ff.

29.E.g. Pind. *Pyth.* 10 51; 11 40; Virg. *Geor.* 2 41; Hor. *O.* 4 15 1 ff; Ov. *Met.* 15 176 f.; *Tr.* 2 548.

30.E.g. Hor. *O.* 4 15 1 ff.; Prop. 3 3 22 ff.; 3 9 3 f., 35 f.; Ov. *Met.* 15 176.

31.Prop. 2 34 61 ff., and see H. Tränkle 'Properz über Virgils *Aeneis*', *Mus. Helvet.* 28 (1971) 60 ff.

32.Mr J. G. Howie intends to treat the subject of advice from dependents in Greek poetry in a future article, and I myself hope to define yet another category of advice to superiors at a later date.

33.See ch. 1, n. 44; ch. 2, n. 28.

34.See ch. 6, n. 15.

35.See ch. 8, n. 39.

36.See Virg. *Ecl.* 1 10 56 ff.

37.See, e.g. Ov. *Rem. Am.* 199 f.

38.See ch. 1, n. 29.

39.See ch. 5, n. 13, and pp. 135, 150, 199.

40.On the genre, see pp. 76, 171 ff., 175.

41.On the genre see Williams 9 f., 103 ff.; N-HI, 243 ff.

42.See pp. 182 f., 188 f.

43.See R. G. M. Nisbet 'Notes on Horace Epistles 1' *CR* NS 9 (1959) pp. 73 f.

44.For ancient eating and drinking see R-E, *s.v. Symposion*, and the other R-E articles cited there.

45.Cp. the schetliasmos in the propemptikon and the typical komastic speech as demonstrations of affection between equals.

46.Cf. Fraenkel, op. cit. (ch. 8, n. 8) p. 418, n. 1; Williams 121 f.

47.For cheap wine in another Horatian uocatio cp. *O.* 1 20 1.

TRANSLATIONS
All quotations of one line or more not translated in the text are literally rendered here. My thanks are due to my colleagues Dr E. K. Borthwick, Mr R. M. Pinkerton, Dr N. K. Rutter, Mr W. K. Smith, Professor P. G. Walsh and Mr J. R. G. Wright who shared the task of overseeing my versions.

CHAPTER ONE
Propertius 1 6, p. 3
I am not afraid now to become acquainted with the sea of Hadria in your company, Tullus; nor to spread my sails in the Aegean swell. With you I could climb the Rhipaean mountains and go beyond the house of Memnon.

But my mistress's words as she embraces me hold me back, as do her earnest pleas and frequent changes of colour. Night after night she nags me about our love, and she complains that, if I leave her, there are no gods. Then she says she does not love me, and she makes the threats a mistress makes when her lover is growing cool and she is unloving in turn. I cannot hold out for an hour in the face of these complaints. The devil take the lover who can control himself! Can it be worth my while to tour learned Athens and to see the ancient riches of Asia if, when my ship has set out, Cynthia is reproaching me, and tearing her face with frenzied hands, saying that she owes kisses to the wind that bars my way, and declaring that there is nothing more cruel than a lover who has broken his faith?

But as for you, try to surpass your uncle's well-earned axes; and give back their ancient rights to our allies who have forgotten them. Your youth has never had leisure for love: your concern has always been for your country in arms; and may the boy Cupid never bring to you sufferings such as mine, and everything familiar to my tears. Allow me, a man willed

by fortune always to lie prostrate, to yield my soul to the limits of decadence. Many have gladly perished in a long-drawn-out love; when the earth covers me, may I be among their number. I was not born for renown or fit for arms: this is the warfare the Fates wish me to endure. But you, if you travel where soft Ionia stretches, or where the waters of Pactolus soak the ploughlands of Lydia; if you go by foot on land or with oars traverse the sea as one in authority; should there come a time when you remember me, you will know I am living under a cruel star.

Tibullus 1 3 3-4, p. 11 (see p. 259)

Horace *Epode* 1 7-8, p. 11 (see p. 268)

Statius *Siluae* 3 2 99-100, p. 11
Why was my love for you so faint-hearted? But my faithful thoughts shall never leave you, and I shall accompany your sails with far-following prayers.

Paulinus *Carmina* 17 93-6, p. 11
I am restrained by the bond of the sickly body; but in my mind I fly behind you and with you hymn the Lord.

Theocritus *Idyll* 12, p. 17
You have come, dear boy! After two days and two nights you have come! But lovers grow old in a day. As spring is sweeter than winter, as the apple is sweeter than the sloe, as the ewe has a thicker fleece than her lamb, as the virgin is better than the thrice-wed woman, as the fawn is swifter-footed than the calf, as the nightingale with its clear voice is the most tuneful of all birds, so you have brought joy to my heart with your coming. I am like a traveller who in the heat of the sun has run beneath the shade of an oak.

I wish that the Cupids blew with equal force upon both of us and that we might become a song for all generations to come: 'God-like were

those two among men of the past;
one the "Inspirer", as a man of
Amyclae might say, the other, to use
the Thessalian term, the "Hearer";
they loved each other in perfect
equality. They were golden men once
again in those days when the beloved
loved in turn.' I wish, Father Zeus,
that this might be; this is my wish,
ageless immortals; and after two
hundred generations a messenger
might come to me in Acheron, from
where no man returns, saying 'The
love of you and of your charming
"Hearer" is on the lips of all, and
especially the young men's lips'.

However, the gods of Olympus have
jurisdiction over these things! It will
be as they desire. But when I praise
you for your beauty, I shall not grow
pimples above my thin nose. If you
hurt me at all, you immediately
heal the hurt, and give me double
measure of joy; and I go off, my cup
overflowing.

Megarians of Nisaea, finest of row-
ers, may you live in prosperity, since
you gave great honour to your Attic
guest, Diocles the lover of boys! At
the beginning of Spring, boys always
assemble around his tomb to compete
for the kissing prize: the boy who
most sweetly presses lips to lips goes
off to his mother loaded with garlands. Happy is the man who judges
the boys' kisses; I am sure that he
prays earnestly to glittering Gany-
mede asking that his mouth shall be
like the Lydian stone against which
the money changers try true gold, to
see if it is false.

Aristophanes *Aves* 680, p. 23
You have come, you have come, we
can see you.

Catullus 9, 1-5, p. 23 (see p. 266)
Poetae Melici Graeci 848 1, p. 23
The swallow has come, has come.

Homer *Odyssey* 23 233-40, p. 24
As when the welcome land appears to
swimmers whose well-made ship

Poseidon has shattered in the sea with
the assault of wind and wave; and a
few, swimming towards land, have
escaped the grey sea and salt scum
is thick upon their bodies; joyfully
they come to land, disaster escaped;
just as welcome to her was the sight
of her husband, and she could not
take her white arms from round his
neck.

Aeschylus *Agamemnon* 895-903, 966-
972, p. 24
Now, after all these sufferings, with
joyful heart I would call this man the
guard-dog of the homestead, the
forestay that saves the ship, the firm-
based pillar of the high roof, the only
child to his father, the land appearing
unexpectedly to sailors, a fine day to
look upon after a storm, a flowing
spring to a thirsty traveller. Every
stress escaped is a joy. I think him
worthy of such welcomes. . . . For
just as while the root remains, the
foliage comes to the house, shading it
from the dogstar, so your return to
the fireside of your home is like
warmth in winter; and when Zeus
is making wine from the bitter grape
[i.e. midsummer], then there is coolness in the house, when its lord and
master is moving in it.

Homer *Odyssey* 16 17-19, p. 24
As when a devoted father welcomes
his son, who has returned home after
ten years in a foreign land, his only
son and his darling, for whom he has
endured many sufferings. . . .

A.P. 12 171 (Dioscorides), p. 25
Zephyr, most gentle of winds, bring
back to me Euphragoras, that beautiful pilgrim, just as you received him.
Do not extend his absence beyond a
few months, since even a short time
is like a thousand years to a lover.

Statius *Siluae* 3 2 132-4, p. 27 (see
p. 271)

Theocritus *Idyll* 7 52-6, p. 27
Agianax shall have a good voyage to
Mitylene – even when the South

Wind drives the wet waves and the Kids are in the evening sky and Orion checks his feet upon the Ocean – if he saves Lycidas, who is being roasted by Aphrodite; for hot love of him burns me.

Pindar *Pythians* 10 1-2, p. 28
Blessed is Lacedaemon, happy is Thessaly.

Hesiod *Opera et Dies* 112-13, p. 28
They lived like gods without care in their heart, without labours and without grief.

Juvenal 12 93-5, p. 29
Do not be suspicious, Corvinus, about my celebrations: Catullus, for whose return I am setting up so many altars, has three little heirs.

Catullus 9 8-9, p. 29 (see p. 266)

Ovid *Amores* 2 11 45-6, p. 30 (see p. 271)

CHAPTER TWO
Homer *Odyssey* 13 38-46, p. 38
King Alkinous, most glorious of all the men, pour a libation to the gods and send me safely on my way. To you I say farewell; for you have already given me all my heart desired, an escort and friendly gifts – may the gods of Olympus ensure that they bring me good fortune. When I return home, may I find my noble wife there and my kinsfolk safe and sound. May you, remaining here, give joy to your wedded wives and children; may the gods give you every prosperity; and may there be no misfortune among your people.

Solon *Fr.* 7 (19) D, p. 40
Now I wish you and your family long rule in this city over the people of Solioi. But as for me, may violet-crowned Kypris ensure the safe departure of my swift ship from this famous isle. To this colony may she give distinction and great glory; to me may she give safe return to my native land.

Sophocles *Philoctetes* 1452-71, p. 41
Philoctetes. Now, as I depart, let me address the land: goodbye, cave that has shared my watching; goodbye, nymphs of streams and meadows; goodbye, deep voice of the sea-lashed headland where often, in my cavern, my head was wetted by the blasts of the South Wind, and where often Mount Hermon echoed my moans in my storm of troubles. Now, fountains and Lycian spring, I am leaving you, leaving you at last, an event beyond my expectation. Goodbye, sea-encircled Lemnos. Send me off with no complaint on a good voyage to the place where mighty fate, the advice of friends, and the omnipotent god who has brought about these things are conveying me.
Chorus. Let us go off now, all together, when we have prayed to the sea-nymphs to come with us and keep us safe on our return voyage.

Catullus 46, p. 44
Now the spring is bringing back the warm weather; now the madness of the equinoctial gales is silent, and the pleasant breezes of the Zephyr are blowing. It is time for you to leave the plains of Phrygia, Catullus, and the rich land of boiling Nicaea: let us be off to the famous cities of Asia! Already my mind is eager and ready to go roaming; my feet are joyful and strong with desire. Goodbye, dear bands of companions, who came far with me from home and now are returning separately by different roads.

Rutilius Namatianus 1 31-6, p. 49
The very springs, if they could speak, and those very woods of ours, had they a voice, could urge me on with justified complaints as I dallied, and could give sails to my longing. Now at last, when the embraces of my beloved Rome are loosened, my love of my country prevails and I can scarcely be patient on this belated journey.

Ovid *Amores* 2 11 7-8, p. 53
Now Corinna is leaving the bed she
knew so well and the house we
shared, and is preparing to go off on
treacherous journeys.

Homer *Iliad* 2 339, p. 57
What will become of our agreement
and oaths?

Propertius 1 6 8, 18, p. 57 (see p. 256)

Propertius 1 8 17, p. 57 (see p. 270)

Virgil *Aeneid* 4 305-8, p. 57 (see
p. 266)

Ovid *Amores* 2 11 7-8, p. 57 (see
above)

Homer *Odyssey* 5 299-312, p. 61
Wretch that I am! What is this latest
blow? I am afraid that the goddess
Calypso prophesied truly to me in
every respect: she said that before I
came home to my country, I would
fill up the measure of troubles on the
sea. All this is now fulfilled. Zeus fills
the broad sky with great clouds, and
he has stirred up the sea; the blasts
of all the winds are upon me; now
my death is certain. Three and four
times blessed were the Greeks who
died in broad Troy serving the
Atreidae. I wish I had died and met
my fate on that day when hordes of
Trojans hurled their bronze-tipped
spears at me beside the body of
Achilles. In that way I would have
received funeral rites and the Greeks
would have spread my fame; but now
I am destined to perish miserably.

Catullus 63 50-73, p. 62
Native land that gave me life! Land
that gave me birth! Wretched as
I am, I left you; and, as runaway
slaves leave their masters, I walked to
the forests of Ida to be at home among
snow and chill lairs of wild beasts and
to go in my madness to all their hid-
ing places. Where or in what region
do I think you lie, my native land?
My eyes long to turn their gaze on
you while for a little my mind is free
of savage frenzy. Shall I be carried

into these forests far from my home?
Shall I be absent from country, from
possessions, from friends, from
parents? Shall I lack the forum, the
wrestling school, the race course, and
the gymnasia? Again and again in my
misery I must complain.
   What role have I not played? I have
been a woman, a young man, an
ephebe and a boy; I was the flower
of the gymnasium, the glory of the
wrestling oil; my door was crowded,
my threshold was warm, my house
was hung with crowns of flowers
when at sunrise I had to leave my
bedchamber. Shall I now be called a
servant of the gods and a handmaid
of Cybele? Shall I be a Maenad, a
eunuch, a barren man? Shall I in-
habit the chill snow-mantled regions
of green Ida? Shall I live out my life
beneath the high summits of Phrygia,
the home of wood-dwelling doe and
forest-roaming boar? Now I repent
what I have done, now I regret it.

Tibullus 1 3 3-34, 83-94, p. 63
You will go over the Aegean waves
without me, Messala; I hope that you
and your staff will remember me. I
am held back sick by Corcyra, a
foreign land: black Death, keep your
greedy hands away from me. I beg
you, black Death, keep your hands
away; I have no mother here to
gather my burnt bones into her sad
breast; I have no sister to scatter
Assyrian perfume on my ashes and to
weep before my tomb with streaming
hair; Delia is not here, Delia who
saw me off from Rome, and first, they
say, consulted all the gods. She three
times took the sacred lots from the
boy: from all three the boy gave her
sure omens. Everything foretold my
return; but she could not be stopped
from weeping and worrying over my
journey. I consoled her myself; and
even when giving her my parting
instructions, I kept on anxiously
seeking excuses for delay. I would use

R*

birds or evil-omens as an excuse, or I would say that the day sacred to Saturn was holding me back; how often did I begin my journey and then say that a stumble at the gate had given me signs of a bad passage! Let no one be so bold as to go away when love forbids it; or let him realise that he has gone against the god's prohibition. What use is your goddess Isis to me now, Delia? What use are the cymbals you clashed so often with your hands, what use the ritual purity you observed in your sacred rites and, I remember it well, your sleeping apart from me in a pure bed? Now, goddess, now is the time to come to my aid – for the many painted tablets in your temple show that you can heal – so that my Delia may pay the vows she made by sitting before the doors of your shrine clad in linen, and twice a day with loosened hair singing your praises, prominent amid the Pharian throng. But be it my good fortune to worship my ancestral Penates and pay monthly offerings of incense to my ancient Lar. . . . But, I beg you, remain chaste; and may the old lady, ever watchful, sit by you as a guardian of your holy purity. Let her tell you stories and, when the lamp is in place, draw off long threads from the full distaff; let the maidservant at her heavy woolmaking in her weariness gradually fall asleep and drop her work. Then may I come, suddenly, without prior announcement, seemingly sent down from heaven to your side. Then run to meet me, just as you are, your long hair in disarray, your feet bare. For this I pray; may white Aurora bring this glittering day to me with her rosy horses.

Propertius 1 17, p. 64

I deserve this, since I had the heart to leave my mistress! Now I have only solitary halcyons to address. Cassiope will not see my ship arrive safely with me, and all my prayers fall uselessly on a thankless shore. Even the winds take your side, Cynthia, absent though you are; look what savage threats the storm utters. Will the blessing of a lull in the storm not come? Will this little beach of sand cover my body?

But I ask you, Cynthia, to turn your savage complaints to something better: be satisfied with this punishment of darkness and unfriendly seas. Will you be able to brush off my death with dry eyes, and not to hold my bones to your bosom? Cursed be the man who first made ships and sails and journeyed over the unwilling sea! Would it not have been better to conquer my mistress's temper (for although hard hearted, she was none the less unique) than to see shores fringed by woods strange to me and look in vain for the longed-for help of Castor and Pollux? If the fates had brought my passion to the grave at home, and if the final stone was standing over my buried love, she would have offered her precious hair at my funeral, and would softly have placed my bones on fresh rose petals; she would have called my name over my last dust, and asked that the earth be light upon me.

But you, watery children of Doris, spread your white sails in wellomened chorus: if ever love has flowed to join your waves, spare your comrade and give him milder shores.

Horace *Odes* 3 27 34-66, p. 66

'My Father', she said, 'my abandoned name of daughter, and my filial devotion overcome by madness, where and from where have I come? A single death is light punishment for this maiden's guilt. Am I awake and do I weep for my evil deed, or am I innocent and does an empty phantom, escaping the ivory gate and bringing a dream, make sport of me? Was it better to travel over the long waves or to pick fresh flowers? If someone would give me, now I am angry, that infamous bull, I would try to cut with steel and shatter the horns of that prodigy I loved so much of late. I was shameless to leave the home of my father, I am shameless to remain alive. O any god who hears this, I want to wander naked among lions. Before foul decay seizes the beauty of my cheeks and the sap of youth leaves the tender prey, I want with my loveliness to feed tigers. "Worthless Europa," my father, although absent, reproaches me, "why do you hesitate to die? You can break your neck by letting it swing from this ash with the waist-band that accompanied you for a good purpose. Or if you prefer the rocks and sharp crags as a means of death, come, entrust yourself to the swift breeze, unless you, a king's daughter, prefer to spin a mistress's wool and be handed over as a concubine to her barbarian mercy".'

Horace *Odes* 3 27 33-4, p. 67 (see p. 275)

CHAPTER THREE

Aeschylus *Prometheus Vinctus* 307-308, 322-3, p. 72
I see your plight, Prometheus, and I wish to give you the best advice. . . . (307-8).
So take me for your teacher, and do not kick against the pricks (322-3).

Callimachus *Iambi* 5 1-2, p. 72
My friend, listen to my heart-felt thoughts – for advice is a sacred thing.

Diegesis, p. 72
Callimachus is satirising a school teacher called Apollonius – or, as others say, Cleon – alleging that he is seducing his own pupils. Callimachus is pretending to be well disposed to him and telling him not to do this in case he is caught.

Callimachus *Iambus* 5 31-2, p. 73
Let me tell you that I am Bacis and

the Sibyl and the laurel and the oak-tree.

Propertius 1 9 5-6, p. 73
When love is in question I am as reliable as the doves of Chaonia at saying which girl is to tame what young man.

Propertius 3 23, p. 76
Well, my tablets and all their learning are lost and so many good writings lost with them! They were worn by my hands' usage, that told them to bear credit even unsealed; even without me they had learned to win over girls and to speak without me in eloquent terms. No gold attachments gave them value: they were made of common wax and ordinary boxwood. Such as they were, they always remained faithful to me and always produced good results. Perhaps this message had been committed to the tablets: 'I am angry because you delayed your coming yesterday, you cold-blooded creature. Was it because you found some other girl more attractive?' Or are you accusing me of some imaginary offence? Or perhaps the girl's words were 'Please come to me today and we shall take time off together. Love has prepared a welcome for you lasting all night', and whatever a clever and ready-tongued girl can devise when she is in love and spends a garrulous hour on coy wit. Oh dear! to think that some miser is doing his accounts on them and putting them among his horrible ledgers. If anyone brings them back to me, he shall be rewarded with gold: who would want to keep wooden tablets and lose riches? Off you go, slave, put this notice on some pillar quickly and give your master's address as the Esquiline.

Corpus Inscriptionum Latinarum 46 n. 6, p. 77
A bronze cauldron has been lost from the tavern. If anyone brings it back he will get 65 sesterces; if he informs

on the thief so that the object can be recovered. . . .

Papyrus Aegyptiaca 146 BC, p. 78
A slave boy has run away in Alexandria. His name is Hermon. He is aged about eighteen and is wearing a cloak and girdle. Whoever brings him back will receive two bronze talents three thousand drachmae. Whoever reveals his presence at a temple will receive one talent two thousand drachmae, at the house of a man of substance against whom a case can be won, three talents five thousand drachmae. Anyone who wishes should give information to the prefect's office.

Another slave called Bion has run away along with him. Whoever brings this slave back will receive as much as for the above. Information about the latter should also be given to the prefect's office.

Petronius Satyricon 97, p. 78
The town crier, accompanied by a public slave, proclaimed as follows: 'A slave boy has recently run away in the bathhouse. He is about sixteen years of age. He is curly haired, effeminate and attractive looking. His name is Giton. Anyone willing to return him or identify him will receive 1000 sesterces.'

Catullus 8 16-18, p. 82
Who will come to you now? Who will think you beautiful? Whom will you love now? Whom will people say you belong to? Whom will you kiss? Whose lips will you bite?

Quintilian Institutio Oratoria 3 4 1-4, p. 84
However, there is a dispute as to whether there are three or more kinds of oratory. Now it is certain that almost all the writers of greatest authority among the ancients have followed Aristotle, who simply employed the term 'public' for 'deliberative' oratory, and have all been content with the three-fold division. But in the

past there was a weak attempt by some Greek orators as well as by Cicero in his *De Oratore* to show that there are not merely more kinds of oratory than three but that there is an almost innumerable number of kinds; and the greatest authority of our own time has supported this view very vigorously. For if we classify the role of blaming and praising under the third section of oratory, in what type of oratory shall we think ourselves to be engaged when we complain, console, calm, excite, terrify, encourage, teach, interpret obscure matters, narrate, plead, thank, congratulate, reproach, abuse, describe, give orders, disclaim, express hopes, opine, etc. etc.? I remain a supporter of the old view and as such am almost obliged to make excuses for myself; and I must enquire what led my predecessors to restrict within such a narrow compass such sprawling subject-matter.

Theocritus Idyll 18 55-7, p. 84
Do not forget to wake at dawn. At dawn we too will come again, when the first singer calls out lifting his fine feathered neck from his bed.

Scholia on Theocritus Idyll 18, p. 85
Some epithalamia are sung in the evening. These are called 'putting to bed songs'; some are sung until midnight; some are dawn songs, which are also called wakening songs [diegertika].

Horace Odes 1 25, p. 87
Not so often now do lusty young men shake your closed windows with constant flinging of stones, nor do they deprive you of your sleep. The door that in days gone by often moved its easy hinges clings to the threshold. Less and less now you hear them saying 'Are you sleeping, Lydia, while I, who love you, am dying of passion through the long night?'
The time shall come when you in your turn will weep as an old woman

over the arrogance of your lovers.
You will stand a worthless creature
in a lonely alley, while the Thracian
wind blows more fiercely as the moon-
less nights approach. Then the burning, lustful love that inflames the
mothers of horses will rage around
your ulcerated liver. Then you will
complain that young men in their
prime take joyful pleasure in green
ivy and dark myrtle but offer with-
ered leaves to Hebrus, the companion
of winter.

Parthenius *Erotika Pathemata* 27,
p. 93
She prayed earnestly to Athena to
revenge her for her unjust deprivation.

Horace *Odes* 4 2 5-12, p. 96
Like a stream running down a mountain, swollen with rain over its familiar banks, Pindar boils and rushes
along, immeasurable with his deep
utterance; the laurel of Apollo is his
whether he rolls down new words
through his bold dithyrambs and
rushes along in undisciplined
rhythms. . . .

Propertius 3 17 39-40, p. 97
These themes are matter for no humble buskin: I shall treat them with
the thunder of Pindaric eloquence.

CHAPTER FOUR
Isocrates 13 12-13, p. 98
Who except these is unaware that
while the use of letters is fixed and
does not change, so that we always
use the same letters for the same
purposes, exactly the opposite is true
of the art of oratory. What one speaker
has said is not as useful to a subsequent speaker; but he is reckoned to
be the most skilful speaker who does
justice to his subject but can invent
material in no way identical with
that used by other speakers. But the
greatest sign of the difference between the two arts is this: oratory is
only good if it suits its occasion and
has propriety and originality; but

letters have no need of these qualities.

Isocrates 4 7-9, p. 98
In addition, were it possible to present the same material in a single
form only, it would be reasonable to
think it superfluous to bore one's audience by speaking in the same way as
previous orators. But the nature of
oratory is such that it is possible to
speak on the same subject in a great
variety of ways – to represent important matters in humble guise, to add
importance to matters of little import,
to recount old material in a new way
and to speak in an antique fashion
about recent events. So we must not
shun subjects which have been treated
by others before us; but must try to
speak better than they have spoken.
The deeds of the past are our common heritage; but to employ them at
the appropriate time and to devise
suitable sentiments for each, and express them fittingly in words – this is
limited to men of ability.

Isocrates 13 16, p. 100
But to choose from these elements
what should be employed in each case,
and to combine them with each other,
and to arrange them in order. . . .

Theocritus *Idyll* 17, p. 100
With Zeus, let us begin our songs,
Muses, and with Zeus end, the best
of the immortals. . . . But among
mortals, Ptolemy should be named at
the beginning, at the end, and in the
middle, for he is the best of men. The
heroes, who were born of old to the
demi-gods, found excellent poets to
celebrate their noble deeds. But I,
who know how to sing well, shall
hymn Ptolemy; hymns are the privilege of the immortals also. The wood-
cutter, when he comes to Ida with its
many forests, looks round, wondering
where to begin his task, since there
are trees everywhere. What shall I
sing of first? for the gods have given
countless blessings, all subjects for
songs, to honour the best of kings.

How outstanding by ancestry Ptolemy, son of Lagus, to perform his mighty work, conceiving in his mind a plan no other could have formed! Zeus made him equal in honour to the immortal gods: a golden throne is set for him in the house of Zeus; and by his side sits Alexander, his friend, a god with glittering diadem, harsh to the Persians. Opposite them is the seat of Hercules, the centaur-slayer, made of solid adamant. There, with the other gods of Olympus, Hercules holds feasts, rejoicing greatly in the sons of his sons because Zeus, son of Cronos, has taken age out of their limbs and these descendants of his are called immortals. The strong son of Hercules was ancestor of both Alexander and Ptolemy; and both traced back their descent in the end to Hercules. So, when Hercules has sated himself with sweet nectar and goes from the feast to the house of his dear wife, he gives to one his bow and the quiver beneath his shoulder, and to the other his iron-hard club, with its raised knots. Carrying his weapons, they escort the bearded son of Zeus to the ambrosial room of white-ankled Hebe.

How outstanding was famous Berenice among women of prudence, and a great benefit to her parents! The noble daughter of Dione, who rules Cyprus, drew her delicate hands over Berenice's bosom and made it fragrant. They say that no woman has ever pleased her husband as much as Ptolemy loved his wife; and he was loved much more in return. A man who goes loving into the bed of a loving wife can hand over his whole house with confidence to his children as their inheritance. But the mind of a woman who does not love her husband is always upon another man; she gives birth easily, but her children do not resemble their father. Lady goddess Aphrodite most beautiful, you cared for Berenice; because

of you beautiful Berenice did not pass over Acheron, the river of mourning. You snatched her away before she came to the dark ship and the ever-gloomy ferryman of the dead; you placed her in your temple and gave her a share of your own honour. Now, gentle towards all mortals, she breathes forth soft love and lightens lovers' cares.

Dark-browed Deipyle of Argos, you bore man-slaying Diomede to Tydeus of Calydon; deep-girdled Thetis bore Achilles the javelin thrower to Peleus the Aeacid; and you, spearman Ptolemy, glorious Berenice bore to spearman Ptolemy.

When you first saw the light, Cos took you from your mother and nursed you, a new born child. The daughter of Antigone, heavy with childbirth, there called upon Ilithyia, who loosens the girdle; Ilithyia stood by her, and helped her, and took the pain from all her limbs; and Ptolemy was born, resembling his father, a well-loved child. Cos saw and cried out with delight; and taking the child in her hands, she said: 'Bless you, my child! May you honour me as much as Phoebus Apollo has honoured Delos of the dark crown. Give equal honour to the hill of Triopos and accord the same privilege to my Dorian neighbours. Lord Apollo also loved Rhenaea.' So spoke the island, and a great eagle, a bird of omen, cried out three times from the clouds above. This was, I think, a sign from Zeus: kings in their majesty are the concern of Zeus, son of Cronos, and greatest among kings is the one whom Zeus loved from birth. Great prosperity is his, many are the lands he rules, many are the seas.

Countless lands and countless tribes of men swell their crops with the help of Zeus' rain; but none of those lands is as fertile as the plains of Egypt, when the rising Nile penetrates the porous soil. Nor has any land so many towns of skilled workmen: there are three hundred cities built in Egypt; and there are three thousand and three times ten thousand besides; and besides them two times three and three times nine; of all these noble Ptolemy is king. He also has part of Phoenicia, of Arabia, of Syria, of Libya, and of the dark Ethiopians. He is lord of all the Pamphylians, of the Cilician spearmen, of the Lycians, of the warrior Carians, and of the Cycladic islands, for his ships are the best that sail upon the sea. Every sea, land, and sounding river is ruled by Ptolemy, and many horsemen and many shield-bearing foot-soldiers assemble about him, equipped with glittering bronze.

In wealth he could surpass all other kings: so much comes from all sides daily to his rich palace; and his people go about their work in peace. No hostile foot-soldier crosses the Nile, full of monstrous fishes, to raise the battle-shout in others' villages; no armoured enemy leaps onto the beach from his swift ship to attack the cattle of the Egyptians – so great is the man who is ruler on the broad plains, fair-haired Ptolemy, a skilled spearman. Like a good king he is concerned to hold all he received from his father; and he has added his own portion to it. But the gold in his rich palace does not lie useless like the wealth of worker ants. The glorious houses of the gods are well-endowed by him, since he always gives tithes along with other privileges. He has given great gifts to strong kings, to cities, and to his trustworthy companions. A man never comes to the sacred contests of Dionysus, knowing how to sing a clear song, but he is given a gift worthy of his craft; and the spokesmen of the Muses sing of Ptolemy in return for his gifts. What is finer for a man of wealth than to win renown among his fellows? This is something the

Atreidae still have; but the innumerable treasures they won when they captured the palace of Priam have vanished into the air, from where there is no return.

Alone of former men, and alone of those whose footsteps still warm the dust beneath their feet, Ptolemy has built fragrant temples for his dear mother and father; and he has set up beautiful statues of them in gold and ivory to help all mortals. As the months go by, he burns many fat thighs of oxen upon the blood-red altars, he and his noble wife; no better woman takes her husband in her arms at home, loving her brother and husband with her whole heart. In this way the sacred marriage of the gods was accomplished, the marriage of those two whom lady Rhea bore to rule Olympus; Iris, still a virgin, her hands purified with myrrh, spreads one bed for Zeus and Hera to sleep in at night. Farewell, King Ptolemy! I shall speak of you as of the other demigods; and I think that my words will not be rejected by men to come. As for excellence, ask it of Zeus.

Tibullus 2 2, p. 112

Let us speak words of good omen: the Birthday-spirit is coming to the altars. Everyone present, man and woman, speak words of good omen! Let holy incense be burnt on the altar; burn perfumes sent by the soft Arabian from his wealthy land. Let the Genius in person come to see the honours paid to him; let pliant garlands deck his holy locks; let his temples drip with pure ointment; and let him be filled with honeycake and soaked with wine. He must grant you, Cornutus, whatever wish you make. Come! Why hesitate? He is agreeing. Ask! I prophesy that you will pray for the faithful love of your wife; I think the gods already know this well. You would prefer this to all the fields that strong countrymen plough with tough oxen throughout the whole world, and all the pearls grown in the rich Indies, where the Eastern sea-wave reddens. Your prayers are made: may Cupid come on beating wings, bringing yellow bands for your wife to endure until dragging age brings wrinkles and whitens her hair. May these things come true, Birthday: give progeny to his ancestors, and may a brood of young play about your feet.

Horace *Odes* 4 5 21-4, p. 114
Our houses are pure and unpolluted by adultery: custom and law have brought this stain of impiety to heel; mothers are praised for their children's likeness to their father; punishment accompanying crime suppresses it.

Isocrates 13 16, p. 118
. . . and also not to miss what is appropriate, but to adorn the whole speech suitably with striking thoughts, and to clothe it in flowing and melodious phrase.

Plato *Phaedrus* 267 A-B, p. 118
But shall we leave undisturbed Tisias and Gorgias, who saw that probability was more worthy of respect than truth, who through their rhetoric could make small things appear large and large small, who could discuss new subjects in an old-fashioned way and vice versa, and who discovered the use of brevity and interminable length upon any subject matter?

Aristotle *Rhetoric* 1418A, p. 119
This was the meaning of Gorgias' dictum, that words never failed him. If he is speaking about Achilles, he praises Peleus and then Aeacus and then the god, and then similarly courage, which does this or that or is like this.

Ovid *Amores* 2 11 7-8, p. 120 (see p. 259)
Ovid *Amores* 2 11 33-7, p. 120
But since the winged breezes are

carrying off my empty words, may Galatea nevertheless be kindly to your ship. Divine Nereids and you, father of the Nereids, it will be your crime if such a splendid girl is lost. Go, and remember me, and return with a favourable wind.

Catullus 9, p. 122
Veranius, of all my friends worth more to me than a million, have you come home to your own roof, to your loving brothers, and to your old mother? You have come indeed. What joyful news this is to me! I shall see you safe and I shall hear you tell tales of the places, deeds and peoples of the Iberians, as is your custom; and drawing you to me, I shall kiss your sweet face and eyes. Of all happy men, who is happier and more joyful than me?

A.P. 12 118 5-6 (Callimachus), p. 123
When I came, I did not cry out, asking, 'who has you?' or 'whose are you?', but I kissed the doorpost. Only if this is wrong, am I wrong.

CHAPTER FIVE
Virgil *Aeneid* 4 305-30, 365-87, p. 131
Did you hope, traitor, to conceal even so great a crime, and to leave my land without a word? Have our love and the pledge once made no power to hold you, nor the thought that Dido will die by a cruel death? Are you even preparing your fleet, heartless man, in the season of winter and hurrying to sail overseas in the full blast of the north winds? What would you do if you were not making for foreign fields and a new home, if Troy remained as of old, if Troy were the goal your fleet was seeking over the stormy sea?

Is it me you are eager to leave? By my tears and your pledge I beseech you – since I have left myself, alas, nothing else – by our wedlock and the marriage we entered into, if I have ever helped you or anything about me has given you pleasure, have pity on my tottering house and, if there is any room left for pleas, abandon your purpose. Because of you the peoples of Libya and the nomad sheiks hate me, my own Tyrians are hostile; because of you my chastity too and my former reputation, my only claim to fame, is gone. To whom are you leaving me, a dying woman, my 'guest' – since only this title is left of your former name 'husband'. For what am I waiting – for my brother Pygmalion to destroy my walls or the Gaetulian Iarbas to lead me captive? If only I had held in my arms a child of yours before you fled, if a little Aeneas played in my palace with features at least recalling you, I would not think myself completely caught and deserted. . . . Traitor, a goddess was not your mother, nor was Dardanus founder of your race; but frozen Caucasus bore you on its hard crags and Hyrcanian tigresses gave you milk. Why should I hide it? For what worse circumstance should I hold myself back? When I wept did he sigh? Did he turn his eyes? Was he overcome, and did he shed tears or show pity for me who loved him? What am I to put first? Now, now neither great Juno nor father Jupiter look on me with friendly eyes; nowhere can I safely place my trust. He was shipwrecked on the shore and in need, and I took him in; and in my madness I gave him a share of my kingdom. I recovered his lost fleet; I saved his companions from death. Ah! I am fired and driven by madness. Now augur Apollo, now the Lycian oracles, now the messenger of the gods, sent by Jupiter himself, conveys awesome commands through the air. Oh yes, that is the god's work! Concern for this troubles their peace!

I do not hold you back, nor do I confute your words. Go, seek Italy before the winds; seek your kingdom through the waves. I hope that, if the gods of justice have any power, you will suffer full punishment on the mid-sea reefs, and will often call out the name of Dido. Although absent, I shall follow you with dark fire; and when cold death has separated my limbs from my spirit, I shall accompany you everywhere as a ghost. You will be punished, impious creature! I shall hear of it, and the tale will come to me in the depths of Hades.

Propertius 1 8 2-4, p. 134 (see p. 270)

Ovid *Amores* 1 1 7-8, p. 134
What if Venus were to seize the arms of golden-haired Minerva, and if golden-haired Minerva were to wave lit torches?

Cato *Pro Rhodiensibus*, p. 134
But they were afraid that if there was no one for us to fear and if we could do as we wished, then they would be enslaved to us under our exclusive dominion.

Virgil *Aeneid* 4 345-7, p. 134
But now Grynean Apollo has ordered me to make for great Italy; Italy is the destination given by the Lycian oracles. This is what I love, this is my country.

Ovid *Tristia* 3 13, p. 135
Look, my birthday has come round again, for no purpose – for what good to me was my birth? Cruel birthday, why have you come to add to an exile's wretched years? You ought to have brought an end to them. If you had any concern for me or any decency at all in you, you would not be following me beyond my country; you would have tried to come for the last time to me in the same place as I first became known to you – evil meeting! – as a child; when I left Rome, you ought sadly to have said to me in the city, as did my friends, 'goodbye'. What have you to do with Pontus? Surely Caesar's anger has not sent you also to the farthest land of the frozen earth? I suppose you

expect the honour customarily paid to you – a white garment hanging from my shoulders, the smoking altar decked with garlands of flowers, a grain of incense sizzling in the festal fire, and myself offering the honey cakes – the special mark of the birthday – and making propitious prayers in well-omened speech.

I am not in such a situation nor are the times such for me that I can be joyful at your approach. An altar of death surrounded by funereal cypress suits my state, and a flame ready for the heaped pyre. It does not please me to offer incense that cannot win over the gods, and in the midst of troubles no words of good omen come to my lips. But if I must make some prayer today, I ask you not to return to these places while Pontus holds me – almost the farthest of lands, falsely named 'kind to strangers'.

CHAPTER SIX
Ovid *Amores* 3 11, p. 139
Love and hate struggle, pulling my faint heart in opposite directions, love this way, hate that. (33-4)
I have borne much and for long: my patience is now overcome by her faults. (1).
Unfortunately for me, your face means more to me than your faults. (44)
Why should I mention the disgraceful lies of your untrustworthy tongue, and the gods forsworn to my loss? (21-2)
Be kind to me, I implore you by the conjugal nights of our bed, by all the gods who often allow you to perjure yourself by them. (45-6)
Now my craft, bound with a garland that shows my wishes are fulfilled . . . (29)
and I seem not to know my own wishes. (40)
now my craft, bound with a garland that shows my wishes are fulfilled, listens indifferently to the swelling

waves of the sea. (29-30)
I would rather set sail and exploit the following winds and willingly love her. For, if I were unwilling, I should be compelled to love her. (51-2)
Horace *Epode* 1, p. 140
You will go in the light galleys, among the tall bulwarks of the hostile fleet, my friend Maecenas, ready to face any danger shared by Caesar. What shall I do whose life is sweet as long as you still live, a burden if you die? Am I to stay at ease by your command, though ease without you is no pleasure? Or shall I undertake this enterprise and bear it as a real man should? I shall endure it! I shall follow you with courageous heart, even across Alpine ridges and through Caucasus unwelcoming to man, or to the farthest bay of the west.

Perhaps you ask how I, unwarlike weakling as I am, can help your efforts with mine? If I go with you, I shall fear less for you, since absence strengthens fear – just as a bird who sits on her naked fledglings fears the wriggling approach of a snake more if she leaves them, even though she could not help them any more if she were there.

I will gladly fight this and any war, hoping to win your favour – not so that ploughs may struggle behind my many oxen; nor that sheep of mine may exchange Lucanian for Calabrian pastures before the onset of the hot dog-star; nor that a white villa of mine may touch the Circean walls of high Tibur. Your generosity has enriched me, enough and more than enough. I shall not have gathered wealth simply to bury it in the earth like miser Chremes or waste it like a dissolute spendthrift.

Theocritus *Idyll* 11 19-79, p. 143
White Galatea, whiter than cream-cheese, softer than a lamb, friskier than a calf, brighter than an unripe grape, why do you reject a lover? Why

do you come to me at once when sweet sleep overcomes me and, when sweet sleep releases me, go off at once, running from me like a ewe that has seen a grey wolf? I fell in love with you, girl, when you first came with my mother to gather hyacinths from the hill, and I showed you the way. From that time to this I cannot take my eyes from you; but you do not care, not a bit.

I know, sweet girl, why you run away from me: it is because my hairy eyebrow stretches over my whole forehead from ear to ear – a single long one – and beneath it is a single eye and I have a flat nose over my lip. But although I am like this, I have a thousand cattle and I milk and drink the best of milk from them. Cheese never fails me in summer or autumn or the end of winter and my cheese-racks are always heavy. I can pipe as no other Cyclops here can pipe, singing of you, sweet apple, and of myself, often, late at night. Eleven fawns I am rearing for you, all with collars, and four bear-cubs.

But come to me and you will not regret it. Leave the grey-green sea to beat against the shore; you will spend the night more pleasurably with me in my grove. In it are bays and thin cypresses; in it are black ivy and vines with sweet grapes; and in it is cold water which tree-covered Etna sends from her white snow, an ambrosial drink. Who would prefer the sea and its waves to these? But if you think I am too hairy, let me tell you that my heart is hot as oak logs for you, and there is an unquenchable fire beneath the ashes. I could endure to have my soul burnt with love of you and my single eye too, which I prize more than anything. I wish my mother had borne me with gills: then I could have come down to you in the sea and kissed your hand – if you will not let me kiss your mouth – and brought you white lilies and soft poppies with

red petals. But one flowers in summer, the other in winter, so I could not bring both at once. Now I shall learn right away to swim, girl, if some stranger sails here in his ship, so I can learn what you find pleasurable about life in the depths.

Come out, Galatea, and when you have come, forget to go home, as I do sitting here now. Consent to follow a shepherd's life with me, and to milk and make cheese, by putting in bitter curdle. My mother, and she alone, does me wrong, and I blame her for it: she has never said a good word to you on my behalf, although she sees me growing thinner daily. I shall tell her that my head and both my feet are sore, so she may be troubled, since I am troubled.

O Cyclops, Cyclops, where has your mind wandered? You would be much more sensible if you went and wove cheese-baskets, and gathered branches and took them to the lambs; milk the ewe to hand – why chase what runs away? You may find perhaps another, more beautiful, Galatea. Many girls ask me to spend a night with them, and they all giggle when I pay attention to them; it is clear that I am a man of importance on the land.

Theocritus *Idyll* 3, p. 146

Do you think me snub-nosed, girl, when you see me close? Does my beard stick out? (8-9)

Look, I bring you ten apples: I picked them at the place you told me; and tomorrow I shall bring you more. (10-11)

I tell you, I am keeping a white she-goat with two kids for you. (34)

I wish I were that buzzing bee so I could come into your cave. (12-13)

Now I know Love: he is a harsh god. A lioness suckled him and his mother reared him in the wilderness. He burns me, hurting me to the bone. (15-17)

Girl of lovely looks, stone-hearted,

S

dark-browed girl, embrace me, your goatherd, so I can kiss you. Even empty kisses have their pleasurable sweetness. (18-20)

You will make me tear to pieces, here and now, the garland of ivy which I wear for you, dear Amaryllis. I wove it with rosebuds and sweet-smelling celery. (21-3)

My head is sore, and you do not care. (52)

Catullus 42 21-4, p. 148

But we are making no progress: she is not at all moved. You must change your plan and alter your approach, to see if you can make more headway. Say: 'respectable and reputable girl, give back the notebooks'.

Propertius 1 8, p. 148

Are you mad then? Does my love not hold you back? Am I less to you than chill Illyria? And that lover of yours, whoever he is, does he mean so much that you are willing to sail before any wind without me? Can you be brave and listen to the murmurings of the raging sea and lie in a hard ship? Can you bear on your tender feet the lying snow? Can you, Cynthia, endure the unaccustomed blizzards?

I wish the season of winter could be doubled, that the Pleiads would not rise and the sailors be idle, that your rope would not cast off from the Tyrrhenian shore and that a wind hostile to me would not carry off my prayers! And may I not see such winds blowing beneath that constellation, when the wave carries your ship off on its way, leaving me rooted on the empty shore, often crying 'Cruel Cynthia' and shaking my fists!

But, perjured girl, whatever you deserve of me, may Galatea accompany your voyage, so that, when you have passed Acroceraunia with good fortune attending your oar, Oricos may receive you with its calm waters. No other woman, my dearest, will be able to seduce me from making my laments at your door. Nor shall I cease constantly to hail sailors and ask 'Tell me, in what harbour is my mistress sheltering?' And I shall say, 'Although she is on the shores of Atracia or of the Hyllaei, mine she will be.'

She has been here all the time! Here she remains, faithful to her oath! May my enemies burst themselves! I have won: she could not resist my constant pleas. Eager envy can now abandon its delusory joy: my Cynthia has decided not to take fresh paths. She says that she loves me and that because of me she loves Rome dearly; without me, she says, a kingdom would not be sweet. She has chosen to sleep with me, even on a narrow bed, and to remain my mistress, whatever the circumstances, rather than have for herself the ancient kingdom of well-dowered Hippodameia and all the wealth that Elis has earned with its horse-races. Although he was giving her great gifts and promising her even greater, she did not yield to greed and leave my arms.

I did not influence her with gold or with Indian shells. I was able to sway her by the devotion of my smooth song. The Muses exist then, nor is Apollo slow to help a lover! These are the gods on whom I, as a lover, rely: the unique Cynthia is mine. Now I can touch the height of heaven with my feet: whether night or day comes, she is mine. No rival takes away from me my assured love; this glory shall remain until my old age.

Ovid *Amores* 1 13, p. 152

Now the golden-haired goddess who brings the day on her frosty chariot is coming over the ocean from her old husband. (1-2)

My reproaches were at an end. You could see that she had heard: she blushed; but day did not dawn more slowly than usual. (47-8)

Tibullus 3 10 = 4 4, p. 155
Come here and drive away this young
girl's disease. Come here, Phoebus,
proud of your long hair! Hurry, I
implore you! You will feel no regret,
Phoebus, for having applied your
healing hands to this beauty. See that
her limbs do not become thin and
pale, that an ugly hue does not mar
her white limbs. Whatever complaint
and whatever mischief we are afraid
of, let the river carry it with its swift
current to the sea. Come, holy god,
and bring with you all the juices and
incantations that relieve bodies weary
with sickness. Do not torment this
young man who is afraid that his girl
may die and who makes innumerable
prayers on his mistress's behalf.
Sometimes he prays, sometimes he
reproaches the immortal gods because
she is ill.

Lay aside your fear, Cerinthus:
the god does not harm lovers – only
you must always love her. Your girl
is restored to health. But now she is
entirely yours: she thinks of you alone
in her beauty, and your mob of rivals
sits disappointed. Phoebus, look favourably upon their love; great praise
will be yours for having saved two
lives by saving one. There is no need
of weeping: it will be more reasonable
to weep if ever she becomes cold to
you. Now you will be distinguished
and happy, when both of you joyfully
compete to pay your vows at the holy
altars of the gods. Then the crowd
worshipping the gods will call you
fortunate, and each of them will wish
for himself skills like yours.

Propertius 2 28 42, p. 155
I shall live if she lives; if she dies, I
shall die.

Ovid *Amores* 2 13 15-16, p. 157
Turn your attention here! Spare the
two of us by sparing one! For you will
give life to my mistress, and she to
me.

CHAPTER SEVEN

Ovid *Amores* 2 11 37-56, p. 160
Go, and remember me; return with
a favourable wind. May a stronger
breeze then fill your sails; may great
Nereus then tilt the sea towards these
shores; may the winds blow here and
the tide drive the waters here. You
yourself must ask that the Zephyrs
alone enter your sails; you must with
your own hand stir the swelling
sheets. I shall be the first to see your
well-known ship from the shore, and
I shall say 'That ship is bringing my
gods'. I shall clasp you in my arms
and seize innumerable kisses; a votive
offering shall be slaughtered in
thanksgiving for your return; the
soft sand will be levelled to make a
couch; and any mound will serve as
a table. Wine will be set by you and
many a tale you will tell – your ship
was almost sunk in the middle of the
waves, and when hurrying back
to me, you were not afraid of the
hostile night or the strong south
winds. I shall believe everything
even though you make it up: why
should I not flatter my own desires?
May the morning star, brightest in
high heaven, bring me this day as
soon as possible, with flying steed.

Statius *Siluae* 3 2 127-43, p. 162
The day will come, then, when Caesar
recalls you from a completed war for
promotion. I shall be standing here on
the shore again looking at the enormous waves and praying for other
winds. How happy I shall be then!
How strongly shall I stir my plectra
in thanksgiving on my lyre! I shall
cling to your mighty neck, and you
will lift me to your shoulders, falling
into my arms first as you come fresh
from the ship; and you will tell me all
the things you have saved up to tell
me, and we shall recount to each
other the doings of the intervening
years. You will describe the fast-
flowing Euphrates, the kingdoms of

Bactria, the sacred treasures of ancient Babylon, and Zeugma, the path of Roman peace; you will tell me how sweetly the grove of flowering Idume smells, of the purple of wealthy Tyre – the dye that reddens clothes twice in Sidonian vats – of the place where the fertile sprigs first sweat from their buds white balsam. I shall tell you what tombs I have given to the conquered Argives and what page brings to an end my laborious Thebaid.

Theocritus *Idyll* 7 63-72, p. 163

And on that day, I shall put on my head a garland of anise or roses or white stocks. Lying by the fire, I shall draw wine of Ptelea from a bowl and on the fire beans will be roasted. My pallet will be heaped up a cubit high of fleabane and asphodel and curling celery; and I shall drink in luxury, remembering Ageanax even in my cups, and pressing my lip to the lees. Two shepherds shall pipe for me, one from Acharnae and one from Lycope; and Tityrus shall sing with them. . . .

Tibullus 1 7, p. 165

This was the day Fates prophesied as they spun their fateful threads, which no god can unravel; this is the man they foretold as one who could turn to flight the tribes of Aquitaine, and make the Atax tremble, defeated by his brave soldiers.

These things have come to pass: the Roman people have seen fresh triumphs, and enemy generals with their captive hands in chains. You, Messalla, your head crowned with the victor's laurels, rode in an ivory chariot drawn by white horses.

It was not without my help that you won your glory: I call as my witnesses Tarbella in the Pyrenees, the shores of the Ocean by Saintonge, Saône, fast-flowing Rhône, great Garonne and Loire, grey stream of the fair-haired men of Chartres.

Or shall I mention the grey Cydnus, twisting with silent wave through its marshes in calm flow? Or huge, cold Taurus, that touches the clouds with its airy head and feeds the long-haired Cilicians? Why should I tell how the white dove flies unharmed from city to city, sacred to the Syrians of Palestine; and how Tyre, that first learnt to trust a ship to the winds, looks out from its towers over the vast surface of the sea; or how, when the dog-star shrivels the burning fields, the Nile, bringing fertility, overflows in its summer flood?

Father Nile, why or in what lands can I say you hide your source? Because of you, your country requires no showers, and the dry grass does not pray to Jupiter the rain-god. The people of Egypt, skilled at mourning for the Memphian bull, chant to you and worship you as their own Osiris.

Osiris was the first to make a plough with his skilled hands and to trouble the tender earth with steel. He was the first to entrust seeds to the untried land and he first gathered fruit from unfamiliar trees. He taught men how to tie the young vine to stakes and how to cut its green foliage with the harsh sickle. For him the ripe grape was first pressed by uncouth feet and yielded up its sweet juices. This liquid taught men to tune their voices to song, and stirred their untutored feet to move in regular rhythms. Bacchus, too, gives release from misery to the heart of the farmer, worn-out by harsh labour. He also brings peace to men in trouble, even though hard chains clank around their legs. Dull cares and mourning are not for you now, Osiris – but dance, song, happy love, mixed flowers, a forehead bound with ivy, a yellow cloak falling to your young feet, purple clothes, a sweet-sounding pipe, and a light basket containing hidden mystic objects.

Come here, Bacchus! Join in worshipping the Genius with a hundred enjoyments and dances; and pour abundance of wine over his temples. Let ointment drip from his shining head, and soft garlands sit on his head and neck. Come to us today for this, Genius! I shall honour you with incense and cakes sweet with Attic honey. I pray that you may have increase of children, who will add new achievements to those of their father, and stand around him, full of distinction, when he is an old man.

Nor should the man who lives in Tusculum or the ancient city of white Alba be silent about that great work, your road. For through your generosity, here there is a deep spread of hard gravel, and there paving-stones are neatly joined. The countryman shall sing your praises, when he returns late in the evening from the great city, and reaches his home without stumbling. But you, Genius, whom we must celebrate for many a year, come each time with ever increasing happiness.

Propertius 3 4 21-2, p. 167 (see p. 274)

Plautus *Truculentus* 490, p. 168
One witness who has seen an event is worth more than ten who have only heard of it.

Theocritus *Idyll* 14, p. 169
Aeschinas. A very good day to my friend Thyonichus.
Thyonichus. And the same to you, Aeschinas. It's been a long time.
A. A long time.
T. What's the matter with you?
A. I'm not doing too well, Thyonichus.
T. So that's why you are so thin and you have that big moustache and unkempt curls. A Pythagorean, looking just like you, passed through the other day – pale and shoeless – an Athenian, or so he said.
A. What, was he in love too?
T. Yes, with white bread.
A. You're just pulling my leg, my friend. But Cynisca, the beauty, is treating me badly: I am going to go out of my mind sooner or later; I'm

a hair's breadth away.
T. Just like you, my dear Aeschinas, a bit over excited. You want everything to go your way; but tell me what has happened.
A. The Argive, Agis the Thessalian cavalryman, Cleonicus the mercenary and I were having a drinking party at my country place. I killed a couple of chickens and a sucking pig and I opened a cask of Biblos wine, four-years old, with a bouquet almost as fresh as when it came from the wine press. An onion and snails were got out; it was a fine party.

When we were becoming well-heated, we agreed that each should toast his beloved in neat wine; but he must say who his beloved was. So we spoke their names and drank, as agreed; but although I was there, Cynisca said nothing. What do you think I felt about that? 'Can't you talk? Have you seen a wolf?' someone joked. 'How clever of you', she said, and blushed; you could have lit a torch from that blush. There is a 'wolf', Lycus, the son of my neighbour Labes, a tall, soft youth; many people think he is handsome. It was for him that Cynisca was burning with that precious love of hers; the business had got to my ears, just by chance, some time before, but I didn't go into it. So much for being a sensible grown man!

Well, we were all four deep in drink by then and the man from Larissa sang 'My Wolf' right from the beginning – a Thessalian song – just to make trouble. Cynisca suddenly began to cry, more than a six year old girl wanting to be dandled in her mother's lap. Then – you know what I'm like – Thyonichus, I punched her on the head, once and then again; she picked up her skirts and ran out quickly. 'So I'm not enough for you, you pest', I said, 'You prefer some other lover? Well, go and keep him warm! You're crying for him, are you? I hope you cry tears big as apples.' When a swallow has given food to her chicks under the roof, she quickly flies back to gather more. Quicker than a swallow Cynisca flew from her soft chair straight through the lobby and doors, where her feet took her.

The fable goes 'The bull once went to the wood': twenty, eight, nine and ten more and today eleven, add two and it is two months since we have been apart; and she doesn't know if my hair is cut Thracian fashion. Lycus is everything to her now; her door is open to Lycus even at night; but I am neither reckoned nor taken account of; I am like the wretched Megarians, in the lowest possible position. If I could stop loving her, all would be well. But how? I am like the mouse who fell into the pitch, as they say, Thyonichus, and I don't know the cure for hopeless love – except that Simus, who was in love with that brazen woman, went across the sea and came back cured, a man of my own age. I will sail across the sea too; a mercenary is not the worst of men, even if he is not the best, but somewhere in the middle.
T. I wish things had gone as you had wanted, Aeschinas; but if you have really decided to go abroad, Ptolemy is the best employer for a gentleman.
A. What's he like in other ways?
T. He is one of the finest – discerning, cultured, amorous, a really pleasant man; he knows his friends and he knows his enemies even more. He frequently gives generous gifts, and doesn't say no when asked, just as a king should; but you mustn't ask all the time, Aeschinas. So if you want to pin the end of your cloak to your right shoulder and have the courage to stand firmly on your two feet and meet the onset of a bold enemy, go to Egypt as quickly as you can. We are all greying at the temples, and time is gradually whitening us to the chin.

We should achieve something while our knees are still supple.

CHAPTER EIGHT

Aristotle *Rhetoric* 1358A-B, p. 177
A speech has three constituents: speaker, subject-matter, and addressee, and its function is directed towards the last – I mean the hearer.

Virgil *Aeneid* 1 78-80, p. 178
You have given me my humble kingdom, you have made Jupiter's power friendly to me, you have granted me the privilege of attending the banquets of the gods and of being lord of storm-cloud and tempest.

Horace *Odes* 3 14, p. 179
Caesar is returning home, people of Rome, victorious from the Spanish shore; lately we heard of his laurels, won, like Hercules, at risk to his life.

His wife, whose joy is her outstanding husband, must come forward after sacrifice to the deserving gods. Our renowned leader's sister must come too and, adorned with suppliant fillets, the mothers of the girls and youths recently saved. You boys and unwed girls, abstain from ill-omened words. This day is truly a feast-day to me: it will take black cares away from me; I shall not fear uprising or violent death while Caesar rules the world.

Slave, go and fetch unguent and garlands and a cask that remembers the Marsian War, if any wine-jar was able to escape wandering Spartacus. Tell high-voiced Neaera quickly to tie in a knot her myrrh-scented hair. But if the doorkeeper is awkward and you are checked, come away. Whitening hair moderates a temper that once welcomed quarrels and assertive bickering; I would not have put up with this when I was hot with youth, in the consulship of Plancus.

Propertius 3 4, p. 185
Divine Caesar is planning to fight the

rich Indians and to divide with his fleet the straits of the gem-bearing sea. Great is the wealth to be won, soldiers: the end of the earth prepares triumphs for you; the Tigris and Euphrates will flow beneath your ordinance. Parthia will become, however late, a province under Italian domination; and the memorials of the Parthian triumph will grow accustomed to Latian Jupiter. Come, set sail, ships inured to war; war-horses, carry out your usual duty. I prophesy that the omens are favourable: expiate the Crassi and their slaughter; take thought of Roman history.

Father Mars and fate-guarded fire of holy Vesta, before my death I pray, may the day come when I see Caesar's chariot loaded with spoil and its horses often shy at the crowd's applause. Leaning on my dear girl's breast may I look, reading on the banners the names of captured cities, and seeing the fleeing cavalry's arrows and the bows of the trousered soldiers and the captured leaders sitting beneath their weapons.

Preserve your offspring, Venus. May this present line, which you see descended from Aeneas, last for ever. Theirs be the reward whose work has won it; it will be enough for me if I can applaud in the Sacred Way.

Horace *Odes* 3 27 1-34, p. 189
May the impious be escorted out by the omen of a squawking owl and a pregnant bitch, or a grey she-wolf running down from the countryside of Lanuvium or a vixen heavy with cubs.

When their journey is begun, may a serpent break it, crossing their path obliquely like an arrow, and terrifying their ponies. When I, an augur with foresight, fear for someone, I shall call with my prayer from the sunrise the bird that presages the coming of rain, the crow of good

omen, before it returns to the stagnant marshes. Be happy wherever you wish and, as while living, remember me, Galatea. May no ill-omened magpie or wandering jackdaw forbid your going.

But do you see what storms surround Orion as he hurries to set? I know the danger of the black gulf of the Adriatic, and the destructive power of the white wind Iapyx. May the wives and children of our enemies feel the dark blasts of the rising south wind and the roaring of the inky water and the banks trembling under its blows.

Just so Europa entrusted her snow-white body to the deceitful bull and grew pale, for all her boldness, at the sea full of monsters and the treachery of mid-ocean. A little before in the fields she had gathered flowers to make a garland she vowed to the nymphs; then in the blackness of night she saw nothing but stars and waves. As soon as she had come to Crete, powerful with its hundred cities. . . .

A.P. 12 131 (Posidippus), p. 192
Goddess who frequents Cyprus and Cythera and Miletus and the lovely plain of Syria, sounding with the hooves of horses, come and be gracious to Kallistion, who has never turned a lover away from the door of her house.

Horace *Odes* 1 30, p. 192
Venus, queen of Cnidos and Paphos, leave your beloved Cyprus and transfer yourself to the lovely temple of Glycera, who calls you with abundance of incense. Let the burning boy, the Graces with loosened girdles, and the Nymphs come in haste with you, and Youth that lacks charm without you, and Mercury.

Theocritus *Idyll* 6 6-40, p. 193
Daphnis. Galatea is throwing apples at your sheep, Polyphemus, and calling you unlucky in love and a goat-

herd. And you, you wretch, do not look at her but sit piping sweetly. Look, she is throwing apples again at the dog that follows you to watch your sheep. The dog barks looking at the sea and the lovely waves reflect it, running along the softly sounding sands. Watch that it does not jump at the girl's knees when she comes out of the sea and tear her beautiful skin. Even from there she is flirting with you: she is like the dry down of thistle, when the lovely summer sears it, flying away from a lover and chasing one who does not love her; and she leaves no stone unturned. To love, Polyphemus, what is not beautiful often seems so.

In reply to him Damoetas began to sing this song.

Damoetas. I saw her, by Pan, I saw her throwing apples at the sheep. She did not escape my notice, I swear by my one sweet eye, with which I hope to see to the end; but the prophet Telemus, who predicted evil for me, may he take it back to his own home and keep it for his children.

I do not look at her, so as to irritate her; but I tell her I have another woman as wife. When she hears this she is jealous, o Paean, and pines away and anxiously spies on me from the sea, looking at my grove and flocks. I have spurred on the dog to bark at her; when I was making love to her, it would put its muzzle in her lap and whine.

Perhaps when she sees me do this often, she will send a messenger; but I will shut my door until she swears to spread her fair bed for me here in this island. In fact, I have not a bad appearance, so they say; I looked into the sea recently when it was calm, and my beard and my one eye were beautiful, in my own judgment, and my teeth glittered more brightly than Parian marble. But I spat into my breast so as to escape the evil eye, as the old woman Cotyttaris taught me.

Horace *Odes* 1 36 8-9, p. 196
. . . boyhood spent with him and no other as a guide and manhood reached together.

Propertius 3 12, p. 197
Were you able, Postumus, to abandon Galla in spite of her tears and to follow as a soldier the brave standards of Augustus? Was any glory from despoiling the Parthians so important to you, that when your Galla begged you incessantly, you would not comply with her requests? If it is not impious, I wish all you greedy men might perish together, and anyone who prefers warfare to a faithful wife.

But you, lunatic, wrapped up in your military cloak, will wearily drink the water of Araxes from your helmet. Meanwhile she will waste away from empty rumours, afraid that your courage may bring you harm, that the arrows of the Medes may rejoice at your slaughter, or the armoured cavalryman on his gilded horse, afraid that some small part of you may come home in an urn to be wept over – that is how men who fall in those parts return.

You are three and four times fortunate in your chaste Galla, Postumus: a man who behaves like this deserved a different sort of wife. What will a girl do, unprotected by fear of anyone, since Rome teaches the looseness she professes? But go and be free from fear: Galla will not be won over by gifts; she will not remember your hard-heartedness to her. Whenever the fates send you home safe, chaste Galla will hang about your neck. Postumus will be a second Ulysses in having a marvellous wife.

Ulysses was not harmed by so many long delays – his ten years on campaign, Ismara, the mountain of the Cicones, Calpe; and then, Polyphemus, your burnt out eye, and Circe's trickery, the lotus – addictive drug – and

Scylla and Charybdis torn asunder with each second wave. It was not to Ulysses' detriment that the oxen of Lampetie lowed on the Ithacan spits – Lampetie daughter of Phoebus had pastured them for her father; that he ran from the weeping girl of Aeaea's room, swam so many stormy nights and days, entered the black house of the silent shades, approached the Sirens' lagoons with his oarsmen's ears stopped up, revitalised his old bow with the slaughter of the suitors, and so brought his wanderings to an end. It was worth his while, since his wife had sat chaste at home; Aelia Galla is more faithful than Penelope.

Theocritus *Idyll* 7 96-127, p. 201

The Cupids sneezed for Simichidas: he, poor wretch, is as much in love with Myrto as goats with the spring; but Aratus, dearest of all my friends, longs for a boy deep in heart. Aristis knows – a fine man, a man of excellence, whom Phoebus himself would be happy to have singing, lyre in hand, beside his tripod – Aristis knows how Aratus is burnt to the bone for love of a boy.

Pan, lord of the lovely plain of Homole, put him unasked into my friend's arms, whether he is the soft Philinus, or some other. If you do this, dear Pan, may the boys of Arcadia not flog you with squills about the sides and shoulders when meat is scarce. But if you will not, may you be bitten by insects all over, and scratch yourself with your nails and sleep among nettles; and may you spend midwinter among the mountains of the Edonians, beside the river Hebrus, up by the North Pole; and in summer may you pasture your flock among the furthest Ethiopians beneath the rock of the Blemyes, from where the Nile is no longer seen.

But you, Cupids like rosy apples, leave the sweet stream of Hyetis and Biblis and Oecus, the lofty seat of fair-haired Dione, shoot lovely Philinus with your bows, I implore you, shoot him, since in his perversity he will not take pity on my friend. Indeed he is riper than a pear and the women say 'Ah, Philinus, your bloom of beauty is passing away.'

Let us no longer watch by the door, Aratus, nor wear out our feet. Let the cock crowing at dawn hand over another man to the misery of chill numbness; and may Molon for one be choked in that wrestling school, my dear friend. But, as for us, may we have peace; and may an old woman spit on us and keep evil things away from us.

Propertius 2 16, p. 204

Your praetor has recently arrived from the lands of Illyria, Cynthia, an enormous prey to you, and an enormous concern to me. Could he not have lost his life on Acroceraunia? Ah, Neptune, what gifts I would be giving you! Now they are banqueting and the table is full – but I am absent; now the door is open all night – but I am not there.

So if you are wise you will not neglect the proferred harvest: you will shear the stupid sheep when his fleece is full-length. Then, when you have eaten up everything he has to give and he is reduced to pauperdom, tell him to sail off again to some other Illyria. Cynthia does not chase after men in office; she cares nothing for magistracies; she weighs one thing only and always, her lovers' purses. But, Venus, come to the aid of my misery now; make him rupture himself with his continuous lechery.

So Love is to be bought for cash by anyone at all; Jupiter, my mistress is lost to me for gain unworthy of her. She is constantly sending me to the Ocean to search for pearls; she orders me to bring gifts from Tyre itself. I wish there were no rich men at Rome, that our very leader could live in a straw hut. If that were so, girls would never be available for cash, and a mistress would grow grey in one home; if that were so, you would never have been sleeping for the last week apart from me, your white arms clutched round such a foul creature. It is not (I call you yourself to witness) for any fault of mine, but because fickleness has always been a friend to beauty. One moment the barbarian is tramping up and down, excluded and lustful; the next he is successful, and holds my kingdom. See what fate Eriphyle found by accepting gifts that brought her harm, and what evil fire consumed new-wedded Creusa!

Will no wrong done by you check my weeping? Or can my suffering love not extricate itself from your faults? So many days have now gone by; and no longing for the theatre touches me or for the Campus Martius; and my table gives me no pleasure. You say I ought to be ashamed! Indeed! I ought. Unless, as they say, disgraceful love is always deaf. Think of that leader, who recently filled the waters of Actium with the empty noise of his doomed soldiery. Degraded love made him turn his ships and run away and seek refuge at the ends of the earth; Caesar's courage and glory is this; with the hand that conquered he laid arms aside.

But the dresses and emeralds and chrysoliths with yellow light which the praetor has given you, may I see swift storms carry them off to nothingness; may they become earth and water to you. Jupiter does not always laugh calmly at the perfidies of lovers, and with deaf ear neglect the pleas of the wronged. You have seen his thunder running through the whole sky; you have seen how his lightnings have leapt down from their home in heaven. It is not the Pleiads or watery Orion who do these things; the wrath of the thunder-storm does not fall as it does for nothing. That is when the god punishes perjured girls – because he too was deceived, and he wept, for all that he was a god. So do not value Sidonian dresses so much that you have to fear whenever the cloudy south wind blows.

Horace *Odes* 3 7, p. 208

Why are you weeping over Gyges, Asterie? That young man is constant in his faith to you and at the beginning of spring cloudless west winds will restore him to you, wealthy with Bithynian merchandise. Driven by the south wind into Oricum after the rising of the raging Goat-star, he is spending cold and sleepless nights, full of tears.

Yet a messenger from his agitated hostess tells him that Chloe is sighing for him, and in her unhappy love desires him as much as you do. Cunningly the messenger tempts him in a thousand ways, telling him how credulous Proetus was stirred on by his treacherous wife with false accusations to hasten death for overchaste Bellerophon and how Peleus was almost sent to Hades for chastely trying to resist Hippolyte of Magnesia. Such stories instructing him to infidelity he cleverly recounts – in vain, since Gyges, when he hears them, is deafer than the rocks of Icarus and still retains his integrity.

But you must be careful that your neighbour Enipeus does not win more favour in your eyes than he should, although no other cunning horseman makes such a fine spectacle on the grass of the Campus Martius and no one swims the stream of the Tiber so quickly. Shut up your house as soon as night falls; do not look down into the street when you hear the sound of the plaintive pipe; and when he often calls you harsh, remain obdurate.

Horace *Odes* 1 7, p. 211

Others will praise famous Rhodes, or Mytilene, or Ephesus, or the walls of

Corinth between its two seas, or Thebes made famous by Bacchus, or Delphi by Apollo, or Thessalian Tempe. There are those whose one task it is to celebrate in long epics the city of virgin Pallas and to wreath their brows with olive gathered from every side. Many a man will tell in Juno's honour of Argos fit for horses and rich Mycenae. I am not charmed so much by Spartan endurance, or by the plain of rich Larissa, as by the house of sounding Albunea, by the rushing Anio, by the grove of Tiburnus and by the orchards watered by running streamlets. The white south wind often drives the clouds away from an overcast sky and does not let rain be bred forever; so you should be wise, Plancus, and remember to set bounds to your seriousness and the toils of life with mellow wine, either when you are in the camp glittering with standards or when you will be in the thick shade of your Tibur.

When Teucer was leaving Salamis and his father for exile they say that nevertheless he bound with a crown of poplar his temples moistened by wine and spoke as follows to his sad companions: 'We shall go, my friends and comrades, wherever fortune kinder than my father carries us. You must not despair under Teucer's leadership and auspices: truthful Apollo promised a second Salamis in a new land. My brave friends, who have often suffered worse fortunes with me, now drive away your cares with wine; tomorrow we shall cross the great sea again.'

Ovid *Epistulae ex Ponto* 1 3 79-82, p.214
Tydeus, exiled from Calydon came to Adrastus, and the land favoured by Venus gave refuge to Teucer. Why should I speak of the old Romans, for whom Tibur was the furthest land of exile?

Ovid *Fasti* 6 665-6, p.215
They leave the city of Rome for exile and retire to Tibur; there was a time when Tibur was a place of exile.

CHAPTER NINE
Horace *Odes* 1 14, p.218
Ship, fresh waves will carry you to sea again. What are you doing? Persist and reach the harbour. Do you not see how your sides are bare of oars, your mast smashed by the swift south-west winds, your yardarms creaking, your sides hardly able to resist the over-violent waves without girding-ropes. You do not have untorn sails; you have no gods to call on when next pressed by trouble. Although you are Pontic pine, daughter of a noble wood, and boast of a useless descent and name, fearful sailors put no trust in painted sterns; unless you owe the winds sport, take care.

Of late I was weary of caring for you; now I feel love for you and no small concern; I hope you avoid the seas lying among the shining Cyclades.

Euripides *Heracleidae* 427-32, p.220
My children, we are like sailors who have escaped the savage strength of the storm; and when they have the land within their grasp, they are driven back to sea again from the shore by the storms. So we too are driven away from this land, when we were already near the beach and thought ourselves safe.

Horace *Odes* 2 17, p.222
Why do you dispirit me with your complaints? It is not the gods' will nor mine that you should die before me, Maecenas, great glory and support of my fortune. Ah! if any untimely disaster should take away you, half of my soul, why should I, the other half, delay? I could not feel so much affection for myself, nor would I be a whole man if I lived on. The same day shall bring death to both

of us: I shall keep the oath of fidelity I have taken. We shall go, we shall go, wherever you lead off, companions ready to walk the last way together. Neither the breath of the fiery Chimaera nor hundred-handed Gyas, should he rise again, will ever separate me from you; this is the decree of powerful Justice and the Fates. Whether it is Libra or terrifying Scorpio that has me under its aspect and is the stronger influence upon my birth-hour; or whether it is Capricorn, tyrant of the western wave; our stars are joined in a marvellous way. The glittering protection of Jupiter has snatched you from evil Saturn and slowed the wing of flying fate – it was then that the assembled populace three times applauded you joyfully in the theatre; the tree would have fallen on my head and carried me off, had not Faunus lightened the blow with his right hand – Faunus who guards men under the influence of Mercury. Remember to pay due sacrificial victims and the temple you vowed; I shall sacrifice a humble ewe-lamb.

Propertius 1 22 1-2, p.224
You ask in the name of our constant friendship, Tullus, my nation and my ancestry and where my home is.

Propertius 2 28 42, p.224 (see p. 271)

Horace *Odes* 1 3, p.231
I wish you, ship, the guidance of the powerful goddess of Cyprus and of those shining stars, the brothers of Helen, and of the father of the winds, once he has shut up all except Iapyx; only, I beg you fulfil your trust, bring Virgil safely to the shores of Attica, and preserve half my soul.

That man had oak and triple bronze about his breast who first entrusted his fragile craft to the angry sea: he was not afraid of the headlong southwest wind battling with the north winds, or of the gloomy Hyades, or of the rage of the south wind, mightiest ruler of the Adriatic, if it wishes to raise or calm the seas. What kind of death did that man fear who could look dry-eyed upon monsters of the deep, the raging sea and the ill-famed cliffs of Acroceraunia?

It was in vain that a kindly god split up the dry land with dividing waters, if impious ships nevertheless cross the tabooed seas. Bold to endure anything, the human race rushes through forbidden sin: the daring son of Iapetus brought fire to men by evil cunning; after his theft of fire from its heavenly home, sickness and a new host of fevers lie heavy on earth, and the slow necessity of death, long-extended before, quickened its step. Daedalus attempted the empty air on wings not given to man; Hercules in one of his labours broke into Acheron; nothing is too difficult for men. In our foolishness we seek heaven itself, and through our crimes we do not allow Jupiter to lay aside his angry thunderbolts.

Propertius 2 19, p.236
You are leaving Rome against my will, Cynthia; but I am pleased that when you are without me, you will be living in the remote countryside. In the fields, that home of chastity, there will be no young man to seduce you and press you to infidelity with his blandishments. No sounds of contention will rise in front of your windows; nor will your sleep be broken by lovers shouting upon you; you will be alone, Cynthia, and you will look upon the lonely mountains and the sheep and the lands of a poor farmer. No games will be able to corrupt you there, no shrines – most often the cause of your infidelities; there you will constantly see oxen ploughing and the vine shedding her leaves under the skilled sickle. There you will offer a few grains of incense at a rustic shrine, where the goat will

fall victim before the altars of the country gods. Why, you will even mimic their dances bare-ankled, so long as you are completely safe from any intruder.

I myself shall hunt: I want now to take up the rites of Diana and lay aside the desires of Venus. I shall start to chase wild beasts, to hang up their horns on the pine-tree, and in person to urge on the bold hounds. Not that I would dare to provoke great lions or come to grips with wild boars in swift pursuit: my boldness shall be to ambush soft hares and to capture birds with jointed pole, where Clitumnus hides his lovely streams in the grove sacred to him, and where his wave washes white cattle.

But you, my darling, whenever you think of being unfaithful, remember that I shall come to you in a few days. The lonely woods and the wandering rivers running down from the mossy hills will not prevent me from constantly repeating your name here on devoted lips. No one is to harm me in my absence!

A.P. 11 44 (Philidemus), p.240
Your friend whom the Muses love, dearest Piso, demands your company tomorrow, in his humble cottage, from the ninth hour onwards, to keep the annual feast of the twentieth. You will not have sow's udders and draughts of Chian wine; but you will see sincere friends and you will hear conversation sweeter than you would hear in Phaeacia. And if you ever look with favour upon me, Piso, we shall celebrate a richer feast of the twentieth instead of a poor one.

Horace *Odes* 1 20, p.240
You will drink cheap Sabine wine from modest cups, dear knight Maecenas – wine I laid down and sealed in a Greek jar when you were applauded in the theatre, and the banks of your ancestral river and the playful echo of the Vatican hill together repeated your praises to you. You will drink [i.e. at home] Caecuban and grapes pressed at Cales; the vines of Falernum and of the Formian hills do not mellow my cups.

Horace *Epistles* 1 5 1-5, p.241
If you can put up with reclining as my guest upon cheap couches made by Archias and if you are not afraid to eat a vegetarian dinner on a humble plate, I shall expect you at my home, Torquatus, at sunset. You will drink wines strained between the marshes of Minturnae and Petrinum near Sinuessa, in the second consulship of Taurus. If you have something better, have it sent – or put up with my choice.

Catullus 13, p.243
You will dine well, my dear Fabullus, at my home, in a few days – the gods willing – if you bring with you a good, big dinner and a beautiful girl, wine, salt, and laughter of every sort. If you bring these things, my dear friend, you will dine well, since your Catullus' purse is full of spiders' webs. But you will get in return affection unadulterated, or anything that is sweeter and more elegant: I shall give you an unguent given to my mistress by the Venuses and Cupids. When you smell it you will ask the gods to make you all nose.

T

friendship–*contd.*
  relation of, as primary element in
    prosphonetikon, *21*
  schetliastic topos of, *57*
  topos: inflation of, *217*; novel
    use of, *4, 123-4*; use in different
    genres, *99*
  willingness to accompany as sign
    of, *4, 99, 141*
funerary poems, animals as
    addressees in, *218*

Galinsky, K., *250n. 55*
Gallus, Cornelius, propemptikon
    to Lycoris, *238*
Gardiner, E. N., *254n. 61*
generic
  alteration: by addition, *129*;
    by transformation, *129*;
    constructive, defined, *129*;
    extent of practice in antiquity,
    127; in form, *127-8*; Menander
    on, *127*; omission of primary
    element, *128-9*; recurrence
    of, *127*
  announcements, *25*
  communication between author
    and audience, *25, 129*
  examples: and Greek lyric poets,
    36; and Homer, *36*; length of,
    50; variation in use of,
    49-50
  expectation, *13, 14-15*
  formulae: and composition, *31*;
    as expansions of Homeric
    prototypes, *36, 37*; as lists of
    primary and secondary
    elements, *37*; as part of
    cultural heritage, *37*; as
    influencing poetry, *13, 14-15*;
    Menandrian prescriptions for,
    37; rhetoricians' influence on,
    73; specifying place for topoi,
    14-15
  patterns, *36, 99*
  sophistication: common
    background of audience and
    author and, *7*; development of,
    50; inclusion and, *13, 54-5*;
    of Archilochus *Fr.* 79a (D) =
    Hipponax *Fr.* 115 (Masson),
    99; of Sappho *Fr.* 94 (LP),

generic, sophistication–*contd.*
    54-5; of Theocritus *Idyll* 12,
    30-1; originality in, *99*
  studies, *7, 16, 31-3, 36*
genethliakon
  addressee in, *137, 221*
  Amor, *113*
  Bacchus in, *168*
  defined, *113*
  examples of, *283*
  features of, *112*
  function of, *136*
  Genius, *113, 136, 168, 250n. 15*
  inverse, *136-7, 221*
  Natalis, *113*
  personification in, *113*
  religious concepts underlying,
    136-7, 167, 168
  topoi of: altar wreathed in
    flowers, *136*; fine clothes, *136*;
    garlands, *168*; generation
    topos, *113, 168*; incense, *113*,
    136, 168; offerings, *113, 136*,
    168; prayers, *136, 168*; wishes,
    113, 136, 169
  triumph-poem: included in,
    167-9; similarity to, *167*
  triumphs and birthdays as
    religious occasions, *167, 168*
genres
  absorption of, *158-9*
  allusions to other, *158*
  antiquity of, *34-6*
  arbitrariness of generic divisions,
    138
  as classification in terms of content, *6*
  as responses to situations, *34, 138*
  assignment of poems to,
    difficulties of, *158*
  before recorded literature, *34*
  belief that Homer invented, *35, 70*
  bipersonality of, *221*
  boundaries of, corresponding to
    human experience, *138*
  categories of, *70-97*
  classifying, difficulties of, *74-5*
  contrast between form and, *6*
  defined, *6*
  development of, *34-69*
  distinguishing characteristics of, *6*
  formal sophistication affecting,
    127-8

U

propemptikon, equal to equal–*contd.*
  breach of comradeship, *57*;
  Menander's reasons for
  exemplifying, *9-10*; Menander
  type 2, *8, 9-10, 20, 235-6*;
  non-schetliastic, *9*; schetliasmos
  as feature of, *237*; schetliastic,
  9-10, 11
excuses of, *284-5*
excusatory, *11-12, 13, 15-16, 141,*
  162-3
excuse/wish to accompany, *115,*
  116-17
excuses for not, *11-12, 15-16,*
  115, 116-17, 246n. 17
excuses, role of in type 2, *11*
friend's, *8, 9, 57*
friendship topos, *99*: assertion of,
  123-4, 141-2; recalling of
  friendship, *52-3*
function of, *129*
gods: help of, *115, 116, 117, 130*;
  sacrifices to, *130*; sea, *190*
good wishes, *115, 116-17, 133, 138*:
  go with, *52*; topos, *27, 190*
governor demitting office, *8-9*
home: departure from, *120*;
  distinction between leaving and
  going, *116*; emphasis on,
  depending on variant, *116*
Homeric, *36*
included in: inverse epibaterion,
  165; inverse syntaktikon, *165*
including: prosphonetikon, *159-65*;
  syntaktikon, *54-5, 128, 165*;
  triumph-poem, *186-7*
inclusion: as substitute for
  topical allusion, *160*; of other
  genres, frequency of, *164-5*;
  of schetliastic in non-schetliastic, *12-13*
inferior to superior, *8-9, 20, 55,*
  186: cases where explicit
  schetliasmos is not possible,
  117, 198; encomium in, *8, 9,*
  10, 14-15, 186, 198, 221, 236;
  excuses in, *11*; Menander
  type 3, *8, 9, 11, 235-6*
injunction to go, *32, 186, 248n. 28*
inverse: examples of, *56-7, 60, 130*;
  topoi of, *130*; vituperation of
  addressee, *130*

propemptikon–*contd.*
  leaving one city for another, *8*
  literary examples of, *10, 20*
  memor sis topos, *see memor*
    sis (remember me) topos
  Menander on, *see* Menander the
    Rhetor on propemptikon
  narration in, *54, 55, 127, 159*
  non-schetliastic: absence of
    prescription for, *9, 115*;
    addressed to persons going
    home, *115-16*; addressed to
    persons leaving home, *115, 116*;
    compensation for lack of
    schetliasmos in, *16*;
    destination, description of,
    115, 116; divine help, *115, 117*;
    encomium to superior, *198-9*;
    equal to equal, *9*; examples
    of, *115, 116-17*; excuses, *115,*
    116-17; good wishes, *115, 116,*
    117; home/accompanying
    clash with absence of
    schetliasmos, *116*; material,
    order of, *115*; Menander on,
    52, 116; ordering of topoi,
    115-17; question of order of
    topoi, *115, 117*; speaker
    leaving own home, *116*; use
    of schetliastic material in, *53-4*;
    wish to accompany, *115, 116,*
    117
  omens: at departure, *186*;
    nature of, *130*
  orator's, to governor, *8, 9, 10*
  ordering of topoi, *115-17*
  post-encomiastic section, *15*
  primary elements of, *6, 18*
  private to private, *10, 20*
  public to public, *8, 20*
  pupil to pupil, *9-10*
  relationship of affection as
    primary element of, *6, 8-9,*
    10-11, 120
  return of departing traveller
    anticipated, *159-60, 186-7*
  return of migratory gods in
    propemptic hymns, *159-60,*
    162
  returning topos, *159-60*
  schetliasmos, *see* schetliasmos
  schetliastic, *see* schetliastic